The Philosophy of Sociality

The Philosophy of Sociality

The Shared Point of View

RAIMO TUOMELA

UNIVERSITY PRESS

2007

OXFORD
UNIVERSITY PRESS

Oxford University Press, Inc., publishes works that further
Oxford University's objective of excellence
in research, scholarship, and education.

Oxford   New York
Auckland   Cape Town   Dar es Salaam   Hong Kong   Karachi
Kuala Lumpur   Madrid   Melbourne   Mexico City   Nairobi
New Delhi   Shanghai   Taipei   Toronto

With offices in
Argentina   Austria   Brazil   Chile   Czech Republic   France   Greece
Guatemala   Hungary   Italy   Japan   Poland   Portugal   Singapore
South Korea   Switzerland   Thailand   Turkey   Ukraine   Vietnam

Published by Oxford University Press, Inc.
198 Madison Avenue, New York, New York 10016

www.oup.com

Library of Congress Cataloging-in-Publication Data

Tuomela, Raimo.
The philosophy of sociality: the shared
point of view / Raimo Tuomela.
p. cm.
Includes bibliographical references.
ISBN 978-0-19-531339-0
1. Collective behavior. 2. Social groups.
3. Social action. 4. Social epistemology.
I. Title.
HM866.T864 2007
302.3—dc22   2007012015

Printed in the United States of America
on acid-free paper

2 4 6 8 9 7 5 3 1

For my family

PREFACE

This book is about the conceptual resources and philosophical prerequisites that a proper understanding and explaining of the social world requires. The main thesis of the book is that this can only be based on a group's point of view, or as I typically will say, the group members' shared "we-perspective." The full-blown we-perspective centrally involves group notions, as used by group members ("us"). Thus what we have collectively accepted as our group's goals, values, beliefs, norms, and so on, and to which we are collectively committed is central. This is what the full we-perspective, also called the "we-mode" in the book, involves and yields. The we-mode essentially involves the idea of thinking and acting as a group member, thus for a group reason. Weaker, individualistic forms of the we-perspective and the shared point of view are also needed in some contexts. Such a weak, "I-mode" perspective involves the idea of thinking and acting as a private person for a reason that is private but can be called a we-perspective when it involves considerations related to a group one belongs to. We-mode concepts are not reducible to I-mode concepts. In other words, it is we-mode collective intentionality that is ultimately needed for understanding social life. While group notions are of course needed for the study of some specific ordinary group phenomena (e.g. the functioning of the state), this book argues that the full we-perspective (involving we-mode collective intentionality) is deeply built into the thinking and acting of human beings. It seems to be a coevolutionary adaptation based on both biological and cultural evolution. The theory created in this book at bottom relies on a naturalistic and evolutionary view of the world, thus of the social world. However, the scarcity of research and empirical evidence on collective intentionality in evolutionary research has prevented me from making the evolutionary perspective more concretely present in the book.

This book systematically and analytically develops the basic group notions for the study of the social world, thinking and acting as a group member being a most central underlying notion here. In a way, this book can be said to present almost a philosophical "theory of everything" in the social world relying on the we-perspective. Accordingly, it is argued that such central social notions as cooperation, social institutions, and the evolution of institutions, as well as collective and group responsibility, do require the full we-perspective as an underlying notion, even if the actors of course need not always be thinking in group terms when going on with their daily business.

This book continues, improves, and expands the work I have earlier done in the field that I now would like to call the philosophy of sociality, taking it to include at least the study of collective intentionality, social ontology, and metaphysics, as well as social epistemology. Philosophy of sociality also branches into normative fields of study such as moral philosophy (think of collective responsibility) and political philosophy (think of social contracts and collective acceptances of basic social institutions as we-notions).

As the book is fairly long and dense, I chose to make the index rather selective. Generally, only the defining and theoretically central uses of technical terms are indexed.

Some chapters of this book make use of my earlier essays. More precisely, I use revised versions of some passages of the following articles with appropriate permission from the publisher and coauthor:

"Acting as a Group Member and Collective Commitment" (jointly with M. Tuomela), 2003, *Protosociology* 18, 7–65.

"We-Intentions Revisited," *Philosophical Studies* 125, 2005, 327–69.

"Cooperation and Trust in Group Context," jointly with M. Tuomela, *Mind and Society* 4, 2005, 49–84.

"Joint Action," in N. Psarros and K. Schulte-Ostermann, eds., *Facets of Sociality*, Ontos Verlag: Frankfurt, 2006, pp. 169–207

"Cooperation and the We-Perspective," in F. Peter and H. B. Schmid, eds., *Rationality and Commitment*, Oxford University Press, forthcoming.

"Joint Intention, We-Mode and I-Mode," *Midwest Studies in Philosophy* 30, 35–58.

I am grateful to several persons for discussions related to the themes of this book. Kaarlo Miller has been my best critic throughout the years. He has commented on most of the manuscript and, as always, his comments have been very sharp and critical. Hans Bernhard Schmid and Frank Hindriks read most of the chapters of an early version and made good comments. My wife Maj read the manuscript right before the book went to print, and her remarks and criticisms made me rethink my points at several places. Special thanks go to her for support during the several years the we-mode approach of this book was being created. In addition to her and Kaarlo Miller, the other members of my research group—Raul Hakli, Pekka Mäkelä, and Antti Saaristo—read parts of the manuscript, and I thank them for their remarks.

I also thank the Academy of Finland for partial support to the members of my research group. A personal grant to me from the Helsinki Collegium for Advanced Studies for the academic year 2003–4 was very helpful. First drafts of several chapters were written during that period. My thanks are extended to the Collegium for providing good conditions for work.

I dedicate this book to my immediate and extended family.

CONTENTS

The Philosophy of Sociality

INTRODUCTION

1   The We-Perspective

Human beings are social beings living and adapted to living in groups. They can think and act as group members and as "private" persons. In modern societies people tend to belong to several groups, and the basic or constitutive goals, values, standards, beliefs, practices, and so on (using one term "ethoses") of these groups may sometimes be in conflict with each other.

In a broad sense, this book is about the group's point of view, namely, the group members' shared *we-perspective*. To use a topical term, we can say that the book concentrates on *collective intentionality* ("aboutness") expressing a we-perspective. The we-perspective will be understood to contain at least the ethos of the group, collective commitment, affective elements (e.g., "we-feeling"), and action based on these components. A we-perspective may be involved both in the case of one's functioning *as a group member* for the group and in the case of one's functioning *as a private person* in a group context. The term *we-mode* (or, equivalently, *group mode*) is in this book applied to the former case and the term *progroup I-mode* to the latter case. The plain I-mode (or private mode) need not involve collective intentionality, but when it does, the mentioned qualifier "progroup" is used. The we-mode level can be spoken of as the proper group level, while the I-mode level gives the private (or purely personal) level of social life.

My technical explicate for the *full* we-perspective (group perspective) is the we-mode. Roughly speaking, the we-mode is concerned with group-involving states and processes that the group itself has at least partly conceptually and ontologically constructed for itself (e.g., the group may simply take as its goal— "our" goal, for the members—to build a bridge). Acting as a group member in the we-mode sense *constitutively* involves acting for a *collectively constructed group reason*—the group gives a group member reasons to think, "emote," and act in certain ways. For instance, the group's constitutive goals, values, and beliefs

3

provide such group reasons. In contrast, the I-mode is concerned *only* with "private" personal and interpersonal reasons and relations, as well as with groups involving such ingredients. Group reasons in a weaker sense may contingently be involved.

For instance, social institutions require special thickly collectively constructed contents (e.g., "Euros are *our* money"), and, arguably, this seems clearly to fall beyond the conceptual resources of the I-mode (see chapter 8). The important divide here is between a group thinking and acting as one agent versus some agents acting and interacting, perhaps in concert, in pursuit of their (possibly shared) private goals. Group reasons (qua we-mode reasons) and I-mode reasons (private reasons) for acting and having attitudes thus are clearly of a different kind. Accordingly, only the we-mode can properly account for the generality that the group level involves with respect to group members (change of membership, future members, etc.) and the kind of (partial) depersonalization that group life involves.

We-mode thinking, feeling, and acting presuppose collective acceptance of the group's ethos (or of some element entailed by the ethos) or of some other, *non*constitutive content as the object of the group's "attitudes." The collectively accepted contents must be taken to be for group use, namely, collectively available and in force for the group members, and, when broadly conceived, for the benefit of the group's goals and interests.

It is often useful to view a group as an agent capable of acting as a unit. Thus it can be taken to accept views, form intentions, act, and be responsible. However, it is not an extra agent over and above the group members. When a group acts, its members must act as group members. In a sense, one can thus redescribe the group's functioning and acting at the group member level in terms of the group members' functioning in appropriate ways as group members. This is basically we-mode activity. It follows from the idea of a group acting or functioning as one agent that the members ought to function appropriately. They can be said to be necessarily "in the same boat," "stand or fall together," or share a "common fate." In the technical terminology of this book, they satisfy the "Collectivity Condition." Formulated for the special case of goal satisfaction, it necessarily connects the members as follows. Necessarily (as based on group construction of a goal as the group's goal), the goal is satisfied for a member if and only if it is satisfied for all other members. The Collectivity Condition is a central constitutive element of the we-mode.

This book focuses on the we-mode, thus we-mode collective intentionality, and on its conceptual and functional relation to the I-mode. As mentioned, the I-mode we-perspective and I-mode collective intentionality also exist, but the we-mode we-perspective is holistic and richer—for example, in that it involves the Collectivity Condition and the group reason requirement, both of which are based on collective construction in the group. We-mode collective intentionality (equaling the we-mode we-perspective) basically amounts to thinking and acting fully as group member. The I-mode case is partly different, for there is also I-mode collective intentionality that does not involve the I-mode we-perspective. Notice, too, that people often, if not typically, act both for we-mode and I-mode reasons, even on the same occasion.

The central distinction from which my theorizing starts is the generally accepted distinction between thinking and acting as a group member (reflecting the group level) versus as a private person. My analysis of thinking and acting as a group member will assume that we are dealing with normal human beings to whom propositional attitudes, other mental states, and actions can meaningfully be attributed. In general, such agents must understand what group membership means and must also know to which groups they belong. In my technical developments, this will require that they understand what the group ethos is, that is to say, what its central or constitutive goals, values, beliefs, norms, and standards are and what it is to take it, or its ingredients, as one's reason for action. Note that even in simple cases of joint action such as two persons doing something together (e.g., lifting a table), the participants form a group with the ethos content of lifting the table: They have collectively accepted lifting the table jointly as their joint goal, hence they jointly intend to achieve this goal.

The second element that is conceptually involved in the we-mode, over and above thinking and acting as a group member, is collective commitment. In order for a group member to act as a group member, it must thus be required that she be committed (bound) to performing actions that further the group's ethos and other matters that the group is pursuing. Indeed, the members should be collectively committed, namely, committed as group members, to participating in group activities. Their collective commitment involves them also being "socially" committed (that is, directly committed to other group members) to each other to act in the right group ways. Collective commitment has two basic, intertwined roles here. First, it "glues" the members together around an ethos. This gives the foundation for the unity and identity of the group. Second, collective commitment serves to give *joint* authority to the group members to pursue ethos-related action. They can and must, in their own thinking and acting, take into account that the group members are collectively committed to the group ethos and to the group members and that they are jointly responsible for promoting the ethos. Every group member is accountable not only to himself for his participatory action but also to the other members. All this shows how group unity, as formed by collective commitment to the ethos, relates to action as a group member.

In view of the above, it can be said that the we-mode is constituted of two elements, a content element and a "practical" (action-related) element, namely, collective commitment. To illustrate, we consider a two-person case in which a goal (or intention, belief, etc.) is collectively accepted (constructed) and held by two persons, you and me. The case involves two elements:

(i) G is *our* goal, where "our goal" satisfies the Collectivity Condition.
(ii) We (you and I together) are collectively committed to goal G as our goal.

I claim that (i) and (ii) give the intuitive "rock bottom" of the we-mode. Actually, (ii) is part and parcel of (i) and can be regarded as entailed by it. The participants' being collectively committed to goal G involves that they are committed to doing their parts of their joint action concerned with their achieving G. The joint goal that they here have constructed for their group serves as their reason for their performing their parts. The notion of a joint goal satisfies the Collectivity Condition. Due to its being satisfied, the notion of "we" is not reducible to the conjunction "you and I," although it entails it.[1]

The we-mode elements (i) and (ii) can intuitively be viewed as partial translations of group-level descriptions of the following kinds.

(i') Group g's goal is G (where g has you and me as its sole members).
(ii') Group g is committed to goal G.

Descriptions (i') and (ii') can be regarded as equivalent. Hence also (i) and (ii) are seen to be equivalent from our present group-level perspective. This point also applies, mutatis mutandis, to intentions, beliefs, and other voluntary attitudes.

While the notions of collective commitment and acting as group member are intimately connected, they can still analytically be kept apart. So conceptually we start with a full notion of a human being as person and the notions of group and group ethos and promoting the group ethos (acting for the group), and we proceed to analyze thinking and acting as a group member on this basis. Adding collective commitment to thinking and acting as a group member gives the notion of the we-mode, which explicates the thick (or full) we-perspective. The fullest notion of the we-mode requires in addition that the group members not only accept the group's ethos and other goals and beliefs, and so on, in their action but also are at least disposed to accept them in the reflective and reflexive sense that the specific constellation of goals, values, beliefs, and so on indeed is the group's ethos and that those other elements indeed are the group's nonconstitutive goals and beliefs, all this being publicly available knowledge in the group. This account applies to normal democratic groups, and it also applies to fleeting groups such as the group formed by some persons carrying jointly a heavy object. Here the group's specific ethos can consist merely of a joint goal and a relevant mutual belief that qualifies as a group ethos.

This book relies on the conception of human beings as persons in the sense of the "framework of agency" that assumes that (normal) persons are thinking, experiencing, feeling, and acting beings capable of communication, cooperation, and following rules and norms. There are important evolutionary considerations related to this. One is the phylogenetic fact that the human species has had at least the general capacity for both we-mode and I-mode attitudes and action for at least hundreds of thousands of years, although not refined by linguistic skills until perhaps one or two hundred thousand years ago. The other is the fact or at least claim that children acquire a rudimentary capacity for shared intentionality toward the end of their first year of life and for we-mode collective intentionality starting as early as in their second year of life.[2] In this process the child learns to make believe and pretend. This capacity is central, for example, for a person's understanding of the notion of institutional status. The disposition to have collectively intentional (we-mode) thoughts and to act in the we-mode seems to be a coevolutionary adaptation (that is, based on a genetic and cultural evolutionary mechanism and history). The precise content of the collectively intentional mental state is nevertheless culturally and socially determined. It has been argued on the basis of experimental results that the most basic feature that distinguishes human beings as a species from higher animals such as chimpanzees is humans' capacity and motivation to have, and act on, collectively intentional states that probably coevolved long ago, perhaps in connection to the emergence of Homo sapiens.[3] (See chapter 9.)

In a nutshell, this book accordingly argues that conceptualizing social life and theorizing about it requires the use of group concepts, indeed the we-perspective and, especially, the we-mode. To think (e.g., believe, intend) or act in the we-mode is to think or act as a group member in a full sense, thus for a group reason. Thinking and acting in the we-mode expresses collective intentionality in its full sense. In contrast, to think or act in the I-mode is to think or act as a private person—even if a group reason might contingently be at play. To what extent and in what contexts group concepts are needed or useful is discussed in detail in the book. An example of where the we-mode (the adoption of the full we-perspective) can do better is the prisoner's dilemma. It simply does not exist—at least on the group-member level—if the group members really act fully as a group. For here the group would rationally choose the cooperative strategy (C) over defection (D) because the C strategy or action yields a joint outcome that is Pareto-preferable to the joint outcome resulting from defection, while, in contrast, the pure I-mode recommends mutual defection, at least for single-shot cases, and the progroup I-mode at best recommends changing the situation into a coordination game.

As to some connections to political philosophy, the kind of collective acceptance account to be constructed in this book to partly explicate the we-perspective shares some features with the "republican" version of democratic theory that communitarianism also represents. Briefly, the ethos in my account represents "common good" (a central element in republicanism) and other joint constitutive elements, while collective acceptance (coming to hold and holding relevant we-attitudes and acting on them) represents the democratic process wherein people, qua group members, express their shared choice of what the common good (etc.) in their group will amount to.[4]

2   Preview and the Basic Theses

Chapter 1 clarifies the central notion, or actually notions, of acting and functioning as a group member. One can function and act as a group member either in the we-mode or in the I-mode. In the latter case, one adopts the group ethos ideas in a private sense. Accordingly, we-mode reasons for actions and mental states are group-based and collectively constructed, while I-mode reasons are private. We-mode acting as a group member will be called the "standard" sense and the latter the "weak" sense of acting as a group member. The notion of collective commitment—viewed as a conceptual entailment of we-mode collective acceptance—is clarified, and its functions in central group contexts are discussed in this chapter. A distinction between we-mode groups and I-mode groups is made and clarified. We-mode groups, in contrast to I-mode groups, are social constructions based on collective acceptance, whereas I-mode groups are not.

Chapter 2 analyzes the notions of the I-mode and the we-mode, or actually several versions of these notions. It also clarifies the central Collectivity Condition (recall section 1) that underlies the full we-perspective (the full shared point of view). The chapter also contains arguments for the importance of the we-mode, and it surveys most of the reasons for either the necessity or the desirability of we-mode thinking and acting that are discussed in more detail later in the book.

Chapter 3 is concerned with I-mode we-attitudes and develops several varieties of them, most of which will be used in later chapters. Indeed, shared we-attitudes are central in all of the remaining chapters. There is also a discussion of a circularity problem that arises in some contexts involving coordination of attitudes and actions.

Chapter 4 gives an account of we-mode we-intentions and joint intentions and their irreducibility. Joint intentions in the we-mode are taken to consist of shared we-intentions in the we-mode. A detailed account of we-intentions is given, and an alleged circularity problem concerning we-intentions is discussed and resolved. This chapter also presents the "bulletin board view" of collective acceptance of collective attitudes and discusses its applicability.

Chapter 5 gives a detailed account of joint action as a group and a brief survey of other available accounts of joint action. While it concentrates on acting jointly as a group (we-mode joint action), weaker kinds of joint action are also briefly considered, for example, I-mode joint action and collective action based on shared we-attitudes.

Chapter 6 analyzes collective acceptance from a semantic-linguistic point of view. The results are used to give an account of group actions and beliefs. Furthermore, a generalized account of group attitudes is given. This central model is based on group authority in the sense of some authorized members' forming attitudes and/or acting for the group, as well as possibly giving orders to group members. In this connection also the central notion of having an attitude as a group member based on a group reason is clarified. The appendix to chapter 6 discusses social groups, I-mode and we-mode groups, mainly from an ontological point of view, and contrasts the entity view with the nonentity view.

Chapter 7 contains an extensive discussion of cooperation, including accounts of both I-mode and we-mode cooperation. These two modes are compared and illustrated in terms of a simple game-theoretical public good acquisition model. It is shown that in some situations we-mode cooperation is preferable to I-mode cooperation even on grounds of instrumental rationality. Cooperation in a group context, thus basically in an institutional context, is also considered, in both its I-mode and we-mode versions.

Chapter 8 presents a detailed account of social institutions in force. Social institutions are regarded as special collectively constructed social practices (recurrent actions as a group member) that are normatively governed—in part by constitutive norms. At bottom, institutions are group-level phenomena accountable in terms of the we-mode. However, in actual life, institutional activities normally also include lots of I-mode activities that accordingly can be said to have colonized the realm of we-mode institutional action. The special institutional status (including a conceptual, social, normative component) is central to a social institution.

Chapter 9 contains a discussion of the evolutionary aspects of acting as a group member and cooperation. It is argued that the disposition to act as a group member (and, accordingly, to cooperate) is a coevolutionary adaptation, a stable feature involving probably both biological and cultural elements. This chapter sketches an account of the dynamics and change of social practices and discusses group change and evolution. The main change mechanism is taken to be social learning (e.g., imitation) based on conformism, thus we-attitudes. This theoretical account squares well with other, empirically supported work in the field.[5]

Chapter 10 presents an account of group responsibility. The main idea it defends is that we-mode groups, namely, groups in which a substantial number of the members are collectively committed to the group (its "ethos" and to each other to promote the ethos), are normatively responsible for their actions and for what their members, also violators and dissidents, do. In contrast, I-mode groups, namely, groups relying only on private commitments to some shared goals or beliefs, and so on, are not responsible as groups for any actions or outcomes, although their members may be jointly responsible for what they jointly (although not as a group) cause.

Chapters 1–6 create the basic theory of the book, and the rest of the chapters make creative use of the theory to give an account of cooperation, social institutions, group evolution, and group responsibility.

The most central theses defended in the book are as follows.

(1) The we-mode is central both for (a) conceptualizing the social world and (b) accounting for the functionality of several kinds of social activities and relationships. As to (a), for example, the concept of social institution is a group concept collectively constructed in the group and thus clearly seems to involve the we-mode. The we-mode is also functionally required (at least to an extent). Thus, in comparison with the I-mode, thinking and acting in the we-mode (thus for a group reason satisfying the Collectivity Condition) will in many cases make joint action, cooperation, and social practices instrumentally more functional. Aspects of the centrality of the we-mode are discussed in all chapters of the book. The shared we-mode (or group) perspective is the basis of the theory created in this book. As the disposition to we-mode thinking and acting arguably is a stable feature based on culture-gene coevolution (an adaptation), this theory connects to our ancestral history and has a naturalistic basis.

(2) A group member thinks or acts in the we-mode if and only if he is (i) "we-committed" (participates in the collective commitment) to a thought (the mental state and its content) or, respectively, to an action that is (ii) collectively accepted in the group as the group's thought or action and that is (iii) for the group's "use" and accordingly gives the group members a group reason for their thinking and acting. We-mode states and actions presuppose for their truth the satisfaction of the Collectivity Condition (involving the members' necessarily "standing or falling together"; see thesis (4)). All of these features are assumed to be mentally represented in the group members' minds in one way or another. Thus we can speak of a group member having we-mode states such as intentions and beliefs. As an empirical claim, it can be argued that we-mode mental states and actions are natural, coevolved capacities of human beings. This fact, if it is one, is also philosophically important, for—although collective intentional attitudes may make things observer-dependent—these attitudes themselves do not depend on any underlying intentional or "preintentional" attitudes. (See chapters 1, 2, and 9.)

(3) In the I-mode case, a social mental attitude (e.g., intention, belief) often involves a conformist element. Such a conformist attitude can be explicated as a we-attitude. Such an attitude is a we-attitude in its grounded sense if and only if its holder (an individual agent) has it and has it in part because he believes that the

others (or the majority of them) have it and because he believes that all this is mutually believed in the group.[6] Here "because" can express either a reason or a cause. The connection of we-attitudes to conformism is discussed in chapters 3 and 9.

One can refine the notion of the I-mode and work with the "plain" or "pure" I-mode, the "progroup" I-mode, the pure private mode (chapter 2), and even the antigroup I-mode. We-attitudes can also be had in the we-mode, as especially chapters 4–6 make clear. In the we-mode case, the because-relation expresses a presupposition (or a "presuppositional reason") rather than a reason in the standard sense. I-mode we-attitudes can also be called "thin" or "weak" we-attitudes, while we-mode we-attitudes are "thick."

(4) Intuitively, genuine group attitudes and actions are based on the Collectivity Condition, which is discussed in detail in chapters 1, 2, and 8. Applied to the satisfaction of a collective goal, this condition says: Necessarily—due to collective acceptance of the goal as the group's goal (note the reflexivity)—a collective goal is satisfied for a participant if and only if it is satisfied for any other participant. Collective acceptance here is in the we-mode if and only if it satisfies (a version of) the Collectivity Condition. Furthermore, it is argued in chapter 8 that the we-mode and the Collectivity Condition also amount to institutionality in a broad sense and, equivalently, to collectively constructed sociality. (The precise treatment and the required qualifications for these four equivalences are discussed in chapter 8.)

The Collectivity Condition gives a reason to say that the depersonalization that occurs in social groups is part of the basic structure of group life (in its we-mode content) and thus is not a mere contingent feature of groups.

(5) The we-mode is not reducible to the I-mode, although progroup I-mode (requiring acting for the group in a private sense) comes functionally (although not conceptually) close to the we-mode. For instance, a person may have a goal to work for the benefit of his group but still do this privately and be only privately committed, although this goal still does not amount to a we-mode goal that the group "reasons." (See chapter 5 for progroup I-mode joint action versus we-mode joint action.) In general, arguments concerning the aspects of the irreducibility of the we-mode to the I-mode are discussed in several chapters, especially in chapters 2 and 4–8.)

(6) Social groups are not agents in an ontological sense, but they can often usefully be treated as agents and persons, and therefore, for example, beliefs, goals, intentions, and actions can be attributed to them. The "positional" account of a group's attitude, discussed in chapter 6, is based on the group members relevantly collectively accepting the attitude as the group's attitude, although a group cannot literally have an attitude, but a group of persons can collectively share an attitude as group members. (See chapter 6.)

(7) While human beings are capable of thinking and acting both in the I-mode and the we-mode, it is a basic problem in which situations which mode is exemplified. We-mode mental states and actions typically are joint states and actions in a strong sense involving an irreducible, thick "we" (that is, a "we-together"), and this makes the ontic "jointness" level central for the construction of the social world. In this connection, the "primacy" problem and the "switch"

problem arise. Primacy concerns the conceptual versus ontological primacy of one mode over the other, and the switch problem has to do with how a person can or does switch from one mode to the other. (These matters are discussed in chapters 4–8.)

(8) Central parts of the social world are socially constructed in terms of collective acceptance. Thus, medieval Finns collectively created money out of squirrel pelt by collectively accepting squirrel pelt to be money. Collective acceptance here amounts to coming to hold and holding, with collective commitment, a relevant "performative" we-attitude, broadly speaking, one in either the intention family or in the belief family. In chapter 6, group actions and attitudes are shown to be based on collective acceptance, and in chapter 8, social institutions are discussed as collectively constructed artifacts. The account of group attitudes and actions involves the idea of there being authorized group members ("operative" members, e.g., leaders) for various group functions. They typically not only form goals and views but also have the power to act for the group and to give orders to members. Note that groups often involve a normatively codified division of tasks and rights, thus constituting power-related positions.

In addition, a group's constitution, its ethos, is based on collective acceptance that satisfies the Collectivity Condition. The goals, values, standards, and so on involved in the ethos (and all other items fully constituted in the we-mode) have the world-to-mind direction of fit of (semantic) satisfaction and function as (we-mode) group reasons for the members' thinking and acting.

(9) There are two centrally different kinds of cooperation, I-mode cooperation and we-mode cooperation. In I-mode cooperation, the participants try to satisfy their own "private" goals by adjusting them and their (private) means actions toward the others' corresponding goals and means actions, purporting that the participants will gain from cooperation, as compared with a situation where cooperation does not take place. We-mode cooperation in turn basically amounts to we-mode joint action. (See chapter 7.)

(10) Social institutions in their core sense are norm systems obeyed in accordance with relevant social practices, often highly routine practices accountable in terms of "collective pattern-governed behaviors." The norm system will include constitutive norms (such as "Squirrel pelt counts as money") that serve to confer a special institutional status on the social practices or some of their element(s). The *institutional status* consists of (i) a *conceptual* (or "symbolizing") component (e.g., squirrel pelt constitutively is money); (ii) a *normative* component ((a) the predicate "money" may be applied to squirrel pelts, and (b) the owner of squirrel pelts has certain *powers* concerning exchange of goods); and (iii) a *social* component (the money institution is a group phenomenon valid in a group context). The concept of social institution is a we-mode concept, and in actual practice, at least some we-mode thinking and acting is required for institutions to function adequately. This book argues that collective sociality and institutionality go together and are in fact truth-equivalent with both the we-mode and the collectivity involved in the Collectivity Condition. (See chapter 8.)

(11) The development and cultural evolution of social institutions toward equilibria is investigated partly in terms of new application of a mathematical model of change that I have developed elsewhere and is only informally explained

in this book.[7] The case of the evolution of institutions requires the addition of suitable assumptions about conformism of various kinds, for example, conformity based on majority (e.g., shared we-attitudes), leaders' opinions, or the plain attractiveness of ideas. (See chapter 9.)

(12) Under a wide variety of conditions, we-mode groups are normatively responsible for their actions and outcomes of their actions, and they are also responsible (to some degree at least) for their members' actions in group contexts, and this also includes violations of the group's ethos (its "constitution").

In the case of I-mode groups, there is only "aggregated," although possibly conditional, private responsibility for what a member does (either alone or in conjunction with the others' I-mode actions). (See chapter 10.)

1

ACTING AS A GROUP MEMBER

1 Group Notions and the Conceptualization of the Social World

Much of human life is spent in group contexts. People are usually members of several social groups—for example, task groups, small social groups, organizations, nations, states, and so on. They act as group members relative to a group, especially in the contexts where that group acts and has committed itself to a task. But what does acting as a group member consist in? This chapter will answer the question, and it will also analyze group commitment on the level of group members. Here we speak of the group members being collectively committed to the group task in question.

On a general level, it is argued in this book that central parts of the social world—including social groups, social practices, and social institutions—conceptually (and, typically, functionally) require we-mode thinking and acting and, more broadly, the full we-perspective. In turn, we-mode thinking and acting require and are (conceptually and factually) based on thinking and acting as a group member and therefore thinking and acting for a group reason (in a full-blown sense requiring the satisfaction of the Collectivity Condition).[1] The former claim will be discussed later in this book, while this chapter focuses on the latter. The notion of collective commitment that is part and parcel of the we-mode can be regarded as a central "glue" in social life. It concerns the group members' collectively binding themselves, for example, to an idea, action, or to the group itself. In its weakest form, collective commitment is "group-socially" normative rather than properly (substantitively) normative, that is, normative in a moral, legal, or a wide prudential sense. There is some previous work on collective commitment, but there seem to have been no serious attempts to analyze the notion of acting as a group member in detail.[2]

Acting as a group member—figuratively on the *group level*—intuitively contrasts with acting as a private person—on the *private level*—even if one also as a private

13

person can, of course, think about groups and act in relation to them. Indeed, in this book I use the word "private" rather than "personal" to represent I-mode thinking and acting, because both the I-mode and the we-mode can be involved when the word "personal" is used in the sense of applying to a particular person.

In groups committed to preserving and furthering matters constitutive of their identity, the notion of acting as a group member in its standard sense amounts to the same thing as the notion of *we-mode* (thus group-reason based) functioning and acting.[3] Furthermore, collective identification (identification with one's group) amounts to functioning as a group member in its full, group-committal sense (i.e., we-mode functioning).

The concept of we-mode in itself contains the notion of group (and expresses part of the group-perspective). It is a holistic institutional notion, while ontologically it can be regarded as being about "groupishly" interrelated group members. Thinking and acting in the we-mode basically amounts to thinking and acting for a group reason, that is, to a group member's taking the group's views and commitments as his authoritative reasons for thinking and acting as the group "requires" or in accordance with what "favors" the group (namely, its goals, etc.). A central notion that is needed is that of a social group. This book focuses on the we-mode group, based on the one hand on a "we" concerned with togetherness and on the other hand on the group's "ethos"—its constitutive goals, values, standards, beliefs, and practices. (This will include the possibility of a group with subgroups with different ethoses, such that the ethos of the full group will consist of the intersection, so to speak, of the subgroups' ethoses.) If and when the members jointly intend to satisfy the ethos, they are collectively bound (committed) to it, because intention can be taken to entail commitment in the relevant sense.

When I speak of the *we-mode* in the general sense (as opposed to the I-mode) it amounts to the *full-blown we-perspective*, and this perspective is a kind of conceptual module that contains several interconnected concepts. These concepts include especially the *thick* notions of *"we"* and *group* as well as *we-mode thoughts* (e.g., "We will perform a joint action X together") and *we-mode reasons* (e.g., "I am doing X because our group's doing Y requires it"), *collective acceptance* (e.g., "We accept that these stones mark the borders of our territory"), and *collective commitment*, especially to the group's *ethos*. Thinking or acting for a we-mode reason (group reason) entails thinking or acting *for the group*.

As a quick survey of the topics treated in this chapter, a review of the section titles will give initial guidance to the reader.[4] Thus the mentioned notions of social group, group ethos, acting as a group member, and collective commitment will be studied below. This chapter is central for the theory being created in the early chapters of the book. There is a good amount of concept analysis and classification here, and the later chapters will throw further light on these notions and their interconnections.

2 Ethos and Social Groups

The notion of a social group is central in this book, and in this section I will discuss both we-mode and I-mode social groups, with an emphasis on we-mode groups.

I will focus on we-mode social groups based on *voluntary* membership. Voluntary membership involves that a person signing on as a member of the group prima facie ought to endorse the basic goals and values, norms, standards, beliefs, practices, and so on—briefly, the ethos—of the group and to act accordingly. In this kind of group, a member cannot in general be coerced to stay in the group. In contrast, there are groups with involuntary membership. Thus, one is typically born into a society, nation, and state. However, one can in principle exit one's society and state, but not one's nation. Thus we have to distinguish between the right or possibility of voluntarily entering a group and that of voluntarily exiting it. These notions do not entail each other.

To keep things simple, I will generally assume that there is internal freedom from coercion in the group. That is, the members' decision-making should not be at least strongly coerced but must express their intentional agency and free will. Of course, in the context of group life and joint action, the participants will have to partially give up their own authority to the group, but this should happen basically without (much) *internal* coercion. Some amount of coercion can be tolerated, but it has to fall short of acting under gunpoint (think of working in a committee with a powerful chairman—the committee members may tolerate some exercise of power against their will).

Furthermore, the groups under discussion are normally taken to be free from *external* coercion in their decision-making and group acceptance. In contrast, a group can be forbidden to exist, can be forbidden to act (e.g., due to its subversive activities), or can be coerced to stop acting, for example, when engaged in illegal or asocial activities.

The notions of the *realm of concern* and the *intentional horizon* of a group are needed for the central notion of the *ethos* of a group. I assume that at least in principle all of these three items are up to the group to determine within a given environmental setting, and this tends to generate that the group is internally and externally free (autonomous). Accordingly, these items are taken to be based on group acceptance, thus on group members' collective acceptance, in the sense that certain specific things are collectively taken to belong to the group's realm of concern, intentional horizon, and/or ethos.

The *realm of concern* of a group will consist of a class of topics that the group has collectively accepted as its topics of concern, that is, as "contents" that are of interest to the group, and are considered in a *group context* (in contrast to a private context). A group context is public to the group members. Basically, the group context–private context distinction is a matter of collective acceptance in the group, taking due account of its broader social environment. When people act as group members, they must be acting in the (socially and normatively) right circumstances. For instance, acting in a group position (task, office) and thus performing one's work duties requires that such circumstances, partly defining the group context, are present.

Concentrating here on propositional attitudes, I take the *intentional horizon* of a group, g, to consist of the subset of topics in its realm of concern that it de facto has some specific attitude about (except for the assumed collective acceptance). For instance, the attitude can be belief, intention, (having a) goal, wish, and so on, but as a group attitude it must be (normally voluntarily) collectively accepted, even if the individual attitudes on which the group acceptance is based need not be voluntarily held.[5]

The *ethos* of group g in its strict sense is defined as the set of the *constitutive* goals, values, beliefs, standards, norms, practices, and/or traditions that give the group motivating reasons for action.[6] The notion of ethos can be understood in the wide sense in which every group can be taken to have an ethos, which in weakest cases may consist just of some basic shared ends or beliefs that are possibly unreflected and not clearly articulated and understood. I will basically speak as if the group were a single-ethos group, but my account also accepts the "multi-cultural" case of a group with several subgroups with partly overlapping sub-ethoses. The intersection of the subethoses will be the group ethos or, if you like, the nuclear ethos of the full group.[7] Below I will normally speak of the ethos of the group, and this can refer either to the case of a single-ethos group or to the multi-ethos case of a group with subgroups. All the group members share the nuclear ethos (but not what is outside it), and this also applies to higher order groups (e.g., the European Union).

The ethos directs the group members' thoughts and actions toward what is important for the group and is generally expected to "benefit" it.[8] Examples range from a state's constitution to a university's goal to provide higher education and promote scientific research to a stamp collector club's ethos to facilitate its members' stamp collecting. When there is no clear-cut distinction between the constitutive and nonconstitutive goals, beliefs, standards, and so on, we can take the ethos in a wider sense to consist of the *central* goals, beliefs, standards, and so on, defining centrality basically in the partly circular terms of the group members' collective acceptance of what is central. The ethos forms a subset of the intentional horizon of the group. The ethos constitutes the content aspect of the identity of the group (and in the multi-ethos case, a partial identity of each subgroup of the group). To give a simple example, the group might have as its constitutive goal (ethos) to make their village wealthy and beautiful.

In general, to be satisfied and maintained, the ethos requires collective action.[9] A group is assumed to accept an ethos for the group with commitment to satisfy it. Typically, although not logically necessarily, the acceptance of the ethos also concerns its maintenance (e.g., the "rules of the house" are typically accepted not only for obedience but for maintaining them). The notion of the promotion (satisfaction and maintenance) of the ethos is a central notion in this book. What promotes the ethos is for the group (i.e., is "shareware" for the group) and satisfies the constitutive *Collectivity Condition*, which involves the idea of the group members necessarily "standing or falling together" concerning group-relevant activities and items (see chapters 2 and 8).

Collective acceptance will be elucidated in chapter 6. The basic idea is that collective acceptance amounts to the participants in question coming to hold and holding a shared "we-attitude."[10] The we-attitude can be in the proattitude family (including, e.g., proattitudes, intentions, and promises) or in the belief family (actually belief understood as acceptance and not "experiential" belief); or, somewhat more generally, the we-attitude can have the world-to-mind or the mind-to-world direction of fit of satisfaction. Roughly, a person has a certain we-attitude (e.g., a we-goal) if she has the attitude on the basis that the others in the group also have or tend to have it and that this is mutual knowledge (see chapter 3). We-attitudes can be either in the we-mode or in the I-mode (in spite of the perhaps misleading term "we-attitude"). A we-mode we-attitude, in contrast to an I-mode one, involves a "thick," or "togetherness," notion of "we" (e.g., "We together intend to do X," "We believe that p as a group," with the group's commitment to these).[11]

Before discussing social groups in more detail, let me present a brief charac-terization of we-mode and I-mode reasons in more precise terms than above. This division of reasons is central not only for an account of social groups but in fact for almost all the central social notions dealt with in this book. My criteria speak of an agent's "main reason" for action—this notion is that for a reason to be a main reason, considered alone, it typically would (or at least ought to) suffice for (his commitment to) the action in question. The criteria are given for a simple case relating to the context of a specific group, assuming that a reason is a fact or a fact-like entity expressible by a that-clause:

> (IMR) Reason R is a group member's motivating *I-mode reason* for performing an action X if and only if R is the agent's main motivating private reason for his performing X. Typically, R is a state that the agent wants or intends to be the case or a state that, according to his belief, obtains; and X is an action that is a means to R or an action that R requires for its obtaining such that the agent is privately committed to performing X for the reason R.

> (WMR) Reason R is a group member's motivating *we-mode reason* for performing an action X if and only if R is the agent's main motivating group reason for his performing X. Typically, R is a state that the group in question wants, intends, or requires to be the case or is a state that, according to the group's belief, obtains; generally speaking R is a state that is "for the group." X is an action that is the individual's part of a collective action that is a means to R or a collective action that R requires for its obtaining, where the group members are collectively com-mitted to performing the collective action for reason R and mutually believing so.

In (WMR), X can be, for example, a collective (or group) action with multiple tokens (e.g., going to church on Sundays) or a joint action (e.g., cleaning up a park as a many-person action). As the group members are collectively committed to performing the collective action in question for reason R (a state expressible by a that-clause), they are also socially committed to the group members to performing their parts of the collective action for reason R. A full-blown (a we-mode) group reason will have to satisfy the Collectivity Condition (see chapter 2).

Having a private commitment means, in (IMR), that the person privately (rather than as a group member) has psychologically bound himself to a "content," for example, to performing an action for a reason. In general, private commitment is dependent on an intention, for example, the intention to reach a goal. Notice that functioning in the we-mode is *necessarily* connected to a thick group reason, to what one's group has committed itself to in the situation at hand, where the group's commitment serves as an authoritative reason for the participants. In contrast, functioning in the I-mode is at most only *contingently* connected to a group reason—that must be an I-mode one, if there is one involved. ((WMR) and (IMR) can be generalized to cover any voluntary attitude and action.)[12]

Typically, the social groups to be discussed in this book are assumed to be capable of acting as groups. What will be called we-mode groups have this capacity. In them the members act at least partly for a group reason. Any group is assumed to have an ethos, and, at least in autonomous groups, the members ought to further and promote (at least respect) the ethos of the group. This requires that its members can collectively commit themselves to doing something together and, accordingly, that the members will understand and mutually believe (at least in a *de dicto* sense) that they are members of the group with a certain ethos—be the group a permanent one or only a group of people acting together on a specific occasion. The descriptions under which the members take themselves and others to be members of the group might be vague, as long as the group still is able to function in the right way as a group. Being a member can then be taken to presuppose a mutually recognized commitment (bond) to the group ethos and social commitment to the other group members relative to promoting the ethos.

To discuss we-mode groups in detail, a central assumption I will make is that the members of a group share an ethos, E, that consists of contents such as goals, beliefs, values, standards, and norms. In simplest cases, a distinctive group ethos might be just the intended goal to lift a table together. Upon analysis, this amounts, roughly, to the members' collective acceptance of E, where the collective acceptance has the world-to-mind direction of fit concerning E. This entails a general joint intention toward E.[13] One can say that the distinctive "content" (or "ideology") of the group is constituted by its ethos.

The full-blown collective acceptance of an ethos as a group's ethos by the members basically results in their forming a *we-mode* group. Such collective acceptance is based on a thick notion of "we" ("we-together"). The result of the collective acceptance is a group that the members qua members construct for themselves and in which there is not only the (*pro tanto* or prima facie) obligation to obey the ethos but also a functionally substantial number of members who are collectively committed to obeying the ethos and maintaining it "for the time being." (See chapter 10 for discussion of dissidents.)

For a group to be able to act as a (we-mode) group, its members must believe (or be disposed to believe) that they are members of the group (under some description of membership) and also that the other group members (noncircularly characterized) belong to the group; and the members must also believe that the others believe so of themselves and of them. Generally put, there must be a mutual belief of these group elements for the group to function properly. If you and I form a group for exchanging stamps, each of us must at least believe that he is a member and that the other is a member; otherwise our group cannot act—we cannot, for example, organize a stamp exhibition.

A we-mode group thus is based on collective acceptance of a group ethos, where the ethos is constitutive and distinctive of the group. Furthermore, the Collectivity Condition is satisfied: Necessarily, E is a member's group ethos if and only if it is every other member's group ethos. As a psychological fact, the acceptance need not be reflected on but might be something that is "seen" in the group members' actions and inferences. (The members might be cleaning a park together as a we-mode group without coming to reflect on the fact that they really are functioning as one agent even if that is their view.) On both conceptual and functional grounds, a member's participation in collective acceptance presupposes that a sufficient number of the others also participate.[14] The collective acceptance in the we-mode case has to involve the idea of one's accepting that one ought to to do *one's part* of the group's satisfying (and maintaining) the ethos. The attitudinal and, especially, actional part structure related to accepting and satisfying the ethos is thus assumed to be involved in the we-mode case. The part structure (thus "position" structure in a general sense) is essential to the we-mode case and indeed involves the idea of *functioning as a group member* in the full sense. The social commitment involved in the collective intention and commitment, as entailed by the we-mode collective acceptance, relies on the part structure being in place. When the part structure is normatively codified by social norms and rules, we are dealing with a normatively structured group involving power relations.

In a nutshell, in this account, a group is viewed as a collectively constructed agent that can have goals, beliefs, and so on and that can act, although that is not literally true. The group intends to satisfy (and uphold) its ethos, and this involves that the members collectively accept their obligation to do their parts of the group's satisfying (and upholding) its ethos. The group is viewed as having authority—via the members' collectively accepted goals and views and their chosen leaders—to give the members reasons to think and act in group contexts (see chapter 6).

My account of *core* we-mode groups is group-internal and based on collective acceptance. In addition, external criteria (such as symbolic markers) often are present in actual life, but the core notion is internal and will be involved in all broader we-mode group notions. External criteria, like objective requirements for membership, can even be "built" into the ethos. Other external requirements, such as that members of various outgroups have to regard a core we-mode group as a group, seem not to be conceptually required (think of secret groups of which outsiders know nothing). Membership is defined in terms of the ethos, E. To be a group member basically requires the acceptance of E.

Let me accordingly reformulate the above account of a we-mode group so as to make the artifactual nature of we-mode groups clearer:[15]

> A collective g consisting of some persons (or in the normatively structured case, position-holders) is a *(core) we-mode social group*
> if and only if
> (1) g has accepted a certain ethos, E, as a group for itself and is committed to it. On the level of its members, this entails that at least a substantial number of the members of g have as group members (thus in a broad sense as position-holders in g) collectively accepted E as g's (namely, their group's, "our") ethos and hence are collectively committed to it, with the understanding that the ethos is to function as providing authoritative reasons for thinking and acting qua a group member;

(2) every member of g as a group member "group-socially" ought to accept E (and accordingly to be committed to it as a group member), at least in part because the group has accepted E as its ethos;

(3) it is a mutual belief in the group that (1) and (2).

Collective acceptance here conceptually requires reflexive acceptance: Necessarily (in a conceptual or quasi-conceptual sense), the members collectively accept (with collective commitment) E as g's ethos if and only if (it is correctly assertable for them that) E is g's ethos.[16] Given this, our account entails that a we-mode group (in contrast to an I-mode group; see below) is a collective artifact and indeed an organized institutional entity (see chapter 8). Group members are viewed as functioning in group positions (be they differentiated or not). Thus, a we-mode group can indeed be said to consist of such positions.[17]

According to (1), it makes (at least functional) sense to attribute mental states (e.g., acceptances, goals, intentions) to a group. The group is taken to be able to reason and act as a unit on the basis of those mental states and to be both intra- and intertemporally committed to what it has accepted. A we-mode group is accordingly taken to be capable of making judgments, molding its physical surroundings, and constructing institutions in virtue of the collective commitment to the group ethos (this contrasts with an I-mode group). In short, a we-mode group is a quasi-person without literally being a person.

From the perspective of ethos satisfaction and maintenance, a group's capacity to act as a group relies on the fact that the ethos has the world-to-mind direction fit and is in this sense goal-like. Collective acceptance of the ethos here amounts to a general joint intention to satisfy the ethos (and what it entails). Because of the joint intention (and the entailed collective commitment) toward the ethos, the agents are organized for joint action, and they can accordingly act jointly as a group.[18]

Clause (1) presupposes that the group members have some mastery of the concepts involved, for example, they must know at least roughly what it is for a group to have an ethos and what it is for them to be collectively committed to the ethos. To illustrate, in a stamp collectors' club, the members typically do accept its ethos of organized stamp collecting and are collectively committed to it. Thus (1) is fulfilled. A group cannot rationally have a goal without being committed to it, and thus its members—especially its new members—ought to accept E and be (collectively) committed to it. This supports clause (2). (See section 3 for "group-social" normativity; also see section 6.)

We-mode groups were argued to be collectively constructed. What is collectively constructed is primarily the (conceptual psychological) entity-nature of the group, that is, that some persons form a group as a kind of entity.[19] Assuming that collective acceptance indeed is reflexive, we have that the members of g collectively accept for the group that E is the ethos of g (thus the members' ethos qua members of g). By their collective acceptance the members then entify or quasi-entify the group in their thoughts, give it an ethos, and in effect think that they "stand or fall together," the Collectivity Condition becoming satisfied. The members have thereby constructed g as a we-mode group. Collective acceptance rationally entails mutual true belief in—or at least "knowability" of—what has been accepted, namely, g as a group with ethos E.

Suppose a group is a secret group in a country where stamp collecting is strictly forbidden. Then the criterion of (we-mode) grouphood might indeed be only internal: The central basis of grouphood then is collective acceptance of E with collective commitment and the entailed mutual belief about collective acceptance (see clause (3)).[20] The group in the core sense is one that exists for the members and between them. Not all we-mode groups need be based on purely internal criteria, though, only what I technically call a core we-mode group. Thus, adding on new conditions is possible, as long as (1)–(3) are satisfied. Conditions (1)–(3) are necessary in the case of any constructed group, because it is basically the members who by their collective acceptance construct the group. No external conditions can by themselves be sufficient for the existence of such a group.

Next, we consider relaxing the ideas that every member need take part in the collective acceptance required by (2) and in the mutual belief in (3).[21] What is needed is a sufficient amount of collective acceptance in the group to the effect that the proposition that g is a group with ethos E is true. Thus "g accepts E" and "a substantial number of the members of g accept E" can be regarded as more or less functionally equivalent with respect to g's actions (see chapter 6 for an in-depth discussion).[22] If a group involves an authority structure with a division of its members into authorized operative and nonoperative members, that might suffice, as long as the nonoperatives go along and function as if they were taking part in the group acceptance. In their case, also, the conceptual demands might be relaxed (their understanding of what an ethos is and what it requires of them might be limited, etc.).

The mutual belief in (3) can be understood in a cognitively undemanding sense; see section 5 of chapter 3. Note, furthermore, that g is typically described in intensional rather than extensional terms, and the group members' descriptions might differ substantially from each other. Still, they cannot differ very much extensionally, on pain of the group failing to have an identity. My above point concerns the criteria of grouphood and group membership. Note that this is different from the practical epistemic matter of how correct or erroneous is their actual classification of individual people into group members and nongroup members.

The members who are collectively committed to the ethos will act appropriately as group members (see section 3 for such we-mode acting as a group member), hence they will trustfully cooperate with each other (see the precise argument in appendix 3 of chapter 7 for this). Commitment comes in degrees, and typically members who are also strongly emotionally committed to the group are central for initiation and carrying out group action.

As my main focus in this book will be we-mode groups, I will be brief on I-mode groups. In contrast to a we-mode group, in an I-mode group the members are assumed to be only privately (that is, as private persons) committed to an ethos. Think of persons who form an I-mode group on the basis of their thinking as follows: "I as a private person intend to help starving people in a context where also some others so intend." Accordingly, an I-mode group is based on its members' interrelations, but it is not constructed by the members as a group in the way a we-mode group is, and it is not capable of acting fully *as a group*: The members do not act as full-blown group members because not even the cognitive content of the Collectivity Condition is satisfied and they are not collectively committed (in an action-generating way) to participation in promoting the group ethos (also this actional aspect is entailed by the Collectivity Condition as I have formulated it). However, the members may act toward the same goal, so that the group can be said to behave in an ordered manner toward the goal, so that *descriptively*, but not on *conceptual* grounds, the group can be taken to act.

> A collective g consisting of some persons is an *I-mode social group*
> if and only if
> (1) The members of g (privately) accept some goals, beliefs, standards, and so on, as constitutive for the collective, forming the (privately) shared ethos E, and accordingly are committed to E at least in part because the others in g (privately) accept E, and this is mutually believed in g.
> (2) The members of g mutually believe that they (noncircularly characterized) are group members—at least in the weak sense that they share the beliefs that they themselves belong to g and that the others believe that they belong to g, under suitable, perhaps collective descriptions of membership.

Note that the social condition in clause (1) that the members accept the ethos in part because the others do also holds in the we-mode case, although in that case this condition is a consequence of the fact that the members take the group's acceptance of E as their reason for accepting E. This point thus concerns those who have not yet accepted E, and a central case in point is where the group has a long history and those who originally established E for the group may not be members anymore. While in a we-mode group, full for-groupness ("g is our group," with an open "we") is conceptually involved because of the collectively accepted E in accordance with the Collectivity Condition, in an I-mode group a kind of for-groupness (I call it "progroupness") exists only in the members' private mental states. The commitment in the I-mode case is weaker because of being only private and therefore more easily changeable.[23] Note that clause (2) is entailed by the definiens of we-mode group.

3   Acting as a Group Member

In any we-mode group, the members may perform *freely* chosen *actions qua a group member* under some provisions. These actions—or, more broadly, activities, including mental ones—must belong to the topics of concern of the group in group contexts, as opposed to private contexts, and in the standard case they must be collectively accepted (or at least collectively accept*able*) as actions correct for a group member to perform. Accordingly, an action is an action as a group member if and only if it is collectively accepted by (or is collectively acceptable to) the group members as an action that promotes, or is at least weakly conducive to, the satisfaction and maintenance of the ethos of the group, and where the ethos is at least a partial reason for the action in question. This is basically what my analyses below will elucidate (but see the qualifications in chapter 10 making room for dissidents).

The notion of ethos presupposes that the realm of concern of the group is given. This presupposition makes it easier to account for the group's changing its ethos and identity and for comparing different (and perhaps competing) groups concerned with the same kinds of topics. Furthermore, the notion of the realm of concern is required for the elucidation of the notion of acting as a group member. The ultimate conceptual *explicans* in the we-mode case is (rational) collective acceptance (as group acceptance) that involves collective commitment to what has been accepted. The realm of concern, the intentional horizon of the group, the ethos, and acting as a group member all ultimately depend on such we-mode collective acceptance (that satisfies the Collectivity Condition).[24]

The general case to be considered is that of a *normatively structured group* with positions (the unstructured case can be regarded as its special case with no specific positions over and above group membership). I will first classify the types of actions within the group's action realm. These actions will all be collectively acceptable and mutually knowable as being at least weakly ethos-promoting and, in general, performed in part because of the ethos (in the reason sense of "because"). They represent *possible actions as a group member* in typical cases. Here are four action classes that I take to be jointly exhaustive:[25]

(1) positional actions (related to a group position or role), which include (i) actions (tasks) that the position-holder in question *ought to* perform, perhaps in a special way, in certain circumstances, and (ii) actions that he may (is permitted to) so perform in some circumstances;[26]

(2) actions that constitutive and other group norms and group standards (e.g., norms and standards which are not position-specific) require or allow;

(3) actions and joint actions that are based on situational intention formation (e.g., agreement making) that have not been codified in the "task-right system" of g or the group norms of g, but that still are consistent with actions in (1) and (2) and are ethos-promoting;

(4) freely chosen actions or activities (and possibly joint actions), that are not incompatible with actions in classes (1)–(3); these freely chosen actions belong to the realm of concern of g and are rationally or reasonably collectively accepted by, or acceptable to, the members of g as ethos-promoting actions.

Acting as a group member in the *core* sense is to act intentionally within the group's realm of concern, promoting (furthering) the satisfaction and maintenance of the ethos—the central, constitutive goals, values, standards, beliefs, norms, and/ or elements of the history of the group. The ethos is supposed to give the members a reason for action when acting as group members. The core sense will below be divided into what may be called *standard* acting and *weak* acting as a group member. The former will also be called the *we-mode sense* and the latter the *I-mode sense* of acting as a group member. Note that in a we-mode group, some amount of I-mode action as a group member can be tolerated, depending on group functionality. Even in the underlying collective acceptance defining the classes (1)–(4), some I-mode acceptance can be present. The ethos can be satisfied and maintained by actions falling within (1)–(4). If the group members *jointly intend* as a group to satisfy the ethos, they are collectively committed (bound) to it. If they only separately intend to satisfy it, they are (only) privately committed to it.

To comment on the above action classes, the actions may also be based on the group's *nonconstitutive* goals (etc.), thus goals that are not central to the group's identity. Still the actions must at least in an indirect sense be "ethos-promoting." Actions in class (1) are typical positional actions, and subclass (ii) of (1) consists of actions that the holder of a position may choose from. The task-right system specifying (i) and (ii) involves internal social power and is based on obligations and rights related to positions.[27] This also basically applies to I-mode groups. Both in I-mode and we-mode cases, the normativity related to positions might be weaker and only concern the rightness and wrongness or appropriateness of acting as a "good" or "proper" group member related to various tasks in a group context. I would also like to emphasize that the *way* or *manner* in which actions both in class (1) and in classes (2)–(4) are performed may matter (consider the various ways of building a boat, making pottery, dining, singing a song, apologizing, etc.). Acting in the right way requires a social, possibly group-specific skill.

In class (2) we have actions that concern all group members. For example, members of a religious organization may be supposed to engage in certain activities on Sundays and respect, often in certain group-specific ways, certain moral norms and an etiquette for dressing. As for (3), the organization may have to react to some special habits of certain newcomers of an unusual ethnic origin. Class (4) in the religious organization could contain demonstrative actions, for example, TV appearances directed against a war or in favor of the freedom to consume certain drugs.

Action as a group member can be either successful or unsuccessful. It is required that the group member will intentionally attempt to act in a way that he takes to be within the group's realm of concern without violating the group's ethos. The ethos is at least an underlying or a "presuppositional" reason for the member's action. It need not be a *salient* motivational reason, as especially classes (3) and (4) indicate (cf. also criteria (iii) and (iv) below).

As said, full success in action will not be required. There may thus be failures due to false beliefs about the group's norms and standards, due to lack of skill or to environmental obstacles. Acting as a group member in the core sense is equivalent to acting intentionally in an ethos-promoting sense by means of performing actions falling into one of the classes (1)–(4)—or at least attempting so to act. However, even if acting as a group member is intentional action, a group member need not promote the ethos in all cases (see below for the various possibilities). Furthermore, the actions in classes (1)–(4) need not (especially in case (4)) be strictly contained in, or specified by, the ethos; it suffices for my present purposes that they at least weakly promote the satisfaction and maintenance of the ethos and are consistent with it. That they promote the ethos is typically a partial motivational reason for these intentionally performed actions, and minimally the agent is assumed to intentionally refrain from violating the ethos.

To go into more detail, by my broad ethos-promoting (and "ethos-respecting") action—concerned with *satisfying* and *maintaining* the ethos—I will mean an action satisfying one of the following criteria.

> (i) An agent intentionally promotes the ethos by acting with the aim and correct belief that his action will promote the ethos. The agent's motivational reason for performing the action here can be taken to be the mentioned aim in conjunction with the belief.

Consider a task group consisting of two agents planning to jointly paint a house. The ethos consists basically of the goal of having the house painted by them. Each agent performed his share of the painting with the correct belief that his part of the performance will promote the goal of the house getting painted. In another example, a conscientious agent may throw the wrap paper of his lunch into a wastebasket with the aim and belief that the ethos thereby gets promoted in the satisfaction sense.

> (ii) The agent intentionally performs a certain action in part for the motivational reason that he (correctly) believes it is what the ethos requires or allows or is "probabilified" by (probabilistically conducive to), but he may lack the aim to truly promote this ethos. This agent is a mere "rule-follower."

For instance, the agent throws the wrap paper of his lunch into a wastebasket believing that this is required by the ethos, but not specifically aiming that the ethos thereby gets promoted. The ethos required his action, and obeying it was a part of his reason, but he did not specifically aim at promoting the ethos.

> (iii) The agent performs a certain action in the wide intentional sense that he does not perform it nonintentionally and performs it in part for the "presuppositional" reason that he at least tacitly correctly believes that the ethos requires or allows or is probabilified by it, but he did not consciously aim at the promotion of the ethos.[28]

For instance, the agent might routinely throw the waste paper into the basket or refrain from violating the traffic rules.

> (iv) The agent conforms to a rule or a standard of action by intentionally acting "correctly" (e.g., "I stop at red signals because it is the socially correct action" instead of "I stop at red signals because this is what the ethos requires"). He acts in part for the reason that it is the "right thing" to do but not for the reason that his action is required by the ethos. Still, the nonaccidentally performed action—a kind of "pattern-governed" action—accidentally is (directly or indirectly) required or allowed by, or (probabilistically) conducive to, the ethos of the group.[29]

All the senses of criteria (i)–(iv) amount to more than mere accidental compatibility with the ethos. Indeed, if the group members intentionally respect the ethos by their actions in the group context in one of these senses and if they are correct in their relevant beliefs (concerning the "external" success conditions of the ethos), then the ethos tends to be objectively promoted, at least to some extent. However, on other occasions, ethos-related goals and intentions need not become satisfied (cases (iii)–(iv)); and the beliefs and standards involved in the ethos, while they will not be contradicted, will not be actively professed and used as premises in theoretical and practical reasoning. As to we-mode acting as a group member, strictly interpreted, the borderline cases (ii)–(iv) might seem not to be possible at all—in (ii) this depends on how "truly" is understood. Similarly, in the we-mode case, collective commitment toward the ethos in (iii) and (iv) is either presuppositional and thus weak (case (iii)) or opaque and weak in this other sense (case (iv)).

One may also speak of *functioning as a group member*, where functioning is broader than acting. Functioning here also includes having propositional attitudes as a group member. We have in effect already encountered this notion when assuming that the group members must have collectively accepted its realm of concern, its intentional horizon, and its ethos, because collective acceptance means coming to hold and holding a relevant we-attitude. While our earlier treatment of the notion of the realm of concern was conducted in terms of "contents" in a broad sense, in my above characterization of acting as a group member we concentrated on classes of actions. Given the earlier notion of content, we can deal with (propositional) attitudes similarly. Thus, we may speak of attitude contents and actions within the realm of concern of group g, and in the above classification we may include also attitudes in addition to actions. The important thing to notice here is that those attitudes (e.g., beliefs) are in the group context (in contrast to a private context) and that they are based on acceptance and thus on something that one can acquire by means of one's intentional action in group contexts.[30]

As seen, collective we-mode acceptance of the ethos basically amounts to joint intention involving collective commitment. This of course presupposes that the members have adopted the "we-perspective" that conceptually requires that the group members are disposed to think of themselves as parties of a "we" that intends, believes, and acts for the use of the group. Under favorable conditions, all this becomes manifest as their thinking and acting as a group.

As to I-mode collective acceptance, it amounts to an aggregate of private acceptances, and here a content (e.g., a goal) is not accepted as a group content, but, contingently, everybody accepts the content as her content, but possibly for the use of the group. As said, even in a we-mode group there may be members functioning in the I-mode in an ethos-respecting way. However, on both conceptual and functional grounds, not all members can at all times act only in the I-mode. When functioning as a group member in the standard or we-mode case, the agent functions on the basis of collective commitment and of the group reasons that collective commitment is based on (in about the sense that intentions are based on wants and interests). Thus she may participate on the basis of the group members' joint decisions, its leaders' directives, the group's ethos, group norms, and so on, and the collective commitments that in turn are based on such factors. On the grounds of achieving functional group activity, I will below require we-mode acceptance at least in the case of a substantial part of the authorized "operative" members who represent the group. In the case of nonoperative members, I-mode acting as a group member can be the case. As for I-mode groups, in them the members are acting as group members in the weak, I-mode sense.

In this book, commitment primarily means being bound to something in a way that gives a sufficient reason for action related to the object of commitment (which object typically gives a group reason in the case of collective commitment). For instance, one can subjectively bind oneself to an idea (e.g., that the earth is flat) even without "proper" or "substantive" normativity being involved, and act accordingly in support of the idea. Here I am assuming that *proper* normativity is moral, legal, prudential (etc.) normativity. As to collective commitment, it is generally attitude-relative (typically dependent on joint intention). It need not be properly normative. For one thing, in contrast to the "proper" cases it only applies to persons qua group members, not qua private persons. A commitment must still be at least "technically" normative, in the sense that, for example, achieving a goal "requires" taking certain action, or in the weaker sense, that just expressing what the right or proper thing to do is.[31] Here we have a *conceptual* ground of technical normativity, which often—for example, when the agent rationally performs relevant practical inferences—combines with a *rationality* ground.[32] These presupposed grounds are in general involved also when we deal with commitments as "oughts" directed to others, that is, as social commitments that are assumed to be entailed by collective commitment. Here social normativity is involved. In general, a social "ought" or "may" is derived from social grounds, given the right conceptual presuppositions. Social "oughts" and "mays" can be *group-social* (or, equivalently, collectively social and based on a group reason, see chapter 8) or merely *privately social*, depending on the underlying grounds or the reasons. Thus, as will be seen below and especially in chapter 6, group-social reasons are we-mode reasons and thus involve group authority, while the private-social reasons (even when concerning a group's welfare) are I-mode reasons. Among the we-mode reasons and the I-mode reasons there can be both moral reasons and quasi-moral reasons. Thus, a social commitment toward another person may involve quasi-moral or moral expectations not to harm or to do something good to him. Such reasons can be involved both in we-mode and in I-mode cases. In the group-social case, harming concerns persons acting as group members. Full-blown moral grounds, in contrast to quasi-moral grounds, involve a Kantian element of universalizability.

To elaborate, in the case of (we-mode) collective commitment, group-social normativity (but not necessarily proper normativity) applicable to persons qua group members is at play. It is constitutively based on the conceptual framework of group concepts (e.g., we-mode group, ethos, acting as a group member, promoting the ethos). This framework is necessarily involved, for example, in the sense that acting as a group member requires thinking and acting in certain ways. There need not always be articulated "oughts" and "mays" involved, but there are at least social expectations and pressures with normative force, and the source of such normativity is group-social (institutional). This kind of normativity is part and parcel of the conceptual framework of group concepts and concerns all group activities involving a thick "we." The "oughts" and "mays" involved in contexts of acting as a group member are at bottom based on the concept of togetherness ("groupness"). Thus, when acting together with others, one ought to do one's part and one has the right to expect that others do theirs, and this normativity has a partial basis in the framework of group concepts—it belongs to the "conceptual logic" of group concepts. When group members are involved in acting together intentionally to bring about a state X, they are collectively committed to X on the basis of their joint intention to achieve X. This collective commitment involves as its central element the idea of the group members' being collectively committed to each other as group members (thus socially committed) to achieve X together and hence to participate in the joint acquisition of X. In the group belief case (e.g., "We believe that the earth is flat") the members are collectively committed to respecting the content of the belief and acting accordingly.[33]

Summing up the above discussion, when people collectively agree to perform an action X together as a group, they collectively (jointly) we-intend in the we-mode to perform it for the (use of the) group being collectively committed to doing what they collectively intend.[34] In general, forming an intention is the central way of becoming committed, and here the resulting commitment is attitude-relative. In the I-mode case, the members may collectively but in a private sense agree to perform X. Here they we-intend only in a weak I-mode sense and are privately committed to what they intend. Their "aggregative" acceptance of action performance consists of each participant's private acceptance of it, either for the group or for herself.

I will use the following specific terminology about commitment: Suppose a group g is *committed* to p. Then, in a well-functioning group the members (or almost all of them or at least its operative members) are *collectively committed* (i.e., *have become collectively bound) to p qua group members.* A single member is here said to *participate in the members' collective commitment* (or, as I also say, to be *we-committed* in the we-mode) and thus in the group's commitment. Viewed as a we-mode we-commitment, such participation involves that the member qua a group member is committed to the nonaccidentally shared content for the use of the group (the Collectivity Condition applies here) and believes that the others are similarly committed and that this is mutually believed among the participants of the collective commitment.[35] Viewed slightly differently, a we-commitment is in the we-mode when it satisfies the Collectivity Condition saying that, in virtue of the participants' collective acceptance of a goal or view (etc.) as the group's goal or view, it is necessarily the case that the accepted proposition is true or correctly assertable for the group if and only if it is so for any member of the group.[36] The Collectivity Condition is indeed a constitutive principle of the we-mode. Accordingly, I-mode commitment does not satisfy it, although the participants might by their private promises to an extent approximate the we-mode commitment situation.

In the case of normatively structured groups (with "task-right systems" and positions defined on the basis of them), in order for the group to be committed, the operative members or a substantial number of them can be required to be we-committed in the we-mode for the group. The operative members are members who have the authority (generally from the group members) to decide and/or act for the group (see chapter 6, section 2). However, my formulations below will best suit the cases where all group members are operative members with their authority derived from their membership.

Note finally that when acting as proper group member one may fail (or succeed) either with respect to group normativity and commitment or with respect to the specific way or manner required by the actions in classes (1)–(4), and one may thus fail or succeed relative to the required social skill.

4   Standard and Weak Acting as a Group Member Defined

Let me now proceed to a systematic characterization of the varieties of acting as a group member.[37] To begin, we consider the wide notion of *acting in a group context*. This notion will not be central below, and thus the following loose characterization will suffice here. Acting in a group context means acting in the public domain of the group, as opposed to acting in the private sphere related to matters that can have some causal significance for the group's functioning. For instance, this kind of action can have consequences for the "social atmosphere" in, and cohesion of, the group. Put slightly differently, people act in a group context when they act within the framework of the group, thus action in group positions or the performance of group tasks are cases in point.[38] The class of actions in group contexts contains actions pertaining to the topics of concern of the group. While all acting as a group member (in one of my senses) is acting in a group context, the converse obviously is not true. Consider an example where a group member in a club spontaneously cleans the floor of the clubroom, with the others' possibly silent acceptance. This might not be acting as a group member, but it is at least acting in a group context. It is also positively causally relevant to group life (and is thus action "for the group"). On the other hand, one can obviously act within the realm of the group's concern but fail to obey the ethos of the group. Another example is treasonable acts against the group and its ethos. (This may be acting in the dissidence-allowing sense of chapter 10.)[39]

Next we consider a weak notion of acting as a group member, also to be called I-mode acting as a group member. This notion is based on the group members' sharing the ethos but being only privately (and not collectively) committed to it. Thus there may be a group of persons who grow flowers in the village commons and intend to make their small village look beautiful in this and perhaps other ways. Each of them is only privately committed to making the village beautiful, and they mutually know or believe that the others are similarly committed. The participants' actions here may—but need not—be interdependent in other ways. The group under discussion is an I-mode group. In a weak, I-mode sense, we here have the following definitions of action as a group member (based on I-mode collective acceptance).

> (AGMW) An action X performed by member A of group g is *an action performed as a group member in a weak sense* if and only if A performed X in the group context in the core sense (X belonging to one of the action classes (1)–(4) of section 3) in part for the purpose of promoting the ethos of g that she privately accepts and to which she is privately committed (and thus privately socially ought to promote).

Here obeying (thus promoting) the ethos means satisfying it either by making it true (in the case of goals) or keeping it true by acting on it (in the case of beliefs and standards). Group g can be either an I-mode or a we-mode group. In both cases the ethos is shared, because that is required in the respective group definitions. In the latter case, the "I-moders" form a subclass of the "we-moders." This case can be called I-mode acting as a group member. In this book, "private" and "I-mode" thinking and acting amount to the same if the group is an "empty group," which possibility I allow.

> (AGMS) An action X performed by member A of we-mode group g is *an action performed as a group member in the standard sense* if and only if (i) either the members of g (or their authorized representatives) rationally (reasonably) collectively accept for the group with collective commitment that X is an action in one of the senses (1)–(3), or (ii) the action X falls in class (4) (and is thus reasonably collectively acceptable as an action within the realm of concern of g and indeed as an action as a group member); X is here assumed to be performed in part for the reason of promoting the ethos of g that the group is committed to—and to which the members (or at least a substantive part of them, including this member A) are collectively committed (and thus group-socially ought to promote).[40]

Definition (AGMS) can be called the standard, we-mode sense of acting as a group member. This is the sense in which the members of a we-mode group are supposed to act as group members and the sense normally meant in this book by acting as a group member. This kind of full-blown acting as a group member "represents" the group level and is the driving force operating on the group level. Acting as a group member is what maintains the generality and stability of the group level and also affects changes on this level. This applies to the maintenance and change of social institutions, for instance. Group members functioning in this way are in principle interchangeable and viewed without taking into consideration their individuality. Note that, from a functional perspective, we-mode groups may be able to tolerate an amount of I-mode acting as a group member and even action deviating from what the ethos prescribes or recommends. A member's reason for promoting the ethos in definition (AGMS) expresses the group's authority to give reasons for the members to think and act in ways compatible with the group's commitment to its ethos. The group's commitment will mean that the members, or their authorized representatives, together have formed the ethos for the group at some point in the group's history.

In general, it holds on the basis of our earlier definition of we-mode social groups that it *ought to be the case* in the group that the members function properly as group members. From this ought-to-be requirement, each member can derive a relevant *ought-to-do* requirement concerning herself. Accordingly, the group members are obligated to perform actions within clauses (1)–(4) (of section 3) and actions that accordingly are required for their performance or are otherwise ethos-promoting (in one of the senses (i)–(iv) of ethos promotion).

Note that in the case of voluntary groups (groups voluntarily entered), signing on for membership can be taken to entail the acceptance of the obligation to obey the ethos (see chapter 6). Thus, it is the normative task of the group members to collectively see to it that the ethos is satisfied and (typically) maintained (see section 5). In the case of acting as a group member in the standard sense, the members will have to act intentionally with the right purpose, even if the environment would not cooperate and even if the acting may be routine.

When a member acts as a group member in the above full sense (AGMS), he can be said to "represent" the group or to act "in the name of" the group. This is analogous to the case where an attorney by his actions represents an agent (i.e., what the latter would rationally and justifiably do) in the court. To discuss representation, briefly, I will consider two kinds of group action.[41] First we consider a group's promoting the ethos in a general sense. Taking a group, g, to be capable of action qua a group, I assume that g intentionally sees to it or brings about the satisfaction of the ethos, or at least tries to act so. This is the case when its members jointly (try to) see to it or bring it about that the ethos is promoted—based on their joint intention expressible by "We together will see to it that the ethos is promoted." When they together see to it that (stit) the ethos is promoted, every group member can be said to have a part or slice in this joint stit-ing. They may act separately or jointly to this effect and use whatever "tools" (e.g., hiring agents to do something) are believed to be useful. Here the members' part actions simply are actions qua a group member in the standard sense, and by these actions they represent (or act in the name of) the group. The totality of the part actions, based on their jointly stit-ing the ethos becomes satisfied (and, normally, maintained), collectively taken, constitutes the group's respective action. The group members can be regarded as "authorized" representatives of the group as long as they act as group members in the standard sense. The group "acts through them," and, conversely, they by their actions represent the group and thus the group's ethos and ethos-related interests. Consequently, their actions weakly represent what the group does (or should ethos-correctly do) in the situation. Ethos-related collective action of the above kind can take place also when there are conflicting elements within the group, as long as some "ground rules" forming a kind of "joint action bottom" are respected. In this respect, such collective action can be compared with a game of tennis: playing tennis is a joint action based on adhering to some ground rules, although it has an obvious competitive, hence conflict-involving, element. The multicultural case with respect to the basis entailed by adherence to the nuclear ethos is a structurally similar case.

Next consider the case where the group performs a specific action, X, mutually believed to promote the ethos (recall section 3). In this case there are specific operative members that carry out the task and act so that the action X can be attributed to g on the basis of their together intentionally stit-ing X (or bringing it about). For instance, the leaders (namely, the authorized operative members) of the group may make a deal in the name of the group. The operatives see to it, or bring it about, that X, and thereby by their actions they doubly represent the group, provided that their actions indeed are "ethos-correct" and based on collective commitment (giving functional unity to the group). This is because, first, they represent the group in the above weak sense, in which acting as a group member means representing the group or, perhaps better, the group's ethos. Second, they also represent the other group members and act for them. Here each operative member performed a part or "slice" of X and thus took part in this kind of strong representation.[42] Furthermore, for this kind of strong representation, it is also required that the actions correctly represent the ethos.

5   Satisfying and Maintaining the Group Ethos

This section investigates satisfying and maintaining the ethos of a we-mode group. What do these notions involve and under what conditions are there reasons to maintain the group ethos? To begin, I consider an autonomous social group, g, with a certain ethos (constitutive goals, values, beliefs, standards, norms, etc.). The content aspect of group g's identity is "defined" by its collectively accepted ethos, E; this is expressible by "We form a group, g, based on ethos E." That this definition holds is a constitutive principle for the group, and its rational collective acceptance already gives a kind of weak normative reason for maintaining it, based on the rationality of the persistence of maintaining the group's identity. The collective acceptance of an ethos normally involves collective acceptance and joint intention (and hence collective commitment) not only to satisfy it but also to maintain it (think of a state's constitution and the in-built resistance toward its change). An autonomous group can of course change its own identity, thus change E.

The collective acceptance of E (involving collective commitment) basically has the world-to-mind direction of fit and is, or is like, an intention, and thus the content E itself is a kind of goal.[43] So we can here speak of g's intention to achieve E. This intention conceptually entails that g ought to achieve E: it ought to be the case that if g intends E, it will try to achieve (satisfy) it.[44] This intention-dependent requirement exists as long as g has the intention; thus it is a different problem, typically one related to rationality, for how long g holds or should hold the intention. It might even rationally give it up before satisfying E when E is a single-shot goal or without satisfying it even once when E is a standing goal.

The collective acceptance of E by g obviously does not *logically* entail that g ought to continue to accept E, unless indeed this collective acceptance also explicitly concerns maintenance (e.g., for the time being or given such and such conditions; recall the earlier example of the collective acceptance of the "rules of the house"). But given that g's having E is like having a goal (with the world-to-mind direction of fit of satisfaction) it may be *rational* for g to try to hold on to E, and this involves the group members' being collectively committed to E not only on rational but also on group-social grounds, that is, on the grounds of being members of a we-mode group. A rational group (*pro tanto*) ought to maintain E as long as no relevant changes in its underlying reasons for acceptance of E have occurred. Thus g will maintain E if and only if its relevant reasons stay the same. There are two pairs of issues that have to be kept distinct. First, there is the issue of maintaining versus changing E. Second, there is the issue of obeying (and thus satisfying) E versus disobeying E. In principle, this gives us four possible combinations, namely, maintaining-obeying, maintaining-disobeying, changing-obeying, changing-disobeying, when we look at a group at different points of time.[45] Below I will concentrate on the maintenance issue together with the entailed group-social obligation to obey, but will not strictly assume that the group has collectively accepted maintaining its ethos, so to speak, blanco. (Note that promoting the ethos in the sense of this book covers both satisfying and maintaining the ethos.)

As seen, if E is a standing goal, g's acceptance of it premise-dependently (where the premises concern its reasons for acceptance) entails that it rationally ought to maintain it as long as the reasons for acceptance are not changed. This kind of normative premise might not be explicit and specific about the reasons. In a rational democratic, self-governing group the reasons might be prevalently group-internal and, for example, amount to "given that the overwhelming majority of group members accepts E as the ethos of the group." In general, the obligation to maintain E can be changed, and it can be rationally changed if the group finds good reasons to do so—it might want to change its identity. E can even contain something about its own critical evaluation and updating.

The group's commitment to E involves *rational persistence* and resistance toward change that is not present in, for example, desires and hopes, and the collective aspect makes solo quitting reproachable in principle. There is a kind of "intrinsic resistance" on rational grounds against the group's changing its constitution (identity). Another route to rational resistance to changing the group's identity may come from functional considerations related to the group's particular nonconstitutive goals and aims: the group ought to be maintained at least as long as it rationally has such goals.

The consideration based on the group's identity gives a partial justification to the statement "It ought-to-be the case in g that E is maintained, given that no relevant change-inducing reasons have come up."[46] It follows that the group members (both on rational grounds and on group-social grounds) ought to perform relevant world-to-mind activities related to the maintenance and upholding of "E is g's ethos." For instance, the Wednesday lunch group ought to maintain its ethos by meeting on Wednesdays as long as the "reason situation" does not change. The group members thus ought to maintain E by their actions and, without further reason, refrain from changing the ethos. Thus, the statement "Given that the reasons for the acceptance of E by g are in place, it ought-to-be the case in g that E is its ethos" can be taken to entail two different ought-to-do requirements for the group members.

As to epistemic matters, there is a difference between the cases where there is mutual knowledge and where there is mere, possibly false, mutual belief about the existence of collective commitment. In the former case, the group members must somehow have made public their intentions and commitments toward the ethos and what it covers. In the case of mutually believed collective commitment, the members might not *know* that the others participate in the collective commitment. Hence they cannot justifiably sanction each other (when needed), because they cannot be sure that the others indeed failed to do something (as the putative violators might actually not have had the intention in question). If there is *mutually known* collective commitment, the group members will be publicly bound (within the group) to maintain and satisfy the ethos and bear responsibility for these two matters, hence for the group members' acting correctly as group members. While with *mutually believed* collective commitment we do get the right kind of collective maintenance and satisfaction behavior, indeed group-binding group action, we do not yet have the publicity and thus the objectively justified demands on the members that we would get with mutually known collective commitment.[47]

As seen, the (ought-to-be) norm that E ought to obtain (given such and such conditions that continue to hold) nondetachably entails that at least rational group members persist in holding it and oppose change. This kind of maintenance must be distinguished from the satisfaction of the content of E. Both the maintaining of the ethos as the group's ethos and the satisfaction of the ethos require the right kind of obeying action, and such action will be ethos-promoting action in the sense clarified in section 3. My basic principles of ethos maintenance and change can schematically be put as follows for suitable rational reasons or conditions C in the case of an externally and internally free group g.

> (i) a free group g rationally ought to maintain its ethos E, given suitable reasons C (e.g., C might involve that the overwhelming majority of the group members rationally collectively accept E as g's ethos);
> (ii) a free group g may rationally change E, given C (C as in (i));
> (iii) change of E or its substantial parts entails change of identity of g, but the group rationally ought to keep its identity, unless strong reasons for changing it emerge (such as – C in (ii));
> (iv) a free group's commitments not related directly to E may rationally require its maintenance.

Clause (iii) serves to justify (i), and the same holds for the commitments in (iv).

If we are to have full-blown group action qua group action, joint intention and (we-mode) we-commitment on the part of the participants are required. I will now consider a weaker sense of group action or collective action that does not require joint intention to promote the ethos or even acting for the reason that the group ethos thereby gets promoted (this is what the I-mode sense (a) of acting as a group member would yield). The group action I have in mind does involve collective commitment to the right kind of ethos-entailed action (and is thus stronger than I-mode collective action), but it does not make the ethos a reason for action. This kind of group action consists of the ethos-promoting cases (iii) or (iv) in section 3. Thus, the action need not amount to more than refraining from action, that is, intentional omission to act in a certain way prohibited by the ethos (this is case (iii) of promoting the ethos). This kind of action can be called *presuppositional group action in the we-mode*, where the essential thing is that the ethos functions as a kind of underlying presuppositional reason for the participants' action.[48]

In such action, the agent can pursue his own (further or immediate) goals as long as he does not violate the ethos. For example, not violating the traffic rules is correct societal behavior, and the group members do not strictly act together when driving in the traffic, although they can be said together to satisfy the traffic rules (part of the ethos)—typically only inadvertently. That there are such traffic rules is assumed to be a presupposed state of affairs that the agent takes as an underlying, constraining reason for his action. Nevertheless, the members' actions need not have the same goals, and they do not involve the agent's intention to maintain or to satisfy the traffic rules and, to switch to a more general case, the ethos. The ethos is only a presupposition of action and its presuppositional reason. If things start going wrong, and the agent gets social sanctions for his behavior, he may realize that he does not operate correctly. There is more going on here than the ethos getting promoted merely as an unintended consequence of what the people do, because there is an underlying structure (e.g., the system of laws of a state) that allows us to say that the group members together promote the ethos, albeit perhaps not intentionally. But had they reflected on the situation, they would possibly have understood that the authorized leaders (operative members) of their society have established the ethos-based norms and standards that they as nonoperatives ought to obey.

There are various mixed possibilities that all serve to create the kind of behavioral order that is demanded by the ethos but that fall short of being proper we-mode group actions based on a joint intention to maintain and satisfy the ethos. There can be a mixture of participants acting in the weak, I-mode sense of acting as a group member and participants acting in the above presuppositional sense (involving one of the cases (iii)–(iv) of promoting the ethos). Such a mixture may of course also contain participants acting in the we-mode for the right ethos-based reason.

6   Arguments for Collective Commitment

In this section I will try to pull together various, interdependent functions that collective commitment has in the analysis of group action. As most of the points have already been mentioned or discussed, this section will be an extensive summary of part of what has been said. In this section I will be dealing with groups functioning as a unit. Thus what is said below gives a kind of justification for the account of we-mode groups that was given earlier—without strictly assuming that the groups dealt with are we-mode groups.

(1) *Group membership in a group functioning as a groupt requires collective commitment.* In this kind of group, the members—or a substantial part of them—are assumed to collectively accept the ethos of the group. A collectively accepted ethos makes it a jointly intended goal state, and joint intention involves collective commitment. This is a conceptual point about full-blown collective acceptance and groups functioning as a unit (such as we-mode groups). What this point assumes is that the members have indeed accepted being members of a group that requires this much "we-togetherness" of them. It suffices, but also seems to be necessary, that they adopt the full we-perspective concerning their group and accept an ethos satisfying (a version of) the Collectivity Condition, which entails that, necessarily, when the ethos is promoted for a member it is promoted for all (and thus for the group). What we get is in effect a we-mode group, in which collective commitment is a central ingredient.

(2) *Group identity in a group functioning as a unit requires collective commitment.* A group's identity consists mainly in the group's ethos to which the group members are required to be committed as a group and as a thick "we" ("we-together"). In addition, the group members' identity and interrelationships may be relevant to group identity, as the case may be (see section 2 and chapters 6 and 8). Sometimes it may also matter whether or not the external social environment views a collection of people as a social group.

The idea here is that a group cannot be a unit unless it forms a strong "we." The group has to be viewed from the inside, from a we-perspective, by the members for proper group activities and functioning as a specific unit to take place. This requires that the group members are attached to the identity-expressing ethos by collective commitment, which keeps the group together as a unit. In such a unit, each member thinks and acts with a we-perspective (the group's perspective)—and is also internally responsible to the others concerning ethos-related activities. The we-perspective is grounded in the shared ethos to which the group is committed and to which thus the members are collectively committed. Thus it involves for-groupness, as expressed by group thoughts of the kind "We intend to do X" or "We believe that p" and collective commitment to these thoughts. In addition, the we-perspective also typically includes we-feelings, that is, affective bonds, in many cases enhanced by rituals and accompanying music.[49] Collective commitment is strengthened if an appropriate we-feeling exists in the group.

Without a substantial amount of collective commitment to the ethos, the group risks losing its identity (or part of it) and falling apart into an aggregate of independent actors furthering the same ethos. Collective commitment functions to guarantee that the identity stays the same, or becomes what the group wants it to become, and such commitment serves to unite the members around that identity.

While the ethos gives the "contentual" part of the identity of the group, collective commitment per se, independently of the nature of the ethos it concerns, accounts for the cohesion and "causal we-ness" in the group. In addition, empirical research supports the idea that identification with a group and commitment to it increases ethos-promoting action. Thus Marilynn Brewer argues on the basis of empirical research that when a collection of individuals believe that they share a common ingroup membership, they are more likely to act in the interest of collective welfare than individuals in the same situation who do not have a sense of group identity.[50] I take collective welfare to include "for-groupness" in promoting the ethos of the group. Hence identification with the group (and, most important, its ethos) tends to yield ethos-promoting action. Brewer also argues that identification with the ingroup can elicit cooperative behavior even in the absence of interpersonal communication among group members. Functioning in an ingroup context, individuals develop trust and a cooperative orientation toward shared problems. Here we have empirical support for the claim that in ingroup contexts, we-mode behavior (or at any rate progroup I-mode behavior) tends to come about and to supersede selfish I-mode activities.[51]

When a committed group has some privately committed members, these members are not full-fledged group members (in the standard sense). Privately committed members may be strongly committed to E, but their commitment does not add to the group's identity, only to their own (social) identity, without "gluing" them to the other members unless "fortified" by extra promises and the like (perhaps even in an iterated way!). As to group action, these members may walk out or do something wrong with less ado than in the collective commitment case. These members are not full-fledged "arms and legs in the collective body" in question. If, on the other hand, they are mutually believed to be collectively committed, they are treated as full-fledged members—and they tend to surprise the group when they act according to their own minds.

(3) *A group's functioning as a group requires collective commitment.* This point does not directly require considering the group's identity but only its acting as a unit. Thus, if a group intends, believes, and acts as a group, as one agent, its members ought to be collectively committed. Collective commitment gives the agent-unity required for functioning as a group. This kind of agent-unity corresponds to the kind of unity we require of a single agent for her to be able to intentionally act. An integrated agent of this kind can be said to have natural authority to act; she is the author of her actions when suitable (mainly mental) conditions obtain. Similarly, a group that is capable of action as a group will be the author of its actions. The problem for a theoretician is to say what is required of the group members for the group to (be able) to act (function) as a group and for the group to be trusted and for its being responsible for its actions.[52] The social glue and cohesion provided by collective commitment should be present and required in these contexts. Part of what is involved here—over and above what aggregated private commitments give—is the social commitment involved in collective commitment: Being committed to each other, the group members can better rely on the others to perform their respective tasks, which, especially in the case of interdependent and joint actions, is central. Social commitment to others and to the group is the core of the reproachability feature involved in collective commitment: a publicly we-committed member who leaves the joint project or intentionally violates the ethos can be criticized by the others, whereas if he had been committed only "to himself" he would in general have been less criticizable socially for letting the others down. In the I-mode case, he can be criticized for causing harm to others and for not being a rationally stable person.[53]

In general, the group needs good reasons to believe that the members are collectively committed in order to dare to act as a group. If all or most of the members were only privately committed to E, it would be like an armada of boats without a commander of the armada. Each captain of a member boat is on his own in his attempt to get to the end port E (or to an end furthering it). Those who decide to take on other goals cannot be controlled or sanctioned for that on group-social grounds. Accordingly, merely privately committed members in interdependent I-mode activities have more possibilities to quit without criticism, as they have preserved their full agency authority in this situation. Other participants may criticize quitters, for example, on grounds of lack of rationality or on moral grounds, but they have no group-based authority behind their demands to make the quitters stay. On functional grounds, we need a group that acts in a coherent way through coherently acting members all of whom participate in seeing to it that they get to the same port. The mutually believed collective commitment gives this and also in general seems necessary or at least better than aggregated private commitment. The social commitment in the collective commitment is the core of the glue that gives them shared authority over the "oughts" and "mays" in question. Thus the members will also each have the authority (their share of group authority, as it were) to criticize and correct violators for their failures to function as proper group members.

A special case of the functionality argument is given by group goals and beliefs. Groups may have goals and interests that the members do not have and that may even conflict with the members' goals and interests (see the positional model of group attitudes in chapter 6). When properly acting as group members, they will also collectively accept goals and views for the group that they would not adopt or have if only acting privately. For such new goals and beliefs to function properly for the group, collective commitment to them is required. This argument is not a direct argument for the requirement of collective commitment, but it indirectly shows also that when the ethos of the group does not coincide with the private views and ideas of the members, collective commitment is a forceful element of the we-mode.

(4) *Group responsibility requires collective commitment.* In order for the group to be able to answer general demands (both group-external and group-internal) for taking responsibility or being responsible, collective commitment must be present, and we must in effect be dealing with a we-mode group. The idea here again is that a group cannot as a group be responsible for its intentional actions and for its dissidents' actions without the unity provided by collective commitment (point (4) is indeed a special case of (3)). Group responsibility will be discussed in detail in chapter 10, where details and qualifications to this thesis formulated in general terms are given.

Generally speaking, collective commitment gives the group members authority to control the other group members' relevant actions, and thus they can be held partly responsible for others' wrongdoings (i.e., actions by group members that violate the ethos and what it derivatively covers). A we-mode group is responsible for not having controlled its members' actions—especially in the case of violations of the ethos and general norms and standards in a society. The responsibility is based on the group's commitment to see to it that the ethos is promoted. This imposes "oughts" and entails "mays"—or if you prefer, "duties" and "rights"—of at least an instrumental, ethos-relative kind on the group members to help, control, pressure and otherwise influence others when needed so as to facilitate achieving the end result in a joint venture. Group activities of this kind are in principle every member's business. A group member's action is "transparent," in the sense that it is open for scrutiny by the other members.

As a conclusion, collective commitment is part and parcel of the we-mode, that is, the full we-perspective, and all arguments for the we-mode over the I-mode will also be arguments for the requirement of collective commitment. As will be shown in more detail later, especially in chapter 4, the we-mode (the group level) is not reducible to the I-mode (the private level), and thus there will be, as it were, a choice between two fundamentally different ways of viewing persons in a social context. Thus, in the we-mode case, "we" is the intentional subject of attitudes and action, while "I" is the respective intentional subject in the I-mode case. The full we-perspective expresses a voluntarily made connection among the group members: because of entering the group, they necessarily are connected as a "we" capable of joint thinking or acting. The we-mode thus conceptually involves the group as an actor, and this will affect the agents' relevant psychological states. In the I-mode case, I may interact with you and act toward the same goal to the extent it is not too costly. However, in the we-mode case the cost argument in general has much less bite. The group member acting qua a group member is supposed not to think of his "fate" in private terms but only as a member of the group in terms of its "fate" and the members' "common fate" (as spelled out by the Collectivity Condition). When acting in the we-mode, a participant cannot as easily leave as in the case of private commitment when it becomes costly for him to stay and participate, because he sees the project as the group's project (as our project) rather than his own private one and is bound by his group-based commitment to the others over and above the other ways (e.g., due to rationality, morality) he may be committed. A participant cannot be jumping on and off or in and out and only take part when it suits him. A group does not want to keep members who are there to free-ride on collective goods but will not pay for the costs when the going gets tough.

7   Commitment and Acting as a Group Member

As seen, the social commitment involved in collective commitment is in many ways central. But there are also other constitutive elements in commitment. I will now classify and discuss them briefly and afterward show the relevance of my classifications to acting as a group member. Commitment will be characterized in terms of seven variables.

First, the subject of commitment is either a private agent or several agents or a (structured or unstructured) social group. *Second*, one can be committed to a propositional content or, if a more externalist language is preferred, to a state of affairs or end, or—in derivative sense—to an item in such a content (or state) such as an object (e.g., person) or property. Every such commitment, nevertheless, gives a sufficient reason to act and entails a *commitment to act* appropriately. For instance, an agent may be committed to good personal relations obtaining in her group, and this entails that he at least in a technical sense ought to see to it and, when obeying the ought, will see to it that that end state obtains. Accordingly, any commitment involves also commitment to action of some kind, to standard singular action or to a part of a joint action. Commitment to a belief analogously involves professing the belief and persistently acting on it. I list the action in question as the *third* constitutive element of commitment (it can be the same action as the one in the content of the commitment, if there is no other content).

Fourth, as seen, commitment can be either private (in the sense of involving private authority only) or collective (involving collective authority). The private authority aspect entails—to use my terminology below—that the agent is committed only to himself and at least in part for himself, taking "for" here to mean "for the benefit of." For example, an agent's intention to open the window typically involves a private commitment.

In contrast, group members' collective commitment is based on what they as a group have committed themselves to or on what their group in a broad sense requires of them. For instance, in the case of a group's intention to paint a house, the group members are assumed to be collectively committed to the joint action of painting the house. Hence they are socially committed to the others to perform their parts of the joint action. This follows basically from the fact that in joint tasks and projects there is only shared control and responsibility over the joint outcome. The joint outcome requires that each participant not only performs his preassigned part but is also prepared to help and perhaps pressure the others to do theirs; thus each participant is expected to perform his tasks and conversely has the justified expectation that the others perform theirs.[54] A collective commitment is for the group and also public—relative to g.

The *fifth* constitutive feature is the already-mentioned one that the committed person can be committed to himself, to the others, or to the group.[55] Here commitment to the others as a group member may be either distributive or nondistributive. The term "group" refers to the two components the ethos and the group members, but in the case of social commitment, only the group member aspect is meant. Commitment to the group seems central in large groups in which the members generally do not know each other.[56]

Commitment to one's group involves supporting and promoting the group's ethos and also advancing its less central goals, interests, standards, beliefs, and so on. The main conceptual and theoretical difference between a commitment to one's group and a commitment to the members (qua members) of the group lies in that— in addition to having (current) members—a group is basically a position-involving entity with a history and an open-ended future. It can be an entity merely in the minds of people but in addition also as a social system consisting of agents and their interrelations as well as an ethos, and so on. If a member is committed to the group (viewed as an entity with a certain ethos) to do her best, she must of course be committed to the group members to function as a group member. In general, commitment to the group increases group cohesion (to the bond between the members and the members and the group) because it involves not only the group members but also the group viewed as an entity to which an ethos is associated.

Consider the following claim in a group context: I intend and am committed to an action if and only if I am committed to myself, or the other(s), or to the group to perform that action, where the "or" is an inclusive one. Assuming that one can only be committed to oneself, the others, and/or the group when acting as a group member, this claim is tenable. The equivalence expressed by it lets us move back and forth between the "to-person" language and the plain action-commitment language. Note that in the case of collective commitment, a social commitment to the group members, including oneself, is entailed. Thus, whenever I am committed to you to open the window I am also committed to myself to open the window, given the assumption of our being collectively committed to seeing to it that I open the window.

Sixth, an agent can be committed before himself (or have only himself privately as his "audience"), before the others in his group, or before his group. Thus, an agent is committed only before himself if he secretly forms the intention to achieve something (e.g., to help another person or to rob a bank). He is committed before the others if the other members of his group or a subset of them are his (public) audience, and he is committed before the group if he, for example, declares publicly that he will fight for his group (say, sports team or country).[57]

Seventh, the item that the commitment is about (i.e., a state of affairs or an action) or the consequences of its being realized (e.g., a goal which is achieved) can be for the purpose and use of the committed agent only, for (all or some) other members in his group, or for the whole group, understood as an entity.

To summarize, we are concerned with a member of group g who is acting as a group member in one of our earlier senses. There are seven variables—some of them with nonexclusive values. They can be written as follows.

(1) agent: (a) single; (b) several agents collectively; (c) social group

(2) content: (a) propositional content or, in a derivative sense, state; (b) non-propositional element, such as object or action, of a propositional content or state of affairs (e.g., ethos, country, swimming)

(3) action: (a) single; (b) joint; (c) group

(4) authority: (a) private; (b) several members collectively; (c) group

(5) agent-object of commitment: (a) oneself; (b) others in the group; (c) the group;

(6) audience: (a) before oneself; (b) before others in the group; (c) before the group

(7) purpose: (a) for oneself; (b) for others in the group; (c) for the group

Accordingly, when participating in a collective commitment, an agent is in principle committed to a certain content, to performing a type of action, with a certain authority, to an agent-object, before a certain audience, and for the use of some person(s) or group. Our seven variables will all apply to commitment, in the sense that one or more of the values (disjuncts) will obtain. For instance, in (2), (a) and (b) both hold true in many cases; similarly, in (3), (4), and (5), both (b) and (c) are often both satisfied. As to (4), group members may be both privately and collectively committed concerning the same action (making (a) and (b) both hold true). On the other hand, for example, within (3), the conjunction (3)(a) and (3)(b) is trivially inconsistent. Similarly, one may study which value combinations concerning different variables are possible. For instance, (3)(c) and (4)(a) is an inconsistent combination. I will not here systematically study all these relationships but only make a few more remarks about interesting possibilities.

As to (7)(c), "for the group" can be related to various kinds of commitment. In collective we-mode commitment it is a constitutive part of the commitment, for such collective commitment has a collective or "jointness" content or entails such a content satisfying the Collectivity Condition. This jointness content basically boils down to our jointly acting together toward a joint end for our group's use and (broadly) benefit. In the case of private commitment, a private for-groupness feature can also be present. (In this case, commitment for the group may be called "progroup commitment," to avoid confusion.) There are some other obvious interpretations concerning our variables—for example, in (5) a group can be taken to be committed to itself, to other groups or to some individuals, or to a group of groups (such as the European Union).

The final task in this section is to reconsider the varieties of acting as a group member in view of what has been said above of collective commitment. In section 4 several notions or senses of acting as a group member were distinguished: acting qua a group member in a weak, I-mode sense, a standard sense, a dissidence sense (possibly with incorrect action; see especially chapter 10), and a representation sense, as well as a strong representation sense. The task ahead is now to say what kinds of commitment are possible in these cases. What follows is a concise and rather obvious account, given the earlier extensive discussion.

Acting qua a Group Member in the Standard Sense

(i) Ideally, there must be collective commitment to ethos E (to uphold E together with others) and thus to intentionally acting in accordance with E, that is, to obeying E or at least trying to obey it. Thus the action classes (1)–(4) of section 3 are included; these classes also contain unsuccessful intentional attempts to obey E. (In weaker cases at least a substantial number of the operative agents is assumed to obey E by performing actions falling within classes (1)–(4).)

(ii) Collective commitment involves social commitment: the group members are not only committed to themselves but committed to each other and to the group to uphold E and to act in ways falling into one of the classes (1)–(4).

(iii) There is commitment to support E and other, nonconstitutive interests, goals, standards, values, beliefs, norms, and so on, and accordingly there is commitment to perform actions in classes (1)–(4) in our classification of section 3.

(iv) In relation to above point (ii), the committed actions should be transparent, out in the open, as knowledge of them is gratis shareware in the group. Thus they cannot be private secrets. They are open for the others to monitor, because the action is part of the group's action or group activities. Each (operative) group member is committed to the others and to the group when he acts, which means that he has given up part of his authority over his own action. He is committed to the others to participate in the members' joint seeing to it that E is upheld or to acting with this effect, and if there are nonconstitutive goals, they should be collectively observed as well. This entails that he should also participate in monitoring what the others are doing. There is shared responsibility for maintaining the ethos by E-congruent actions (and possibly other acceptable group actions) and for the consequences all this has for a third party (audience, external observer). Commitment "before" others is thus recommendable.

(v) For-groupness, as discussed in the previous section, is a feature of the collective commitment to E and E-congruent actions (i.e., actions falling within the classes (1)–(4) of section 3).

(vi) Commitment to the group in general (involving its ethos, structure, history, expected future, past, current, and perhaps future members) can ideally be required: it adds strength to the "to," "for," and "before" aspects of commitment. (For instance, one can be committed to a country, university, or firm.)

Acting as a Group Member in the Representation Sense

Recall the standard sense for what kinds of commitment are required, as they apply here as well. While mistaken actions are acceptable in the case of acting as a group member in the standard sense, for acting as a group member in the strong representation sense, correct actions for the right reason (i.e., actions obeying the ethos) are required.

Weak Sense of Acting as a Group Member

This is the I-mode case with (a) private commitment to E, (b) private commitment to oneself or the others or possibly to the group, (c) private commitment to E and to actions conducive to E, (d) commitment before others or only before oneself, (e) commitment (in part) for the group or merely for oneself.

Acting as a Group Member in an Organization

Finally, let us briefly consider an organization such as a university or a business corporation (this discussion also relates to several issues in this book; see especially chapters 6 and 10). An organization has a certain ethos, basic goals, values, standards, and so on. It can be viewed as a we-mode group, if its members (or a substantial number of them) collectively construct (interpret) it in we-mode terms (as the phrase "This is *our* organization and we are working together as a unit" indicates). The ethos gives the content of the organization. Apart from its content, an organization basically consists of a set of positions that are normatively interlocked with each other. Specifically, the interrelations between the positions contain power relations and informational relations. For instance, a position-holder can have the power to order the holder of another position to do something within the ethos-induced domain, and different position-holders may have, and have the right to have, differing amounts and kinds of knowledge concerning the organization's activities.

When the organization makes decisions, it makes them in virtue of its authorized operatives' (typically joint) decisions, and when it acts, it performs its actions in virtue of its possibly different authorized operatives' actions. The operative members may vary from occasion and task to another, and they may also include nonmember operatives on some occasions. Thus when a business company does X—for example, selling a new brand of goods or builds a new building for its own use—the operative members are presumably different and possibly not group members at all. The Hobbesian Author behind the company's actions is constituted by the shareholders. They collectively have the power to select a governing board for the company, and derivatively they have the power to select the functional position-holders—from the CEO down to a salesperson and truck driver. The Author (i.e., the group formed of the shareholders) is a core-level group in an organization, while the functioning operatives (the CEO, various kinds of managers, workers, and what have you) form its hired personnel and indeed a group taking care of the daily affairs of the organization. It is in virtue of their action that specific actions are attributed to the organization, for in general they in daily life represent the organization. Thus the hired personnel can be seen as a subgroup of the full group.

In a typical business corporation, all the position-holders are hired ones (the shareholders are not position-holders in the organization itself). Even though they are hired, when performing company jobs they will act in the codified or institutionalized way that the company charter and other ethos-principles involve. So company functions may, and at least in some cases will, involve (codified) we-mode activities. Both under the we-mode and the I-mode interpretation there is also a codified social commitment between the position-holders: a position-holder may be responsible to another one (if they are in interlocking positions or are somehow in suitable power relation to each other). In any case, a position-holder is socially committed to the company to perform her tasks. All the position-holders who are hired by a company can be operative members or, when they are not members, operative "agents" for some tasks. However, hired agents who are not position-holders but only temporarily connected to the organization in order to perform some tasks are not operative *members* but rather more like the company's "means" or "tools." As seen, the ultimate core of an organization is constituted on the one hand by its owners (if it has owners in the legal sense) and on the other hand by the positions that constitute it. The owners determine (often via suitable operative members) the ethos (and thus the general content) of the organization, and the position-holders act to achieve and/or maintain it. Some position-holders may in fact have as their task the reformulation of the ethos within certain boundaries.

What kinds of commitment are there in an organization constructed as a we-mode group? At least ideally, there is codified collective (hence social) commitment that involves the position-holders binding themselves qua position-holders to the organization to perform certain tasks and indeed to obey the task-right system pertaining to their positions. This codified collective and social commitment is based on the obligations and rights involved in the organizational norms. In addition, there may well be uncodified we-mode collective and social commitment involved in the freely chosen joint and jointly accountable activities that the position-holders choose to perform (but that are still promotive of the organization's ethos). The we-mode activities and commitments that we are considering here of course need not be in agreement with what the position holders might have privately preferred in those situations. However, the more "genuine" (i.e., in the sense of backed by private preferences and wants) the we-mode activities and commitments are, the better the organization is likely to function in the long run.

8   Summary

In this long chapter, several central notions to be used in this book have been defined and discussed. It is argued that (autonomous) social groups can be partly defined in terms of their constitutive goals, values, beliefs, norms, and standards collectively accepted by the members acting. They are collectively called the *ethos* of the group. A group is assumed to try to satisfy and normally also to maintain its ethos. Understanding the ethos widely enough, every social group is seen to have an ethos. Groups are divided into *we-mode groups* and *I-mode groups*. A we-mode group is a group that involves the *we-perspective in the full sense* (involves, e.g., the idea of the Collectivity Condition, to be discussed in chapter 2) and in which ideally the members function in the we-mode in a collectively committed way, and thus necessarily on the basis of a group reason. In contrast to an I-mode group, it is based on its members' collectively constructing it as a group, and it in effect consists of the group members functioning in the we-mode as full-blown group members (to be discussed in detail in chapter 2). A we-mode group can accordingly perform actions as a group. This book focuses on we-mode groups.

This chapter has concentrated on the two central social, group-based notions of *thinking and acting as a group member* and *collective commitment*. Ethos-related acting as a group member is a central notion that obviously must be understood when speaking of the we-perspective, group life, and social life more generally. Thus, not only philosophy of sociality, philosophy of social science, political and moral philosophy but also the various social sciences need this notion and should benefit from these analyses and arguments.

Collective commitment is the other "we-perspective" notion studied in this chapter. It is a kind of social glue needed for group members when thinking and acting as a group. Its many other functions were also discussed. In contrast to that of some other studies, my most elementary notion of collective commitment is not normative in the moral or quasi-moral sense but is group-socially normative and intention-relative.

2

THE WE-MODE AND THE I-MODE

1 Collectivity

As stated in chapter 1, the social world cannot be adequately studied without making use of the distinction between the notions of having an attitude and acting *as a group member* versus *as a private person*. These intuitive notions are the core of my distinction between the *we-mode* and the *I-mode*.[1] In this chapter I will present detailed analyses of these two notions and argue for the importance of the we-mode over the I-mode.[2] I will also consider the problem whether thinking and acting in the we-mode is required in some contexts or is better or more adequate than thinking and acting in the I-mode. This contains the subproblem of whether we-mode collective intentionality will in some sense win over I-mode collective intentionality (usually called "progroup I-mode" in this book), supposing that some kind of collective intentionality (specifically, a shared point of view) is needed instead of merely aggregated individual mental states and actions. This problem is hard, and I will consider it in several chapters. Yet another problem is whether, on the whole, the distinction between the we-mode and the I-mode is merely a conventional matter, something dependent only on our social practices, or whether there are both we-mode states and dispositions and I-mode states and dispositions in a causal ontological sense. I will not accept this dichotomy but defend a middle-ground position that yet allows that both kinds of states exist in causal sense.

To give a simple illustration of the I-mode/we-mode distinction, consider the following sentence: "We intend to go to Alfonzo's for lunch." Here "we" could consist of you and me. Two main interpretations are that you and I have the separate intentions (intended goals) to go to Alfonzo's for lunch even if we might mutually know about each other's intentions. This is the I-mode case of shared intention. Here your having had your lunch at Alfonzo's satisfies your intention. However, in the we-mode case, we together intend to go to Alfonzo's (whether we go there together or separately need not matter). In this case your intention is a proper we-intention, and your personal lunch-going intention is to participate in our going to Alfonzo's for lunch. Obviously your intention here is not satisfied merely by your going to Alfonzo's for lunch; it is satisfied only after I have done my part and gone to Alfonzo's as well. The Collectivity Condition (of chapter 1 and below) is satisfied by our joint intention to go to Alfonzo's but not by shared I-mode intentions.

The harder problem of showing that we-mode collective intentionality is sometimes required or desirable over (progroup) I-mode concerns cases like this: Suppose you and I are driving on a country road in opposite directions. We have separate private goals. We arrive from different directions at a tree trunk lying on the road and blocking our way. We realize that in order to be able to continue we must jointly remove the trunk, and we quickly do it. Your activity was helpful and indeed required for my being able to reach my goal, and conversely. We both intended in the I-mode to remove the trunk and did it. The result was joint action in the I-mode. In general, joint actions can be performed in a functional sense in the progroup I-mode. Thus trunks can get moved, bridges built, and so on in this way. In all such cases of course we-mode joint action is also possible. Often in actual life there is no recognizable overt difference but only difference in mental attitude. In principle, though, as mental attitudes involve dispositions to action, there is also a potential overt difference (e.g., collective commitment shows this in practice). One of the theses of this book is that in some cases we-mode (joint) action is required both *hermeneutically* (for the right understanding) and *explanatorily*. A strong case in point is institutional action, because institutions are based on constitutive we-mode collective construction (see chapter 8).

In chapter 1, the we-mode was said to involve the idea of one's functioning because of a group reason rather than a private reason. The group reason involves that the resulting attitudes and actions are for (the use and benefit of) the group, the participants being collectively committed to function together, as a group (recall chapter 1). Here "for-groupness" contains the group-level reason that the we-mode requires: what is collectively constructed for the group serves as the group members' reason for participation. The we-mode group reason for action (such as that a group's plan to build a bridge is a reason for its members' participation) involves the satisfaction of the Collectivity Condition and the participants' being collectively committed to the goal (or belief). While building a bridge jointly in the I-mode is functionally possible, in the we-mode the participants form a stronger "we" than in the I-mode. They act as one agent, being glued together by the Collectivity Condition and collective commitment. When a group functions as a group, its members must appropriately function as group members. The group member level is, as it were, an appropriate translation or redescription of the group level. If our group has a goal (that then is our goal as a group) we are supposed to accept the goal as our group goal (although not perhaps as our private goal) and to be collectively committed to acting appropriately as group members related to the satisfaction of the goal.

The we-mode essentially involves thick collective construction. For instance, a state G is collectively constructed to be "our goal" with collective commitment.

In the I-mode, collective construction is not involved but only the participants' private acceptance of a shared goal. The most central elements underlying the we-mode are that the group is viewed as an agent capable of collective construction (in a conceptual and ontological sense) and that on the group member level (the we-mode level, it can be said), the Collectivity Condition holds true. This principle is a conceptually necessary principle about the we-mode (we-mode attitudes and actions) and one that the I-mode does not satisfy. The Collectivity Condition makes the individual members' collective attitudes and actions in a sense interchangeable and depersonalized, at least in an egalitarian group: It is necessarily the case that if one group member has a (distributive and distributed) collective group attribute, then all the others who occupy a similar position will have it. Strict individuality is thus blocked and this shows that the Collectivity Condition represents the group level on the level of group members.

In more precise terms, a we-mode collective goal based on the participants' collective acceptance and distributed among the participants in an "egalitarian" group will have to satisfy the following Collectivity Condition concerning semantic satisfaction.

> (CC) It is true on "quasi-conceptual" grounds and hence necessarily that a goal content p is satisfied in the case of a member (qua a member) of an egalitarian collective g if and only if it is satisfied for every other member of g (qua a member of g).

Here the qualification "on quasi-conceptual grounds" is taken to entail that the collective goal-content p is collective due to the group's acceptance of it as its goal, which is taken to amount to its collective acceptance ("construction"), involving collective commitment, by the members of g as their collective goal when functioning as group members in the standard sense. Thus, what is quasi-conceptually true can be regarded as being analytic a posteriori. The collective acceptance in the goal case, putting the matter in linguistic terms, concerns the conative proposition "Our goal is p" (or, equivalently, "We will achieve p") and is assumed to be necessarily truth-equivalent to the correct assertability of the proposition for the group members. Collective acceptance here entails that each participant, functioning as group member in the standard sense, has accepted the goal as the group's ("our") goal and hence aims at contributing to the satisfaction of p.[3]

A common goal is by its conceptual nature simultaneously fulfilled for the participants, but in the case of a we-mode collective goal, the simultaneously satisfied tokens of the individuals' collective intentions to act together are *necessarily connected due to the collective acceptance*. Collective acceptance can vary in strength, so to speak, and range from joint, plan-based acceptance to shared "acceptance-belief" (belief that p amounts to acceptance that p is true; see chapter 6). The stronger the kind of collective acceptance, the stronger is the necessity. In general, the content of (CC) must be assumed to be mutually known to the participants. However, the agents need not have beliefs directly about (CC)— the connection can be generated in a roundabout way due to their beliefs that they are engaged in the same project. An I-mode attitude does not satisfy (CC), even if the members' private but shared goal would contingently happen to be simultaneously satisfied in the case of all the members of g and even if the participants had promised to each other to try to satisfy their shared goals simultaneously—the goal still would not be a proper collective or group goal; and in the we-mode case, only the group goal ("our" goal) is under consideration, not private goals.[4]

(CC) generalizes to any attitude, say, want, wish, belief, and so on, and also to action as a group member, thus to participation in joint projects. As we will in this book concentrate on the satisfaction of attitudes, I will technically formulate a generalized version only for that case. Considering an attitude ATT and assuming that its content is p, we thus get the following version of the Collectivity Condition:

> (GCC) It is necessarily true (on quasi-conceptual grounds, thus on analytic a posteriori grounds) that the participants' shared we-attitude toward p (here assumed equivalent to the group's attitude toward p, that is, $ATT(g,p)$) is satisfied for a member A_i of g (qua a member of g) if and only if it is satisfied for every other member of g (qua a member of g).[5]

Shared we-attitudes will be discussed in detail in the next chapter. In general, a sentence of the kind $ATT(g,p)$ is an attitude-expressing sentence. In the case of intended collective goals (and intentions) the surface form of the attitude-expressing proposition, say, s, could be "We will achieve p," where "will" expresses intending and p represents a goal state. In the case of collective beliefs (acceptances) the formula s may take the form "We believe that p" or "It is our view that p", and analogously for other attitudes. In addition, actions can be taken to be covered by ATT.

Let me now sketch how to proceed in the other central cases the Collectivity Condition is claimed to apply to: all cases involving group-constructed collectivity. In the case of egalitarian groups and distributive properties, it is easy to generalize the Collectivity Condition to having an attitude (instead of merely speaking of *satisfying* an attitude) and *participation* (or "involvement") as group members in group projects. As coming to have an attitude and having it are based on voluntary activity in the group case—as will be argued in chapter 6—we can speak of participation in having an attitude and performing one's part of a joint action at the same time. Both notions rely on the normative notion of acting as a group member in the standard sense (recall section 3 of chapter 1). I will below idealize the situation and assume that indeed all the group members act as proper, "good" group members and satisfy the participation norms in question.

If a group accepts doing something, then its members will participate in doing it (or at least try to). Thus, if the group members jointly intend to do X, and will do it, then necessarily (because of this) all members will relevantly participate, that is, to be "involved" or "play a role," possibly in a passive sense, with respect to X. In the case of a dyad formed by you and me, then, necessarily, I will participate (be involved, play a role), and you will similarly participate, if we act as group members. It follows that, necessarily, I am involved as a group member with respect to X if and only if you are. If you are not involved as a group member, that would mean that a group project concerning X is not underway, and then I cannot be involved (and analogously for you). More generally, we have this:

(i) Necessarily (because of the group members' having agreed to X, where X is an ethos-compatible attitude or action in the group's realm of concern), a group member is qua a group member involved in the group's X-ing (its having or doing X) if and only if any other member also is analogously involved as a group member in X-ing.

There is also a group version of this general collectivity idea. It says, very roughly formulated, the following.

(ii) Necessarily, based on group acceptance, a group X-s (has attitude X or does X, as the case may be) if and only if every group member qua a group member is involved (or plays a role) in X-ing, be this involvement or role potential or actual participation in the coming about or holding of X.

This collectivity principle lies at the bottom of the analysis of group action and group attitudes in this book (see chapter 6, especially the discussion of (GATT), section 4). The group's X-ing (and thus the members' joint X-ing) gives the members a reason to participate, to perform their parts of, or play their role with respect to, X. In this situation characterized by (i) and (ii), the members necessarily are "in the same boat," and this expresses what collectivity and the we-mode involve.[6]

This account can be applied also to structured groups (e.g. organizations) with a division of tasks, roles, and positions—in general, "norm-based task-right systems."[7] Thus social power in this in-built structural sense will be involved. Some qualifications are of course needed. The same goes for group properties that do not distribute to a group's members, although even in such a case it is true that all the members necessarily are "in the same boat" regarding the property, in the sense that the statement of the group's having that property is collectively available to them (is "premisible" for them, in the terminology of chapter 6). Note, too, that the Collectivity Condition interestingly gives a reason to say that the depersonalization that occurs in social groups shows up in the basic structure of group life (in its we-mode content) and thus is not a mere contingent feature of groups.

Note that a position-holder in a structured group can act as a group member in the weak, I-mode sense (AGMW) of chapter 1. Allowing for the weak sense of ethos promotion discussed in that chapter (recall the senses (i)–(iv)), a member can instrumentally function (or, better, quasi-function) as a group member just by doing his "work," even if not for the ethos-serving reason (that satisfies the Collectivity Condition). He would then, so to speak, be exhibiting the right actions, but his *reason* for performing a group-task T would be, roughly, the I-mode reason expressible by "I perform T because it is conducive to my personal interests" and not the we-mode reason expressible by "I perform T at least in part because it is my duty and furthers, or at least does not contradict, the group's ethos." A person can accept the ethos of a group in a private sense (under his description of it) without participating in its we-mode acceptance and without participating in the group members' collective commitment to satisfy and maintain it.[8]

Paradigmatic examples of the we-mode are provided by full-blown joint intention and joint action. Here the agents, in distinction from the I-mode case, jointly accept a plan (intention) for the group and collectively commit themselves to act, the collective commitment here being generated (even in a conceptual sense) by the joint intention. As already seen in chapter 1, three central characteristics of the we-mode concerned with a reason, attitude, or action are these: The content in question must be (i) collectively accepted (ii) with collective commitment (iii) for (the use and the benefit of) the group. This kind of we-mode acceptance presupposes the satisfaction of the Collectivity Condition. However, there can be I-mode joint intention and action as well as agreements, depending on the participants' relevant attitudes and interpretations (see chapters 3 and 5). Furthermore, in many cases of many-person joint action in the we-mode, some persons can be allowed to participate in the I-mode without the joint or collective action losing its we-mode character. There will be much discussion of we-mode functioning later in the book, for example, in relation to cooperation and social institutions.

2   Basic Kinds of We-Mode and I-Mode

To discuss the we-mode and the I-mode in detail, I will assume below that A is a member of the group g in question, and I will regard the collective acceptance of an attitude as coming to hold and committedly holding a *we-attitude* (see chapters 3, 6, and 8). As collective acceptance is attitude-dependent, collective commitment is also attitude-dependent and lasts only as long as the attitude is held. In the case of private commitment, a proper normative aspect need not be present: the agent need only bind herself in a descriptive sense—so that she, at least if relevantly rational, to some extent persists in holding the attitude.

Group membership—where both I-mode groups and we-mode groups in the sense of chapter 1 are under discussion—need not in this context involve more than that A regards himself as a member of an ethos-involving group g and typically also that the other members of g tend to regard him as a member of g; and A must also be disposed to act as a group member.

Let us consider the case of a group's belief. It amounts to the group's acceptance of a view, say, p, with "view-commitment."[9] Group g thus has bound itself to the view that p. The members of g accordingly are collectively view-committed to p. The members accordingly have collectively committed themselves to using content p in their relevant inferences (via the proposition s in which p occurs as an element) and to acting on the basis of s's truth when acting as group members.[10] The group case is in general more "intellectually loaded" than the private case, and the group ("we") is not relevantly comparable with "I." While a single agent can have beliefs in such terms of direct confrontation with reality as are rendered by "This is a brown table," in the group case, the concept "we" requires conceptualized thinking, in that a judgment about what we believe is involved. Thus in the full-blown group case (where the group functions as a unit) the corresponding formulation is "We believe as a group that this is a brown table" or something analogous. The idea is that the subject of the belief must be committed to the content and that this needs grammatical expression as well. At least in all "conative" (action-related) cases, such as planning and executing collective action, reflection of the attitude (e.g., belief) is required.

My we-mode and I-mode notions depend on the notion of acting as a group member in the core sense (see chapter 1). The we-mode is the mode of the thick we-perspective (or group perspective), and it gets a central part of its content from *for-groupness*, which means thinking and acting for the group so that all the activities and results of them that are *collectively accepted* by the group are group "shareware" and thus for the use of, and collectively available to, the group members in their thinking and acting as group members. This is in part based on the Collectivity Condition as applied to we-mode for-groupness. Typically, what is for the group is also for the benefit of the group, as the ethos of the group must be respected (e.g., "We intend to uphold E for our group by means of actions as a group member"; "We believe that p for our group").[11] Altruistic actions like helping poor people can be for the group in my general sense, as long as the ethos is not violated. The other central element is *collective commitment*, which, especially the involved *social commitment*, dynamically "glues" the members to each other and, more generally, to the group (think of a group with changing members). We recall that for-groupness involves the idea of the group ethos being a "presuppositional" reason or precondition for action, which will accordingly amount to action as a group member when collective commitment to the ethos is in place.[12]

An attitude is in the I-mode or in the we-mode if, respectively, it is held for an I-mode reason or for a we-mode reason, and the analogous principle applies to actions (recall the accounts (WMR) and (IMR) of chapter 1). We will, however, need somewhat more precise we-mode and I-mode notions in this book, and therefore I will below define some such notions. Consider a case where some people have some attitude, ATT, toward a content p. For instance, they both intend to go to Alfonzo's for lunch. Now, some such cases are we-mode cases while some others are I-mode cases. Ordinary language does not by itself determine when the we-mode is at stake. Thus, for instance, the statement "We intend to paint the house together" can be made true at least in some cases by shared progroup I-mode intention and not by shared we-mode joint intention. Normal common-sense understanding will normally make sufficiently clear which is at stake, although there may still be room for differing philosophical and conceptual interpretations.

In the analyses below, the group, g, in question can be either normatively structured or unstructured. We are dealing with a group member who acts as a group member in a relevant sense (or, in the case of the last I-mode notion, only in a group context), and we ask in which different modes he could have an attitude (ATT). The attitude ATT may but need not be one that the ethos of g is directly about. I propose the following definitions.[13]

(WM) Agent A, a member of group g, has ATT(p), the attitude ATT with content p, in the *we-mode* relative to group g in situation C if and only if A has ATT(p) in part because (i) he is functioning (i.e., experiencing, thinking, and/or acting) as a member of g in the standard sense (AGMS) of Chapter 1 and because (ii) ATT(p) has been collectively accepted, with collective commitment, under conditions of mutual belief in g as g's ethos-promoting attitude in C; hence (iii) because of (ii), A is participating in the members' collective commitment, in the

ATT-way, to content p, at least in part for g (i.e., for the benefit and use of g) in C.[14] (It is presupposed that the collectively accepted attitude ATT(p) satisfies the Collectivity Condition.)

(IM1) Agent A, a member of group g, has ATT(p) in the *plain I-mode* relative to g in situation C if and only if A has ATT(p) in part because he is functioning as a group member of g in the weak sense (AGMW) of chapter 1 and is hence privately committed, in the ATT-way, to content p, at least in part, for himself in C.

(IM2) Agent A, a member of group g, has ATT(p) in the *progroup I-mode* relative to g in situation C if and only if A has ATT(p) in part because she is functioning as a member of g in sense (AGMW) and is privately committed, in the ATT-way, to content p at least in part for g in C.[15]

Action modes can now be accounted for by means of attitude modes and the because-of relation ("because" in general expressing both reason and cause): An action is performed in a certain kind of mode if and only if it is performed because of (or on the basis of) an attitude had in that same mode. Furthermore, we can take the psychologically effective reasons for action to be contents of attitudes or, in some special cases, the attitudes themselves.[16] Then this account of an action performed because of an attitude in a certain mode typically amounts to saying that this action is performed for the reason expressed by the content of that attitude such that the reason here is in the mode that the attitude is in (recall (WMR) and (IMR) of chapter 1).

Due to ethos-related for-groupness, the reason for a person performing action X as a group member in the we-mode case can be "that X is what the group's ethos requires or what serves it." When the members collectively accept such contents for the group, they can use them in their inferences and act on them (see chapter 6, section 5). In the I-mode case, a "progroup" reason (the term is used to avoid confusion with we-mode for-groupness) is also possible (and even required in case (IM2)) and amounts to advancing the group's goals and interests (it is to its benefit, in short). However, in contrast to the we-mode case, the Collectivity Condition is not satisfied in the I-mode case. (IM1) requires the presence of a "for herself" reason (e.g., "I do X because it furthers my private, possibly altruistic, interests and goals").

One can also speak of a sense of I-mode, more private than that involved in (IM1), according to which an agent is concerned wholly privately, independent of any group. Thus, if in (IM1) no relativity to a group is present (and g is deleted or, so to speak, shrinks into the "empty" group) we arrive at the pure private mode: A has a certain attitude ATT with content p in the *pure private mode* in a certain situation C if and only if A has ATT and is privately ATT-committed to content p only for herself in C.

In (WM), in contrast to the I-mode cases, agent A is required to function as a group member in the standard sense—because the Collectivity Condition and the requirement of collective commitment must be satisfied. Due to our present focus on action in a group context (in contrast to acting fully privately), (IM1) and (IM2) also require acting as a group member in the weak sense (AGMW).

A central point about (IM2) is that it mimics we-mode group activity in a sense without really motivationally engaging in it. Note that (WM) requires disposition to correct action but allows for acting against one's private interests.

In (WM), A is assumed to be we-committed in the we-mode to content p (a content within the group's realm of concern) in the ATT way, meaning that she is participating in the members' collective commitment in the way that is special to the attitude ATT in question. In the case of an intention, for instance, she is supposed to respect the world-to-mind direction of fit of the satisfaction of intention. Note that agent A may have committed herself to functioning as a group member because she takes the group to have intrinsic value or to have instrumental value for her. The former case gives the fullest sense in which she can *identify with the group*.

Paradigm cases of we-mode attitudes and actions satisfying (WM) in normal conditions are full-blown joint intentions (shared we-intentions) and joint actions based on shared we-intentions, as well as normative, group-binding group attitudes and actions. (These notions will be discussed later in this book, and I-mode counterparts of these full-blown notions are also considered.)

(WM) contains the requirement of the collective acceptance of the attitude as the group's attitude (see chapter 8 for the reflexive "(CAT) formula"). By entailment, this account makes ATT satisfy the Collectivity Condition. However, to emphasize this matter, it has also been explicitly required in (WM) that this condition must be satisfied. If there is a conflict between individual motivation and group motivation in the we-mode case, the latter wins or has more weight. Thus, when acting as a group member in the we-mode, an agent will perform the right positional action. When an agent rationally acts for her group, her motivation to act for it is larger than that for herself.

There are interesting possibilities of weakening (WM). First, the requirement of reflexive collective acceptance can be relaxed.[17] Second, one can consider a case in which the participants are only privately committed to ATT(p) while still acting as group members in the standard sense (and thus being collectively committed to the ethos). Suppose a group has as its realm of concern collecting small objects of value. Its current ethos might just make it a stamp collectors' club ("Our goal is to collect stamps"), while the members would also be privately committed to collecting coins. This would satisfy this weakened definiens, and we might call this notion the mixed we-mode and I-mode notion.

Case (IM1) of the (plain) I-mode is simple, as it contains no group considerations, except that A is taken to be a group member but has the attitude and acts as a group member in the weak sense (AGMW). There is group-relativity with respect to group g, and A is allowed to have his attitude in the we-mode concerning some other group.

As to (IM2), A is here trying to satisfy the attitude largely privately and at least partly for the group. Note that while (IM2) is compatible with (IM1), it does not quite entail it, for such entailment requires the additional premise that A is acting also in part for herself. What happens if there is a conflict between individual and group motivation? Suppose the group goal requires A to perform X while his individual goals would lead him to perform -X. Then we have a case of genuine conflict (and we are dealing with a special case of the switch problem, to be commented on in chapter 7). Group life cannot, at least in the long run, prosper in this kind of case.

Note that even with no direct conflict, we-mode action wins over progroup I-mode action in the sense that, while both modes lead to the performance of X, there is collective commitment in the we-mode case but only private commitment in the I-mode case. As collective commitment contains social commitment toward other participants, A is disposed more easily to give up (the consummation of) X in the I-mode case than in the we-mode case (see chapter 7). The presumption here is that the effect of social pressure is stronger than that of private interests.

Obviously, our above technical notions are just an interesting sample of a variety of modes. For other purposes different notions may be needed.

In the we-mode case (WM), participating in collective commitment entails being committed to the others and/or to the group (recall these notions from chapter 1). In contrast, private commitment in (IM1) and (IM2) is to oneself and/or to the others and/or to the group. We may also ask for whom a commitment is made. In the we-mode case, the we-commitment is for (the use of) the group (in addition to being to and, in typical cases also "before," the others or the group). In the I-mode cases (IM1) and (IM2), the private commitment in principle can be for oneself (only partly so in (IM2)), for the others, or for the group (where the conjunction of all these is a possibility). In general, progroupness in our I-mode definitions can be taken to range from very little to maximal progroupness.

Note that one can act in a kind of "quasi" I-mode-progroup way in a group context without strictly acting as a group member in the weak sense (one might, e.g., accidentally conform to the ethos or do things that indirectly contribute to the ethos). To make the we-mode and the I-mode analyses more analogous and better comparable, I have nevertheless required acting as a group member in the weak sense in (IM1) and (IM2). The "groupish" I-mode case (IM2) requires private commitment that is (partly) to the group.[18] In cases that are only for the group, the for-herself part shrinks to zero, although the agent will still reason in terms of I-thoughts rather than we-thoughts and may at bottom be motivated by selfish motives. Similarly, functioning in the we-mode may be based on selfish motives, or at least this is allowed as a conceptual possibility.[19] Thus we have:

(i) Both I-mode and we-mode thinking and acting can be, but need not be, based either on selfish or on altruistic motives.

As to group identification, a group member can identify with the group (basically, adopt the group's ethos as part of his social identity) in various ways (cf. (WM) and (IM2)). (IM2) involves a weak element of group (or collective) identification. Clearly, the more we-mode thinking and acting in the group there is, the more cohesive it is, the primary factor accounting for cohesion being of course collective commitment (recall the comments in chapter 1).

Here are some further points related to the above analyses. As the we-mode is based on a group reason, while the I-mode is based a private reason—recall (WMR) and (IMR)—the following observations can be made.

(ii) The I-mode (i.e., (IM1), (IM2)) does not entail the we-mode (i.e., (WM)).

(iii) The we-mode (i.e., (WM)) does not entail the I-mode (i.e., (IM1), (IM2)).

Obviously, there can be mixed we-mode/I-mode cases. For instance, people working in an organization agree to act in the we-mode concerning the basic rules of the organization serving its ethos. In the same context they may act in the I-mode and, for example, compete with each other (think of competing salesmen in the same business company). Let us state this as follows.

(iv) Social activities such as group actions and social practices can involve mixtures of we-mode and I-mode actions.

According to (ii) and (iii), the we-mode is not (deductively) reducible to the I-mode (nor does the converse hold), and they can recommend conflicting actions (see chapter 4, section 4, for a detailed discussion of the irreducibility claim and chapters 6 and 7 for the latter claim). Note that the we-mode is in the minds and actions of individuals. While the we-mode represents group-level thinking and acting and as a concept thus is holistic, ontologically it pertains to individuals and does not postulate supraindividual agents. This entails that the we-mode (involving, e.g., agents having thoughts about groups and social structures) does not add anything "dramatically" different to the ontology, although states of we-thinking and I-thinking are ontologically different kinds of states.[20]

Several aspects distinguishing the we-mode from the I-mode have been discussed above. The most central is the reason aspect incorporated in the for-groupness idea: the we-mode conceptually requires thinking (including "emoting") and acting because of a group reason, whereas the I-mode requires only private reasons, which may contingently involve satisfying the ethos of the group. A factor incorporated in the group reason element that was emphasized especially in chapter 1 is that in the we-mode case, the group has the authority, so to speak, and thus the group members acting as group members share the authority and responsibility for whatever they do as a group; and the participants count on each other's being so involved (no matter if there is actual overt causal dependence between the participants or not). In contrast, in the I-mode case each person has full authority over what he is doing. The collective commitment involved in the we-mode entails that everyone is committed to furthering what everyone is jointly doing and to doing his or her part of it. It is not a question of who does what in each situation. The participants' plans in principle involve open elements, as new situations may and do come up. In the we-mode case a participant may even do all the parts if needed. In contrast, in the I-mode case, a participant is not supposed "automatically" (e.g., without further agreements) to do all the parts if needed; for her it is a matter of individual costs or other considerations related to her private reasons.[21] As emphasized earlier, the participants in we-mode contexts are socially committed to each other to participate. They can count on the others' help when needed. Only the group can release one from this commitment. In contrast, in the I-mode case, the participant is basically committed only to herself to participate, unless further agreements and promises are made.

In the we-mode case, actions as a group member are in the public group domain—for example, for-groupness and collective (and the entailed social) commitment require it. For-groupness licenses the use of collectively accepted ideas in practical inference and action related to the group domain. When intending jointly and being collectively committed, the participants give away part of their autonomy to the group, so to speak, and thus to the public domain. Their we-mode actions are out in the open. In principle, everybody is assumed to contribute to the group good, to do her fair share, but is also allowed to have her piece of the group cake (products of the joint enterprise), so to speak.

3   Why the We-Mode?

In this section the we-mode and the I-mode (especially the progroup I-mode) will be compared further. Let us start by asking the following question: Which of the modes is conceptually and/or psychologically primary? Our above analyses do not yet give an answer to this question. To comment on the issue, we first recall that the full (we-mode) we-perspective involves the disposition to use we-thoughts (e.g., "We ATT(p) as a group") and act on them, whereas the I-perspective (and I-mode) involves the disposition to reason and act on I-thoughts (e.g., "I will do X in this group context"). Human agents generally seem to engage in both kinds of thinking or at least to be disposed to do so, and our common-sense conceptual framework of agency does not seem to make one of the perspectives conceptually primary.

People are able to engage both in we-mode and I-mode thinking and acting—even simultaneously—but these two modes are not reducible to each other. In particular, this irreducibility point applies also to progroup thinking and acting. Furthermore, there is the simple general point for requiring we-mode notions that the social world cannot be understood and accordingly cannot be fully explained without them (or their suitable "successor concepts") without change of topic, so to speak. (On the other hand, obviously the social world cannot be fully understood without I-mode concepts either.)

However, the following quasi-conceptual or, rather, "anthropological" consideration seems to favor the primacy of the I-mode: We-mode thinking of course presupposes that the thinker has a body. Thoughts will show up in action; for example, a person cannot in general intend to open the window or raise his arm without being disposed to move his body in the appropriate way. This kind of bodily action typically is I-mode action. However, against this point it can be said that when the agent acts as a group member, he will have to perform appropriate actions (such as opening the window or raising his arm) that are "we-derivative" and performed for a group reason, thus in the we-mode. While there are also pure, group-independent I-mode bodily actions (e.g., a person may typically move her little finger quite independently of any group), it would seem that we-mode actions and attitudes do not always require I-mode intermediaries but can, so to speak, be mapped directly onto neural states and events. There seem to be at least no in-principle barriers to the we-mode "going all the way down"—not only conceptually but also in this factual psychological sense.[22]

We-mode acting as a group member requires that the ethos of the group be respected at least as far as the reason for the action is concerned. This is a kind of *cooperation-generating* feature (see chapter 7). Furthermore, this central feature tends to lead to harmonious social relations between group members. Because of the cooperative design of organizations and institutions, this often requires of the members that their resulting we-mode action, governed by the group's goals and interests, not be *strategic* action vis-à-vis the internal affairs taking place in the group (although it of course may be strategic concerning other groups). In particular, group members are supposed not to take private advantage of other members. However, as we-mode activities are often mixed with strategic I-mode acting in real life, people might do all that X requires but might still harm others and try to satisfy their own private interests by strategic means (e.g., a member secretly plotting against some other members to achieve leadership while still performing his "official" tasks satisfactorily). This is something relating to the way or manner of the agents collectively doing X but not to the achievement of X itself. Note that (WM) requires acting as a group member for the group, and this basically prohibits harming other group members. Nevertheless, if it allows for some amount of we-mode competition (e.g., sports games, competing businessmen adhering to the same company rules).

What about negative consequences that we-mode thinking and acting can have? Without entering this topic properly, let me just remind the reader of various "crowding" effects (primarily an I-mode phenomenon: "Too many cooks spoil the broth"). Of course morally bad things may be involved, too. The we-mode/I-mode distinction as such is morally neutral: An ethos can be either morally good or morally bad, and the we-mode can be put both to morally good and morally bad use.

While full-blown we-perspective notions form a somewhat holistic and irreducible conceptual package, it might be thought that all events, states, and processes that are conceptualized and described in terms of we-perspective notions nevertheless can be described equally correctly in terms of I-mode (especially progroup I-mode) notions. This would require comparability of the two perspectives, in that the topics dealt with in one perspective should be the same or at least be overlapping with those dealt with in the other perspective. This is a moot point, as we-mode notions are not generally reducible to I-mode notions (see the irreducibility theses (*ii*) and (*iii*) above, and see chapter 4). Later in the book I will, however, perform some "local" comparisons (e.g., in chapter 7). The two perspectives in question are wholesale perspectives but are at least functionally comparable with each other, it seems. The I-mode generally will do with much weaker and less interdependent collective primitives than the we-mode. By suitable additional assumptions (e.g., about participants' special agreements), at least some functional convergence can yet be achieved. In this book I argue, at any rate, that strong, irreducible we-mode concepts are needed for an adequate description and explanation of the social world.

As a kind of preview of what will come in later chapters, I will now consider some interesting cases in which we-mode thinking and acting (rather than I-mode thinking) is required or desired for successful social activities—mainly in addition to the considerations already presented in chapter 1 (recall, e.g., the discussion of the functions of collective commitment). I will argue that the we-mode can be *descriptively* and/or *explanatorily* better than the I-mode. The reasons favoring we-mode thinking and acting can be *conceptual* and/or *constitutive*, they can be *rational* in the sense that either instrumental or end rationality favors the we-mode over the I-mode, or they can be factual (or contingent, in philosophical terminology) in some looser sense than strict rationality involves. Strictly speaking, some of the reasons to be discussed are reasons for the shared point of view, that is, the group perspective, but not necessarily for the we-mode group perspective. Points (i)–(v) are basically connected to we-mode reasons, while the rest, points (vi)–(ix), are for the group perspective in general, be it we-mode or I-mode.

I will begin with points related to conceptual and rational issues and then proceed to contingent factual reasons:

(i) A strong we-mode case is formed by the important class of *group properties*, such as binding group attitudes, that a group qua a group has. Such group-binding properties in general require the we-mode.[23] Full-blown group beliefs and goals as well as other group attitudes are based on the group members' functioning fully as group members and in unison. They accept views and goals for the group, and these views can be regarded as group beliefs and goals.[24] What they do is in the we-mode, and the group can in a sense be regarded as the basic agent and not the individual (as in the I-mode). We-mode attitudes are causally real, and they obviously may affect the persons' actions in ways differing from the causal impact of their relevant I-mode attitudes. Partly for this reason but also for other reasons, we-mode group properties are needed for the correct description and explanation of social life, and this gives a necessity argument of the constitutive kind for the need for we-mode thinking and acting.

As to the belief case, individual group members' belief states (I-mode beliefs) can only be dealt with "statistically," as they do not form a unified group state. What is required for full-blown group belief that p is that the members collectively accept the view that p for the group (e.g., as expressed by "We as a group believe that p").[25] This is a we-mode judgment, and as a result the group has the "acceptance belief" that p—whether or not the members have the "experiential" belief that p. New things (relative to the members' I-mode experiential beliefs) may emerge in this kind of a group context. For instance, we-mode group beliefs may involve group standards and norms deriving from the group's ethos. There may also be compromise beliefs (beliefs with contents due to compromises) that possibly no single member finds privately acceptable (e.g., a case of voting in which no one's first choice is elected). In this kind of case, acting against one's private belief (goal, etc.) in group contexts becomes possible even within one and the same group.[26]

In his recent work on "discursive dilemmas," Philip Pettit concentrates on a voting type of situation, where the group's view is determined by a simple rule such as the majority principle. He shows that the group members' reasons for a conclusion (view) may lead them to collectively accept a view for (deductively sufficient) reasons that they individually reject. This is an interesting group phenomenon, although perhaps not very representative of group decision-making (see section 2 of chapter 4).[27] This phenomenon—concerned with two incompatible ways of inferring and arriving at a solution—does not, however, entail that groups are persons, contrary to what I take Pettit to claim (inference and existence are not that close).[28]

(ii) There are cases of joint action in which the we-mode normally is taken to be required. Thus, there are cases of *necessarily* many-person actions—such as certain games (e.g., tennis), ceremonies (e.g., graduation), and many-person speech acts (e.g., discussion)—where we-mode action generally is assumed on conceptual grounds (although one may think of simulating, for example, a tennis game on the basis of private commitments and agreements in the progroup I-mode). There are cases of joint activity (e.g., having a discussion) in which we-mode joint action is required or preferable on contingent grounds. (See chapter 5.)

(iii) Rational cooperation at least on some occasions gives better results when conducted in the we-mode than in the I-mode (see chapter 7). Thus, we-mode joint action can be both *individually and collectively more rational* than I-mode "joint action."[29] In particular, the acceptance of the we-mode group perspective entails that collective action dilemmas disappear in principle. This is because the group, if rational, here goes for cooperation and requires mutual cooperation of its members. On the ingroup level, there will then be no conflict between collective and individual rationality (this conflict is the defining feature of a collective action dilemma), if the group members genuinely function as group members. This is of course a big "if" in actual practice, but collective commitment associated with social and other sanctions will help when private desires create obstacles (see chapter 7). In this way, cooperation even in a single-shot prisoner's dilemma (PD) can be viewed as both collectively and individually rational, given that individual rationality is understood as rationality qua a group member. In contrast, within the plain I-mode, the only individually rational strategy in the single-shot PD is (mutual) defection, and within the progroup I-mode the PD might be changed into an assurance game, with some of the conflict remaining (see Chapter 7, appendix 2, for the assurance game).[30]

(iv) We-mode cooperation is also relevant to moral and social philosophy, for it can be argued that we-mode cooperation typically plays a decisive role when accounting for moral and just behavior. While extreme liberalism in social philosophy deals only (or at least primarily) with individual actions and private goals, other forms of liberalism (such as Rawls's) employ collective goal notions that might be analyzable as we-mode notions (e.g., the notion of a political good or egalitarian liberty). Rawls's political liberalism regards justice as fairness, as a society-wide collective goal to be achieved by cooperative collective action that might be construable as cooperation in the we-mode sense.[31] We-mode cooperation and we-mode attitudes in general are relevant also to other political philosophies relying on collective goals such as common goods—for example, communitarianism, republicanism, and socialism.

Similar remarks can be made concerning moral theories emphasizing the role of cooperation: In general these theories require each person to do her part, perhaps conditionally on others doing their parts, of collective activities leading to the common good or actions that are good for all. We-mode cooperation (in the sense of chapter 7) is clearly relevant to this kind of moral theory. The distinction between I-mode and we-mode action (especially cooperation) can also be used to clarify the distinction between situations in which a person treats others merely as means to his ends (I-mode case) and situations where others (and their welfare)

are, so to speak, part of one's end (typically a we-mode case). Indeed, we-mode cooperation in its fullest sense incorporates the idea of mutual nonharming and helping, this idea being generally accepted as a moral principle—as remarked in a note, the Collectivity Condition is a special case of the golden rule. Also fairness can be commented on in terms of the Collectivity Condition (e.g., "Necessarily, I do—and get—my share if and only if others similarly do and get their share").

Furthermore, group responsibility involves we-mode considerations. As this matter will be discussed in detail in chapter 10, I will not here consider it.

(v) Social institutions in their standard sense are collectively constructed arti-facts consisting in special normatively governed social practices where group members are supposed to act qua group members in a collectively committed way. Specifically, social institutions arguably must be *constituted* by we-mode collective acceptance, and arguably an I-mode account of them is not possible (as indicated in the introduction and as will be shown in chapter 8). For instance, such economic activities as selling and buying require some amount of we-mode exchange, even if the institution can tolerate a considerable amount of relevant I-mode activity. More generally, we-mode thinking and acting are crucial in the conceptual construction of much of the social world, and basically we-mode groups and acting as a group member can be argued to generate institutional reality (although also I-mode activities of course take place in institutional contexts, but only in a nonconstitutive sense).[32]

(vi) Even when we-mode acting is not strictly required, there are often specific *contingent instrumental gains* that we-mode thinking and action can bring forth.[33] These instrumental or "economy" gains include many familiar kinds of things. The participants of we-mode joint action can often achieve better results as compared with (even progroup) I-mode action (but sometimes achieve poorer results, as shown in experiments by social psychologists). Here we should think not only of the case of people acting separately but of the case in which they act "jointly" (with the kind of coordination that a task requires) in the progroup I-mode sense. Various economy gains can be achieved, for example, in terms of saving energy, resources, and time, and in terms of achieving better quality of products, better reliability of performance, risk reduction, and higher likelihood of success. We-mode action, with its cooperative atmosphere, can also be more pleasant and socially more desirable to the participants than I-mode action.

(vii) There are also contingent experimentally achieved results that support the thesis that people often act for (we-mode or I-mode) group reasons.[34] Let me list some arguments for motivational group reasons that are based on social psychological experiments related to the social identity paradigm:

- Experiments on relative deprivation show that the distinction between the individual and the group level is central and leads to different consequences. Respectively, comparing oneself with other group members involves optimiz-ing one's absolute I-mode utilities while optimization of the relative gain of one's group relative to other groups is at stake in the latter case.

- The speech style people use typically depends on which groups they mo-mentarily choose to take as salient for the communicative situation at hand.

- Identification with a group is a precondition of group polarization: Attitudes associated with salient social identities may be more polarized than personal attitudes, even in the absence of communication or direct social influence.

- Ingroup favoritism can occur in the absence of interpersonal attraction or its antecedents.

- As mentioned in chapter 1, when a collection of individuals believe that they share a common ingroup membership, they are more likely to act in the interest of collective welfare than individuals in the same situation who do not have a sense of group identity.

- As also said in chapter 1, identification with the ingroup can elicit cooperative behavior even in the absence of interpersonal communication among group members. Functioning in ingroup context, in contrast to an outgroup, individuals develop trust and a cooperative orientation toward shared problems.

Brewer sums up the relevant research on the need for "we-ness" thus:

The evidence from a number of different domains of social behavior supports a distinction between behavior motivated by identification with social groups and behavior motivated by personal self-interest. When a particular group identity is engaged, individuals act in ways that represent and maintain distinctive group characteristics, even when that behavior is not consistent with individual egocentric motives. On the one side, social identity enhances liking, trust and cooperation toward fellow ingroup members, and actions that promote collective welfare. On the other hand, social identity also engages preferential biases, extreme attitudes and competitive orientation toward members of outgroups— all conditions that promote the likelihood of intergroup conflict. Thus, motives and behaviors that derive from attachment and loyalty to ingroups have important implications for intergroup relations.[35]

Note, however, that because of the possibility of progroup I-mode behavior, we do not get a clear and unambiguous evidential argument for the we-mode we-perspective from these social psychological investigations.

(viii) There are *evolutionary and developmental* arguments for the we-mode or at least the shared point of view coming from recent research in evolutionary anthropology and developmental psychology. Some researchers claim that collective intentionality is the most central feature that distinguishes human beings from other higher animals such as chimpanzees. Thus, Tomasello and his colleagues have studied the ontogenetic development of collective intentionality in humans and claim that the first, rudimentary kind of shared intentionality appears already at the age of nine to twelve months, and that fuller collective intentionality starts to become available in the second year.[36] Furthermore, a baby a few weeks old already forms a kind of emotional and "protoconversational" symbiosis with its mother. We might here consider "proto-we-mode" or perhaps simply "not-yet-any-mode." It might thus be argued that such a proto-we-mode has primacy to the I-mode. Only at a later stage can the infant experience himself as a separate "I," and then I-mode thinking and acting begins. The proper we-mode may take several years to develop.

The research results available today speak for collective intentionality, be it couched in the I-mode or in the we-mode. In older children and adults, the we-mode is operative anyhow. Notice that the emergence of full-blown we-mode seems to be in part due to children having been reared appropriately, thus to their having been socialized into we-mode functioning.

The above ontogenetic results fit well with the common hypothesis that in the development of the human species, acting as a group member and cooperation, and indeed collective intentionality, viewed as dispositions, are adaptations that have developed by means of culture-gene coevolution toward the late Pleistocene.[37] Accordingly, one may argue not only that group life has been and is central for humans but that collective intentionality (be it of the we-mode or progroup I-mode kind) has been a fitness-generating factor in the evolution of humans and even that we-mode groups (that can act and function like agents) have proved to be evolutionarily fitter (fitter biologically and/or culturally) than I-mode groups. The closely similar point can be made that cooperative and well-organized groups and their attitudinal properties seem to have fared better than uncooperative and poorly organized groups. (See chapter 9 for discussion.)

(ix) Finally, we consider the factual, contingent problem of whether the we-mode or the I-mode works better in *ordinary life* according to recent sociological and social psychological investigations. One may also speak of society-level institutional design in this connection. For instance, Triandis has compared "individualism" and "collectivism" with each other in light of recent empirical sociological research. At least loosely, these two correspond to the I-mode and the we-mode.[38] According to Triandis, in a collectivist group or community, people perceive themselves in terms of the groups to which they belong, while the opposite is true of individualistic collectives. In a collectivist group there is generally coherence between individual aims and collective aims, but in the case of incoherence, collective aims prevail, while the in individualistic groups individual aims win over collective aims. In the former, behavior is guided by obligations and duties, whereas rights are more important in the latter. Furthermore, in the former, private gains are much less important than in the latter. Triandis's account of collectivism fairly accurately applies to the we-mode, while his points about individualism square well with the factual consequences of the I-mode (especially the plain I-mode).

He arrives at the general conclusion (pp. 170–71) that "collectivism has definite advantages for those social relationships that include small groups, such as family and co-workers, where people are dealing with face-to-face situations and with people they are going to be interacting for a long time." In this kind of "interpersonal situation," achievement is mostly not the central purpose; rather, "people are either enjoying themselves or are consuming goods." In contrast, he takes individualism to have major advantages in situations where the individual is dealing with large collectives, such as the state, or in situations where achievement within the world economy is a central concern. He calls these "large collective situations." In short, from the point of view of individuals, in interpersonal situations, Triandis argues that there should be collectivism, and in large collective situations individualism.[39]

4 Summary

In this chapter the conceptual features of we-mode and I-mode mental states (and actions) have been considered in detail. For instance, a we-mode belief expressible by "We, the members of group g, believe that p" is a belief collectively accepted as the group's belief that is meant for the use (and typically benefit) of the group members (this, especially, involves a group reason) and to which the group members (ideally) are collectively committed. A we-mode attitude or action (in contrast to an I-mode one) is argued to presuppose the satisfaction of the Collectivity Condition. This condition is central for the theory created in this book. In a way, the Collectivity Condition is a group-version of the golden rule, and it explicates the colloquial musketeer's principle "All for one and one for all" as well as related ideas about standing or falling together and sharing a common fate. A plain I-mode attitude is a self-regarding and typically selfish one to which an individual is privately committed, while a progroup I-mode attitude is based on an individual's privately committing himself to regarding the group's goals and interests as central.

A preliminary survey of the functions and advantages of the we-mode and the I-mode is given in this chapter. Among the several points discussed, there are conceptual reasons related to taking the group's view instead of an individual's view of various social matters. Thus, the we-mode is central for our understanding ourselves as social beings and as group members, as well as especially for understanding such macrosocial notions as group attitudes and social institutions (see chapter 8). There are evolutionary reasons as well as instrumental reasons supporting the we-mode, as well as reasons concerned with rational functioning in social contexts. Cooperation in collective action dilemma situations can rationally be brought about in terms of we-mode action in typical cases, although that may not be strictly needed on instrumental grounds (see chapters 7 and 8). The basic hypothesis in this book actually is the centrality of the we-perspective for understanding and explaining social life, and the we-perspective need not always be the we-mode perspective but may sometimes be the weaker I-mode we-perspective, at least when the real functioning of people in large groups is concerned. In chapter 7, the I-mode we-perspective or, equivalently, the progroup I-mode is discussed in functional context and compared with the we-mode. Practically every chapter contains a discussion of the we-mode and also of its relationship to the progroup I-mode.

3

SHARED WE-ATTITUDES

1 Collective Intentionality and Shared We-Attitudes

Collectively intentional mental states can be divided basically into three kinds. There are shared states that dispose the subjects to act suitably, for example, wants and intentions. These are states with the world-to-mind direction of fit of semantic satisfaction. Next, there are cognitive states such as beliefs that people can share. These are states that generally have the mind-to-world direction of fit. Finally, there are shared emotions, that is, mental states with the "null" direction of fit concerning their feeling components.[1] Furthermore, these states can be either in the I-mode or the we-mode. In this chapter I will discuss *I-mode* notions of the first two kinds, and in later chapters we-mode notions. Except for some occasional remarks and points, collective emotions will not be discussed in this book.

People commonly think and act socially in the sense of responding to the demands of their social surroundings, that is, to what the others think and how they act. Especially if the others normatively expect certain behavior from group members, this may be a strong incentive to comply. But there are weaker cases, for example, people imitating others by wearing certain kinds of clothes. In general, in this kind of case there is typically an underlying disposition (proattitude) to conform or, perhaps, conform to some extent while still desiring to distinguish oneself from others in some publicly noticeable aspects. Another example of conformity is provided by acquiring knowledge by testimony: people adopt views from authorities, for instance by reading scientific books by acknowledged scientists.

In this chapter I will focus on conformative social attitudes that an agent holds in part because others in the group hold them. These attitudes are called "we-attitudes." A we-attitude can be either in the I-mode or in the we-mode. Roughly, the I-mode version says that a person has the attitude in question because some other fellow group members have it, while the we-mode version says that a person has the attitude because her group has it. The I-mode version is the purely interpersonal version, and the we-mode version is the group-based one. Both versions deal with central kinds of sociality.[2]

This chapter concentrates on I-mode we-attitudes (see section 2). Section 3 discusses a circularity problem related to I-mode social attitudes, including I-mode we-attitudes. Section 4 gives an account of mutual beliefs as shared we-beliefs. Finally, the concluding section 5 makes some preliminary comments on we-mode we-attitudes, especially shared we-mode beliefs, which will later, in chapters 4 and 6, be discussed in full.

2   I-Mode We-Attitude

We-attitudes are attitudes involving social beliefs in a group, say, g, which typically is characterized intensionally (in terms of a property or a description) rather than extensionally (in terms of listing its members). We consider a person's we-attitude, WATT, related to an attitude, ATT, which has content p. For instance, we can have ATT = want and p = "Our clubhouse is beautifully decorated." The variable ATT can be a plain want, goal, intention, belief, even an emotion like "we-feeling," in the sense of we-pride, or a feeling of togetherness, and so on. (We can, in addition, let ATT be exemplified by an action performed with a certain intention or purpose.)

Let me propose the following definitions.

> (WATT) x has the *we-attitude* ATT with content p, in short, WATT(p), if and only if
> (a) A has ATT(p),
> (b) he believes that also the others in the group, g, have ATT(p), and
> (c) he also believes (or at least is disposed to believe) that it is mutually believed (or in a weaker case plainly believed) that the members have ATT(p).[3]

> (WATTS) A has the *socially grounded we-attitude* ATT with content p if and only if
> (d) A has the we-attitude ATT with content p, and
> (e) (a) in part because (b) and (c),
> where "because" can, broadly speaking, express either reason (thus influence through the person's "intentional channel") or cause (influence through a non-intentional, subpersonal "channel").

Accordingly,

> (WATTR) A has the *reason-based we-attitude* ATT with content p if and only if
> (d) A has the we-attitude ATT with content p, and
> (f) (b) and (c) are x's (partial) reason for (a).[4]

Condition (f) is to be understood widely so that not only actively accepted (or "occurrent") reasons count but also "presuppositional reasons," that is, reasons that are conceptually required and taken for granted, and a person having them must be disposed to make them active if needed.[5] (WATT), (WATTS), and (WATTR) all obviously are *conformative* we-attitudes.

Acting for a we-attitude related to ATT(p) entails acting in the right "ATT-realizing" way for the reason content p. It also involves acting for the social reason that, at least in favorable circumstances, the others in the group have ATT(p) and are satisfying it or at least are disposed to satisfy it (see clause (b)), and also acting in part on the mutual belief in question (clause (c)).[6] In our above example, when some persons act because of (or on the basis of) the we-want to have the house beautifully decorated, this collective end gives each of them a reason to act. This reason consists in his wanting to have the house beautifully decorated and his believing that also the others want so and his also believing that it is mutually believed that the members want to have the house beautifully decorated.

Acting for a social reason of the above conformative kind may not be a good reason (e.g., mimicking may sometimes lead to disastrous consequences). I am trying to give an account of a social phenomenon that nevertheless is rather frequent in social life. The above account of reason-based we-attitudes and of the above kind of cause-based we-attitudes consists of two components. There is the component of what is conceptually presupposed of one's we-attitude, and this "precondition" component consists of conditions (b) and (c). The second component is the motivational component that the agent indeed has the attitude (or acts) for the social reason (expressed by (b) and (c)) in question or that the social state consisting of (b) and (c) indeed causally motivates the person to acquire the attitude (or to act).[7]

While I will conduct most of my discussion as if the content p were a propositional content, that is not a central requirement. Thus p could in principle represent an object by description (A sees a dog) or have a vague, unspecific content (A sees a moving object) or be a nonarticulated content (A sees *this* object), and so on.

The reason-based we-attitude (WATTR) (as well as the we-attitude (WATTS) based on a social cause or reason) is central, but the plain, socially weaker notion (WATT) also has applications. Furthermore, when discussing social action, a central context is that of actions performed because of a social reason, where the social reason is a we-attitude. In such a context, it normally does not make much difference whether the standard notion or the reason-based notion of we-attitude is used. However, there are "toxin puzzle" types of cases that are trying to drive a wedge between intending to perform an action and performing it, and there are arguments against the transitivity of reasons.[8]

How can the conditions (a)–(c) defining a plain we-attitude (WATT) be justified? First, it must be said that they are obviously somewhat idealized in requiring without exception that all the members satisfy the condition. That can easily be remedied, although I will not do it here. As to (a), which may be called the *genuineness* condition, it can be thought of as a rather obvious requirement for distributable (and distributed) group properties that in principle must apply to all individual group members. This is a central idea when speaking of we-attitudes, since they are basically attitudes that individuals can have—as distinct from group properties like group cohesion. An individual's we-attitude is simply a socially enriched attitude, and thus it must refer to the other individuals.

When an attitude is in the we-mode, it requires that the participants must hold it *as group members*, hence they must collectively accept it as their group attitude and must be collectively committed to its content, which is "collectively available" to them (or, equivalently, is meant "for the use and benefit of the group"). We recall that, in general, an I-mode attitude is not based on functioning as a group member and the person having it is only privately committed. Unless otherwise said, it is assumed below that the we-attitudes under discussion are I-mode attitudes (although perhaps progroup I-mode we-attitudes).

Concerning (b), the *conformity* condition, belief is an obvious element for "gluing" the attitudes together, as we are speaking of attitudes distributed among the group members. The appropriate doxastic connection between the participants consists in their belief that the others share the attitude; and this can be a person's reason (or cause, as, e.g., in the case of "we-feeling" in the sense of we-pride or we-solidarity, etc.) for conforming.[9] Belief is the basic cognitive notion for getting information about the social world, and accordingly, conformity may be of the *informational* kind. In this case, a person accepts as true what the majority or what some experts or some other group thinks or says. In contrast, normative conformity is based on normative expectations and perhaps pressure by the group. Thus, an agent having a we-attitude because the others in the group have it may (correctly or not) view the others' beliefs that the members have the attitude as *normative expectations*, and this of course creates normative pressure to conform. Notice, too, that at least in the case of large groups such as societies, the pressure will be largely anonymous. The others in the group thus might not be known to the agent in question under a more informative description than "member of our community," and this may, furthermore, amount in the agent's mind to the Durkheimian idea of "the community demanding" conforming. Social norms are the standard codified normative exemplifications of societal or group demands.

A related aspect is that, as we know, people generally want to be appreciated and valued by their fellow members. So, to put the matter in simple colloquial terms, suppose I am a person who appreciates your thinking well of me. So I conform to your expectations of me—that I should have certain attitudes and act in a certain way, say, X, in a situation. Thus, in order to be such a "good" person (in your eyes) I believe that I must do X. More generally, I should have certain thoughts and perform certain actions because you expect me to have those attitudes and to perform those actions. Expectation here amounts to your belief that I ought to have those attitudes, and so on. To put the matter in general terms, I have the reason-based we-attitude WATT toward a content p, where p is either an attitude or an action, if and only if I have ATT(p) in part because I believe that the others in the group normatively expect me to have ATT(p) and I also believe that this is mutually believed in the group. This is a norm-involving we-attitude of the form defined above. Underlying this we-attitude and explaining it, there often is a conformist attitude such as that I want you to regard me as a good person or as a good group member. Satisfying this proattitude may require conforming—adopting a certain attitude or acting in a certain way.

As to the external social sources of conformism, I will below consider conformism based on majority and that based on minority. In the case of the latter, the sources will primarily be valued persons ("idols") or successful persons (whether valued as persons or not). There seem to be many psychological mechanisms that can account for conformism, depending on the situation. To mention just a few conditions promoting conformism that social psychologists have found, informational conformism is the likelier the more difficult it is to arrive at the correct answer or the more ambiguous the situation (task) is. In such cases the majority or some experts may be relied on. Normative conformity is likely to occur when people regard the group and the group members' views as important for them or, partly alternatively, when nonconformity is socially sanctioned.[10] Furthermore, it has recently been shown that on the subpersonal level there are neural mechanisms to account for conformity (especially when conforming itself is subconscious). Thus research on "mirror neurons" interestingly shows that people are subpersonally disposed to mimic each other.[11] A related well-known phenomenon is that laughing and yawning are highly "contagious" phenomena. Mirror neuron research may show why that is the case.

What about the mutual belief requirement (c), which may be called the *social awareness* condition? The basic idea is that everyone is aware that the others are socially conscious, and are disposed to act on the social, intersubjective consciousness afforded by mutual belief. Thus, a group member will not only believe that the others have the attitude in question but will also believe that the others believe that he has it. Often this involves experiencing or believing that there is social pressure, since the agent may also think that the others think he should (and should continue to) have the attitude in question. A way to defend such a loop belief derives from the assumptions that the others are relevantly *similar* to him: If he believes that the others have the attitude (assumption (b)), he should also believe that on the basis of such similarity the others believe that he, too, has the attitude; and this reasoning can be replicated, resulting in mutual belief, in the sense of replication or iteration.[12] There will also be similar replicable loop beliefs between all group members, at least if the group is small, and our reference point member will believe so (e.g., A believes that B believes that C believes that B has the attitude in question). This is A's belief about a replicable loop belief, and it should be allowed that his belief about such loop beliefs between other members can be wrong. Thus, one can speak of a member's belief that there is a mutual belief that every member has the attitude in question. (At least a fixed point characterization of mutual belief can allow that there be beliefs about mutual beliefs and even mutual beliefs about mutual beliefs—see section 5.)

Instead of the assumption of similarity, an agent can also reason in terms of *rationality* in an analogous way, taking the others to be relevantly rational. This could be called the argument for rational and reliable action.[13]

Weaker forms of the above notion of we-attitude may be considered. In one such case, the belief in (c) only is a plain rather than a mutual belief. The beliefs and mutual beliefs might concern only the majority of group members, and the mutual belief need not be taken to require that everyone participates in the mutual belief. Furthermore, when speaking of a shared we-attitude, the sharing may be complete or only partial. In the latter case, one might speak of percentages and say that p percent of the members of a collective have the we-attitude in question. When I discuss shared we-attitudes below, I basically speak in terms of the above standard notion (involving 100 percent sharing). However, almost all of my points also will apply to the we-attitudes with a weakened clause (c), and many apply also to the rudimentary we-attitudes defined merely by (a) and (b). Further-more, it does not seem necessary to require 100 percent sharing, as that would seriously affect the applicability of this account to real life. What seems a more reasonable requirement is that most group members share the we-attitude in question. This statistical majority criterion entails that the social practice is preva-lent, supposing that the people in question indeed act on their we-attitudes.[14]

To be sure, sometimes people think and act in nonconforming or even opposing ways. Although my account emphasizes conformity, it is easy to define a notion of we-attitude in which the reason for one's attitudes and actions is to be different from others and, perhaps, deliberately to think and act in opposing ways. To account for a nonconformative we-attitude in our (WATT), we replace ATT in clauses (a)–(c) with ATT*, where ATT* equals the opposite of ATT either in the sense that ATT*(p) = ATT(−p) (content negated) or that ATT*(p) = −ATT(p) (attitude type negated). The first of these cases can be called an opposing we-attitude or *contra-attitude*, while the second case expresses a *nonconformative* attitude, in the weak sense of lack of conforming attitude.

Another important variation is where ATT is an intention (or goal) and ATT* is an expectation or normative belief. For instance, the members may expect that each member ought to do X in circumstances C. A person having the reason-based we-attitude then forms the intention (or goal) to do X and does X because she is expected by the group members to do X, under conditions of mutual belief. This is also a clear case of conformity.

In addition to majority conformity, other kinds of conformity are also rele-vant, as said. A person can also respond to and mimic other things than what the others (or their majority) are doing.[15] Thus there can be (statistically) unbiased transmission (you get the feature from your parents, for instance) or there is plain bias (sweet tastes better than sour) or a person can acquire his attitude from an idol or model by imitation. Only the idol pattern here truly involves conformist social transmission.[16]

In the case of a reason-based we-attitude, the reason can be a necessary condition, a sufficient condition, or both, to mention some interesting possibili-ties. In general, I will assume that a reason must be at least a necessary condition, on the ground that the satisfaction of the reason content is indeed taken to be conceptually necessary for the we-attitude WATT to be satisfied.[17]

3   I-Mode We-Intention

In this section mainly I-mode we-intentions will be considered. Agents we-intending in the I-mode need only be connected via their beliefs, although it is possible to have I-mode we-intentions in an epistemically stronger sense. In a typical case, an agent comes to we-intend to bring about something p by taking some others' we-intention to be a contingent de facto ground for his forming and having his we-intention (e.g., I see some people jointly pushing a car and join in).[18]

Let us here concentrate on the simple case directly obtainable from the account (WATTR) of section 2: An agent we-intends by his actions to contribute to the bringing about of p. His partial reason is that the others are also intending similarly and that this is mutually believed. No group reason (in the full sense) is involved here. The content of p would be, for example, that the house is painted or, perhaps, that it will be painted by you and me. The joint action here must be seen as a weak kind of joint action, one in the I-mode. It need not involve more than that I paint the front of the house and you paint its back, without our really doing it together as a group, whereas a full-blown joint action does require the latter. In the I-mode case, there can be a shared plan, roughly in the sense of each of the participants forming the intention to paint the house "together" with the other agent, in the sense that each is going to do a certain part such that the aggregation of the parts results in the full action. As painting the house is a typical we-mode action, where the participants take themselves to be in a shared we-mode project satisfying the Collectivity Condition, we are here invited to think differently. That may be easier if the number of participants would be large. Here the others' intention to participate is an *"external"* rationality condition for a participant's forming his intention to participate (and privately commit himself to p). He makes his decision to participate on the basis of his private wants and preferences (that may concern the group's goals, of course). Here the social reason or, rather, the potential social reason is a contingent condition of the participant's intention, a condition either in the content of the intention or a causal condition for the agent's intending categorically.

In contrast, in the case of a proper we-mode we-intention, the social group reason is conceptually and in this sense *internally* connected to the content of the we-intention—or at least the agent's intention *conceptually presupposes* such connection to the group reason. The agent's we-mode reason here involves that he will act fully as a group member and do what he does as a member of the group. Necessarily, he would not intend to contribute to bringing about p unless that happened for a group reason, that is, our joint doing it as a group.[19] If no group yet exists, we can speak of the agent's prospective we-mode attitude toward a future joint action and the resulting we-mode group membership.

Notice that the (weak or strong) we-intention to contribute to p in this kind of case has satisfaction conditions involving two directions of fit: The intention statement (namely, the statement that x we-intends p) requires that the agent understands that p has the world-to-mind direction of fit and that the conceptually in-built reason (expressed by "for the reason that...") has the mind-to-world direction of fit (e.g., "Agent x's reason for his intending that p is that...").[20] The satisfaction of an internally reason-based we-intention requires that the following must have taken place, using the "seeing to it" interpretation of action: conceptually necessarily, agent x intentionally saw to it that p in accordance with and partly because of a group reason (e.g., we jointly planned and intended to bring about p).[21]

Given the above, I will connect my above account to Michael Bratman's analysis of *shared intentions* in terms of the locutions "We intend to J," where J is a joint action.[22] This account is basically an I-mode account of joint intention, as will be seen. Indeed it is rather close to a weak we-intention in our present sense. His final analysis is as follows.

We intend to J if and only if

(i) (a) I intend that we J and (b) you intend that we J;

(ii) (a) I intend that we J in accordance with and because of meshing subplans of (i)(a) and (i)(b); (b) you intend that we J in accordance with and because of meshing subplans of (i)(a) and (i)(b);

(iii) (i) and (ii) are common knowledge between us.

Here the requirement that the participants intend that their subplans mesh in my view is not a strictly conceptual condition for the agents' having a shared intention. Rather it is a rationality condition that should not be applied to all agents who share intentions that they will act jointly.[23] In addition, somewhat irrational agents can have we-intentions. Building in the meshing thus is not conceptually necessary. If this is accepted, we should rather consider the following account that Bratman calls "View 3."

We intend to J if and only if

(i) (a) I intend that we J and (b) you intend that we J;

(ii) (a) I intend that we J because of (i)(a) and (i)(b); you intend that we J because of (i)(a) and (i)(b);

(iii) (i) and (ii) are common knowledge between us.

Bratman's View 3 expresses a reason-based weak we-intention in our sense, except that he does not make the common knowledge (in my account, belief—the knowledge requirement seems too demanding) a reason (not even a presuppositional reason) for the intention. This in fact makes his account somewhat defective— recall the justification for the social awareness condition. Notice that the content of the intentions here is collective, thus our p = we J. Bratman requires, to avoid circularity, that J-ing be a joint action type that does not entail shared intention:[24] "For example, we will want to use a notion of painting the house together that does not itself require that the agents have a shared intention." "Think of a case in which we paint it during the same time period but we are each ignorant of the other's activity." My critical point here is that when the participants intend that they J, the joint action's intentional performance must be something grasped by the participants, because an intention cannot, strictly speaking, be satisfied by nonintentional actions and because a full-blown joint intention had as a group cannot be satisfied by nonintentional joint action. What is crucial here is, as will be argued in chapter 4, that the converse also holds in a wide sense: every joint action must involve a joint intention of some relevant kind (e.g., mistakes in belief must be allowed).[25] Let us note, too, that the agents' intentions in Bratman's account are based on interdependence, not a group reason. I intend because you do and vice versa, and according to his account, a person may act purely for his private reason and not for the group (for the "use" and "shareware" of the group) that the participants can be taken to form. The problem about the missing group reason will be further commented on in chapter 4.

Using my approach, the following account of I-mode shared intention, a special version of weak we-intention that might also be termed "mere shared interpersonal intention" and that does not require group reason, can now be proposed (substituting X for J in the above account, without any change of meaning).

You and I *share in the I-mode sense the intention to jointly perform* X if and only if
(a) I intend that we X in the external reason-based we-attitude sense, namely, I intend that we X in part because I believe that you intend in the reason-based sense that we X and that we mutually believe that each of us so intends, and
(b) you intend that we X in the external reason-based we–attitude sense.

Here the reason-based intention in (a) is external in the earlier sense. Thus the kind of tight conceptual connection that I required in the internal case does not pertain to this account of shared I-mode intention, and the "we" here is only a thin "we."

A shared *I-mode we-intention* can give rise to collective action (without collective commitment), as will be seen in chapter 5. While this kind of collective action is defective by some standards, such as persistence, and does not qualify as acting *as a group*, we are here still dealing with an important phenomenon.

4 A Circularity Problem for I-Mode Intentions

I-mode we-intentions face a circularity problem that may also affect the functionality of these kinds of intentions. The problem arises in the case of conditional intentions, where the condition is a potential reason for categorical intending. This reason becomes an actual reason for the categorical intention after the agent has deconditionalized the conditional intention. Then the agent has a reason-based intention in the sense defined earlier in this chapter. However, the deconditionalization involves a regress problem in the case of typical coordination situations. (In chapter 6 I will discuss another kind of circularity problem that faces we-mode we-attitudes, thus we-intentions.)

Before discussing coordination of intentions in detail, let me make some more general remarks related to the situation at hand. We-attitudes involve coordination, as we have seen. In the case of conformative we-attitudes, the coordination principle is, to simplify a bit, that a person has an attitude (or action) ATT given that the others have ATT. This coordination principle is most central for generating harmonious coordination in social life: Cooperative action is important, and so is similar opinion, in many cases at least. Obviously, groups operate better when there is far-reaching consensus about goals and means, and so on. It is desirable for group members to speak with one voice and to act as a unit when group matters are concerned. Coordination is required in all these cases, and the coordination in question can be modeled in terms of shared we-attitudes. Shared we-attitudes involve, and provide, the required coordination principles. In more complex cases with division of tasks, the coordination may involve coordinating an attitude $ATT(p)$ with $ATT^*(q)$ with a different content and where ATT^* might differ from ATT.[26] I will not here discuss the various relevant nonharmonious principles.

It is important to see that we can meaningfully speak of coordination not only in the case of such voluntarily formed attitudes as intentions and acceptances of views, actions, and so on but also in the case of involuntary attitudes such as wants, beliefs, hopes, and nonintentional activities. Think of contagious cases of laughter and yawning and collective pattern-governed behaviors.[27] In their case, the coordinating connections take place on a subpersonal level (recall the mirror neuron account mentioned earlier).

In game-theoretical literature there is much discussion of coordination. In philosophical literature the work by David Lewis is central.[28] I will below start with a setup similar to the one Lewis uses, except that I will concentrate on the coordination of intentions and the resulting actions rather than desires and preferences, which the Lewisian account relies on. Accordingly, I will be speaking of pure coordination situations and the formation of personal intentions to act in such a situation. The coordination of other attitudes than intentions will also be commented on.

Intention coordination involves a kind of circularity problem in certain kinds of coordination cases. This problem relates to rational intention formation and intention satisfaction in coordination situations. A paradigm case is a coordination game with two or more equally good equilibria. There is a dilemma when the agents lack a reason to deconditionalize their conditional intentions to arrive at the same choice alternative. Let me give a simple illustration. Suppose that we wish to meet and that this can take place either by both going to the station (X) or to the church (Y). Our meeting of course requires that we go to the same place. Accordingly, choosing X, the agents' rational formation and satisfaction of the intentions expressed by "I will do X" and "you will do X" are interdependent on conceptual grounds, and in this sense the satisfaction conditions of the intentions in question are also conceptually interdependent. The interdependence can be formulated, at least in part, in terms of a biconditional, respectively, "I will do X if and only if you will do X" and "I will do Y if and only if you will do Y." As, however, at least in the intention case, the relationship, in addition, involves a reason connection, I will in general use the locution "given that," thus understood to express not only a necessary and sufficient condition but also a potential reason for categorical intention.[29] We also arrive at this same biconditional simply by assuming that the agents act rationally to satisfy their preferences. For their preferences to be satisfied, they must both go to the station or go to the church. (Note that a many-person version is obtained if we generalize our conditional intention expression into "I will do X if and only if sufficiently many persons do X—or do whatever a rational equilibrium solution requires.")

A structurally similar case can be at stake when forming an intention to participate in a proper joint action such as taking a walk together. There is a similar circularity problem embedded here concerning intentions, although this problem need not epistemically come into the surface for ordinary actors, as common sense contains ways of circumventing the problem. (I do not claim that all cases of joint intention to perform a joint action involve a coordination problem of the kind leading to the above kind of conditional intentions. For instance, conflict-involving cases such as involved in a single-shot PD do not yield this kind of conditional participation intention concerning cooperation in the case of fully rational players.)

More generally, we can speak of acceptance of an attitude in general, understanding acceptance in a wide sense not to require intentional or even voluntary action.[30] We can nevertheless speak of a coordination situation here as well, if you and I have the same belief (want, wish, hope, fear, etc.) concerning the same matter, say, p, which might be rewarding to both of us. The connection principle then could simply be "I believe (want, wish, hope, fear, etc.) that p if and only if you similarly believe (etc.) that p" or some more complex, situationally conditioned variant of this.

Let us now return to intending and be concerned with a special, but central, case of application of the conditional intention expression "I will do X given that you will do X," where "given that" has the logical force of a necessary and sufficient condition and, in intentional cases, of a potential reason (that will be the agent's actual reason after successful deconditionalization). This special case is the case of a pure coordination situation with a finite number of alternatives (such as X = going to the station and Y = going to the church) with the additional assumption that an equilibrium state is to be reached so that the agents "meet" (at least in the sense of arriving at the same place). One can see that the satisfaction conditions of their intentions to perform their part actions will be logically connected in a circular way, assuming fully rational intending. When I speak below of rationality, my claims in general concern rationality relative to the mentioned assumptions, not rationality *tout court*.[31] Thus I will also speak of "r-rationality" meaning "restricted rationality" or "robot-rationality," that is, rationality relative to merely the assumptions so far built into the software of the agent that can be simplistically conceived of as a robot.

In this case, an agent cannot rationally (i.e., r-rationally) form and satisfy his action intention without a circular reference to the other agent's intention. To make this point clearer, consider this formulation:

(P_{int}) I will do X given that you will do X, but you will do X given that I will do X, but I will do X given that you will do X, but you . . . ad infinitum.

This principle can easily be generalized for other attitudes, but it is not necessary to go into detail here.[32] The point of principle (P_{int}) and its generalizations is to show that in pure coordination situations (presupposing meeting or rational arrival at an equilibrium, or something closely like that) fully r-rational conditional intention expressions of the kind "I will do X given that you will do X" or respectively "You will accept p given that I will accept p" in the agents' practical inferences really are infinitary in principle.

I will now reformulate (P_{int}) more perspicuously so that the hierarchical nature of its layers becomes explicit. Let me now use the symbol / for "given that." Then the content of (P_{int}) can be put as follows using the symbols a and b for the respective intention expressions "I, namely, A, will do X" and "You, that is, B, will do X":

(P'_{int})
(1) a / b,
such that the rational (specifically, r-rational) formation of the intention expressed by b, hence its rational satisfaction by agent B in (1), requires that
(2) b / a,
such that the rational formation of the intention expressed by a, hence its rational satisfaction by agent A in (1), requires that

(3) a / b,

such that the rational formation of the intention expressed by b, hence its rational satisfaction by agent B in (1), requires that

(4) b / a,

such that the rational formation of the intention expressed by A, hence its rational satisfaction by agent A in (1), requires that

... (ad infinitum).

Here is an infinite level-hierarchy for the rational formation and satisfaction of the intention-expressing sentences (in the sense of r-rationality). Thus, considering (1), agent A cannot rationally deconditionalize this conditional intention without taking into account the other levels in the hierarchy—unless something further is assumed. In this sense, the sentence does not and cannot have a rationally assignable finitary satisfaction value based on the satisfaction values of its component sentences, because these satisfaction values are intrinsically ("logically") connected prior to their use in (1) (and the analogous point can be made in the case of any other level in (P'_{int})). (P'_{int}) is true of *fully r-rational intentions in pure coordination situations*, as anybody can easily verify for himself. The regress is an in-built feature of the situation. I have spoken here of the nature of the conceptual circularity as ultimately concerning the rationality of intention formation and acting on the intention. I could also have spoken of epistemic circularity in the agents' practical inferences. Thus, unless more is assumed, in (1) of (P'_{int}), agent A cannot fully r-rationally come to know what B unconditionally intends without knowing what the whole hierarchy of levels contains.

This example and other pure coordination cases require for their rational solution ("meeting," etc., resulting in the satisfaction of the participants' preferences) that both of the agents at least personally ("privately") commit themselves to the same specific alternative. The coordination problem is rationally solved if and only if the agents not only perform the same, coordination-conferring action but do it on the basis of their rationally formed intention to do so. In the meeting case, there must accordingly be interdependent categorical (i.e., unconditional) intentions (or goals) to perform a certain one, say, X, of the alternatives. The rationality of the intention here requires that the participants correctly mutually believe (or at least share the belief) that each of them is committed to doing X. The intention need only be an I-mode intention; my thesis also applies to Hi-Lo coordination cases (to be commented on in chapter 7). However, solving the problem in the case of meeting as a joint action requires a joint we-mode "aim intention," that is, that both agents together aim at meeting each other. In this eventuality there is proper joint commitment.

Let me now consider in more detail how to rationally solve the kind of coordination case at hand. As seen, such a solution is not entailed if only the situation of coordination is given and mutual belief or knowledge concerning it is assumed. Fortunately, common sense typically gives us solutions, and often we have rational ways or arriving at such a solution. (Here and below I will use "rational" in a more comprehensive, "social-relational" sense than r-rationality, unless the latter is explicitly referred to.) For instance, our agents might prefer being together, and the problem is whether to go to the station or to the church, or in the joint action case, whether to take a walk together or to stay at home. Such a solution requires that the agents rationally form intentions to act in a specific way. One general line of solution depends on the possibility of communication. Given this, one of the agents may unilaterally and unconditionally bind himself to one alternative and see to it that the other agent comes to know this. Then the latter can rationally form the intention to do the same thing. This is a kind of deconditionalization that is rational from the initiator's point of view only if the other agent is rational (namely, rational in the sense of picking up the information and regarding it as reliable for action) and is believed or known to be rational. If that assumption fails to hold true, we do not get a rational solution. Let us put this line of thought in the following schematic form in the case of two actors, A ("I") and B ("you").

(RC) (i) A commits himself to one of the alternatives, say, X, correctly believing that B has not committed himself to the other alternative Y;
(ii) B believes that A has committed himself to X (possibly but necessarily on the basis of A's communicatively having seen to it that B comes to believe this);
(iii) A believes that B is relevantly rational;
(iv) B believes that A is relevantly rational;
(C_a) A (rationally) performs X (given that nothing outlandish occurs);
(C_b) B (rationally) performs X (given that nothing outlandish occurs).

Here relevant rationality involves that the agent in question is able to deconditionalize intentions correctly (given the belief about the other's commitment) and to perform action X, given his intention and beliefs, and is not weak-willed. Outlandishness is supposed to rule out internal and external factors blocking the performance of X. Given schema (RC) and the discussion preceding it, the fulfillment of (RC) can be seen as not only sufficient but also necessary for a rational unilaterally initiated solution of the kind of coordination problem at hand.[33]

Notice that there is no way epistemically to guarantee fully that the above kind of unilateral solution attempts and, indeed, bilateral solution attempts falling short of the formation of a joint intention will work, even in an epistemically ideal possible world, for there is no object of knowledge in the pure coordination case assuming fully r-rational agents—that is, rational in the restricted sense of r-rationality pertaining only to the features of the coordination situation. Of course, there can be and are cases in which A wills something and B wills the same thing and the intentions are *factually* connected—rather than connected on rational and noncontingent grounds—so that statements of the kind "I will do X given that you will do X" have categorical satisfaction values (see later discussion).

To wit, consider an agent's (let it be "me") attempt to solve the situation simply by forming a categorical intention to act. But here is a problem. To see it once more, consider my practical reasoning where the first premise must be understood as involving the hierarchical principle (P'_{int}):

(P1) You will do X given that I will do X; but I will do X given that you will do X, but you will do X given that I will do X, but I . . . ad infinitum.
(P2) I will do X.
(C) You will do X.

Here (C) expresses my expectation that you will form the intention to do X and my prediction that you will do X. This inference schema is meant to express deconditionalization.

We need (P1) because of the circularity problem for a rational agent arising in a situation of pure coordination. Given (P1), the premise (P2) is not fully "r-rational." It disregards the in-built hierarchical circularity and tries to make a shortcut. Accordingly, the argument is not correct, as (P2) contains only a part of the condition in (P1). (Notice that the deconditionalization involved in the earlier schema (RC) is of this simplified kind.)

Alternatively we could try:

(P2*) I will do X given that you will do X; but you will do X given that I will do X, but I will do X given that you will do X, but you... ad infinitum.

But this premise is not deconditionalizable in the full r-rational sense.

So there is a problem with the second premise in any case. This is the central problem in the intention formation. Of course, it may on grounds other than (P1) be highly rational in many cases for me to assert, in our example, that I will go to the station. Then you, if rational at all, will of course come to the station as well. But the rationality assumption (see (iii) and (iv) in (RC)) may fail or the agent may change her mind, etc.). Furthermore, in cases where no communication is possible in fact and the agents are complete strangers to each other, they may try to guess what the other one will do. This is perhaps not highly rational, but it may be the most rational thing to do.

To sum up, the basic problems with unilateral strategies like promising or forming the intention to do X independently of what the other agent does are the following. (a) Such a strategy is not fully r-rational as it involves a kind of "change of mind" in the sense that, instead of the complete premise (P2*), the premise (P2) is used. Notice that this creates an epistemic problem for the other agent (you wonder if I really "changed" my mind). (b) It must be assumed that the other agent is relevantly rational in the sense that he is able to deconditionalize and arrive at the categorical intention to perform X and that he will also perform X. (As argued, this is problematic; furthermore, if there are many participants involved, quite a lot of deconditionalization is needed.) How serious, if serious at all, these problems will be for rational intention formation depends on the participants and the situation at hand.

In normal life, unilateral promising typically is rational (even if not r-rational as such) and works well. From a conceptual point of view, unilaterality is not essential, because both agents could bilaterally and simultaneously indicate that they will perform X (without yet forming a joint intention to perform X). This is a special case of schema (RC), in which no deconditionalization is needed, but the above problem (a) still persists. Note that even here direct communication seems not to be essential for belief formation, but of course it can help epistemically. Note, too, that the agents may, of course, move to the we-mode level and, for instance, make an agreement or adopt a joint plan according to which both are to perform X, in which case we have a solution to the coordination problem—that is, we have the participants' commitments to X such that there is a shared or mutual belief about this. (In order for the participants' performances of X to occur, the participants of course must carry out the plan, but the epistemic risks involved here are more like the standard kinds of risks that the coordination of activities and the performance of joint actions generally involve.)

In all, in the I-mode case we can have rational unilateral and bilateral solutions, and in the we-mode case we can have rationally formed joint intentions. These exhaust the rational (or "rational-enough") solutions to coordination problems (or "I will, given that you will" problems) in this kind of context; and note that all of the mentioned solutions involve some epistemic risks to the agents. But these solutions still are sufficiently rational, in the instrumental r-rational sense, for the participants to perform the right kinds of actions. The kinds of rational solutions to coordination problems we have discussed may be *institutionalized*, but this matter cannot be discussed here.[34]

To comment on less rational, practical solutions, the pragmatic factors may be such—and in real life very often seem to be such—that they de facto give a kind of solution to the circularity problem, and they may do it in a way that is weaker than unilateral commitment. Suppose, for instance, I may accept this: "I will do X given that you *indicate* (or express) that you will do X given that I will do X." Using this as my premise, I come to believe that a certain real event occurs, that is, an event I take to have the content that you indicate that you will do X given that I will do X; and then I can rationally infer the conclusion "I will do X." Deconditionalization is possible here because the condition for the intention is only contingently connected to the intention—recall the discussion in section 3 concerning essentially the same problem related to internal and external connection. You could use the same line of thinking. In this case, you need not have committed yourself to doing X, even if I in a sense assume that much in my practical inference. This type of solution of course is by itself less rational than the one assuming actual unilateral commitment. Even weaker pragmatic solutions are possible. Thus we might know on the basis of our previous experience that, being an atheist, you tend to avoid churches, and then I reason that going to the station (X) will be our rational meeting place. The much-touted feature of *salience* may or may not work, and it is in any case based on an additional psychological assumption (resembling others in this paragraph).

In addition, in the less rational cases, shared I-mode personal intentions basically suffice, and they may come about because of the agents' shared history and need not be based on communication in the situation in question. Once more, the circularity problem in question very seldom becomes explicit in actual social life, and this is in part because people in the course of time have devised various methods of dealing with the coordination problem question and have even incorporated relevant tools in their language (e.g., the concepts of promise and contract).[35]

The remarks in the last few pages related to the intention principle (P'_{int}) generalize, mutatis mutandis, to (P_{gen}), the general principle basically applicable to any attitude formulated in note 32, even if that may require some enrichments and modifications. In the case of intentional acceptance, the generalization is rather straightforward. In the case of nonintentional acceptance, more should be said, but I will leave that for another occasion.

5   Mutual Belief

Mutual belief is a central social notion, indeed a shared we-attitude notion.[36] Mutual belief represents a second important type of collective intentionality on a par with intentions and goals. The importance of the notion of mutual belief has been emphasized by philosophers, economists, sociologists, and psychologists at least since the 1960s.[37] The central point here is that mutual beliefs serve to characterize social or intersubjective existence in a sense that does not rely on the participants making agreements or contracts. Thus, many social relations, properties, and events can be argued to involve mutual beliefs.[38] As a simple example, think of the practice of two persons, A and B, shaking hands. It is presupposed here that A believes that B and A are shaking hands and that A also believes that B believes similarly; and B must believe analogously. Many philosophers, especially Grice, have argued that communication must involve mutual belief.[39] Furthermore, while mutual belief (almost) amounts to shared we-belief (see below), the characterization of we-attitudes also depends on the notion of mutual belief, here viewed as an I-mode notion.

The notion of *consensus*—viewed as mutual belief of some kind—has been regarded as relevant to such topics as public opinion, values, mass action, norms, roles, communication, socialization, and group cohesion. In addition, fads, fashions, crazes, religious movements, and many other related phenomena have been analyzed partly in terms of shared beliefs, consensus, shared consensus, mutual belief, or some similar notions. Such analyses have sometimes gone wrong because they have treated consensus merely as shared first-order belief. Thus, consensus as mere first-order agreement does not properly account for *pluralistic ignorance* (where people agree but do not realize it) and *false consensus* (where people mistakenly believe that they all agree). Basically, pluralistic ignorance and false consensus are second-level phenomena. The third level will have to be brought in when speaking about people's awareness of these phenomena. Other well-known social psychological notions requiring more than shared belief are Mead's concept of "taking the role of the generalized other," Dewey's "interpenetration of perspectives," and Laing's metaperspectives.[40]

There are two different conceptual-logical approaches to understanding the notion of mutual (or, to use an equivalent term, common) belief: (1) the *iterative* account, and (2) the *reflexive* or *fixed point* account. According to the iterative account, mutual belief is assumed to mean iteratable beliefs or dispositions to believe.[41] In the two-person case, mutual belief thus amounts to the following: A and B believe that p, A believes that B believes that p (and similarly for B), A believes that B believes that A believes that p (and similarly for B); and the iteration can continue indefinitely in principle and thus at least as far as the situation demands. (E.g., depending on the case at hand, two levels might be categorically required, and from there on it is required that the subjects do not believe the negation of p at any higher level; or there would be a rule of inference allowing higher level iteration, if needed.[42]) In the case of loop beliefs, there is, accordingly, mutual awareness only in a somewhat rudimentary sense. As to the connection between shared we-beliefs and mutual beliefs, the very definition of a we-belief of course uses the notion of mutual belief. Operating within the iterative account, a we-belief and a mutual belief are very close. A shared we-belief that p amounts to everyone believing that p and that everyone believes that everyone believes...that everyone believes that p, while a mutual belief amounts to everyone believing that everyone believes...that everyone believes that p. Thus, apart from the small difference that the mutual belief in this case occurs within the scope of the agents' beliefs, there is no other difference.[43]

The fixed point notion of mutual belief can be defined as follows: x and y mutually believe that p if and only if they believe that p and that it is mutually believed by them that p. No iteration of beliefs is at least explicitly involved in this "doxastically circular" definition. Correspondingly, a clear distinction can be made between the iterative or the level-account and the fixed point account. Shared we-beliefs can be related to the reflexive or fixed point account of mutual belief. According to the simplest fixed point account, mutual belief is defined as follows. It is a mutual belief in a group that p if and only if everyone in the group believes (that p and that it is mutually believed in the group that p). In the fixed point approach, the syntactical infinity involved in the iterative approach is cut short by a finite fixed point formula, that is, an impredicative construct in which the joint notion to be "defined" already occurs in the definiens. Under certain rationality assumptions about the notion of belief, it can be proved that the iterative approach, which continues iterations ad infinitum, gives the fixed point property as a theorem.[44]

As compared with the iterative analysis, the fixed point account is in some contexts psychologically more realistic, as people are not required to keep iterative hierarchies in their minds. Note, however, that it depends on context whether the iterative approach or the fixed point approach is more appropriate. Thus, in the case of successful joint action, at least loop beliefs must be required.

6   Summary

This chapter introduced the notion of a shared we-attitude, mainly in the I-mode or private sense (for the we-mode case, see chapter 6). For example, an individual functioning in a group context has the (reason-based) goal to achieve something p just in case she has the goal to achieve p and has it in part because the others in the group have that goal, in conditions of mutual belief. This is the simplest version of a conformative we-attitude that the person here assumes to be shared in the group. The "we" in the I-mode case can be a weak one, representing an I-mode group. Accordingly, in any collective with some intersubjective identity (based on mutual knowledge or belief) the members can have shared we-attitudes. For instance, people waiting for a train can share some we-belief, say, concerning why the train is late. The chapter also discussed specifically shared I-mode we-intentions that are used later in the book. While in a full-blown, we-mode we-intention a group reason is necessarily (or internally) present, in the corresponding I-mode case, the connection is only contingent and in this sense external.

In many I-mode cases involving coordination, there is a circularity problem that in the two-person case can be called the "I will if you will" problem. For instance, in a typical coordination dilemma I will do X (one of the action alternatives) if and only you will do X, but you will do X if and only if I will do X, and so on. A regress is created. Solutions to this problem were presented and discussed. (A circularity problem concerning we-mode attitudes also exists, but it is of a different kind; see chapter 6.)

The chapter also discussed mutual beliefs and connected them to shared we-beliefs. Both iterative and fixed point I-mode beliefs were commented on. In the belief case, the we-mode sense is concerned with believing (here: accepting as true) a proposition or sentence qua a group member. A we-mode belief, expressible by "We, as a group, believe (accept) that p," requires that the group in question is collectively committed to upholding and acting on its mutual belief or at least to keeping the members informed about whether it is or can be upheld. This contrasts with mutual belief in an aggregative individual mode involving only purely private commitments to upholding and acting on the belief in question. A we-mode we-belief in a group often concerns the constitutive features of the group (namely, the ethos of the group, see chapters 6 and 8). It follows that the I-mode analyses (the iterative and the fixed point accounts) discussed in section 5 can at best give necessary conditions for we-mode we-beliefs.

4

JOINT INTENTION AND WE-INTENTION

1 Intending Jointly as a Group

The central aim of this chapter is to study the notion of joint intention to perform a joint action or to bring about a certain state. Here are some examples of such joint action: You and I share the plan to carry a heavy table jointly upstairs; to realize this plan, we sing a duet together; we clean up our backyard together; I cash a check by acting jointly with you, a bank teller; we together elect a new president for our country. In such cases of intentional joint action, the participants can be taken to have a joint intention jointly (*as a group*) to carry the table upstairs (etc.). The content of the joint intention expressible by "We will carry the table jointly" involves our performing something together, and the pronoun "we" refers to us, namely, you and me and the possible other participants considered together. When we jointly intend to carry the table, each of us can be said to *we-intend* to do it.

The main purpose of this chapter is to discuss joint intention and we-intention in the we-mode. In this sense, the participants intend as group members because of a full-blown group reason (one satisfying the Collectivity Condition). This contrasts with I-mode joint or shared intention. When the participants intend in the I-mode, they intend solely as private persons—in contrast to the we-mode case, where they must function as group members and where intending for a group reason must be at play.[1] In contrast to the I-mode case, functioning in the we-mode is necessarily connected to a group reason.

Joint intentions can often be expressed by means of locutions of the form "We will do X," where the word "will" is used conatively (rather than predictively, in the future tense) and X is a joint action type.[2] I will below sometimes speak of the jointly intending agents' *jointly seeing to it that* (*jstit*) a state or event obtains. This is a general umbrella term for joint action. It covers many kinds of activities—for example, jointly performing actions in a direct or in an indirect sense, jointly bringing about states, jointly maintaining states, and so on.[3] To see how broad this notion is, consider a trivial example where the participants jointly *stit* the gate to the town is open. The following cases of intentional activity fall under their seeing to it that the gate is open. The agent opens the gate (by his own direct actions), if it is closed; he keeps it open, if some other agent or something else tries to close it; the agent gets some other agent to open the gate, if it is closed; if it is closed, he refrains from preventing another agent from opening it. I take *jstit* to be necessarily intentional. This fits well with its appearance in the content of joint intention, as one cannot nonintentionally satisfy an intention.

The content of a (we-mode) joint intention has, as it were, two parts. In the case of joint agency (here the dyadic case), "A and B jointly intend jointly to see to it that X" (or, from their perspective, "We will perform X together"). The first part of the joint intention could be just *jstit*-ing something. *What* is to be *jstit*-ed constitutes the second, "variable" part of the content, and this part need not be performed as a joint action. The first part is basically the same in all joint intentions. It indicates that the joint intention is oriented toward joint action. We can add that *jstit*-ing involves that each participant of joint intention is in principle "actionally" involved: he has a share or part in the participants' *jstit*-ing X. Thus we have: Agents A and B jointly intend to see to it jointly that X. Here X can be the participants' joint action, somebody else's action, some other agents' joint action, a state in the world (like that a house is painted or the window is open). Consider the special but central case in which X is a joint action to be performed by A and B. Then we get, using *jstit* for joint action allover: A and B jointly intend to *jstit* they *jstit* X, which due to the "collapsing" property of *jstit* amounts simply to "A and B jointly intend to see to it jointly that X."[4]

All intentions are necessarily related to one's own actions. In the single-agent case, an agent may intend to see to it that his car is fixed. This intention has as its satisfaction condition that the agent by his own actions sees to it that his car becomes fixed—for example, he can either get a mechanic to fix the car or fix it himself. The agent must thus intend by his actions to do something required for his original intention to become satisfied. This kind of intention I will call (direct) "action-intention." A generally accepted conceptual condition for an action-intention, at least a prior intention, is that the agent must at least believe that it is not impossible for him to perform the action.

An action-intention contrasts with an "aim-intention." In the latter case it is not required that the agent believes that he with nonzero probability can alone bring about or see to it that the action or its result event comes about. Rather the agent is assumed *by his actions to contribute* to the aimed result.[5] The kind of aim-intention that will concern us in this chapter is we-intention. A we-intention is—in a nonliteral sense—a participant's "slice" of the joint intention, and an aim-intention based on a group reason. One can conversely and technically say that a joint intention consists of the participants' we-intentions about the existence of which they have mutual belief. Jointly intending agents are assumed, by their participatory actions, to bring about the jointly intended (hence we-intended) state or event. We-intentions are different from ordinary action-intentions not only in being aim-intentions but also in that they conceptually depend on the joint intention in question.

A we-intention thus involves that the agent we-intends to see to it jointly with the others that a certain state or event comes about. The central condition of satisfaction of the we-intention is that the we-intending agent *intends to participate* and accordingly intentionally participates in the *jstit*, namely, the joint action. In other words, he intends by his own action, his part or share, to contribute to the joint action. This is an action-intention, which a rational agent believes he can, at least with some probability, satisfy by his own action (presupposing, of course, that the others perform their parts).

There is the rationality constraint on we-intention that an agent cannot rationally we-intend unless he believes not only that he can perform his part of their joint action, X, with some probability, but also that he together with his fellow participants can perform X jointly (can *jstit* X with them), at least with some nonzero probability. The jointly intending agents must believe that the "*jstit* opportunities" for an intentional *jstit*-ing of X are (or will be) there, at least with some probability. Yet another property of a we-intention is that, in each participant's view, it must be mutually believed by the participants that the presuppositions for the (intentional) *jstit*-ing of X hold or will hold with some probability.

The formation of a joint intention (hence a we-intention, a personal "slice" of the joint intention) requires that the participants jointly and, typically, intentionally make up their minds to *jstit* something, thus exercising joint control over the possible courses of action and settling for a particular content of *jstit*-ing. Joint intentions (hence shared we-intentions) entail collective (or, if you prefer, joint) commitments to action, and this collective commitment also includes that the participants are socially committed to each other to perform their parts of the *jstit*-ing.

Section 2 discusses the conceptual and "structural" aspects of joint intention formation (and, for that matter, the formation of joint beliefs as well). It also discusses in more detail the epistemic and normative bonds between jointly intending participants. Section 3 gives a summary account of my theory of joint intention and adds some new aspects to the account. Section 4 shows what the main differences between I-mode and we-mode shared intentions are. Section 5 presents an extended summary of the chapter. Taken together, sections 2–5 give an up-to-date theory of joint intention and we-intention.

2   Joint Intention Formation: The Bulletin Board View

In joint intention formation, each participating agent agrees to take part in the agents' seeing to it jointly that some state or event X obtains. Concentrating on the central case in which X is a joint action (such as lifting a piano, painting a house, making a contract), the agents jointly intend *as a group*, or as one agent, to see to it that they perform X jointly. We can think of the situation in analogy with the case of a single agent: An agent intends X and performs X on the basis of the intention. If the agent is a collective one, a we-mode group, the same can be said of it. A collective agent's (group's) intending and acting amount to the group members' jointly intending X and jointly acting on the basis of their joint intention. They must act on their joint intention for their satisfying action to be jointly intentional (and not only intentional in the weak sense that all the participants act intentionally). Otherwise the analogy view would not work, and the participants would not act as a unit.

I will below concentrate on the we-mode case and assume that agents jointly intend as a group and thus in the we-mode to realize the content of the joint intention that they—by the very formation of the joint intention—have jointly accepted for the group as the group's intended goal. The joint intention entails collective commitment to the content in analogy with the single-agent case. The group is thus committed to satisfying its intention, and the group members are collectively committed to satisfying their joint intention and are also socially committed to each other to performing their parts of the joint action that the intention is about. The collective commitment serves to keep the members together as a unit. The group members function as group members toward achieving the content of the joint intention (and in the general ethos case they function to further the group's constitutive or main interests, goals, beliefs, and standards). Collective commitment need not be stronger than what joint intention conceptually entails: When our agents jointly intend X (e.g., a joint action) they must collectively bind themselves to X and what its satisfaction requires. As seen in chapter 1, the minimal sense of such binding results in an intention-relative and, as such, merely group-socially normative collective commitment.[6]

In the we-mode case of joint intention, the participants, forming a thick, togetherness "we" (hence a we-mode group), must have collectively accepted doing X (the shared content) together, thereby collectively committing themselves to X. Here the intention expression "We together will do X" (assumed to satisfy the Collectivity Condition) applies to each participant, and it expresses his we-intention and hence the entailed (unconditional) participation intention.[7] In chapter 3 we discussed the approach dealing with conditional intentions of the kind "I will do X if you will do X" and the resulting regress problem. I will below sketch an approach, the "bulletin board" view, which helps to avoid the problem basically by switching from the assumption of conditional participation intentions to intentions with presuppositions. Accordingly, I will consider the presuppositions of joint intention and the central conceptual elements involved in joint intention formation and will focus on public antecedently formed and, broadly speaking, plan-based joint intentions that express jointly intending as a group. A central subclass of such joint intentions is formed by joint intentions based on the participants' explicit or implicit agreement to act jointly. The point about emphasizing the plan-based case is obviously that it is conceptually central and also common in actual social life.[8]

A we-mode joint intention presupposes that the participants understand—at least in some rudimentary sense—that a joint action in some sense is involved. The joint action must be taken to include a "slot" for each participant's intention. In general, all the relevant generic action concepts need to be possessed to a degree by the participants—a kind of "hermeneutic circle" is at play. Thus the notion of joint action opportunity needs to be available to the participants together with the background knowledge that it in turn presupposes. Next, certain situation-specific information must be presupposed. If the performance of joint action X in a situation S is at stake, the concept of X must be possessed—at least in an "actional," if not in a reflective cognitive sense—by the potential participants, and they must also understand what S involves concerning the performance of X. It is also required that, at least ideally, each participant believes that the participants mutually believe that the joint action opportunities for X hold in S (see the third clause in my analysis (WI) of we-intentions in section 3). Some direct or indirect communication (or signaling) between the participants is needed, for the reason that the participants are autonomous agents who, nevertheless, must make up their minds depending on what the others are thinking and doing. More concretely, communication is required for them rationally to arrive at unconditional intentions (we-intentions as well as intentions to perform one's part of the joint action) in the presupposition-dependent sense to be discussed. The indirect communication may be previously "codified" and may relate to certain kinds of situations (e.g., "In situation S we always have a joint plan of a certain kind and act together appropriately").

From a group's perspective, there will have to be unified group action as a result of a group's intention being properly satisfied. This involves that the group members' actions must be suitably bound together and coordinated with each other to yield jointly intentional joint action, namely, joint action based on the participants' joint intention. The bond here is the group's intention and commitment to action, which makes the members collectively (jointly) committed to the action. As seen, arriving at the required kind of joint intention in general requires public, at least group-wide, exchange of information if it is to lead to mutually known (thus public and not only mutually believed) unconditional participation intentions. Another reason for publicity is that such central social notions as the speech acts of agreement making, promising, commanding, and informing—all relevant to joint-intention formation—are in their core sense not only language-dependent but also public.

The view to be developed below tries to take all this into account. I will analyze the conceptually central elements in the formation of a full-blown joint intention to act together in terms of a metaphor, the bulletin board metaphor. The resulting view bases (we-mode) joint intentions on a publicly shared plan of joint action and thereby emphasizes the epistemic publicity (the public availability of relevant information) of full-blown joint intention, as will be seen.

Suppose that one of the members of a community (initially possibly only an I-mode group) comes up with the idea of cleaning a park. This is the proposed joint action content. That person may publicly communicate this to other group members. We may conceptualize and illustrate this situation in terms of the following *bulletin board view* (BBV) of joint intention formation (and, for that matter, the formation of joint voluntary "acceptance" beliefs). The initiating member's or organizer's proposal (or, more generally, plan for joint action) can be thought to be written on a public bulletin board: "Members of group g will clean the park next Saturday. Those who will participate, please sign up here." Here "will" in the latter sentence is taken to express intention and not only prediction. Supposing that the ensuing communicative signaling of acceptance to participate (under the presupposition that sufficiently many others participate) results in the taking up and "whole-hearted" collective acceptance of this proposal, then—given (communication-based) mutual knowledge about this—there will be an adequate plan involving a joint intention to clean the park. The participants' collective acceptance is assumed to entail that the participants form the joint intention to participate in joint action. As seen, this is a two-faced intention, so to speak. There is, first, each signed-up participant's we-intention to clean the park and, second, his intention to carry out his part or share of the cleaning (qua his share of it). Furthermore, the participants—because of having expressed their personal participation intentions—have jointly exercised control over what to do together and made up their minds to clean the park. Thus their joint intention to clean the park has come into existence.[9]

In a slightly stronger case, the participants not only accept a shared plan of joint action but also in effect make an explicit or implicit we-mode agreement to perform it.[10] Making an agreement gives each participant a reason for action, namely, his promise. Furthermore, it also gives a reason for each participant to normatively expect that the other participants indeed will participate. Thus, a participant has the right to expect that the others will perform their parts and is also obliged to respect their analogous rights. In this sense they are normatively socially committed.

The central thing about the BBV is its general content, although I have used language metaphorically to state the view. From a conceptual and theoretical point of view, this model of joint intention formation involves the following elements. First, what the joint intention is about must have been brought to the participants' attention. I call this the topic issue. There may be an initiator who proposes a topic, or the participants may arrive at it by negotiation or joint decision making. In other cases, a topic may be suggested to them by their shared history or background knowledge in conjunction with some relevant contextual information. For instance, the participants may share the standing desire to keep the park clean, and when they learn that a garbage collector will arrive the next morning, they may gather that park cleaning is the thing to do tonight. In the BBV, this can be indicated by the appearance on the bulletin board of the description of the topic (here park cleaning).

Second, the set of potential participants will be the members of group g, and this must be knowable to the potential participants. The actual participants—or at least a suitable subset of them sufficient to get the joint action initiated and under way—will have to be publicly indicated. Third, the central element again is the public availability of the information about the intention to participate; this aspect is also relevant to newcomers and persons who have to change plans for some reason. The participants will pick up that information, and this will lead them to believe that those who have signed up will participate. What is more, they will also be able to acquire mutual knowledge (or minimally mutual true belief) about this, for they will come to know that the others know that those persons will participate; and this can be iterated if needed. In the present we-mode case, there will be a group intention (based, e.g., on majority decision), and therefore all the group members ought to participate in the group intention.

The publicity requirement in the BBV is a kind of public communication requirement in the sense discussed earlier. It is a particular contingent feature of the BBV that the information gathering and delivery is centralized so that, for example, pairwise communication is not needed. However, this is a practical feature that is not conceptually essential. But publicity in group context is still philosophically central, in that it creates a realm that is objective for the participants, and is more prone to lead to actual objective knowledge than weaker views. There is thus a kind of group-relative objectivity both ontically and epistemically involved here. Furthermore, in the case of large groups, new participants, and participants who have changed their intentions, and so on, knowledge can then better be gathered and checked than otherwise.

In our metaphor, there may be information written on the board, and there is also information in a special box beneath the board called "Presuppositions and Background Knowledge." Typically only situational information is written on the board, and the rest, for example, general background assumptions, is available in the presuppositions box. Somewhere there should also be information about whether the participants are only forming a shared plan for joint action based on publicly expressed intentions or are also making a full-blown agreement to act jointly and in this "thick" normative sense accept a joint plan.

The BBV has several virtues. (1) It explicates collective and joint acceptance of attitudes (intentions, "acceptance" beliefs, and other voluntary attitudes) and does it by showing that the idea of a collective enterprise—for example, that some agents will have a joint plan or joint belief—is taken as an underlying *presupposition* (rather than only a contingent condition or a causal determinant). The agents, so to speak, individually sign up for the project in question. If the presupposition fails—for example, the joint intention or a joint belief proposal does not gain enough support—the signing up of course leads to nothing. But when it succeeds, in the joint intention case it gives *categorical*, unconditional participation intentions and joint intentions. The BBV is not concerned with proper conditional intentions in the first place. That sufficiently many participate is a noncontingent *presupposition* (an underlying presuppositional reason in the sense of section 3 of chapter 3) rather than a contingent condition. (2) The BBV binds together all the participants. This is because a version of the Collectivity Condition is at play here, as the question is about the group's attitude in the first-person-plural sense. A participant categorically commits herself when signing up, although she may retract her commitment if she comes to believe that a relevant presupposition is not satisfied. (3) There is no need for a prior joint intention to form a joint intention, as personal we-mode intentions to take part in a joint intention are enough for entering one's signature on the board. (4) The view can treat the participants either symmetrically or asymmetrically, depending on the demands of the situation. (5) The BBV is capable of yielding epistemically strong joint intentions, in the sense that all the information in the joint intention is publicly available and publicly checkable. (6) Although I will not discuss the matter here, it is easily seen that the basic structure of the BBV can be applied also to the I-mode case.

Let us still consider the kind of discursive dilemma of group decision-making that Philip Pettit has discussed in his recent works. This dilemma concerns the conclusion-driven versus the premise-driven way of making group decisions. To illustrate, suppose the group discusses whether to clean the park on Sunday or not. Suppose, for simplicity's sake, that there are three participants, A, B, and C. A rational decision to clean the park makes the matter depend conjunctively on three kinds of judgments. The members have to judge whether the ground is dry enough, whether the wind will be weak enough, and whether the park will not be too crowded for the cleaning to succeed. It might so happen that A, B, and C, respectively, judge A: Y, Y, N, B: Y, N, Y, and C: N, Y, Y concerning these premises. This gives the standard pattern in which the collectivization in the premise-driven way gives Y (yes) to all the premises by the majority principle, while the conclusion-driven collectivization based on the individual members' deductively formed conclusion gives N (no) for all the three participants. The BBV can now be applied in two different ways, either to the individual conclusions or to the conclusion that premise-driven collectivization gives. So there might seem to be a problem also for the BBV, if it is meant to give an answer to the formation of group intention and group beliefs in all cases. I respond as follows. First, in the above kind of deductive case, a rational group may discuss and decide on the premises separately and form the group view of the premises by the majority principle (this is Pettit's favored way for groups that are persons or at least person-like). In our example, the group would decide for cleaning the park. But of course it is not possible that there is a group intention without any participation intentions. So using merely the premise-driven reasoning does not lead to what is wanted, the participants' or their majority's joint intention involving the appropriate participation intentions. If the group indeed agrees on the importance of having a unified view of the premises (which accepting the majority principle for deciding about the premises here gives) they would have to change their conclusions, and they would also have a group reason to do that. Second, the main purpose of the BBV, anyway, is to show how to arrive at categorical participation intentions in a joint intention case (or, correspondingly, categorical acceptances of beliefs in a group belief case). If the members are asked to express their view about what the group is to do, we can speak of a single-stage application of the BBV; if they are asked to evaluate each premise separately, we have a multistage application of the BBV. The former goes together with the conclusion-driven approach, while the latter corresponds to the premise-driven approach. There discursive dilemma does not as such affect the BBV, as the whole issue basically depends on what the group members are asked to do. Third, the above deductive case is not typical; more usually the decisions are made on the basis of *pro tanto* reasons, and showing that there is a discursive dilemma in such cases is a different matter.

The BBV covers all publicly indicated and accepted we-mode joint intentions and joint beliefs, be the acceptance thick or thin, and all "group-public" cases subsumable under the label "jointly intending as a group." In such cases, it will typically also be correct to attribute the joint intention to the group and to say that the group intends to perform the action.[11] The beliefs here must be "acceptance beliefs," namely, the group members' acceptances of contents or views for the group qua functioning as group members.

In contrast to the public BBV dealt with above, one can also formulate and deal with a purely intersubjective and nonpublic BBV in which everything is based only on subjective beliefs and mutual beliefs. Thus, if the participants accept a content (intention content or belief content) that they purport to be for the group, if they are collectively (and socially) committed to the content, and if there is mutual belief (but perhaps not mutual knowledge) about the participants' acceptances, then the group intersubjectively intends as a group.[12] In the case of the merely intersubjective kind of BBV, the metaphorical bulletin board will exist only in the minds of the participants—or believed participants—and no communication is required. Between the epistemically full-blown BBV and the purely subjective BBV there are various intermediate views or models, depending on what is assumed of objectivity and of the reasons for the participants' beliefs.[13]

Let me finally summarize my classifications of the different cases that the BBV allows (my examples tend to concern joint intentions, but beliefs, to be discussed in chapter 6, and, mutatis mutandis, actions, to be discussed in chapter 5, are also included below). Cases (1)–(3) are covered by the public BBV, while case (4) falls under the intersubjective BBV.

(1) *Full-blown joint content (intention, belief).* There are two cases: (a) agreement-based joint content, a strong case of the BBV involving agreement making in conditions of mutual knowability, and (b) expressed acceptance of plan in conditions of mutual knowledge or knowability.[14]

Speaking of joint intention, in (a) the participants make an agreement to act jointly; for instance, the participants make an agreement to paint a house together. In contrast, (b) includes the somewhat wider kind of case where the participants can sign up for joint action. Thus, if sufficiently many persons sign up, for example, for a bus tour, then joint intention is created and, normally, action ensues. Analogously, we can give examples of the group's acceptance of views (beliefs). A very simple example of (a) is the case in which the group uses voting and the majority principle to arrive at an acceptance belief (e.g., that terrorist attacks will diminish if the government of Ruritania is changed). In case (b), the view—such as the one just mentioned—is proposed by someone, and the others express their acceptance.

Put in general terms, case (1) is (strongly) *normatively group-binding* on the basis of a *joint obligation* and *collective commitment*.

(2) *Weakly normative joint content (intention or belief).* In these cases, there are normative participation expectations based on an agent's leading the others to normatively expect that he will participate in the joint action in question.[15] When all the agents do the same, there will be a base for the participants' mutual belief about collective commitment to participate and thus about the others' participation intentions. We may speak of this case as being based on mutual weak promises to participate. Example: By expressing—by his words or by his actual action—that he will help to clean the park, an agent leads the others normatively to expect that he will participate in the joint action. When this kind of weak promise is mutual (and understood to be mutual among the participants), a weakly normative joint intention to participate is at stake. Each of the participants is committed to this joint task under conditions of mutual belief, and thus we have collective commitment here. (Recall, however, that there can be a joint intention to clean the park, and so on, also in a nonnormative sense.)

(3) *Nonnormative joint content (intention or belief).* In this case, there is a publicly shared, plan-based joint intention or view (belief) that falls short of

being even a weak promise in the sense of case (2). In this case there will be, because of the publicity requirement, an expression of intention, which nevertheless is based on nonnormative, thin acceptance (for example, I intend to participate but I do not promise that I will).[16] In all, we can say that this type of case of the BBV relies on the mutual-knowledge-based, explicitly expressed intention to share a plan (involving merely "technically" normative acceptance of the plan). The participants will be collectively (or jointly) committed to the plan partly because of the mutual knowledge that they share a plan, and thus intention.

(4) *Nonpublic joint content.* This is the weakest case of joint content (intention or belief) and involves the weakest kind of collective acceptance. While the publicity requirement is not satisfied and while there thus are no public participation expressions, there must still be *mutual belief* concerning the acceptance of the content. This case thus falls outside the standard BBV (but not the intersubjective version of it). Even this weak case may be group-binding if it involves collective commitment and for-groupness based on mutual belief only. For instance, a participant is personally collectively committed, I say "we-committed," to the joint action in question on the grounds that he will not achieve his goal—that the joint action comes about—without the others performing their parts properly; thus he and the others commit themselves to the action in this instrumental sense. This case does not allow for objectively justified criticism of violation, because such justified criticism would have to be based on public facts relevant to the truth of the mutual belief.

In all, cases (1)–(4) entail *group-binding* contents (intentions or beliefs). Thus, in the joint intention case, group-binding group action will normally come about (and may come about also in the belief case, even if individual acting as a group member seems more typical). Cases (1) and (2) are normative cases, while in (3) only joint "thin" acceptance of content (e.g., expressed we-mode we-acceptance in the defined sense) is involved. In (4) the joint content is based on some kind of shared implicit understanding of the situation and the other participants' relevant mental attitudes.

In general, intending and believing as a group is to take place either in terms of the standard public BBV or in terms of the intersubjective BBV.

3   We-Intentions and Joint Intentions Analytically Elucidated

In accordance with the grounds presented in the previous section, I will next discuss social we-intentions and joint intentions in a more analytical and precise fashion—keeping in mind such examples as the joint intention jointly to lift a table, sing a song, or make a contract. Although the conceptual distinction between we-mode and I-mode intention is clear in view of what was said above, both kinds of social intentions can in a sense be viewed in terms of the notion of a shared we-attitude (in the sense of chapter 3).[17] Put somewhat loosely, a person has the we-intention to do (or bring about) X if and only if he has the intention to do (or bring about) X and has it in part because, according to his belief, the others in the collective have that intention, there being mutual belief among the participants about this. When there is shared we-intention in this sense, we have a weak joint intention, one in the I-mode. In the we-mode case, we can say that the participant intends to perform her part of X at least in part for the ("internal") reason that the group intends as a group to perform X. This will in simple unstructured groups amount to, or at least entail, the participants'—or at least the operative agents'—having formed the joint intention to perform X as a group. A group member intends to perform her part of X primarily because the group intends to perform X—and only derivatively because the others (distributively considered) intend to participate. The group reason here is a conceptual condition for a participant's we-intention and a reason for her intending to perform her part (and for her performing it). That also the others or a sufficient number of them participate is both a conceptual and a rationality condition for one's intention to participate. In the we-mode case, the participants are functioning as group members and taking the group as their authority for their intention formation. This contrasts with the I-mode case, where they are functioning merely as private persons privately committed to a goal.

A we-mode joint intention is expressible by "We as a group will perform X jointly" (that I take to entail "We will perform X jointly as a group"). Here the participants are assumed to take themselves to form a thick "we" ("we-together" or "we-as-a-group"), which is not a mere aggregative "we" that signifies "the two (or more) of us" (the basic I-mode sense of "we"). The "we-as-a-group" notion indicates the we-mode sense of "we." We can say that the *intentional subject* of a we-intention is "we," while the *ontological subject* of a we-intention is a single agent.[18]

Suppose now that the joint intention to perform X together is attributed to m real agents, say, $A_1, \ldots, A_i, \ldots, A_m$, assumed to understand what the joint action X involves. (The participants need not be identified by their standard names but, e.g., as position-holders in a group.) In this case, every participant A_i has, as his personal "slice" of the participants' joint intention, the we-intention to perform X together with the others. The group reason that each A_i here has for participating in the performance of the joint action X is that their group so intends, which upon analysis amounts to the fact that the participants jointly intend X (see chapter 6 for the bootstrapping allegedly involved). They form a group here already because their having a joint intention means that they take themselves to be capable of acting as a group, and this will in effect make them a social group.

My analysis of we-mode we-intention can be summarily formulated as follows.[19]

(WI) A member A_i of a collective g *we-intends* to do X if and only if

(i) A_i intends to do his part of X (as his part of X);

(ii) A_i has a belief to the effect that the joint action opportunities for an intentional performance of X will obtain (or at least probably will obtain), especially that a right number of the full-fledged and adequately informed members of g, as required for the performance of X, will (or at least probably will) perform their parts of X, which under normal conditions will result in an intentional joint performance of X by the participants;

(iii) A_i believes that there is (or will be) a mutual belief among the participating members of g (or at least among those participants who perform their parts of

X intentionally as their parts of X there is or will be a mutual belief) to the effect
that the joint action opportunities for an intentional performance of X will obtain
(or at least probably will obtain);
(iv) (i) in part because of (ii) and (iii).

I have assumed that the participants actually exist, but I allow that a participant might in some contexts be mistaken in his (rationally presupposed) beliefs
(ii) and (iii). (On pain of not we-intending at all, he cannot be mistaken about the
general situation at stake, namely, that there are some agents about to perform a
joint action.) Thus, in such abnormal circumstances, a single agent can in
principle have a we-intention, and here a we-intention is not objectively a
"slice" of a joint intention. Below I will, however, assume that the acceptance
of "We will do X together" must be veridical and entail the existence of a joint
intention. Thus it will be assumed below that all the agents in question really have
the we-intention.[20] As to (iv), it lays bare the fact that the presuppositional beliefs
cannot be idle and serve to make the participation intention rational.

As indicated, it is a mutually believed conceptual (presuppositional) condition for an agent's we-intending to participate in performing X with the others
and for her intention to perform her part of X that also the others (of sufficiently
many of them for X getting performed) similarly participate. Furthermore, that
they all (or even some of them) actually have formed the intention to participate
in X is a contingent fact that a rational agent will take as a proximate reason for
taking part. As said, the primary reason for a participant's intention to perform
her part of X in the we-mode case—on conceptually "internal" grounds—is the
group's intention (here based on the agents' joint intention). The group's intention conceptually—and often also causally—precedes an agent's we-intention,
and it is always a partial reason for the agent's performing her part.[21] The joint
intention, accordingly, is the participant's reason at least for her intention to
perform her part (see the inference schemas (W1) and (W2) below) and will, in
the case of an antecedently existing joint intention, be a "newcomer's" reason
for her joining in, namely, for her forming her we-intention on the basis of the
group's previously formed intention. Recall that the participants are collectively
committed to seeing to it that their intention to perform X together will be
satisfied. This collective commitment is a conceptual feature involved in their
intention.[22]

The presupposed beliefs (ii) and (iii), expressing the minimal rationality of
the we-intender concerning what a we-intention conceptually involves, as well as
condition (iv) will not be commented on in detail here.[23] Let me only say that the
joint action opportunity conditions include, besides the relevant mental and
physical abilities of the participants, also that the others (or at least sufficiently
many of the "right" kinds of them, as required for an intentional performance of
X) will indeed participate.[24]

It is presupposed by my analysis that a minimally rational we-intender should
in the standard case of direct joint action be disposed to reason in accordance with
the following two schemas (W1) and (W2) of practical inference (or in terms of
their variants).

(*W1*) (i) We will do X.

Therefore,

(ii) I will do my part of X.

Here the we-intention qua a slice of the participants' joint intention to perform X gives the agent a reason to (intend to) perform his part of X.

(*W2*) (i) We will do X.
(ii) X cannot be performed by us unless we perform action Z (for instance, teach agent A, who is one of us, to do something required of him for X).

Therefore,

(iii) We will do Z.
(iv) Unless I perform Y we cannot perform Z.

Therefore (because of (iii) and (iv)),

(v) I will do Y (as my contribution to Z).

The second of the schemas applies to all "normally rational" we-intenders, too, but of course only when the contingent clauses (ii) and (iv) apply, and it is to be exhibited by the we-intenders' dispositions to reason in appropriate circumstances. This schema expresses part of what is involved in saying that a we-intention involves a collective commitment to contribute to the realization of the content of the we-intention. This collective commitment also involves social commitment, namely, that the participants are committed to one another to participate in the joint performance of X. Accordingly, (*W2*) clearly makes we-intentions cooperative to a considerable extent by requiring relevant interaction—or at least disposition to interact—among the participants (see chapter 7). Schema (*W2*) also indicates that the notion of one's part of joint action X cannot be fully fixed in advance and constructed out of antecedently available individual actions.

Supposing that joint intentions can be expressed by "We as a group will do X" or its variants, in order to cover "standing" intentions in addition to directly action-generating intentions, we must also take into account dispositions to we-intend.[25] The following can accordingly be regarded as a true claim intending jointly as a group (or in the we-mode).[26]

(*JI*) Agents $A_1, \ldots, A_m$ have the *joint intention to perform a joint action* X if and only if
(a) these agents have the we-intention (or are disposed to form the we-intention) to perform X; and
(b) there is a mutual belief among them to the effect that (a).[27]

The entailment from left to right is obvious. As to the entailment of the joint intention by clauses (a) and (b), notice that there is a kind of holistic interaction effect here, because the agents' we-intentions presuppose joint intention (see the circularity discussion below). This fact guarantees the truth of the entailment in question. The joint intention toward X is assumed to entail collective commitment toward X.

Another point that still needs to be made here concerns broader cases in which a group can be said to intend to perform an action. The simple intuition here is the consensus intention: a group intends as a group when its members qua group members so intend. However, in the case of structured groups, the matter can be viewed somewhat differently. Here one can make a distinction between group members who are somehow authorized (typically by the group members) to form intentions for the group and possibly to realize these intentions. (There can be several hierarchical layers connected by the authority-relation, but so as not to complicate issues unnecessarily, only the two-layered case is considered). The authorized members are called operative members. On the basis of the more general and more detailed account to be given in chapter 6, the following summary analysis of group intentions seems adequate for groups that are externally and internally free (e.g., dictators are thus not allowed by this formulation):[28]

> (GINT) Group g *intends as a group to perform action* X (or intends that a state X obtain) as a group if and only if there are operative members of g such that
> (1) these agents, when acting as group members in the we-mode sense (and accordingly performing their positional tasks due to their exercising the relevant decision-making system of g), intentionally collectively form the joint intention toward X (e.g., partly by accepting the conative expression "We will do X" or one of its cognates for g) and are collectively committed to bringing about X;
> (2) there is mutual belief among the operative members to the effect that (1);
> (3) because of (1), the (full-fledged and adequately informed) nonoperative members qua members of g tend to tacitly accept with collective commitment—or at least ought so to accept—that their group g intends to perform X (as specified in clause (1));
> (4) there is mutual belief in g to the effect that (3).

Clauses (1) and (3) express the most central ideas here. Clauses (2) and (4) express rationality conditions that might not be properly fulfilled, while there still is a group intention on the basis of the fulfillment of (1) and (3).

We can see from this account that the nonoperative members can in a central way take part in the group's intention simply by functioning as group members and (tacitly) accepting the operatives' joint intention—or at least being normatively obligated to such acceptance. This tacit acceptance can amount to the nonoperatives' endorsing the operatives' joint intention qua members of g, but they can be "in reserve," for example, concerning the execution of the intention. For instance, the sales personnel of a department store (an organization) can take part in the organization's intentions and actions just by doing their work and without perhaps knowing very much about what the operatives for decision-making are doing. Accordingly, they need not actually have the we-intention in question but only take it to be the case that the operatives have accepted "We will do X" for the group. They still can be said to (weakly) participate in the group's intention. It is even possible that the analysans of (GINT) is satisfied even when some nonoperatives fail to tacitly accept "We will do X" for g and the participation intentions that this intention expression entails for them (together with other relevant information). Such persons may be dissidents, but persons hired to help the group to achieve X may also be a case in point.[29]

My account of we-mode joint intention and we-intention is conceptually nonreductive, although it is ontically individualistic or, rather, interrelational.[30] In (WI), the participants are assumed to believe that they will perform the joint action X intentionally—as arguably an intention cannot be satisfied by means of nonintentional action. Assuming the standard case that the beliefs are true and assuming also that intentional action X requires a relevant intention (here typically X), we can in this case take this (joint) intention to be one having the content to perform X, and we arrive at the view that (i) of (WI) entails for the first-person case:

(*) I intend to perform my part of our joint action X as my part of X that we perform jointly intentionally as a group *on the basis of our joint intention to perform* X.

Generally speaking, (*) is perhaps more circular that one may want to tolerate.[31] The notion of joint intention can here be understood in a somewhat vague, preanalytic sense, namely, in terms of what the agents actually "have in mind" in everyday life when they jointly intend, and this is what analytical theories of collective intentionality analyze and elucidate in terms of (partly) technical notions such as we-intentions. There is circularity but not vicious circularity here, because the elements in my analysis are not independently existing "building blocks" of joint intentions but are only analytically isolated parts that presuppose the whole of which they are parts.

My first point to rebut circularity here is that, as seen from (GINT), when some operative members jointly intend as a group to bring about X, the non-operatives need not have the we-intention but only need to go along with the operatives' decision and, if needed, intentionally perform their parts of X (without aim-intending X). Thus, at least in the case of such members, the italicized part in (*) that creates the circularity can be omitted without change of truth value (as indeed clause (i) of (WI) does). Let us thus go back to the following claim (in view of the second clause of (WI)):

(**) I intend to perform my part of our joint action X (that we will perform as a group) as my part of our performing X intentionally.

My second point against circularity is that the participants are assumed to be able to perform X intentionally as a group with an adequate functional under-standing of joint action X, at least as some participants do aim-intend X. This blocks general circularity. Furthermore, we may take the participants to be able to perform X intentionally (in the most rudimentary sense as a kind of "collective pattern-governed action") even if they (and this applies to all participants) do not have the full concept of intentionally performed joint action and may lack the ability to use it in their practical reasoning. Nor do the participants need to have the concept of joint intention in a reflective sense. We can functionally stop the analysis of the intentional performance of joint action X without proceeding to speak of their joint intention. Accordingly, (**) can replace (*) not only in the case of nonoperatives but in the case of all participants. Generally speaking, they must be able to act together (perform X) before being able to form the joint intention to perform X. So practice is central—the intention requires the practice.[32]

4   I-Mode and We-Mode Joint Intentions Contrasted

In this section, I-mode and we-mode attitudes and especially joint intentions will be revisited and the main differences between them pointed out. The section also argues for the irreducibility of the we-mode to the I-mode in the case of joint intention. According to the analysis in the previous section, jointly intending agents intend because of their conative collective acceptance of the "content" in question as the group's content to which the participants have collectively bound themselves. We-mode joint intention and action satisfy the Collectivity Condition. The joint intention (and attitudes underlying it) in effect serve as a participant's group reason for her intention to perform her part of X. In the corresponding I-mode case, there are only the participants' (possibly interdependent) private acceptances of a content with private commitments to it. The Collectivity Condition is not satisfied in this case (although perhaps the participants are merely contingently connected in an analogous way). In the I-mode case, the shared intention (goal) might serve as a participant's "group reason" for her intention to perform her participatory action.

Typical I-mode joint action is interpersonal, dependent action directed toward the same goal.[33] No matter how workable, in a functional sense, such a view is or may be, it deals with interpersonal, "I-thou" action that falls short of being based on a full-blown group reason satisfying the Collectivity Condition. The central distinction in joint or shared attitudes and actions is whether the participants on purpose function as a group (as one agent, as it were) or whether there is only private interpersonal action (possibly action based on a shared private group goal). The kind of "oneness" involved in functioning as a group member in the we-mode case is not as such involved in the kind of interaction pattern that the corresponding I-mode case contains.

Consider common-sense examples like the multiagent action of lifting a table or the multiagent action of going to Rome or watching a football game. Such cases can have we-mode and I-mode instances ("tokens"). These modes are irreducible to each other. Actually, this is a trivial claim, because the former but not the latter *necessarily* involves a group reason. However, here my irreducibility theses concern preanalytic or colloquial notions, the kind of idea that is involved when we say that we will go to the movies tonight or lift this table or will have coffee in a nearby cafeteria. In such examples there is only one content, however vaguely stated, in each case, and our philosophical analysis is supposed to clarify the situation and to show that in one case we are dealing with an I-mode joint action of lifting a table, whereas in another case there was we-mode joint lifting of a table. Note that the for-groupness, collective commitment, and group reason features generally are not explicit in the content of the intention, nor do they appear in the surface of common-sense parlance and thinking. They can be regarded as underlying conceptual presuppositions that philosophical analysis has revealed.

Let us now consider the following simple argument for the ontological irreducibility of we-mode states (the group level, so to speak), using joint intention as an example.

(a) The concepts of joint intention as a group and joint action as a group (in technical terms, in the we-mode) are not reducible to concepts expressing private intentions and actions (namely, intentions and actions based on a private, namely, I-mode reason) and what can be conceptually constructed out of I-mode resources.

(b) If there actually are joint intentions and joint actions that can be correctly described as joint intentions and actions *as a group*, then they differ ontologically from private intentions and actions with the same content (or with a "counterpart" content).

I will here assume that the antecedent of (b) is true as plain common-sense fact and that thus we-mode concepts are not idle.

(c) Some joint intentions and joint actions as a group in fact exist (and indeed are needed in many cases, e.g., for suitable tasks or many-person activities such as tennis and dialogue).

Therefore,

(d) Some ontologically irreducible joint intentions and actions as a group that exemplify the corresponding conceptually irreducible concepts in fact exist (and, to make an additional point, are needed in many cases). (From (a), (b), and (c).)

What is at stake in premise (a) is basically the concepts of joint intention and joint action as a group. (My explication of the colloquial phrase "as a group" is precisely the we-mode.) If concepts are irreducible, then it is reasonable to think in this case that the states and events to which they correctly apply are ontologically irreducible as well. The conceptual side, so to speak, induces naturalistically different ways of thinking and acting in the cases under comparison, and this means ontological difference (that very likely exists in the brain as well). Premise (b) refers to really existing activities. As such, (a) does not entail the antecedent of (b). There are ontologically idle concepts.

To defend (a), a central argument for the claim that joint intention and action in the we-mode are irreducible to I-mode interpersonal intention and action is simply that the former are based on a full-blown group reason satisfying the Collectivity Condition, while the latter are based on private, possibly progroup reasons. Such a group reason (e.g., "Our group intends to lift this heavy table") for a participant's intention and action to participate is different from an I-mode reason, as emphasized. Supposing that the relevant epistemic requirements for the participants are in place, the participant's reason (at least when reconstructed by a theoretician) in the we-mode case involves the features of collective acceptance, for-groupness, and collective commitment. This contrasts with an I-mode reason which is conceptually based on the idea that I participate because of my private, possibly progroup reason, given that you also participate. There is no proper collective commitment here, only your and my private commitments, and you and I do not act, at least necessarily, for our group. To be sure, in real life one often acts both for group reasons and private reasons when performing an action.[34]

Assumption (b) can be argued on the basis of plain common sense. When two agents jointly lift the table, it must be based on their joint intention. Each agent performs her part of the joint lifting, where her part of table lifting is ontologically and functionally dependent on the notion of joint table lifting, and its ontological content might be fully determinable only after the performance of the joint action. However, a table can be lifted also in the I-mode in terms of interpersonal action directed toward the shared end of the table being lifted.[35] My central point here is that, as seen, there are full-blown we-mode cases, such as lifting a table as a group with collective commitment (see below).

My overall judgment concerning the above irreducibility argument is that its conclusion (d) not only follows from the premises argued for but that the argument is about as "sound" as it can be in this kind of field of research. Furthermore, I would like to point out that my basic we-mode argument (the need of irreducible we-mode mental states) seems to be applicable, mutatis mutandis, to any other attitude or action involving jointness.

To briefly comment on other approaches concerning the I-mode/we-mode issue, Seumas Miller would say about the table lifting case that the participants shared the collective end of having the table lifted and they acted dependently to achieve that.[36] His theory gives an I-mode answer. There is no joint intention, there is no we-action, no thick "we," and there is no collective commitment (unless perhaps such a requirement is added as a separate requirement). Bratman's theory says for the case with you and me as participants that I intend that we lift the table (not necessarily as a joint action; recall chapter 3) and you intend similarly, our intentions being suitably interdependent; and then we carry out our intentions (I-mode intentions, in my classification). Gilbert would say that the participants are jointly committed to lifting the table and therefore form a plural subject, and somehow act in light of their joint commitment to lift the table (see chapter 5). Her "plural subject" account can be viewed as a kind of we-mode account.[37] In addition, Searle's account resembles the we-mode view, although it faces problems.[38]

To deepen the discussion, recall from chapter 3 Bratman's analysis of shared intentions in terms of the locutions "We intend to J," where J is a joint action. I claim that his account is an I-mode account of joint intention. Indeed it is rather close to an I-mode we-intention in the sense of chapter 3. His final analysis is as follows.

> We intend to J if and only if
> (1) (a) I intend that we J and (b) you intend that we J;
> (2) (a) I intend that we J in accordance with and because of meshing subplans of (1) (a) and (1)(b); (b) you intend that we J in accordance with and because of meshing subplans of (1)(a) and (1)(b);
> (3) (1) and (2) are common knowledge between us.

Why is this an I-mode account? Basically this is because the analysans does not entail a full-blown group reason, namely, that the agents have their intentions of the form "I intend that we J" (for each participant) necessarily because of a group reason satisfying the Collectivity Condition. Hence the we-mode is not entailed, and thus there need not be (we-mode) collective acceptance of the joint action J as the group's jointly intended content to which the group members are collectively committed. What may thus also be missing is the social commitment involved in collective commitment. There need be no group-based intention and proattitude that "reasons" the agents' intentions to perform their parts in Bratman's account. The agents have their personal intentions on the basis of their private reasons.[39]

The following thesis connecting joint intention and joint action seems defensible: It is necessarily the case that if there is joint intention it can only be satisfied by joint action as a group (recall note 4 in chapter 2 on c-action and m-action). The converse also seems to hold in the following sense. If there is joint action (i.e., if a token instance of collective behavior is joint action), then it must be (jointly) intentional "under some description" (there must be something relevant that the agents did jointly intentionally), and this in turn entails that there must be a relevant joint intention on the basis of which the agents performed the action jointly. In typical cases, this joint intention has the content X, if X is the action to be jointly intentionally (and not only "separately" intentionally) performed. To argue for this thesis, consider a successful case of satisfaction of joint intention. You and I ("we") have the joint intention to lift the table in ten seconds, . . . , in one second, . . . , now, and as a result we are jointly lifting the table with the joint intention-in-action (or joint "we-willing") to lift the table. We are jointly intentionally lifting the table by means of each of us intentionally lifting his side of the table and we are jointly lifting the table in accordance with and partly because of our joint intention to lift the table (or to do something closely related). Because of our joint intention we are collectively committed to the task. All this is in the we-mode—we have thus collectively accepted the joint intention (plan) for us as a group.

The joint action satisfying a joint intention cannot be (using the example just under discussion) just the aggregate action consisting of your and my private actions of my lifting my end and your lifting your end of the table. Rather, it is *our* joint action of lifting the table. That it is our joint action means that we take it to be an action that we have chosen to perform jointly, as our joint action that satisfies the Collectivity Condition (see the account (AT^*) in Chapter 5). There is a full-blown group reason for the action and not (only) private reasons. We are collectively committed to this joint action, the collective commitment being based on the joint intention. Thus our action here necessarily is in the we-mode and involves our acting together fully as group members.[40]

We can, however, lift the table "jointly" in the I-mode. I take Bratman's account to show it (also see ($AT\#$) in chapter 5). However, let us also recall from chapter 3 that in Bratman's account the action J need not even be a joint action based on a shared intention. We have here a second line of argument for showing that Bratman's account is an I-mode one, if we assume—as just argued—that a joint intention can only be satisfied by a joint action based on that intention and that joint action must be based on joint intention with some relevant content (mistakes and the like must be allowed). The point is, of course, that in his account such a joint action is not required and that therefore there need be no joint intention as a group.[41]

There are also other we-mode features characteristic of the we-mode. For instance, as noted, there is *shared authority* (and responsibility) in the we-mode case over the joint action X and its parts. This contrasts with the I-mode case, where every participant has full (private) authority over his action in the aggregate action (but of course not over the aggregate action).

5   Joint Intention and Group Reason

An I-mode account of joint intention is concerned with putting together individuals' private intentions when they for some reason want to act together or achieve something together.[42] To exaggerate somewhat, the basic model in the two-person case is as follows: I regard you as a (cooperative) part of my environment rather than as a proper fellow group member and we face a task to be solved together by our actions.[43] In contrast, in my we-mode account, you and I form a thick "we," a group, that acts possibly in order to solve a jointly accepted task, or we just act together as a group for purely social reasons ("Each of us values and enjoys the company of the others, basically no matter what we are doing together"). I use the colloquial phrase "as a group" here, and it will be interpreted as "in the we-mode" in my account.

In this we-mode account, the intention-dependencies go as follows in an unstructured group g that has formed an intention along the lines of the BBV.

(1) Group g, consisting of the agents $A_1, \ldots, A_m$, intends to bring about X (or see to it that X) as a group, where X may in principle be any state or event (as long as no rationality constraints on g are imposed).

As groups are not literally agents (see the discussion in chapter 6), we must speak of the group members' relevant states and actions:

(2) The members $A_1, \ldots, A_m$ of g jointly, as a group, intend to bring about X; put in more linguistic terms, these agents jointly accept that the intention expression "We will bring about X," satisfying the Collectivity Condition, is true of them collectively (and also individually; see (3)) as group members.

A more general way to arrive at group members' joint intentions here is to speak of the group's relevant authority over them. Note that in (2) the members' (and in the normatively structured case, the operative members') joint intentions may have been formed for the reason that the group's previous decisions and plans play an authoritative role for them (see chapter 6).

After (2), the next step is the following "distribution" assumptions (3) and (4)(i), as well as their consequences (4)(ii) and (5):

(3) Each one of the current members $A_1, \ldots, A_m$ of g in effect accepts, qua a member of g, in this situation that "We will bring about X" is true of himself.
(4) Each member must reason or be disposed to reason as follows:
(i) We will bring about X jointly.

Therefore, taking (i) as my reason (group or we-mode reason),

(ii) I will participate in our (namely, here $A_1, \ldots, A_m$'s) jointly bringing about X or jointly seeing to it that X.

As a paraphrase of (ii) we have:

(5) I will perform my part of our jointly seeing to it that X.

It is inessential here what exactly a part of X involves—it can even be passive and conditional, according to what the functionality of the group's performance of X requires. In general, the participants must at least rationally hope that X will come about due to their joint effort involving their part performances. This serves to give a partial indirect characterization of what "a part" and "participation" involve.

Given that $A_1, \ldots, A_m$ have the right presupposed mutual beliefs about the action opportunities for jointly *stit*-ing X and given that the analogy between single agents and group agents (as "jointified" basically by (2) above) holds true, we can make (5) more specific. This requires that the analogy assumption is based on the two ideas that (a) an intention to act can only be satisfied by means of intentional action and that (b) intentional action must be analyzed as action performed on the basis of a relevant intention—for example, the intention to bring about X (this is what I assume here). So we get

(6) I intend to perform my part of our jointly seeing to it that X as my part of X when acting as a member of g.

Conclusion (6) presupposes that our jointly seeing to it that X is our jointly intentional action performed as jointly intended (that is, for the reason that we jointly intended, possibly in a rudimentary, preanalytic sense only, to jointly see to it that X as a group).

Conclusion (6) gives the main individual-level content of what my notion of we-intention involves. Its group-level content is given by (1) and its jointness-level content is basically given by (2), while (3)–(6) concern the individual level of acting as a group member. Note that any collection of agents that satisfy (1)–(6) forms a we-mode group or at least one capable of action, and so does a collection capable of forming a joint intention (and having mutual belief about this).

Notice still that the concept of joint intention can be taken to entail:

(7) If the members $A_1, \ldots, A_m$ of g jointly intend to bring about X, then they are collectively committed (bound) to (continue) intending and to bringing about X.

We may leave it to psychologists to find out how people in ordinary life, as it were, simplify (6) when intending and acting jointly so that the instrumentally and functionally right things come about. There is some circularity here: a person's intention to perform his part comes to depend on joint intention, although perhaps only on an unarticulated, preanalytic notion of joint intention. This does not matter much, as long as people function satisfactorily in terms of the above account and produce X in about the right way. (Recall the functionally adequate formulation (2) discussed in section 3.)

6 Summary

In this chapter, joint intentions and, to some extent, their formation have been studied. The kind of joint intention focused on is we-mode joint intention explicating the notion of jointly intending as a group. Using the notion of jointly seeing to it that something is the case, the basic content of a joint intention was argued to be "The participants jointly see to it as a group that X," where X can be a state of affairs or a joint action. When some participants jointly intend as a group, in typical cases, each of them is said to "we-intend" the content X. A we-intention is an "aim-intention" in contrast to an "action-intention" (that a participant can rationally intend to bring about by his actions). An agent's we-intention consists of her intention to perform her part of X (here typically a joint action) and some conceptually and rationally required presuppositions that the agent must assume to be satisfied. The participation intention is an action-intention. The nature of we-intentions was analyzed in detail in section 3.

Section 2 presented a view of the general conceptual features of the formation of joint intention (as well as belief) in terms of the BBV. This view relies on relevant presuppositions but is argued not to fall prey to the kind of "I will if you will" regress problem that I-mode shared intentions may face (recall chapter 3). We-mode joint intentions with stronger and weaker bonds between the participants were covered by the account. In section 4 it was argued that we-mode attitudes, including joint intentions, are irreducible to I-mode attitudes. Finally, section 5 discussed how group members' intentions to participate in joint action get their justification (group reason basis).

While this chapter has strongly focused on we-mode joint intentions, it may be pointed out that it is largely an empirical matter, a matter of upbringing, teaching, and education, as well as, more generally, the surrounding culture whether people tend to function prevalently in the we-mode or in the I-mode. In some cases, people weigh their we-mode and I-mode reasons relative to each other (see chapter 7).

Appendix: On the Properties of Intention

Bratman's account of shared intention has been criticized, for example, by Velleman and Stoutland, on the ground that his notion of a person's intending that we (his group) perform a joint action, J, or briefly "I intend that we J" is not an intention notion at all.[44] This discussion, of course, is closely related to the issues considered above. The following principles have been suggested for single-agent intentions.[45]

(1) *Own action condition* (OA): One can intend only to do something oneself.

(2) *Control condition* (C): One cannot intend what one does not take oneself to control.

(3) *Settle condition (S)*: One can only intend what one believes one's so intending settles.

The settle condition entails that "for me to intend that we J I must . . . see my intention as settling whether we J." We may also consider the following additional principle:

(4) *Responsibility condition (R)*: To intend to do something is to commit oneself to do X so as to thereby commit oneself to take full responsibility for having done X (if and when one does X).

I take conditions (1)–(4) to be on the right track and (almost) acceptable for *action*-intentions. (I say "almost" because the control condition, at least, seems somewhat too strongly formulated—less than full control will suffice—and full responsibility in (4) also needs relaxation.) These conditions do not—at least without modification—apply to aim-intentions such as we-intentions.[46] However, as a participant cannot in the standard case we-intend X without all the participants we-intending X, then the control and settle conditions are satisfied in the wider sense that one's we-intending entails that X is settled and under control.

Assuming for simplicity's sake that the presupposition beliefs (ii) and (iii) in the analysis (WI) of we-intention in section 3 are true, our discussion in that section (and section 2) then warrants the following claims, remembering that we-intentions are personal "slices" of joint intentions.

(1J) *Our action condition (WA)*: A person A_i, can we-intend to perform X together with some persons $A_1, . . . , A_m$ only if these persons jointly intend to perform X together such that his action-intention is to participate in these agents' joint performance of X. (If we were dealing with the "irrational" case with false beliefs (i) and (ii) in (WI), the analysans would have to be relativized to A_i's belief.)

(2J) *Joint control condition (JC)*: $A_1, . . . , A_m$ cannot jointly intend to perform an action X jointly and cannot we-intend to perform X in this case unless they mutually believe that they can control X to a substantial degree (at least these agents should mutually believe that their performing X together is not impossible in the circumstances in question).

(3J) *Joint settle condition (JS)*: If $A_1, . . . , A_m$ we-intend to perform X under conditions of mutual belief, they must also mutually believe that their so intending (psychologically, not perhaps in an overt action sense) settles that they will perform X together.

(4J) *Joint responsibility condition (JR)*: For a person A_i to we-intend to do something X (together with other persons) is in part to commit himself to X (in a context where some agents $A_1, . . . , A_m$, of which A_i is one, jointly intend to perform X), so as to thereby commit himself to take partial responsibility for their having performed X together and to take responsibility for his having participated in the performance of X (if and when he actually does participate). (See (1J) for the qualification concerning the case of false beliefs (i) and (ii).)

5

JOINT SOCIAL ACTION

1 Acting Jointly as a Group

In this chapter I will discuss joint action from a philosophical and theoretical point of view. My basic question will be: What is an intentional joint action? Standard examples of joint action are carrying a table jointly, singing a duet, or to have a less cooperative example, playing a game of chess. Joint action can be informal, it can be based on strict rules or agreements, or it can be highly institutionalized (e.g. a wedding ceremony). All full-blown joint actions—in my terminology, joint actions *as a group* or, equivalently, in the "we-mode"—are constitutively cooperative, at least to some extent. Many joint actions are or have a communicative element, and all of them arguably are communicative in a sense involving some—prior or concurrent and direct or indirect—transfer of meaningful information. Furthermore, joint action as a group (here explicated as we-mode joint action) amounts to more than a collection of interdependent individual actions ("I-mode" joint action): recall section 4 of chapter 4. In intuitive terms, joint action as a group entails that the group consisting of the participants in joint action can be taken to have performed or brought about the action in question.

In this chapter I will present an account of joint action "as a group."[1] This I will do in sections 3 and 4 after a discussion in section 2 of topics that a philosophical account of joint action must deal with. Section 5 discusses two main topics: we-mode joint action in an institutionalized context and collective action as action based on a shared we-attitude (and here also I-mode joint action counts). Having presented and defended my account, I turn to a discussion of more recent philosophical accounts of joint action by other authors in section 6. Section 7 concludes the chapter.

As to my terminology, I will use the phrases "joint action" and "acting together" as interchangeable in this chapter. However, when I say "joint action as a group," we-mode joint acting is entailed in my construal. There is also joint action in a *mere* interpersonal sense that I will explicate as I-mode joint action. I will

106

mostly deal with *noninstitutional* joint action (as a group), by which I mean we-mode joint action where there are no institutional power relations between the participants. In section 5 I will briefly consider institutional joint action in which some members have been authorized by other group members to act for the group (see also chapters 6 and 8). As to "collective action," I will below usually treat it also as extensionally equivalent to "joint action," be it in the we-mode or in the I-mode.[2]

2   Conceptually Required Elements of Joint Action

Generally speaking, in a joint action some agents jointly see to it that something is or will be the case, jointly bring about something, or jointly perform something. I will below deal only with actions having an achievement aspect. This means that, epistemically speaking, there is a criterion for deciding whether the action (action type) has been successfully performed or not. Speaking ontically, we can say that with each action under discussion there is a criterial result event or state associated such that this result must on conceptual grounds occur or be there when the action has been performed. Thus there is a task to be performed in the case of each action under discussion, and in the case of joint action, there must of course be participants who bring about the state in the right way—or in some other contexts, maintain the state, and so on (recall section 1 of chapter 4).

When a (noninstitutional) joint action is getting performed, each participant, on conceptual grounds, has a part (perhaps only "being in reserve") to perform, and the participants must understand this and that a joint action of a certain kind is underway. The performances of the parts will be assumed to generate the resulting event, at least when the situation is judged *ex post actu*. The participants are assumed to exercise joint control over the action. However, full antecedent control is not necessary, because the environment will affect the situation. Thus, for example, you and I may jointly close the window by acting together or by our jointly seeing to it that a third party brings about this result event. The parts are all that the participants, strictly speaking, do, but what a part is may not always be decidable *ex ante actu*, for the agents are collectively committed to perform the joint action and thus to monitor also the activities of the other participants until the joint action has been performed (or, in some cases, jointly given up).

In this chapter I will be mainly concerned with *jointly intentional joint action as a group*. An account of the intentionality of joint action must thus be given. Going along with the standard account of intentional single-agent action, I will account for the intentionality of joint action in terms of the participants' (we-mode) joint intention to perform the action in question, and this makes the joint action a we-mode action. Conceptually, we may think of a joint action in close analogy with taking a group as an agent performing an action. The group acts on its intention, and this translates into the participants' (group members') action on their joint intention.

I accordingly distinguish between "I-mode" and "we-mode" joint action, of which only the latter serves to explicate joint action as a group. More precisely, jointly intentional joint action is based on a joint intention, and this makes it joint action as a group. Consider the following example. Some workers at a department store may generally go to Alfonzo's for lunch. There are two centrally different cases. The first is one in which they go to Alfonzo's with mutual knowledge that the others go and perhaps even only on the condition that (a certain number of) the others go. This is I-mode joint action (or acting together). In contrast, the workers may have formed a joint plan and joint intention to go to Alfonzo's together. This is acting jointly as a group, in the we-mode.[3] When I speak of joint intention and joint action simpliciter below, I mean the we-mode joint intention and action unless the context clearly indicates otherwise.

The following features are central in a joint action (as a group), and any account of joint action is required to take a stand on this (nonexhaustive) list of issues:

(1) The *type* of the joint performance or action, X, is to be determined. For instance, there can be direct or indirect performance of action X (e.g., you and I jointly carrying a table upstairs), bringing about the result event of X (e.g., our bringing it about that the table gets moved upstairs).

(2) Given a specification of the type of joint action, its *division into parts* is to be accounted for. For instance, are there antecedently fixed parts? What is each participant's part? It should also be shown how the (we-mode) performances of parts tend to generate the result event of the joint action.

(3) Intentional joint action requires that it be performed in accordance with and in part because of the agents' relevant *joint intention*, thus, in my account, because of what the group intends to do. A conceptually precise account of these "intentionality-generating" elements will have to be given.

(4) The participants must be shown to exercise *joint control* over the performance of the joint action and hence, at least to some extent, over the result event.

(5) The conceptually required interpersonal *dependencies* between the participants and their part performances are to be laid bare. Briefly, the participants in my account are dependent because of their joint intention and because of their part performances, assumed to (conceptually or causally) generate or constitute the result event of the joint action. Part actions are factually dependent or fail to be so, depending on the task and the circumstances of performance.

(6) An account of joint actions having different "*conceptual strength*" is to be given. In particular, we-mode joint action (joint acting as a group) is to be distinguished from mere interpersonal or I-mode joint action, which may also include weak forms of interdependent action.

(7) The participants can jointly act as a group in different kinds of *contexts*, for example, in contexts where they have publicly made an agreement to act jointly and are thus socially obligated to act jointly, and in contexts where they have formed a joint plan to act jointly but are not strongly obligated to act jointly. It seems that many of the disputes concerning the nature of joint action have to do with the context problem rather than with what a joint action conceptually requires.

3   The Basic Account of Joint Action

If one accepts in the single-agent case the analysis that to act intentionally is to act from a relevant intention, which is what I do, then the joint action case can be modeled in partial analogy with this. Consider thus the following account of acting together or jointly, more specifically of joint action as a group, hence in the we-mode (upon explication).[4]

> (AT) You and I *(jointly) intentionally performed X jointly* if and only if
>
> (1) X is a collective action type, namely, an "achievement-whole" divisible—either ex ante actu or ex post actu—into my and your parts;
>
> (2) we jointly intended to perform X (or some "closely related" action) jointly;
>
> (3) we performed X together in accordance with and partly because of our joint intention to perform X jointly.

For the sake of precision, the *analysandum* speaks of jointly intentional joint action (as a group) rather than something like aggregates of intentional single-agent actions. *Joint* intentionality is and must be based on the effective presence of a (we-mode) joint intention. Clause (1) is needed because X must be ontologically of the right kind. It involves the idea that a joint action necessarily has parts the performance of which under favorable conditions generates the joint action X in question. As seen in chapter 4, the joint intention requirement gives the participants a full-blown group reason to perform their parts of the joint action. Clauses (2) and (3) are modeled on the singular case by using the idea that intentional joint acting is acting as a group and that the analogy between a group and an individual is strong enough. Furthermore, these conditions build on the generally accepted idea that intentional action is necessarily based on the agent's intention (not necessarily a preformed intention). In the joint action case, the intention might thus be only a "we-willing" or "we-intention-in-action"). Thus also in (2) the joint intention might be merely a joint willing, and at any rate it can be assumed to have resulted in one. Here a we-willing is conceptually regarded as an *effective* intending to perform the contributing or part action now.[5]

In clause (2), the content of the intention typically is the joint action X (or, more precisely, "We will perform X jointly"), but it might be a goal for which X is the means.[6] I will not here discuss the problem in detail and will below generally simplify the exposition by assuming that the content is X. I will here treat intended collective goals and joint goals as equivalent. Accordingly, intended collective goals will be joint intentions with the goals as their contents.[7] As explained in chapter 4, joint intentions as a group (we-mode joint intentions) will have to satisfy the Collectivity Condition, and the same basically goes for we-mode action. Thus, the participants are assumed to understand "under some description" that, necessarily, they have not performed the action jointly as a group without the satisfaction of this condition. Accordingly, acting jointly (or, equivalently, together) in the sense of (AT) is we-mode joint action.

Clause (2) can be understood liberally so as to allow that the participants need only have an intention-in-action to participate in the collective performance of X.[8] Thus the joint or collective telos in their part performances is to participate in acting together relative to X. (2) also is meant to allow for the possibility of intentions in which a participant intends to perform X either together or alone (the latter possibly only if the first disjunct cannot in his view be realized). This is often a realistic possibility, which leads to a shared collective goal and joint action only when the first possibility is realized (which must happen in the context of

(AT)). The intention can be conditional on the others' participation in a sense different from the others' participation being a presupposition of joint action. In the former but not in the latter case, it would be merely contingent on what the participant notices about his environment. An intention initiating joint action, such as cleaning a yard, can clearly be of this kind ("if you do not show up, I will do the whole thing myself"). The assumption of acting in part because of an intention to act jointly must still hold true at the moment of acting jointly.

In analogy with the case of joint intention, as discussed in chapter 4, it is a conceptual presupposition of one's participation in a joint action that a sufficient number of others, as required by the joint action concept in question, participate. Checking that this presupposition holds is an underlying rationality requirement in a joint action. In any we-mode joint action, there is intentionally created dependence, or at least subjective or believed dependence, between the participants. This dependence comes about through the participants' formation of the joint intention to act jointly. Whether or not there is some kind of behavioral dependence is not central; the important element is that the participants collectively intentionally create relevant action-dependence.

Account (AT) is somewhat circular, as its *analysans* in a sense relies on joint action. But I wish to argue that the following three kinds of considerations will help to make the circularity palatable. First, there are evolutionary considerations of two kinds that emphasize the partly genetic (or, better, coevolutionary) basis of joint action and thus give an objective basis to it. First, higher animals, at least, seem to be capable of rudimentary joint action; an example is provided by lions hunting together. Here we are dealing with a (presumably) preconceptual disposition to joint action that becomes realized in purposeful, although probably not intention-based, joint action. Second, as investigations concerning the prehistory of humans indicate, or so it has been argued, the disposition to joint action in humans seems to be a coevolutionary adaptation, because they have evolved in a group context (see chapters 7 and 9).[9] Accordingly, it can be suggested that at least rudimentary joint thinking and acting (either in a rudimentary we-mode sense or in the progroup I-mode sense of jointness) is a coevolutionary adaptation. Next, considerations from developmental child psychology indicate that jointness phenomena begin early. Even nine- to twelve-month-old babies are capable of rudimentary joint attention activities (e.g., they follow the movement of the same object as their mothers and show features of overt joint action).[10] The third type of consideration is that joint action is deeply ingrained in common sense (recall chapter 4, section 3). Due to their socialization, people understand what jointly carrying a table or walking together are, even though they might not have sophisticated understanding of the notions themselves. They may just act jointly as more or less a routine matter.[11]

All the above three types of considerations indicate that there is an objective, genetically or culturally adapted behavior pattern that is available to, and realized by, humans that does not require much more conceptual capacity than plain single-agent action. If we take single-agent action as a conceptually primitive notion, the analogous statement plausibly applies to joint action as well. Thus the basic idea in clause (1), according to which there are functional, purposively performable parts involved, coupled with the additional idea that there is a "we" as some kind of purposively functioning group involved already help to explicate a primitive notion of joint action (indeed, an evolutionarily primitive notion and a notion that is a conceptual primitive).[12] In accordance with what was just said, we need not generally require that the participants have an *articulated* concept of acting together, although they must have an idea of performing something together with others to make the joint action functionally work. The agents must come to have the understanding that a collective project is underway, and this covers not only occurrent acting but also, for example, cooperative sequences of actions with "dispositional" elements (part actions possibly to be performed on a later occasion; think of the project of writing a book jointly).

The above view of joint action is largely based on the analogy between the single-agent and joint cases. Another way to go is to use examples such as the following to argue for the view. Suppose we discuss and argue about a philosophical problem and, unthinkingly, end up in a heated discussion that amounts to quarreling. However, we did not jointly intend to quarrel; we only jointly intended to discuss a problem. Accordingly, here quarreling was only our unintended joint action. Joint intention (shared we-intention) thus seems necessary for intentional joint action in this case. Furthermore, in parallel with single-agent action, every full-blown joint action can be regarded as jointly intentional and jointly intended *under some description*. (This claim might not be true of animal and rudimentary joint action, not at least in a conceptually demanding sense of "intentional" and "intention.")

Account (AT), in a sense, gives the conceptual satisfaction conditions for statements about the occurrence of intentional joint action, but in other respects it is not at all informative. So we need to spell out its conditions, especially (2) and (3). As joint intention entails shared we-intention, (2) is taken to entail

(2*) you and I we-intended to perform X jointly.

Clause (3) accordingly entails

(3*) you and I performed our parts of X in accordance with and partly because of our we-intentions to perform X jointly.

Furthermore, we obviously need to assume that (3) also entails

(3**) your performance of your part of X and my performance of my part of X in the circumstances in question generated a joint action token of X.

Now we have a full analysis of the satisfaction conditions of "you and I intentionally perform X jointly." That is (1), (2), (2*), (3), (3*), and (3**) are necessary and sufficient for the *analysandum* "you and I intentionally perform X jointly." While even (1), (2), and (3) are jointly sufficient and individually necessary, the present point is that the expanded list is more informative. In addition, here (joint) intention and (joint) action are seen to be conceptually interconnected.

In intentional joint action, each participant is assumed to perform her part of X with the commitment (aim, purpose) to furthering the performance of X (recall chapter 4 for this). Not only should she not negatively interfere with the others' performing their parts but also she should contribute in additional, subsidiary ways if things go wrong, against their joint plan. Accordingly, (we-mode) joint action is cooperative by its nature (see chapter 7).[13]

4 The Basic Account Expanded

The account (AT) of joint action will be complemented below by considerations of minimal rationality and by further remarks related to the circularity issue and the conceptual presuppositions involved.

As to circularity, in chapter 4 I chose *jstit* (jointly seeing to it that...) as my umbrella term, as it covers many kinds of activities—for example, jointly performing actions in a direct or in an indirect sense, jointly bringing about states, jointly maintaining states, and so on. Preanalytically, *jstit* can be assumed to cover all of these action concepts. To make the circularity of (AT) concerning joint action still more palatable, let us consider a relevant end, say, E (that may be the in-built *result* event of a joint action or even a group ethos) to be a state jointly *stit*-ed by the agents. In this case, there is no direct circularity problem relative to the *analysandum*, for joint *stit*-ing can be analyzed in terms of mathematical tree structures without any vicious reference to joint action. However, when this jointly *stit*-ed "state" E is a joint action (e.g., E = the agents jointly perform action X) there is, of course, circularity. But as not all instances of E are of this kind, we can live with this amount of circularity. Furthermore, the notion of *jstit*-ing an E (independently of what E precisely is) can be a given a rigorous logical analysis.[14]

A fuller account of joint action requires also that the doxastic elements needed for making the joint action to an extent rational will have to be included. Briefly, the participants must have the relevant beliefs concerning what is going on in joint action (as a group), and this is what the following expanded analysis takes into account.

> (AT*) You and I *(jointly) intentionally performed* X *jointly* if and only if
> (1) X is a collective action type, that is, an "achievement-whole" divisible—either *ex ante actu* or *ex post actu*—into your and my parts;
> (2) we jointly intended to perform X jointly;
> (3) we performed X jointly in accordance with and partly because of our joint intention to perform X (or some "closely related" action) jointly;
> (4) you and I mutually believed—or at least shared the belief—that (1), (2), and (3);
> (5) (2) in part because of (4).

In the weakest cases satisfying (AT*), the intentionality of the action is subjective, in the sense that it is based on first-degree beliefs (in clause (4)). In stronger cases, it is intersubjective (when based on mutual belief) or "objective" (when based on agreement making and mutual knowledge).

The intention content in (2) is presuppositionally based on participants' beliefs (not necessarily mutual beliefs in a loop-involving sense) that the other(s) will participate with some probability. The participants must share the presupposition belief (clause (4)) that they cannot rationally realize their intentions without the other participating, and each has acquired the belief that indeed the other will participate with some probability. Clause (5) says that the beliefs in (4) cannot be idle but function as a reason for the agents' joint intention.

Consider now clause (4), which requires mutual belief about (1)–(3): Unless I believe that you will participate in the joint intention to perform X jointly and hence intend to perform your part of X, it is not in general rational for me similarly to participate—on pain of my part action being performed in vain. Mere hope is not in general sufficient (although admittedly in some cases one might rationally act on a mere hope, for example, when the matter is important and there is no other reasonable choice). Furthermore, unless I believe that you believe that I intend so to participate, it would not be rational for you to participate and thus not rational for me to start acting either—and so on. (Actually, the loop belief need not be a "positive" one, but the requirement can be of the form that I am *not* to have the belief that you believe that I will *not* perform my part.) Another possibility is to require mutual beliefs in the fixed point sense, in which sense we mutually believe that p if and only if we believe that p and that we mutually believe that p (recall section 5 of chapter 3).

Account (AT*) includes "standard" tokens of yard cleaning and also some cases involving conflict between the agents' parts (e.g., as in playing tennis together), as long as a "joint action bottom" is preserved. But it can be taken to exclude the following case. Suppose that some persons intentionally refrain from polluting the Gulf of Finland with the hope that this would eventually make the gulf unpolluted. They might intend to contribute to "cleaning up" the gulf. However, even if they believed that many other agents also similarly would refrain from polluting and also believed that this collective activity might result in the gulf getting sufficiently clean, all this need not give acting together. Clause (3) need not be satisfied, as the participants only need to have a shared I-mode goal here; and, of course, neither are then clauses (4) and (5) satisfied. All that we are guaranteed to have here is a kind of contingent, causally connected aggregate of individual actions contributing to the same goal. The agents need not here be connected in a way that makes them collectively committed to the end, and they could interrupt their participatory activities without the criticism of letting down the others.

Account (AT*) is my best explicate of (at least minimally) rational acting together in the we-mode, namely, joint action as a group or as one agent. This much can be said only when the joint intention on which the joint action is based indeed is a full-blown joint intention satisfying the Collectivity Condition (recall section 5 of chapter 4). Accordingly, the participants' part actions in the joint action must also satisfy a general version of the Collectivity Condition (recall section 1 of chapter 2). In weaker cases, we only have I-mode joint action based on interdependence and shared I-mode goals.[15]

As remarked in chapter 4, various contexts of acting together related to the BBV obviously can be classified by the same scheme as joint intentions (and beliefs) were classified there. Let the intentions simply be carried out, and you arrive at the respective joint actions.

Having ended my account of we-mode joint action, we can consider the conceptual and other central prerequisites of joint action discussed in section 2 (I follow the earlier numbering):

(1) My account given in this chapter in sections 3–5 basically fits all the action types mentioned. Thus it can be applied to (direct and indirect) performance, bringing about, and to seeing to it that something is the case.

(2) In my approach, the notion of a *part* of joint action is central. It is regarded as a conceptual truth that any joint action token has parts and that thus joint action types are dividable into parts on each occasion of performance, at least *ex post actu*. It is equally a conceptual feature of the notion of joint action that the performances of its parts serve to generate a joint action token.

(3) The intentionality of joint action was argued to depend on its being performed in accordance with and in part because of the participants' relevant joint intention serving as a full-blown group reason for the part performances. The joint intention need not be a prior one but can be a mere joint we-willing. Even here it is entailed that the agents intentionally participated because of a group reason.

(4) The participants exercise joint control over the joint action and especially its result event—basically because of the joint intention involved (see section 3 and the appendix to chapter 4).[16]

(5) In the account given, the participants' bodily activities may have been physically dependent in the sense of (perhaps even counterfactually) requiring each other (for instance, jointly carrying a sofa), or, depending on the nature of the task, they may at the other extreme have been physically independent (for instance, our writing a paper jointly). The central dependence-creating element in joint action is the joint intention on which it is based.

(6) My account explicates acting jointly as a group as we-mode joint action. There is also I-mode joint action in a sense that does not satisfy the Collectivity Condition. It will be discussed in the next section.

(7) The contexts of joint action were briefly commented on by reference to chapter 4. It was seen that a joint action can be based on a public joint plan that is accepted either in a strong normative sense or only in a nonnormative sense. Furthermore, there is joint action based on the intersubjective, mutual-belief-based joint intention of the participants, and there is weaker joint action in which the joint action is based on only subjectively (and not even intersubjectively) shared joint intention.

5   Weaker Kinds of Joint Action

The account of joint action given above has concerned we-mode joint action (acting jointly as a group) in largely "egalitarian" cases that have no normatively structured power relations concerning the joint action. I will briefly comment below on a simple case of power relation, but the main topic below will be weak cases of joint action.

First we can consider a situation in which a group performs an action as a group. For instance, a sports team scores a goal, or a business company overtakes another one. Here the action is attributed to the group. Let us consider a very trivial case of a group, a dyad, whose members, A and B, are in symmetric positions as group members. Suppose A and B jointly carry a table upstairs. Then we can also say that the group (dyad) consisting of A and B carried the table upstairs. In general, suppose g consists of members $A_1, \ldots, A_m$ in symmetric positions so that there is no internal normative power structure in the group. Then "$A_1, \ldots, A_m$ jointly performed X" is truth-equivalent to "g performed X."

However, social groups typically have some normative power structure that often is based on authorization by other group members. In my account of group action, to be presented in chapter 6, the basic idea is that there are some authorized operative members who act for the group on the basis of their shared we-intention and produce the right outcome or activity required for the attributability of the action to the group. Authorized members may also issue orders to other members ("Your part is to do Y," etc.). The nonoperatives tacitly accept this, or at least they ought to. Assume that the operatives, say, $A_1, \ldots, A_m$, jointly intended to perform an action, X, for example, to build a house or score a goal for the group, while the nonoperatives $B_1, \ldots, B_k$ tacitly accepted this. Suppose now that the operatives successfully carried out their joint intention and performed X. Then we can also say that $A_1, \ldots, A_m, B_1, \ldots, B_k$ as a group performed X, although the nonoperatives did not actually participate in the direct causal production of X. Accordingly, actions attributed to a group can in general also be attributed to the members of the group (each member can say "We did X"), and this results in joint action in a broad institutional sense. It is broader than the joint action considered above because the nonoperatives need not have had the we-intention and need not actually have been directly involved in the production of the action. Thus, even intentional we-mode joint action does not always require a joint intention (shared we-intention) by all participants toward the action (or a closely related action; recall (AT^*) and section 3 of chapter 4).

There can also be a kind of joint action in the I-mode. We-mode joint action (joint action as a group) requires that the participants (at least the operatives) have jointly accepted a joint "project" (action, task) as the group's joint project and are collectively committed to realizing the project for the group in the full sense involving the Collectivity Condition. In the I-mode case, these central features are lacking. There is only private acceptance and private commitment. Furthermore, the participants' activities must be suitably interdependent, as the case demands.

In a standard case of I-mode joint action, the participants intend to achieve a certain goal that typically cannot be achieved by any participant's action alone.[17] An example of I-mode joint action is given by Michael Bratman's account. In accordance with chapter 3, his *analysandum* might be termed "mere interpersonal joint action," as no group reason is required to be involved. In my technical account such action is *I-mode joint action*. A certain formulation of Bratman's view will be discussed in section 6, but I will give my version here. It simply replaces (we-mode) joint intention in (AT^*) by shared I-mode intention as defined in chapter 3. We get the following.

(AT#) You and I *intentionally performed X jointly in the I-mode sense* if and only if
(1) X is a collective action type, specifically, an "achievement-whole" divisible— either *ex ante actu* or *ex post actu*—into my and your parts;
(2) you and I shared the I-mode intention to perform X jointly (see *(IMJI)* below);
(3) you and I performed X jointly in accordance with and partly because of our shared I-mode intention to perform X (or some "closely related" action) jointly;

(4) you and I mutually believed—or at least shared the belief—that (1), (2), and (3);

(5) (2) in part because of (4).

In (2) we use the following analysis of I-mode intention from chapter 3:

(IMJI) You and I *share in the I-mode intention to jointly perform* X if and only if

(1) I intend that we X in the external reason-based we-attitude sense (I intend that we X in part because I believe that you intend in the external reason-based sense that we X and that we mutually believe that each of us so intends), and

(2) you similarly intend that we X in the external reason-based we-attitude sense.[18]

What is the difference between the we-mode account (AT*) and its I-mode counterpart (AT#)? Account (AT*) involves the group level because of the idea of jointly intending as a group and thus a full-blown group reason. This somewhat holistic idea, making reference to a "we" understood as a social group in the sense of a collective agent, entails collective commitment to intending to perform one's part of X and to performing X. Joint action in the sense of (AT*) satisfies the Collectivity Condition, while (AT#) does not. Note, too, that in (AT#) there is no assumption of group identification or of the presence of a thick "we" involved, and the reasoning depicted in the concluding section of chapter 4, when applied to joint action, does not apply.[19]

It was noticed that, for example, in institutionalized collective actions, not all the participants need to share a we-intention or—considering analogous I-mode joint action—a shared I-mode intention. There are still other cases. For instance, you and I may intend to remove a tree lying on the road and blocking our driving. Thus I intend to do my part of this task and similarly for you. You and I are operating in the I-mode, and we do not intend to act as a group for our group (not at least in a sense satisfying the Collectivity Condition). While we share an end and thus operate on the basis of weak, I-mode collective intentionality, not even the I-mode we-perspective needs to be involved here for the log to be removed by us (thus this case may even fall short of satisfying the group-involving account (AT#)). Furthermore, note that a third person might join the action without fully knowing what is going on. He might just have the intention to show off by lifting one end of the log with one hand or something like that. However, his activities might be functional with respect to satisfying the core intention, but he still would not qualify as a participant in the I-mode joint action.

There are also broader kinds or categories of collective action involving some jointness. Thus collective social action can be based on a shared we-attitude, and a suitable, broad subclass of it involves jointness to the extent that it amounts to joint action.[20] Such collective action can be divided into three broad categories, as follows.

The first main category, the *commonality* category, is concerned with collective action consisting of independent individual action for a shared, mutually believed social reason of which the following is an example. Suppose that the members of a collective, for example, the teenage girls in a town, prefer to dress similarly, say, wear miniskirts. This is an I-mode collective social action performed for the shared, mutually believed social reason (but not at least a full-blown group reason) of acting as others, for example, wearing a miniskirt—possibly with the underlying motive of looking like the others. For having this kind of reason, the agents must believe that the others act similarly (wear a miniskirt) and that they all are mutually aware of all this. The catchword here is commonality. Clearly, there thus is an element of jointness involved even in this simple kind of parallel collective social action.

The second main category may be termed I-mode *mutual dependence*. The agents' component actions in a collective social action here are assumed to be dependent on each other in a kind of game-theoretic sense. The essence of dependence here is "necessity," in the sense that it is necessary for a participant to take into account the others' actions for an optimal or satisfactory achievement of his goal. There must be a shared we-belief concerning such dependence, and it will constitute at least a part of the social reason in question. An example is people avoiding bumping into each other when walking in the street. Here the agents may be said to act for the social reason that they are in a specific way physically dependent on the other agents—or at least believe so. The second category, accordingly, concerns collective action consisting of mutually dependent I-mode actions (by two or more persons), and I-mode joint activity belongs here.[21] There is an element of cooperation that depends on compatible actions and goals.

The third category is *we-mode jointness*. It involves all we-mode joint actions. Here the shared we-attitude can simply be taken to be a shared we-intention, as in (AT*). Joint action in this category (as well as in (AT*)) can involve some conflict, as long as there is a shared "joint action bottom" (for instance, playing a game of tennis).

In this context of collective social action, some persons' having, and acting for, the same social reason, accordingly, amounts to their sharing, and acting because of, the same we-attitude. We now have the following.

(i) In the commonality category, the shared social reason involves a shared undivided goal (a goal that has not been divided into parts). More precisely, the shared social reason is the content of an undivided shared we-goal (in a weak aggregative sense, without the we-mode).

(ii) In the I-mode mutual dependence category, the social reason is based either on a mutual dependence belief, a we-belief about dependence, or on such a we-belief plus a shared divided we-goal in the I-mode.

(iii) In the we-mode jointness category, the social reason is basically a jointly intended collective goal to act together (a shared we-mode we-goal), with entailed action dependence.

This account can be extended to the "dynamic" or "iterated" case constituted by "core" social practices, be they in the I-mode or the we-mode.[22]

6   Other Approaches

In his recent analytical article, Frederick Schmitt discusses various accounts of joint action and criticizes individualistic approaches. In this section I will critically discuss this article and also state my own views of various authors' accounts.[23]

Specifically, Schmitt discusses Seumas Miller's and Bratman's theories and to some extent Gilbert's and also puts forth his own account, termed "supraindividualism." In the course of the discussion my own account also will be tested.

I will now consider Miller's theory briefly, as I have read and understood it (my reading contradicts Schmitt's reading).[24] Miller's two most important analytic notions in his book are collective end and joint action. He defines a collective end as an individual end that more than one agent has, and that is such that, if it is realized, it is realized by all, or most, of the actions of the agents involved; the individual action of any given agent is only part of the means by which the end is achieved.[25] Having a collective end is an at least partly conscious conative state of an individual. While "conation" is usually taken to mean intention, Miller does not accept this. According to him, one can only intend contents that one can by one's own actions achieve. However, collective ends in general—although the above definition does not entail it (the necessity part is missing in the definition)—seem to be achievable only by the interdependent actions of several individuals. Seemingly against Miller, I claim that one can justifiably speak of intentions also in this kind of case. Thus some individuals can jointly intend to build a bridge, and each of them can aim at and we-intend the joint building of the bridge even if none of them alone can perform this task. Such a joint intention entails the individuals' intentions by their actions to bring about their part of the participants' intentional joint action resulting in the bridge getting built.[26]

Schmitt presents a long and detailed criticism of Seumas Miller's theory.[27] He has many good points to make against strict individualism, but he may have misinterpreted Miller's theory to some extent. Especially, if my above point that collective ends are basically aim-intentions is right, Schmitt's arguments that a joint action does not entail a collective end and that interdependence under a collective end does not entail joint action would not then seem to have much bite against Miller's theory.[28]

Consider next joint action, on which such wider social action categories as joint procedures (conventions) and practices and joint enterprises, as well as social norms, organizations, and institutions, are built in Miller's theory. According to him, groups cannot act, but his counterpart to group action is group members' joint and other actions. A joint action consists of at least two interdependent individual actions directed to the realization of a collective end. Thus,

> individual actions x and y performed by agents A and B (respectively) in situation s, constitute a joint action if and only if (1) A intentionally performs x in s (and B intentionally performs y in s); (2) A x-s in s if and only if (he believes) B has y-ed, is y-ing or will y in s (and B y-s in s if and only if (he believes) A has x-ed, is x-ing or will x in s); (3) A has end e, and A x-s in s in order to realize e (B has end e, and B y-s in s in order to realize e); (4) A and B each mutually truly believes that A has performed, is performing or will perform x in s and that B has performed, is performing or will perform y in s; (5) each agent mutually truly believes that (2) and (3).[29]

Miller's notion of joint action is mutual-belief-based joint action with the additional requirement that here A's action is both a necessary and sufficient condition for B's action, relative to (collective?) end e. Miller's analysis is concerned with a kind of minimal joint action—minimality involving, for example, the lack of collective commitment. (I would add that (2) must hold because of (3) and that all the "joint action opportunities" must obtain.)

However, this analysis still seems both too strong and too weak. Miller gives an example of two persons traveling from Oxford to London; one has a car and enough gas for the trip, and the other one has some money (to pay for his share of the consumed gas) but not enough to get to London alone.[30] According to Miller, this is not a joint action, because the car owner is not relevantly dependent on the other person in the sense demanded by clause (2). But I claim that it may be—for example, if the agents simply agree to travel together. Analogously, we can take a walk together but equally well walk alone: we may decide whether or not to make ourselves relevantly dependent on each other (and thus make (2) satisfied). Miller's account thus is too demanding.

The analysis is too weak, in that it does not capture acting jointly as a group. Joint acting as a group, thus full-blown joint action (in my terminology, we-mode action), would seem not to be capturable with this conceptual machinery (recall the arguments in section 4 of chapter 4), although a behavioral simulation of the we-mode may be feasible.

The basic missing element in Miller's above account is intended group end—a group's end *as a group*, something the agents have jointly accepted as their collective end, namely, for their group, and that involves their collective commitment to it. Such an intended group end amounts to we-mode joint intention.[31] Miller's collective ends can in my terminology be only shared I-mode ends and not we-mode ones.

Going back to Schmitt's article, he correctly argues that joint actions are not constituted by separately characterizable individual actions. Recall that in my account the individual participants are assumed to perform their *parts* of the joint action in question. These parts can, but need not, be antecedently given. Schmitt shows that it is not feasible to start with some singular actions and claim that they can individualistically be put together to form a joint action. In some cases, the parts exist and are recognizable only after the joint action, X, has been performed. Parts of joint action, while necessarily conceptually connected via their descriptions, are, however, individual actions by participants, and—due to their conceptual connection—they can be supposed to generate the total joint action X under normal conditions. I think that Schmitt has not presented tenable arguments against the more holistic idea that individual part actions be understood in this X-dependent sense. For instance, in one of Schmitt's cases, two people are taken to walk arm-in-arm in a drunken stupor (p. 143): "They jointly walk, but quite a few of their motions do not correspond to singular actions on their part. They twist and careen and inadvertently prop one another up—all part of the joint walk but not of any singular actions." However, at least if the joint walk is intentional, I would say that it is still constituted by part actions performed by these agents, no matter how intertwined behaviorally those parts may be. The part actions can have been based on prior intentions to act, but there is also the more realistic possibility available that they are based on we-willings (we-intentions-in-action).

Schmitt argues against individualism that individuals do not perform joint actions as individuals but only as group members. This is a thesis that also I have long advocated in my work. In my terminology, the individuals can perform full-blown joint actions only in the we-mode, which involves that they must act as group members.[32] I have claimed that the very fact of joint intending makes the intenders in question a group. So, as a full intentional joint action must be based on a joint intention (shared we-intentions), all cases of joint action are based on acting as a group member. Put in more precise terms, in the case of intentional joint action, these agents jointly intend to perform X (or something closely related such as a proximate goal that X is a means to), which involves that they share a we-intention with the same content and they perform X jointly in accordance with and in part because of their joint intention, and mutually believe all this. Because of their joint intention and acting on it, the agents form a group.[33] Thus, when there is joint action, there is acting as a group. We can thus say that acting jointly as a group should be taken to contain an implicit quantifier over groups. Put concisely, joint acting as a group = joint acting as a we-mode group = (Eg)(A and B act jointly as a group relative to we-mode group g).[34]

An additional argument for group-relativity, indeed relativity to an intensionally understood group, is given by Schmitt. Considering Gilbert's example of the library committee and the food committee that happen to have the same members, Schmitt discusses the possibility that the library committee makes a certain recommendation but the food committee makes the opposite one.[35] Here we have a case of a joint action X relative to a certain group g_L but also the opposite joint action–X relative to another group g_F. The central point here again is that all joint action is group-relative and relative to how groups are described or characterized.

So far, the criticisms that Schmitt has presented against individualism have had no bite against my account—basically because it is not individualistic in the relevant sense. Distinguishing between conceptual and ontological issues (which Schmitt does not do satisfactorily; see above), I can say that my theory is conceptually rather anti-individualistic, even if ontologically it is, if not individualistic, at least interrelationistic and eschews collective agents and actions in a literal ontological sense.

Schmitt proceeds to present Bratman's aforementioned account of joint action as follows.[36]

> Our J-ing is a joint action of A and B only if
> (a) we J;
> (b) A intends that we J, and B intends that we J;
> (c) we J because A intends that we J and B intends that we J.

Schmitt criticizes this theory on two counts. First, it faces a problem of circularity, in that the joint action type J occurs both in the *analysandum* and in the *analysans*. For an individualist, this is bad news, as he strives for a reductive analysis. So Bratman's move, according to Schmitt, is to restrict J to action types that do not entail joint actions. Schmitt doubts that Bratman's theory has a nonquestion-begging answer to the circularity problem at hand. I will not here go into detail, as I have already commented on Bratman in chapters 3 and 4 and above and have responded to the circularity claim in the case of my own theory.[37]

The second point against Bratman is that his notion of intention as exemplified by clause (b) does not satisfy the settle condition. This is the condition that says that an individual should be able to fully settle what his intentions are, but Bratmanian intentions that we J depend on other agents' intentions. However, the settle condition simply need not be accepted (recall the appendix to chapter 4). Thus a joint intention, hence a we-intention, is something that depends on others. Suppose that two agents jointly decide to move a sofa jointly and thus form a joint intention. Their joint intention will settle what they are to do jointly. This is enough, because the joint intention then leads to the agents' moving the sofa jointly (or at least trying to). We may speak of the joint settle condition here.[38]

As to Margaret Gilbert's account of joint action, in her recent article she proposes the following general schema for all psychological predicates, and I will here understand action predicates to be psychological:

> Gilbert's Schema S: For the relevant psychological predicate "X" and persons P1 and P2, P1 or P2 may truly say "We X" with respect to P1 and P2 if and only if P1 and P2 are *jointly committed* to X-ing *as a body*.[39]

Applied to action, this gives as the only condition for joint acting (expressed by "We X") that the participants P1 and P2 be jointly committed to acting, that is, X-ing, as a body. However, even if we would understand what being jointly committed as a body is, we must make sure that the persons indeed act, do their parts. For Gilbert, joint commitment entails being obligated to act and having the right toward the other person's acting. But it seems that there can be such normative joint commitment without any action.

However, Gilbert does require individual action. This is what she says in another context when specifically discussing acting together:[40]

> Two or more people are acting together if they are jointly committed to espousing as a body a certain goal, and each one is acting in a way appropriate to the achievement of that goal, where each one is doing this in light of the fact that he or she is subject to a joint commitment to espouse the goal in question as a body.

We learn from this that the participants in an activity indeed must concretely participate in the activity in question. Let me, accordingly, give the following account—that also gives a necessary condition—for an action predicate allowing for two or more persons to participate:

> Schema S for joint action: For the relevant psychological action predicate "X" and persons P1 and P2, P1 or P2 may truly say "We X" with respect to P1 and P2 if and only if P1 and P2 are jointly committed to X-ing as a body and in light of this joint commitment participate in the action X.

This analysis I take to be a candidate for explicating (intentional) joint action based on an (explicit or implicit) obligation. However, the participation must be not only intentional but jointly intentional, and my requirement for achieving this has been joint intention. This feature at least is not explicit in Gilbert's account. It should be said that joint commitment as a body and participating in light of it entail joint intention and hence P1's and P2's intention to participate. I conclude that, with the central qualification just made, Gilbert's account may work for obligation-based joint action (the first kind of joint action in my earlier classification). However, the account does not seem to apply to weaker cases of joint action as a group. For instance, joint action involving only joint intention and mutual belief would be a case in point. To be sure, joint intention (at least according to my account) entails joint commitment to action, but the commitment in question is intention-dependent and nonintrinsic. The obligation in this kind of case is group-social (recall chapter 1). Gilbert's obligations seem to be something stronger.

Let me finally proceed to Schmitt's own account. Let j be a joint action (token) of a type J. Schmitt gives the following necessary conditions for joint action.[41]

> An action j is a joint action only if
> (1) there is an agent C who performs j from C's intention of performing j, and
> (2) C is not an individual.

I assume that this analysis is meant to elucidate *intentional* joint action, although it does not say so. But if it were to account also for the nonintentional performance of j (e.g., agent C makes a mistake), clause (1) would be false, for j could not have been performed from C's intention of performing j. Assuming that Schmitt is analyzing an intentional joint action, I have two critical points to make, the first being a mild criticism and the second a rather damaging one:

(i) I gather from the accompanying text that C is meant to be a nonindividual of the supraindividual agent type (although it presumably is meant to be an *individual* supraindividual agent rather than, for example, a type of agent). There is the odd—but perhaps merely linguistic—point that a supraindividual agent can perform a *joint* action. The standard idea, of course, is that only two or more agents can perform a joint action and that one agent cannot perform a joint action. But I regard the use of "joint" here merely as a misnomer.

(ii) As Schmitt himself argues, the conjunction (1) & (2) cannot be satisfied—for a metaphysical reason: there are no supraindividual agents, according to him. The conclusion is that there are no joint actions. So one may now consider two cases: In the first case, a table is carried to the other room by one person. This is a single-agent action, which is as real as actions can be. In the second case the table is carried, instead, by two persons acting jointly (in the preanalytic sense). Here, according to Schmitt, no joint action takes place. It is not clear to me what is taking place in this situation, according to Schmitt's theory. Are there two persons acting and both carrying the table (without carrying it jointly) or what? It is obvious that Schmitt's account is absurd, as a joint action can be—and here is—as real as a singular action.

Point (ii) accordingly is a strong critical point and I take it to suffice for the rejection of Schmitt's theory without further ado.

7 Summary

In this chapter I have presented a philosophical account of joint action, trying to answer the question "What is a joint action?" Here joint action is understood to be joint action *as a group*. The treatment has mainly concerned conceptual issues, but some ontological questions were also addressed.

An intentional we-mode joint action is basically joint action performed because of a joint intention together with relevant beliefs that guaranteed that the joint action opportunities are present. The final account (AT*) of joint action (section 3) makes this precise. Its focus is on jointly intentional joint action, but the notion of joint action itself is relied on this analysis. However, the general idea of acting jointly was also clarified. Account (AT*) strongly relies on what was said in chapter 4 about joint intention. In all, this makes all jointly intentional joint action cooperative (see chapter 7). Account (AT*) was also tested—at least to some extent—by considering some current accounts of joint action in the market and especially the critical points directed against them in the recent article by Schmitt. The result of this test is that my account is, or at least seems, tenable.

This chapter has also discussed weaker forms of joint action. First, an account—(AT#)—of *mere interpersonal joint action* or, in my technical terminology, *I-mode joint action* was presented. This kind of joint action is based on I-mode shared intention. Second, it was shown that when a group intentionally performs an action, not all the group members need to be performing active parts but can rather be in reserve and need not even have the relevant we-intention. Third, one can also speak of joint action, or rather collective action, in cases where the participants share a we-attitude for which they all act. There need be no shared or joint intention involved in those cases.

6

GROUP ACTION AND GROUP ATTITUDES

1 Collective Acceptance

In this chapter the main topic is to give an account of group attitudes and of having an attitude as a group member. My approach assumes that groups are not literally agents or persons but that anyhow they can be regarded as persons, in accordance with how common sense normally treats groups. Treating groups as persons instrumentally works in our daily lives. Within this account one can say that groups really want, intend, believe, and act, but that this amounts to the relevant group members' respectively wanting, intending, believing, and acting in certain ways as group members. To simplify slightly, it can be said, accordingly, that a group ontologically consists of its members functioning as group members with collective commitment to its ethos.

In the account below, the group level will be analyzed basically in terms of the jointness level, in terms of collective acceptance. In chapter 4, I presented the Bulletin Board View (BBV) of collective and joint acceptance. In the present chapter I will still discuss some more technical, logical aspects of this view. The chapter starts with a discussion of group acceptance and collective acceptance (section 1). After that, group action (section 2), group beliefs (section 3), and group attitudes in general (section 4) will be analyzed in terms of collective accep-tance, as elucidated in section 1. There is also an appendix on the ontology of groups.

The notion of a group member's having an attitude will be accounted for largely on the basis of chapters 1 and 2 (section 5), where the notions of acting as a group member and the we-mode were elucidated. It will be seen that, parallel to my treatment of we-intentions, also my account of group attitudes will involve circularity problems. I will comment on them below.

We recall from chapter 1 that the members of a we-mode group collectively accept that they form a group. They view themselves as a group with a certain ethos; minimally there is a mutual belief to the effect that they form a group.

Typically such groups have names or descriptions (e.g., "Black Panthers," "Texaco") and are thus symbolically marked. The members of a we-mode group ought to be collectively committed to its ethos (for them: "our ethos"), and a substantial number of members actually are assumed to have collectively committed themselves to it. In contrast, in I-mode groups, the members are privately committed to a common ethos. Here the ethos is just a privately shared content, such as some villagers gathering to play football in the field on Sunday mornings. Collective acceptance and construction play no role in the case of I-mode groups, in contrast to we-mode groups.

Let me now move on to discuss, partly in linguistic terms, what a we-mode group's acceptance of propositional contents involves. The formulations concern simple unstructured groups in which the group's acceptance amounts to its members' collective or joint acceptance of the content. My discussion is based on some ideas about acceptance in the single-agent case and will concentrate on acceptance as voluntary or as involving a voluntary element. The discussion will complement the account of conceptual presuppositions of collective acceptance in terms of the BBV of chapter 4. The account to be given will be made use of later in this chapter and in chapter 8.

Let us start with the following acceptance statement.

(1) A accepts content p.

Here p can be a descriptive proposition, for example, "Grass is green," an intention expression such as "I will do X," or a normative proposition, for example, "Everyone ought to do X in C." Given a Tarskian view of truth, (1) is equivalent to

(1′) A accepts that p is true,

where p is used autonomously (as mostly below) and where the truth predicate "true" means either correspondence truth or correct assertability, depending on the case (see below). (1) can also be paraphrased as or at least taken to entail

(2) p is premisible for A.

Statement (2) is here taken to involve that A may in a materially sound sense involving truth (or correct assertability) use p as a premise in her theoretical and practical reasoning and to act on the entailed truth (or correct assertability) of p.[1]

Statements (1) and (2) thus support

(3) A may use p as a premise in her (theoretical and practical) reasoning and act "in the right way" in relation to p.

Yet another central paraphrase for (1) goes in terms of voluntary commitment (binding oneself):

(4) A is committed "in the right way" to p (to its truth or correct assertability).

If A has accepted a nonindexical proposition p, then if asked whether p or –p is true or correct she will normally answer that p is correct. If A wants to get some cool juice and believes that the juice is in the fridge, she, acting on her belief, will go to the fridge (the "right" way to act). The notion of commitment in (4) is topic neutral as such, but the required right way of being committed gives specific action content to it. I propose that the "right" way be accountable in terms of the notion of the direction of fit of semantic satisfaction.[2] The two basic directions of fit that a mental attitude or a speech act can have are the world-to-mind (briefly, wm) direction of fit (df, for short) and the mind-to-world (briefly, mw) direction of fit. There is also the possibility of having both directions of fit or the null direction of fit. Intentions have the wmdf, while beliefs typically, except in the case of constitutive beliefs (see chapter 8), have the mwdf. The basic element in A's understanding the use of language is that she understands the directions of fit that different attitudes have. She is assumed to be able to classify the content in the right way, involving the right direction of fit.[3]

If p is a content having mwdf, then its truth depends on whether it fits the world. Thus, if A is to have a true representation of the world in this case, she must accept a proposition (content) p that fits the world (rather than make the world fit a given proposition p, which would be the case if p would have wmdf). Having accepted p as true, A will be committed to using p (and therefore in general be disposed to use p) in her theoretical and practical reasoning when the need arises. (This is analogous to the requirement in speech act theory that the speaker be committed to the content of the act, for example, to what she asserts.) For instance, if A believes that it will soon rain, she may reason that she should carry her umbrella with her. Being committed to the truth of the premise, she will act on it when needed. Next, supposing that p is a content having wmdf, then, if A accepts p, making p true requires some agent's (in the case of intention, A's) relevantly seeing to it that the world fits her mind.

Given the two elements of an agent's acceptance as true or correct of a content and his understanding what its df is, we can account for group acceptance and collective acceptance. Let us assume that an action conceptually is grounded in intentions and beliefs and that also in the case of a group (viewed as an "as-if agent") intentions and beliefs are the two central grounds of action. Intentions (and other proattitudes) have the wmdf and beliefs the mwdf. Thus the direction of fit of the collective acceptance of contents that can directly connect to action is either wm or mw (and thus at least typically belongs to the proattitude family or the belief family, broadly understood). As to groups, both their intentions and beliefs can be taken to involve commitment to the respective contents. Such commitments involve the commitment to see to it that the accepted content is premisible. Accordingly, my counterpart notion for intention will be commitment to a content involving wmdf, and that for belief (namely, "belief as a group") will be commitment involving mwdf, and in addition both cases involve the commitment to seeing to it that the intention-expressing proposition and the belief-expressing proposition are premisible—under the present evidential circumstances. Suppose the group believes that the earth is flat. Then there is a commitment to the premisibility of the content, but as the belief content is a natural one and one that it is not up to the group to make true, additional evidence may require it to change its view. Thus the belief has the mwdf. Only in the case of purely institutional attitude contents does the group have the power to construct their truth or satisfaction (such as in the case of the belief that squirrel pelt is money, to be discussed in chapter 8), and here the attitude has the wmdf with respect to that content.

My idea is to analyze a group g's collective acceptance (as a group) of a content p (in symbols, CA(g, p)) in terms of its commitment, of its having bound itself, to see to it or to act on it that the content p is premisible in group contexts with the right attitude-dependent df. The content p could be, for example, "We will perform X jointly," "Grass is green," or "Squirrel pelt is money." Here g's acceptance of p (namely, CA(g, p)) is acceptance of p for the group; thus it is the "group-perspectival" truth of p that is involved ("g takes p to be true or correct"). The group is assumed to be an unstructured ("egalitarian") we-mode group and thus treatable as an agent and capable of action. The following theses can now be proposed for group acceptance, in terms of intentional "seeing to it that" (*stit*) action.

> (i) Group g qua a group accepts p as correctly premisible (assertable) for g if and only if g is committed to seeing to it that p is premisible for g with the right direction of fit of semantic satisfiability, given that g knows what the direction of fit of p is.[4]

The group's intending or believing amounts to the group members' jointly intending and believing, joint intention and belief here being collectively accepted. The joint intention and belief satisfy the Collectivity Condition and are thus in the we-mode (see the equivalence argument in chapter 8).[5]

I propose the following member-level sharpening of (i) for the case of unstructured, egalitarian groups—the basic intuitive case.[6]

> (ii) Group g qua a group accepts p as correctly premisible for g if and only if the members of g qua members come to share a joint attitude (with content p) that has wmdf (in the intention family of attitudes) or mwdf (in the belief family), and where the having of the joint attitude entails the satisfaction of the relevant Collectivity Condition, the members being collectively committed to seeing to it that p is premisible, in conditions of shared we-knowledge of what the df of p is.[7]

The central aspect of the joint attitude (the "acceptance state") that matters in this context is its direction of fit rather than its being of a certain specific mental kind: The members of g are assumed to be collectively committed to seeing to it in the right way (namely, in terms of action obeying the direction of fit associated with p on that occasion) that p is premisible, given the mutual understanding and knowledge about p and its direction of fit here.[8]

The strongest case of collective acceptance is based on the group members' making an agreement to the effect that a certain content having a certain df will be accepted (and thus regarded as premisible and, equivalently, as correctly assertable) in the group and that it consequently is accepted by more or less all members (or, in the case of normatively structured groups, by more or less all operative members). Truth or correct assertability will, in this context, again be group-relative or "group-perspectival." In the case of structured groups, we cannot strictly require that all the members participate in the collective acceptance. If, for example, the United States accepts that invading Iraq is necessary, this is compatible with many U.S. citizens having no knowledge of this view or a great many opposing this view. Still, a case can be made for the requirement that they ought to accept it as group requirement (recall chapter 1 and see below). When acceptance is viewed as an action, group acceptance can accordingly be analyzed in terms of the account (IGA) to be presented in section 2.

To recapitulate, collective acceptance may take various forms extending from an established, rule-based system to reach formal agreement at the one extreme to a rather unstructured buildup of shared we-belief or we-intention at the other. What is common to all these forms is that the participants in a performative sense come to hold a relevant we-mode we-attitude—one with wmdf or mwdf.[9]

2 Group Action

This section will give an account of actions performed by groups in terms of collective or joint acceptance, and the next section will do the same for group beliefs.

The basic account (AT*) of we-mode joint action, namely, joint action as a group, given in chapter 5 concerned we-mode joint action in cases where the participants all acted for the group without special representatives acting for them. In such a case we can say, for example, that you and I perform an action together in the we-mode if and only if the dyad consisting of you and me performs this action as a group. However, in cases of normatively structured groups performing actions, the situation is more complex. Before considering that kind of case I will comment on the underlying presuppositions.

To make a point about the difference between the I-mode and the we-mode, in the we-mode case there is a "we" that acts as an agent (as a group, unit) and makes choices. Thus in the case of two individuals A and B, assuming that WE(A, B) (i.e., that A and B satisfy the "togetherness-we" predicate "WE" and thus form a we-group) it is only the we-group here that makes autonomous choices and acts. A and B act as group members and are in principle bound to what the group has decided (e.g., what they have come to jointly intend to do). In contrast, in the I-mode case, the group members make autonomous choices as private persons. Thus both A and B make choices, and when their choices and actions are suitably coordinated, they can be said to act together in the I-mode sense. But in the we-mode case there is, as it were, only the group agent that makes choices. However, there is not literally a group agent or person present, but we can still instrumentally speak in the mentioned as-if way. The group agent is accordingly taken to intend and therefore to be committed to some action, which amounts to the individuals A and B acting together as group members and, as it were, making a single choice (i.e., their dependent choices are viewed jointly as making up the group's independent choice). Their space of choice alternatives is the group agent's space of alternatives, which they can perform as a group by each performing a part of it, these parts being suitably correlated. However, in the individual or I-mode case, the space of choice consists of those alternatives that the individuals have, and the group action is built out of these individual actions (choices). In the we-mode case, the members A and B act together as a group, as one agent. A and B literally form a "we" and a group (a we-group) but not a group agent or person. But we can still say that A and B think and act as one agent (person) here and that the group gives them their central reason for performing their parts.

Let us now consider in more detail a situation in which a group acts as a group and in effect is a we-mode group (recall chapter 1). Examples of such group action are: a sports team's scoring a goal, a business company's selling a house, and a scientific association's organizing a lecture. We can describe the matter at the level of the group members. When a group forms an intention or a belief (etc.) and acts as a group, the intuitive requirement is that everyone in the group functions appropriately—for example, participates in the intention forming and acting. This *consensus* intuition also applies to the action of collective acceptance. However, in some cases, the intuitive authority that a group member has for action and formation of attitudes is, possibly on practical grounds, transferred to other members or persons. Accordingly, there are then some authorized "operative" members who act for the group on the basis of their shared we-intention and produce the right outcome or activity required for the attributability of the action to the group. These operatives either are authorized to act for the group by the other group members or have obtained their authority from some group-external source.[10] My formulations and analyses below only cover the case of internal authorization—and accordingly the case of externally and internally free groups, especially democratic ones. The authority system for decision-making in the group thus basically consists of the operative members who have been suitably authorized to decide and/or act for the group and/or to give orders and directives for others. The nonoperatives have delegated their "natural" authority concerning some topics to the operatives, who thus represent all group members—possibly in responsive interaction with them.

The operative-nonoperative distinction may be task-relative. For instance, a member (or type of member, a position) may be an operative for action (e.g., building a bridge) while subject to obeying orders for another operative. The authority system (all the operative-nonoperative distinctions for various tasks) can be hierarchical in a multi-layered sense (organizations that involve groups as their elements), but it suffices here to present the main ideas for the two-layered case. The authority system can be codified and might thus consist just of a voting procedure or of the rule to act as in the past, and in such cases no specially authorized persons are needed.[11] Still, the directives and orders that the system yields can be authoritative.

A short digression into the problems of authority is now in place, because authority and authorization are central for my account of group reasons, group action, group belief, and indeed actively accepted attitudes generally. According to my "positional" account, there is in a structured group a division of the members into operative members and nonoperative members for attitude formation, where the operatives are assumed to be (internally) authorized for the type of task in question. The nonoperatives only tacitly accept or at least (*pro tanto*) ought to accept what (e.g., what intentions or views) the operative members have jointly accepted for the group. This "ought" may be only a weak group-social obligation related to authorization of operatives and the group's functioning as a unit when it has the attitude in question. (Put simplistically, if I have authorized you to make decisions in our dyad, I am obligated at least in this sense to accept what you decide for us.)

What does the meant kind of group-social authority of the operative members consist in? Joseph Raz has given an account that I find largely plausible.[12] On Raz's view, the essence of authority is what he calls "preemption." An authoritative directive is preemptive in the sense that it excludes and replaces the agent's own judgment about what is to be done in the case in question. The operative members of the group give directives on which the group members are supposed to act. Thereby they intend that the group members qua group members perform something X for the preemptive reason (fact) that the operatives have issued the directive for them to perform X. Such a directive has *de facto authority* in the group when most—or a substantial number of—the group members indeed regard the directives issued by the operatives as preemptive reasons for action. A simple case is one where all the members are operative and where they form an intention for the group to do X. This amounts to their joint intention to do X (or at least something that generates X), and the fact of the existence of this joint intention serves as the group members' shared group reason for intending to perform their parts of X and for carrying out this intention. When the members regard the existence of the joint intention as a preemptive reason, this we-mode joint intention (and, equivalently, the group's intention) is an *authoritative group reason* for them. (Recall the point in section 5 of chapter 1 according to which an intention entails a normative requirement. It can be understood to be a preemptive reason as such—but see below.)

However, the requirement that reasons be preemptive in the case of the nonoperatives seems unrealistic in general, and accordingly I allow combining (authoritative) we-mode (namely, group) reasons and I-mode reasons at least in some cases, for example, cases that are not central to the group's constitutive ideas—see section 4 of chapter 7. This is compatible with the operatives intending the reasons to be preemptive. In general, group reasons may be normative requirements—e.g. in cases where the ethos presents the group members with an either all-things-considered ought-to-do norm or a *pro tanto* ought-to-do norm that on the occasion in question has no acceptable exceptions. But the members might not take them always as preemptive reasons but rather as *pro tanto* reasons (think of norm conflicts and conflicts with private reasons), and when not, they in many cases (especially if they take private reasons into account) cannot be acting fully as group members. However, these cases are constantly encountered in real life and we must be prepared to live with them.

A joint intention—as a jointness-level counterpart of a group reason—can be a reason both for the members' joint action and for their performing their parts of it. To show this, consider the example of some agents forming the joint intention to paint a house together. Then the preformed joint intention will collectively serve as their reason (at least in the sense of normative requirement) for their painting the house together, and it also serves as each participant's reason for his performing his part of the joint action. Notice that the joint case is different from the singular case, where an intention cannot (at least in many cases) be a reason for the action that the intention is about. This is because one can rather arbitrarily form an intention and act on it. Such bootstrapping need not be involved in the case of a joint intention.[13] First, there may be a prior group intention or belief that is a group reason for each group member acting as a group member to think and act according to it, and no bootstrapping gets involved. But when the group member concurrently participates in the very formation of the group intention or belief— for example, by agreeing with the others that they are to do something together or accept a view for the group—there is a kind of bootstrapping involved. However, we are here dealing with a jointness phenomenon that is centrally involved in the group's acceptance and, on the group-member level, in the collective acceptance. No single member can of course create this jointness, nor in general can mere aggregation do it. Thus, the jointness is in general nonaggregative and emergent ("creative") relative to the member's I-mode attitudes (or his "proposed" we-mode attitude input). Let me add that if the participants have an underlying joint want, then that want (or its content, rather) may sometimes serve as a deeper joint reason than does the joint intention formed on its basis. But think of cases involving negotiations and bargaining between the participants that finally lead to a joint intention that is a compromise and is against some participants' underlying wants (at least first choices). Here the jointness of the intention indeed is creative and can serve as the meant kind of group reason (and the we-mode proattitude that it involves can serve as a distant motivational reason). Once the group attitude is in existence, the group members, when functioning qua group members, can, and ought to, use it as their reason for thinking and acting. It follows that no harmful bootstrapping needs to be involved. (Recall also the comments on bootstrapping in section 3 of chapter 4.)

De facto authority can be regarded as *legitimate* when the directives constitute justified preemptive reasons for the group members' action. Such justified reasons can, according to my account, be analyzed in terms of for-groupness: they ought to promote the group's ethos. Thus, the group members' we-mode reasons, namely, the group reasons on which they function, are intersubjectively and group-relatively justified in the case at hand. In democratic groups, the authorities (operatives) have been internally authorized by the group members, and on pain of inconsistency the nonoperatives should then regard the operatives' directives as justified.

As emphasized, in this book, functioning on the basis of we-mode group reasons plays a central role. The talk about such group reasons, of course, means in this terminology that the group is regarded as an authority in the defined sense, and this ontologically boils down to the relevant operatives—acting as group members in their positions—having that authority (recall here especially section 5 of chapter 4).

All the above stress on we-mode group reasons still leaves it as a possibility that there are *pro tanto* I-mode reasons (possibly private group reasons) that are sufficient for functionally (e.g., in terms of maximization of utility) overriding the we-mode group reasons on an occasion. But when indeed the we-mode reason is a preemptive reason, it is exclusionary, and this suffices even in such cases to exclude I-mode reasons. It might not be preemptive, though, especially in cases that have no direct bearing on the group's ethos (although such cases still may be within the limits of authorization). Then, even when justified, a reason might fail to be a de facto reason—for example, if a member does not understand the force of justification or is otherwise mistaken or just wants to oppose the operatives. Of course, in normal internally authorized cases, the operative members have the legitimate authority and right to rule (concerning a specified set of topics) that entails a correlated obligation to obey.[14] There is then appropriate justification for the nonoperative members to take the operative members' decisions (directives, orders, etc.) as "desire-independent" preemptive reasons for action, although they might not do it and fail to act as full group members. It cannot perhaps always be realistically required that the operative members have more than de facto authority in the case of a we-mode group, which nevertheless must be required for the group to be able to function as a group (this allows for some dissidents, sometimes even morally justified ones).

To concentrate on group action, the operative members have de facto authority simply if the members are disposed to obey what the operative members choose as the group's plan for action. At least in the case of internal authorization (which is my sole concern here) the *nonoperative* members are *pro tanto* (or prima facie) obligated to at least tacitly accept what the operatives do within the limits of the authorization. This is because of the fact that they have authorized the operatives. Had the nonoperatives not so authorized anybody, they would still be obligated to do their share of what they have jointly intended to achieve; here, due to authorization, their share is more passive. Accordingly, a central argument for the obligation in question is that when a group intentionally acts, it must intend to act, and when it intends to act, it is in a group-social sense normatively required to perform the action in question, given its intention to act (recall the discussion in section 5 of chapter 1). Thus, at the level of group members, both operative and nonoperative members are group-socially normatively (although perhaps not in the sense of *proper* normativity as set out in chapter 1) required to participate in a relevant way. This argument in fact applies to all cases where the group intentionally accepts something, for example, an intention or a view, for itself. (Thus it applies also to our later general account (GATT) in section 4.)

Here is my detailed account of full-blown intentional group action, to be clarified afterward:[15]

> (IGA) A group g *brought about an action or state* X *intentionally* (or, alternatively, saw to it that X was the case) as a group in the social and normative circumstances C if and only if in C there were specific operative agents $A_1, \ldots, A_m$ of g such that
>
> (1) $A_1, \ldots, A_m$, when acting qua group members in the we-mode sense (and accordingly performing their positional tasks due to their exercising the relevant decision making system of g), intentionally together brought about X (i.e., there was an action Y such that the operative agents intentionally together brought about Y in the sense of (AT*) and this performance of Y generated X, and was correctly believed and purported by the operative members to generate X), or, respectively, these operative agents saw to it that X;
>
> (2) because of (1), the (full-fledged and adequately informed) nonoperative members of g, as members of g, tacitly accepted the operative agents' intentional bringing about (or seeing to it that) Y—or at least ought to have accepted it;

(3) there was a mutual belief in g to the effect that there was at least a chance that
(1) and to the effect that (2).

For simplicity's sake, this analytic formulation assumes that there are no dissidents, at least not among operatives (but see chapter 10). Clause (3) is a rationality condition that the very concept of group action does not require to hold true.

What we have here is we-mode joint action in a broader sense than the
symmetric, egalitarian case. The group has a power structure that, furthermore,
can be iterated to create hierarchical layers of operatives (e.g. in the case of an
organization such as a business company). The members of the group can be taken
to act jointly on the basis of the operatives acting and the others suitably
complying. Only the operatives need to have an actual we-intention, hence
joint intention, in a strict sense. They are assumed to have collectively accepted
the intention expression "We will do X" for the group. They act jointly as a group
(or as one agent) on the basis of the joint intention in question that amounts to
the group's intention to bring about Y.

The BBV applies to the joint action in clause (1), and the classifications of
the various circumstances in which group action can occur also apply here.
Account (*IGA*) corresponds to the first category of cases in section 2 of chapter 4,
the strongest case. I will not here explicitly discuss the weaker cases. A reason
for the sentence in the parentheses in (1) is provided by examples such as a state's
declaring war (X). The relevant operative members collectively performed an
action Y (the cabinet members did something, and the president, too, did his part,
as the law prescribes) that generated it.

In (2) we can also speak of the nonoperatives being obligated to endorse what
the operative members are doing for them. Clause (2) can be required because,
first, the nonoperatives have already authorized the operatives to decide and act
for them; thus, to be consistent, they should also accept the result of the action.
While the nonoperatives need not have the full we-intention to *stit* X, they—if
obedient—can still be understood to have a more generally and vaguely described
we-intention; for example, "There is a joint end that we in this country are
pursuing or ought to be pursuing, and that is why we should pay our taxes." So
they ought to have a participatory intention that is a we-intention, at least in the
above loose sense (with existential quantification). If they are aware of what
exactly the operatives' joint intention (shared we-intention) is, a joint intention
expression of the form "We will *stit* X" will apply to them.[16] However, they are not
required to have the we-intention and the intention to perform their part of the
joint action—for instance, the nonoperatives might be in reserve for being
operatives and thus only have the general disposition to we-intend.

In this context, the group is assumed to act as a group; in addition, on
functional grounds, this requires that the nonoperatives endorse what the operatives do. To see what this involves, we consider a simplified societal case with a
state involved. We actually need several layers of operative members and groups
consisting of them. In any case, we have the parliament making laws and the
cabinet executing them via the various ministries. The police and the army are
enforcing agents controlling and monitoring the group members in accordance

with the judicial system of the country. The state employees are hired rather than elected members, but they might still be operatives acting for and representing the group. Ordinary citizens, who in a democratic society have authorized the mentioned operatives to act for them, are pursuing their private business. But while doing it, they also participate in the public promotion of the ethos, E: They ought to respect the laws and standards that the operatives have made for them. In the grand societal collective action amounting to the group's (society's, state's) seeing to it that E, their share is to intentionally stop at red light, make their children go to school, pay taxes, and so on. They thus ought to have the intention to participate in the grand action, but not necessarily under the description of "I intend to participate in our seeing to it that E" but perhaps rather "I intend to stop at red light," and so on. The degree of reflection can vary (in some cases there may only be an unreflected intention-in-action in a routine action, and then the intention and the beliefs related to it form only a "presuppositional" reason), but many will be acting in the we-mode. While clause (2) can still be satisfied without the nonoperatives having the we-intention, the operatives (at least collectively) must have it. Thus, for example, the legislators must know what they are doing: passing laws for promoting the ethos of the country.

To summarize, this view is the "positional," authority-based account of group action, positionality referring basically to we-mode action as a group member (see below and section 4 for remarks). It concerns all groups in principle, thus also groups that have no prior normative structure (positions, task-right system) before the possible introduction of specially authorized operatives. The task of the (internally or externally) authorized operative members is to create group-binding, indeed normatively and publicly binding decisions (intentions, plans, etc.) and/or to act for the group in light of their collective acceptance. The authorized members (leaders) may have the authority to issue directives and orders for the nonoperatives concerning the group action in question (e.g., the division of tasks). They are assumed to act as members of the group in the standard sense, being group-socially normatively collectively committed to what they accept for the group. Thus, what they do is in the we-mode, and indeed one can say that positional thinking and acting in the last analysis is thinking and acting in the we-mode.

3 Group Belief

A group can be said to believe that snakes are dangerous. This may just be a shared I-mode belief that snakes are dangerous (recall chapter 3). Below I will rather concentrate on we-mode group beliefs and among them especially on normatively group-binding ones (where the normativity is the based on agreements), but I will also make some remarks on the other cases that the BBV of chapter 4 covers. In other words, I will apply my positional collective acceptance account in terms of the BBV to the case of group beliefs.

The positional account of group beliefs is concerned with normatively group-binding group beliefs and concentrates on structured groups with positions, viewing positional activities in the broadest sense as just appropriate we-mode activities.[17] As in the case of group action, we often have to deal with a distinction between operative and nonoperative members, the operatives being suitably authorized to form views, although again here there is the consensus intuition that ideally all group members qua group members would have to directly take part in belief formation.[18] For instance, the group members may accept as their group belief that capitalism is the best economic system, that stars determine their fate, or that they ought to help poor people and be collectively committed to the belief in question.

With the operative-nonoperative division in place, a group can be taken to believe ("acceptance believe") something p if it accepts p as its view, and this is based on the operative members' collective acceptance (in terms of agreement making or other obligating acceptance) of p for the group. The collective acceptance in this account is thick, group-obligation-involving collective acceptance of a view for the group. This is basically because the operative members have been authorized to collectively accept—typically by agreements—normatively binding views and goals for the group. In the positional model of group attitudes, the authorized operative members have a special status of having political power concerning some shared group affairs.[19] The nonoperative members of the group must tacitly accept, or at least put up with, what the operative members accept as the group's views. They need not even have detailed knowledge about what is so being accepted. But they are still collectively committed to the accepted items in cases where they have authorized the operative members to form views for the group, or at least they ought to be so committed.

More precisely, the positional account of normatively group-binding group beliefs can be summarized as follows.[20]

(GB) Group g *believes that p as a group in the normative, group-binding sense* in the social and normative circumstances C if and only if in C there are operative members $A_1, \ldots, A_m$ of g such that
(1) the agents $A_1, \ldots, A_m$, when acting as group members in the we-mode sense (and accordingly performing their positional tasks and due to their exercising the relevant decision-making system of g) intentionally jointly accept p, as a group, for g as the group's view and because of this exercise of the authority system (joint decision making system) they ought to continue to accept and positionally believe it (i.e., accept it in the we-mode);[21]
(2) there is mutual belief (possibly only I-mode belief) among the operative members $A_1, \ldots, A_m$ to the effect that (1);
(3) because of (1), the (full-fledged and adequately informed) nonoperative members of g tend to tacitly accept—or at least ought to accept—p, as members of g;
(4) there is mutual belief in g to the effect that (3).[22]

As in the similar analysis of group action, the mutual belief requirements (2) and (4) are rationality conditions that the concept of group belief as such does not require.

Let me further elucidate the positional account by making some central points:

(i) There appears to be some circularity in the group belief as it comes to depend on the group's view (when taken to amount to belief), according to clause (1). I will defer my discussion of this problem until section 4.

(ii) Group beliefs (in the sense of expressing what groups as groups believe) are, or involve, acceptances.[23] The acceptance element involved is simply expressed by "We believe that p" entailing that the content p is accepted by the group. At least all operative members must in accordance with (GB) at least implicitly accept the content p, and, at least on reflection, they must be disposed to make the judgment "We believe that p." Acceptance of p in this sense is crucial for the group belief that p. It is not needed in the case of individual belief. Suppose I am standing in front of an old oak tree and perceptually acquire the belief that over there is an old oak tree. This need not be accepted by me in any nontrivial sense (namely, in a sense going beyond plain belief attribution). However, if you and I are both standing in front of the oak tree, for our dyad to believe that there is an oak tree over there, we must accept or be disposed, on reflection, to accept that belief content for our dyad. There is thus more cognitive content in the case of the group belief, and this extra cognitive content requires that we conceptualize the situation in the we-mode. It is not only that I believe so and believe that you believe similarly, and similarly for you. These I-mode beliefs just lead to shared we-beliefs and need not involve acceptances. The we-mode conceptualization accordingly requires that we must accept or at least be disposed to accept that we as a group believe that there is an oak tree and understand that this content has the mind-to-world direction of fit. In addition, to guarantee group unity in this matter, we must be collectively committed (at least momentarily) in the right way to the content.[24]

(iii) This kind of normative group belief is institutionalized and thus institutional in a broad sense, because it is based on a group's creation of something normative for the group. For it to be fully institutional in a strict sense, it must be required of the group belief that it be relatively stable and backed by the members' relevant social practices.[25] Those social practices include making relevant use of the belief in inferences and acting on the truth of the belief. Generally speaking, among institutional beliefs are included we-mode we-beliefs and in typical cases normatively binding group beliefs. We have here a strong, constitutive connection between institutions (institutionality) and we-mode notions. (See chapter 8 for further discussion and (iv) below for two kinds of institutional beliefs.)

(iv) Here is a point about group knowledge, namely, justified true group belief. Suppose g believes that p in the normative, group-binding sense and p is a true or correctly assertable proposition; then we can speak of group-binding "quasi knowledge"—which still may lack warrant. When it is up to the group-external world to determine whether p is true (the case with the mind-to-world direction of fit), we are dealing with knowledge in a sense different from the case in which it is up to the group to determine what is correct or true. For instance, if p = "The earth is flat," we are dealing with a case where it is not up to the group to determine the truth of the belief, although they may dogmatically try to stick to it. In contrast, if p = "Squirrel pelt is money" and if the group is Finns in the thirteenth century, we have knowledge, namely, constitutive, purely institutional knowledge, which in contrast is collectively self-made and self-validating and has the world-to-mind direction of fit—the latter because the group has itself created a piece of reality that is completely up to it to create and uphold (see chapter 8).

(v) As in chapter 2, I wish to emphasize that totally new things may emerge especially in this kind of a group context. For instance, there will be we-mode beliefs, which, first, are acceptances, and second, may involve group standards and norms deriving from the group's basic goals and interests (think of a group's belief that a supernatural god exists or that the earth is flat). Thus new kinds of beliefs (acceptances) arise and give the group members qua group members emergent new ways of "seeing the world" and may in a sense bring new social things into existence (see chapter 8). There will also be compromise beliefs (with compromised contents) that possibly no single member finds privately acceptable (think of a case of voting in which no one's first choice is elected). In this kind of case acting against one's private belief (goal, etc.) in group contexts becomes possible.[26]

The general thesis that finds support from these kinds of considerations is that while group beliefs do supervene on group members' we-mode activities, they need not supervene on their I-mode activities.

(vi) This account can be used to clarify the beliefs that higher order groups, such as the European Union, have. Thus it suits the purposes of the study of international relations. Indeed, the above account can be directly applied to such higher order contexts, as it only speaks of agents and members of groups. The agents can be, for instance, states (or groups of states, etc.); the iteration can be continued as far as needed. In this hierarchical system, the levels are not reducible to lower levels, but they nevertheless supervene on them. Accordingly, a group of states such as the European Union can have normative group-binding beliefs in the sense of my analysis. The beliefs are acceptance beliefs. In addition, even in the higher order cases, there will always have to be some human beings, persons, acting in the we-mode (relative to the highest order group) at the lowest level to make the system work. Thus, in the case of the European Union, there will be human agents engaged in collective acceptance for the European Union (although they must of course be functioning as position-holders of the European Union rather than of its member states).

(vii) This positional model or account applies not only to beliefs of higher level groups but also to other voluntary attitudes that groups may have (e.g., goals and intentions). (See section 4.)

The reader should recall the discussion in section 2 of chapter 4 of normatively binding group attitudes analyzed in terms of the BBV. The normatively binding group beliefs belong to case (1) in the classification given in that context. However, not all group beliefs (qua group beliefs that a group has and can act on) are normatively group-binding in the above sense, although I believe that my above account concerns the most central notion of normative group belief. It involves an intrinsic group obligation—resulting from explicit or implicit agreement making—to maintain the belief in question as the group's belief. A violation of the obligation will in general lead to at least social sanctions (criticism, disapproval, related to a failure to be a "proper" group member, "one of us").

Other cases of group belief include weakly normative cases (category (2) in the BBV) based on the participants' leading each other to have normative participation expectations. These normative expectations are personal expectations having the objective justification coming from the others' promising-like behavior (language use is not required here, though). For instance, you and I may thus both lead the other one to normatively expect that we will take part in a certain joint activity. Here the obligations are person-related rather than group-related. The basis of criticism in the case of "violation" here is in general much shakier than in the agreement-based cases. There are also nonnormative group-binding cases, and they form my case (3) in chapter 4 (e.g., shared we-mode we-beliefs involving collective commitment). Finally, there are cases of collective beliefs that are not group-binding (case (4), for example, shared I-mode we-beliefs).

Finally, to illustrate part of what has been said in this section, consider the following examples of group beliefs with brief commentaries.

> (a) The Catholic Church believes that miracles happen. (Case (1) of the BBV in chapter 4, section 3: Normatively group-binding, namely, based on group obligation; possibly correlated with private I-mode beliefs with the same content.)
>
> (b) The Communist Party of Ruritania believes that capitalist countries will soon perish, but none of its members really believes so. (Case (1): Normatively group-binding but not correlated with private, I-mode beliefs with the same content.)
>
> (c) This group believes that Smith is a traitor. (Case (2): Weakly normative, no group-obligation, but weakly group-binding as the leaders have led the others to believe that they ought to treat Smith as a traitor, which resulted in collective commitment.)
>
> (d) The team believes that it will win today's game. (Case (3): Nonnormative; the case is assumed still to be group-binding, based on a joint plan, which is personally accepted in a nonnormative, thin sense by the participants and which involves collective commitment but no group obligation.)
>
> (e) The Finns (tend to) believe that sauna originated in Finland. (Case (4) if there is collective commitment. In other cases, it falls outside the scope of even the intersubjective BBV. This is merely a shared I-mode we-belief—one of the kind that Gallup investigations typically study.)

These cases show that there are a variety of group beliefs. The most important and typical of them are the normatively group-binding group beliefs (case (1)) and the nonnormative beliefs in the sense of case (3). The above examples (a)–(d) are all covered by the BBV.

To recapitulate, the following central results about group beliefs have been arrived at.

First, there are two kinds of group beliefs: group beliefs about the natural world (e.g., "Grass is green," "The earth is flat") and purely institutional group beliefs such as "Euros are our money."[27] In the latter case, the content of the belief is completely artifactually created. These group beliefs are acceptance beliefs, in the sense of being based on voluntary acceptance. They are something that it is up to the group to accept. The group can thus accept as its view that the earth is flat, but of course it cannot make the earth flat, nor can it guarantee the truth of this belief, while in the institutional euro case, it can itself validate its belief.

Second, the only group beliefs incorporating the idea of believing *as a group* are we-mode acceptances. The group cannot have normal beliefs, as it has no mind. The aggregative shared we-beliefs are just a kind of sum of individual beliefs and not yet beliefs qua a group. Given such a shared we-belief, in order for the group to come to believe as a group, members must still share the judgment to the effect that "this is what we as a group believe," and this judgment belongs to the acceptance side of the belief-acceptance debate in the literature.[28]

Third, if a group belief is to guide one's action, it must be or entail for the agent a judgment, something like "We together (or as a group) believe that p," that satisfies the Collectivity Condition. Given the kind of identification with the group here expressed by "We together," the agent, as a group member, is supposed to infer from this premise that she may and in some cases should use p in her further reasoning and in her nonverbal action. The group belief may thus be her reason for action.

4   A General Account of Group Attitudes

I will below formulate a general analysis of group attitudes. Let us start by considering beliefs in a general sense. In our above model (GB), we have the following elements. The *analysandum* is that a group, g, believes that p as a group. This is viewed from the jointness-level point of view of the members' collective acceptance of a belief content for g. In the case of a single member, we must accordingly require that he participates in the collective or joint acceptance. (I will again use the terms "collective" and "joint" interchangeably.) So, more precisely, we have the following.

> (1) g believes that p;
> (2) the operative members $A_1, \ldots, A_m$ collectively accept p for g ("us" for them) as its view;
> (3) A_i participates in $A_1, \ldots, A_m$'s collective (or joint) acceptance of p for g as g's belief content.

Clause (1) states what we have on the group level, (2) states what goes on at the jointness level and gives partial jointness-level truth conditions for (1), and (3) says what a single group member's role in this case is when taking the group reason (1) (as explicated in terms of (2)) as her reason for action. We can here assume that all the members are operatives. I will later give the conditions for nonoperatives in a precise way.

It can be seen that we have circularity of the same kind as in the joint intention or we-intention case, because (2) and (3) are characterized by reference to the group. Thus, in (2), the operative members are taken to believe (accept) that p as a group, for this is what the we-mode collective acceptance involved here amounts to. By the same token, (3) is partly circular, as it involves reference to group acceptance (belief). This kind of circularity problem applies within the positional account of group attitudes to any actively formed attitude ATT that the group may have. Yet this is nonvicious circularity, because it is informative, in the sense of giving a kind of transformation rule for going from the group level (macro level) to the jointness level (intermediate level) and because it can be made to work in a functional sense along the lines shown in section 4 of chapter 4 in the case of group-based joint intention. The formation of a group reason (a group's attitude in terms of the members' joint decision or agreement, etc.) can take place without an antecedent group reason, although some kind of general proattitude toward the group may have to be involved on contingent psychological grounds. There is also another kind of circularity problem, termed the bootstrapping problem, looming here. It was discussed and answered in section 2.

This account assumes that it is meaningful to attribute attitudes to groups, although groups are not literally agents. What is going on ontologically is this: The micro level and the jointness level are regarded as ontologically and causally real, whereas the macro level is viewed as nonreal if seen as involving a superindividual agent. The causal powers attributed to social groups accordingly are the causal powers owned by group members, individually or jointly, but there are no extra higher order agents with causal powers going beyond group members' powers. However, group-level concepts, although supervenient on we-mode notions, are here regarded as irreducible and taken to be instrumentally needed for an adequate analysis of social life in general and for adequately describing and conceptualizing such group phenomena as actions performed by groups (recall section 5 of chapter 4). The group level is conceptually and psychologically central, as it accounts, and gives reasons, for much of group members' thinking and acting in group contexts, and especially as it accounts for the kind of we-mode thinking and acting that a group's having an attitude as a group (our present analysandum) requires.

We are here somewhat metaphorically viewing groups as analogous to individual agents (persons). Thus wants, beliefs, intentions, and other mental states attributed to groups are in the first place to be understood analogously with those attributed to individual agents. However, when attributed to groups, the attitudes have to be voluntary and acceptance-based.[29] As groups have no minds and bodies, they cannot have experiential beliefs, and they cannot literally have emotions. Yet the group members can accept views for the group, and they can even accept that the group members ought to like or hate something in their voluntary thoughts and actions. We may thus speak of as-if emotions in the case of groups, and nothing, of course, prevents the group members from having those emotions in their genuine sense.

In my positional analysis, it is the we-mode joint attitudes and actions that cash out the macro level or group attitudes and actions: Group attitudes and actions basically amount to the group members' relevant we-mode joint attitudes and actions. The group is in part a social action system in which the agents jointly want, intend, (as-if) believe, (as-if) feel, and so on, where they thus "inferentially and actionally" function in the right ways. The jointness-level concepts must of course be sufficiently well understood. For instance, in chapters 3–5, it has been shown in detail what joint intentions and actions as well as mutual beliefs amount to. Although irreducible, these notions are sufficiently well understood, and people can and do "live" with them in actual social practice.[30]

My above formulation of the general account assumes that any attitude ATT has a certain direction of fit of semantic satisfaction. When elucidating the group level in terms of the jointness level for an attitude ATT concerning p, there will have to be collective acceptance of p for the group with the right direction of fit of semantic satisfaction; and in ideal cases, all group members will be assumed to participate in this collective acceptance, although in actual practice we typically have to deal with the authority-based operative-nonoperative division. As seen, in the positional, we-mode attitude model, we accordingly have the elements of the group level, the jointness level "transforming" the group-level attitudes and actions into jointness-level (and, in part, into individual member-level) attitudes and actions. The supervenience-based relationship between the group level and the jointness level for attitudes was analyzed in the terms of acceptance in section 1—recall especially theses (i) and (ii). I will below use those ideas for a precise formulation of what a group's having an attitude amounts to.

When we speak of the positional model, "positional functioning" must be understood so widely as to become equivalent to acting as a group member in the standard sense, thus to broadly institutional acting. In the intuitively basic case of unorganized groups, acting as a group member amounts just to plain participation by all members, participation being based on group-social norms (at least those that partly define the group). Thus in this general sense there need not even be differentiated positions in the group. But in the general case specific task-right systems, based on specific group-social norms will define the group positions.

I will below—as was done in the case of (GINT), (GIA), and (GB)—relax the consensus idea for normatively structured groups and specifically deal with simple cases involving a two-layered account of authorization. In those cases, there are specific operative members for g who are authorized by the group members to form attitudes for g. I speak of the acceptance of a voluntary attitude (say ATT) with a certain content (say p), briefly ATT(p). This locution means, for example, in the case of belief, simply that the group members collectively accept a certain content as their belief; and the same goes for intentions, wishes, and so on, as follows.

> (GATT) Group g *has ATT with content p as a group* if and only if there are specific operative members of g such that
> (1) these agents, when acting as group members in the we-mode sense (and accordingly performing their positional tasks and due to their exercising the relevant decision-making system of g), intentionally collectively accept as a group that ATT with content p or accept that p as the content of ATT (e.g., "We believe that p" or "We accept p as our belief") for g with the right ATT-specific direction of fit of semantic satisfaction and with collective commitment to content p in the right way (namely, they jointly accept ATT(p) for g in the we-mode and with the right df);[31]
> (2) there is mutual belief among the operative members to the effect that (1);
> (3) because of (1), the (full-fledged and adequately informed) nonoperative members qua members of g tend to tacitly accept with collective commitment—or at least ought so to accept—that their group g has ATT(p);
> (4) there is mutual belief in g to the effect that (3).

Analogously with our earlier analyses, (2) and (4) are both epistemic rationality requirements for a group attitude to be there, but they also contain the presupposed conceptual conditions. The presuppositions are that the members must understand that the group attitude is based on (1) and that they are all bound to it (see (3) and the argument given in section 2).

What are we to require, more specifically, of a group member's participation in the case where a group has a certain attitude ATT with certain content? According to our analysis, a group cannot have an attitude without at least some members, the operative members, having the attitude and having brought about the group's attitude when acting as group members. The operatives may by their joint decision create a group view and use this group view as their reason for their (further) participatory actions, and indeed all members are supposed similarly to act on the group reason. We noticed (especially in section 2 in the context of discussing the bootstrap problem) that the jointness and we-ness of the operatives' joint attitude (generating the group's attitude) and what it involves (most importantly, the Collectivity Condition) is central for the formation of the group's view. To quote an old saying: *Non mihi, non tibi, sed nobis.*

Suppose that group g has attitude ATT toward p (in the sense of (GATT)). This involves at the jointness level that the (operative) members of g collectively accept ATT(p) for g and that each of the (operative) members participates in this joint acceptance, and the other members at least ought to tacitly accept what the operative members, authorized by them, have accepted for the group. Then, parallel to what was said in chapter 4 about joint intention, each group-socially rational member must have the reason-based we-attitude with content ATT(p) as a group member in the standard sense. The central matter here is of course having ATT as a member of g. This involves that the member in question intentionally performs, or is disposed to perform, actions related to ATT(p) as a group member such that the ethos of g is respected. The agent need not know exactly how ATT(p) relates to the ethos, and he does not even have to know precisely what the ethos of the group is. But, on group-functional grounds, he must believe that *there is* a (unique) group ethos such that his actions related to ATT(p) when meant to be actions as a group member at least weakly promote the ethos (recall chapter 1).

The primary (and indeed a presuppositional) reason in the group member's we-attitude toward ATT(p) is that the group has ATT(p) (be it antecedently or currently formed as the group's attitude). The assumed derived reason for the we-attitude is that the other members, or at least the operative ones, have ATT, under conditions of mutual belief (which makes the definition of a shared we-attitude satisfied). If the group's attitude is formed by the current operative members, the primary reason and the derived reason necessarily are the same, but in other cases the derived reason may be based on the agent's belief that indeed there are sufficiently many others accepting ATT for the group and in that sense serving to satisfy the ethos. If there are not, the group cannot, on conceptual grounds, actually have the attitude. (Recall section 5 of chapter 4.)

To elucidate the view that the group's attitude is involved in having an attitude as a group member, we note that having ATT(p) as a group member (in obvious symbols, ATT(x, p, agms)) involves member x's having the attitude while functioning in a group context such that x's actions realizing ATT(p) are ethos-promoting in g. Here agms means acting as a group member in the standard sense (AGMS), which consists of the intentional promotion of ethos by means of action classes (1)–(4) (of chapter 1) with collectively committed participation. We can give the following clarification of having an attitude fully as a group member (agms) in the case of an operative member x.

Operative x has the attitude ATT(p) in the full sense as a member of group g (namely, ATT(x, p, agms)) if and only if she has ATT(p) (namely, ATT(x, p)) and is participating in the group members' collective commitment in the group context related to g to make the group's attitude ATT satisfied or to maintain it as true (depending on the nature of the direction of fit of ATT) in congruence with the ethos E of g, the attitude and the commitment here being conceptually based on, and "reasoned" by, ATT(g, p).[32]

That ATT(x, p) is based on ATT(g, p) is taken to mean that, noncontingently, x would not have her attitude without the group's having ATT(p) and indeed that she may have inferred (and, when reflective enough, would have inferred) her attitude from the group's ("our") attitude (e.g., simply "I, functioning agms, have ATT(p) because ATT(g, p)," with "because" expressing reason).[33]

Having ATT fully as a group member in the standard sense, namely, ATT(x, p, agms), amounts to having ATT in the we-mode (namely, ATT(x, p, wm)), where x is an operative member. This is because the central elements of the we-mode—as analyzed by (WM) of chapter 2, namely, collective acceptance, for-groupness (thus group reason), and collective commitment—clearly are present in (ii), and we recall that the acceptance for the group with collective commitment has all along been assumed to satisfy the Collectivity Condition. This concludes my account of an operative member's share in a group's having an attitude.

Analogously with the above account of having an attitude in the we-mode, we can also analyze having an attitude in the progroup I-mode or in other I-mode senses. A central difference between the progroup I-mode and the standard we-mode is that only the latter satisfies the Collectivity Condition and is constitutively based on group reasons. The former, accordingly, is based on private rather than collective acceptance and on private rather than collective commitment. Notice that it is possible to have an attitude ATT(p) as a group member or in the we-mode while at the same time failing to have ATT(p) in the I-mode or even having ATT(–p). Given the above symbolism, we can see that there is no formal conflict between ATT(x, p, wm) and ATT(x, –p). Yet there is inconsistency at a deeper level: The agent x cannot satisfy both attitudes at the same time. For instance, she may intend to achieve p (requiring the performance of X) in the we-mode while intending to achieve –p (requiring the performance of –X) in the I-mode. The agent cannot rationally intend and do both X and –X on the same occasion. The essential difference between a we-mode and an I-mode intention with the same content is that they are held for different kinds of reasons—only the we-mode reason satisfies the Collectivity Condition. This does not make intentions in these different modes intentions of different kinds. Thus they are comparable, at least in the above actional sense.

When ATT(g,p), does every member of g have to have ATT(p) to participate in the collective commitment to ATT(p)? Compatibly with (GATT), this is not a conceptual requirement. Being so committed is nevertheless a functional adequacy desideratum, because extensive collective commitment entails group coherence and disposition to act as a unity. As for the nonoperatives, they are *pro tanto* required only to tacitly accept and participate in the attitude that the group has (recall again section 2 for an argument). Such tacit acceptance involves the right kind of behavior but not necessarily the right group reason. The nonoperatives at least ought to know that the operatives have made a specific decision or know that this information is available, and they ought to go along with the decision—although that might happen for the wrong reason. Note that those nonoperatives who adopt the full we-perspective do accept and are collectively committed to what the operatives have accepted for the group; and they will act in the we-mode—there is the required kind of collective acceptance, collective commitment, and for-groupness, but the other nonoperatives will be acting in the I-mode relative to g. What percentage of group members, for example, in large (we-mode) groups can act only in the I-mode without making the group seriously dysfunctional is a contingent matter that will not be discussed here.

Finally, to make a specific logical point related to nonoperatives, consider again clause (3) of (GATT), which can be taken to contain the following requirement: "It ought to be that case that if (1), then the nonoperative members of g tacitly accept ATT(p) for g, that is, tacitly accept and endorse that g has p in the ATT-way." Here the *pro tanto* "ought" is in front of the rest of what (3) says. In this kind of normative requirement, the consequent cannot be formally detached from the antecedent, and thus it cannot generally be detachably inferred that the nonoperatives ought to tacitly accept the content in question (for that would involve a fallacy in deontic logic). The normative consistency requirement is there in the first place because of the intrinsic connection between the operatives and the nonoperatives that is entailed by their group membership in general and their relationship of commitment to authorization in particular. The "ought" operator in the requirement thus signifies the authorization-based obligation that is dependent on the operatives' having accepted ATT(p) for g. Given the "ought" concerning the nonoperatives, it follows that a nonoperative member is not "as he should be" if he does not acquire ATT(p) and if he is not disposed to act for this desire-independent group reason. Thus we can say that at least on "informal" grounds the nonoperatives are obligated and that we have informal "actional" detachment.[34]

5 Summary

This chapter has analyzed collective acceptance and group attitudes (e.g., beliefs, intentions, and also actions) and created the so-called positional account of group attitudes. Detailed analyses of group action ((IGA), section 2), group beliefs ((GB), section 3) and voluntary group attitudes in general ((GATT), section 4) have been central in this chapter. These analyses depend on my view of authorization and authorized group members, namely, operatives for the task in question, as discussed especially in section 2. The general account can be applied to positions and to authorized decision mechanisms as well. The notion of group attitude was assumed to be conceptually central and to have an authoritative role in the group members' relevant practical reasoning—recall section 5 of chapter 4, which can be generalized for any group attitude. A group's having an attitude amounts to its members' or at least its authorized members' sharing that attitude in the we-mode, qua group members. There is a kind of circularity problem here, as a group's attitude, for example, belief, is elucidated by reference to the operatives' acceptance of it. This problem was found not to be serious to the account. Furthermore, there is a bootstrapping problem potentially involved, as the members both form the group and are assumed to rely on the group as authority. This problem was discussed in section 2, with an emphasis on the creative nature of the jointness level.

The main ontological and thus causal operations relevant to group life take place because of the jointness-level events and facts (i.e., the group members thinking thus-and-so and acting appropriately in view of their joint and other, we-mode or I-mode, thoughts.). The ontology of groups is briefly discussed in the appendix to this chapter.

As both collective acceptance and group attitudes are central for the theory created in this book, the basic theoretical machinery has now been created (in chapters 1–6) that is needed for discussing such social topics as social institutions, cooperation, cultural evolution, and group responsibility (see chapters 7–10).

Appendix: The Ontological Nature of Social Groups

According to the *singular entity view*, social groups can be regarded as singular entities consisting of persons and relevant interrelations (construed, e.g., as tropes) between them or, perhaps, as singular mereological entities. Accordingly, groups are taken to exist as some kind of singular conglomeration or fusion. The other view I will consider is the *nonentity view*, according to which groups are not entities of any kind. Rather, individual persons form social groups in terms of their social relationships and (collective) activities of suitable kinds. Even under this construal, the group members may, and arguably sometimes must, think in terms of social groups, in the sense that their thoughts involve groups as entities analogously to the way one may be said to be thinking about flowers, cars, or numbers.

Groups are not persons, because they have neither bodies nor minds. A group cannot exercise agency if the members do not.[35] However, it is often highly useful and meaningful to say that groups intend, have beliefs, and act, and I am also willing to say that a group's intending, believing, and so on amounts to its appropriate members' intending, believing, and so on. In a nutshell, my view is that groups can (but need not) be taken as (singular) entities, and they are agents and persons only in a metaphorical sense. Much of what is said in this book prima facie treats groups as real but nonagentive social systems supervenient on the members functioning qua group members.

Let us next consider the view of social groups—be they normatively structured or not—as suitable kinds of conglomerations of persons at each point of time at which the group exists. A group may be spatially (and temporally) dispersed, in the sense that the group members are not spatially (or temporally) connected in a causal sense. The fusion or "sum" of the elements of such a conglomeration existing at certain times over space and time yields a singular group entity. We may thus speak loosely of ordered sequences of the kind $(g^1, \ldots, g^k)$ corresponding to the times $t^1, \ldots, t^k$ at which the group exists. Each $g^i, i = 1, \ldots, k$, is a fusion over space of the group members existing at t^i. I will below use the material mode exposition, but later I will speak of linguistic entities as well. Below, a group name "g" will in general be taken to refer to a real group entity and a group predicate "G" will be taken to represent a specific group aspect G of some agents' behavior. G stands for "groupish" thinking and acting relative to g (here regarded as a singular entity, a suitable network). Such thinking and acting involves the existence of an ethos, namely, some constitutive goals, values, standards, and norms and we-mode thinking and acting relative to them.

Consider now this definition:

(SG) Singular entity g is a *social group* if and only if there are times in $t^1, \ldots, t^k$ such that for all these times t^i (where $i = 1, \ldots, m$) there is some (typically complex) aspect G such that

(1) g, viewed as a fused sequence $(g^1, \ldots, g^k)$ has some persons, $A_1^i, \ldots, A_m^i$, as its members at t^i;

(2) these members $A_1^i, \ldots, A_m^i$ think and act (function) in the special G-way related to g.[36]

We can now say that g is a social group in a diachronic sense if and only if for all times t^i, $G(A_1^i, \ldots, A_m^i)$ is satisfied by $A_1^i, \ldots, A_m^i$.

In this analysis, g is a singular rather than a generic entity. A generic entity is one that can be multiply instantiated, in contrast to a singular entity. The basic argument for the singular (as opposed to the generic) entity view is that it does not postulate "unrequired" new entities in the world. Thus, (a) one can account for the behavior of groups (e.g., actions performed by groups); (b) using the above "adverbial" account, which puts the main burden on the predicate "G," one can account for the continuity of groups (ontically: the continuity in a consecutive series of the existence of singular entities $(g^1, \ldots, g^k)$; and (c) one can accommodate common sense locutions in this kind of context (e.g., "g performed X," "g is responsible for X," "g is cohesive," "g is egalitarian").[37]

Social groups often are normatively organized and structured. Organizations and (formal) associations are typical examples of such groups. Consider thus a structured group, g, with positions P_i, $i = 1, \ldots, m$. A structured group consists of (1) an open domain, D, of position-holders, (2) positions $P_1, \ldots, P_m$, and (3) a task-right system, TR, defining and governing these positions.[38] TR typically consists of general group norms (ought-to-be, ought-to-do, may-be, and may-do norms) and norms specific to the positions P_i. Thus we can say that g = <D, $P_1, \ldots, P_m$, TR>. I wish to emphasize that a position is a general entity in the sense that the class of position-holders is potentially infinite. Thus, considering a position P, $(x)P(x)$ indicates the open class of position-holders. What this means is that a structured group cannot be reduced to a finite collection of group members. Such a group involves more than its current position-holders or any finite set of previous, current, or future position-holders. Our above definition of groups covers also normatively structured ones if we take the group predicate "G" in principle to cover positions and task-right systems.[39]

Let us consider the nonentity view of social groups.[40] We consider two accounts, starting with a statement saying that an entity is a social group of a certain kind, for example, "The University of Helsinki is a social group." Here the noun phrase "social group" is used predicatively to apply to a proper name ("The University of Helsinki"), and it corresponds to our above predicate G. Consider next a statement that says that certain persons form a group or are members of a group, for example, "g has $A_1,\ldots,A_m$ as its members" or "$A_1,\ldots,A_m$ form group g." In these cases, in contrast, "g" can be seen as a singular term referring to something like a singular nominalistically conceived network with the mentioned individuals as its members (or, perhaps, to a mereological sum with the members as its parts). However, in this case, "g" may alternatively be regarded as a nonreferring singular term. Consider the following solution relying on the "vicarious existence" of groups.[41]

The sentence "g is a social group with the persons $A_1,\ldots,A_m$ as its members" is true in the *vicarious* sense if and only if

(1) the names "A_1," ...,"A_m" in the mentioned sentence succeed in referring to some real persons $A_1,\ldots,A_m$, and

(2) these persons $A_1,\ldots,A_m$ think and act (function) in a special G-way, and "g" (in the analysandum sentence) is regarded as a nonreferring term serving to "specify" the predicate "G" (referring to the G-way).

(Note that if we in clause (2) instead take the view that "g" is a singular term referring to a singular group entity, a suitable kind of network, we do not need the last specification about g.)

We can now say this: The sentence "g is a social group with the persons $A_1,\ldots,A_m$ as its members" is true in the vicarious sense if and only if $A_1,\ldots,A_m$ form a group relative to g if and only if the sentence "$G(A_1,\ldots,A_m)$" is true. Notice that things are even simpler if we take "g" to be a singular term for singular group entities, for then we can say, given our specifications about the relationship between the group entity and its parts, that g is a group if and only if $G(A_1,\ldots,A_m)$.

As seen, the group predicate "G" (as applicable to group members collectively) and the truth-equivalent "is a group" (as applicable to the group entity) involve the group ethos (and this may apply even to I-mode groups), which serves to define (at lest partly) group identity and which is assumed to be preserved through time when the group exists at various times.

Taking causality to be the central criterion of real existence (to exist is to be capable of occurring in causal contexts as a—partial or total—cause or effect), these two views arguably are causally equivalent, and thus, in particular, the singular entity view does not have causal entailments that the nonentity view does not have. The basic reason for this is that the entity view is only a redescription of the nonentity view. Groups can be viewed in either way, depending on the existing collective, especially linguistic, practices. In the case of we-mode groups, it is pertinent to impose the requirement, based on the very nature of we-mode groups as involving a "togetherness-we," that the group members be disposed to think in group terms, for example, "Our group will do X." Groups can well have "intentional existence" in this sense and also have objective existence in the sense of the members interacting in some ways specific to the group in question—all this without an ontological necessity to conceptualize and describe the group even as a singular entity. However, the instrumental advantages of describing groups as entities are often considerable, and this has been widely acknowledged among group theorists, not to mention ordinary people.[42]

Let us finally consider collective identity (or group identity). In the literature the phrase "collective identity" is often used in the place of "group identity." Kay Mathiesen gives a partial, sufficient-condition analysis of collective identity in this sense.[43] My account is indebted to her account, although I depart from it in some respects and use my own technical terminology.

Briefly, my definition goes as follows.

g at t is (largely) *the same* as g' (or g is largely *"collectively identical"* with g') at t' if and only if
(i) the content of the ethos of g' at t' is obtained from that of g in terms of a family-resemblance transformation based on collective acceptance;
(ii) g' is a causal descendant of g;
(iii) the members of g' collectively accept in effect (i) and (ii) as true;
(iv) it is a mutual belief among the members of g' that (iii).

We say that the ethos E' of g' is obtained from the ethos E of g by means of a family-resemblance transformation if and only if for every time t_i that lies between t and t', the ethos E_i at t_i has been obtained from the ethos E_{i-1} at t_{i-1} by means of the collective acceptance (here perhaps only tacit "going along with") that the transformation preserves collective identity.

Analogously, we can define causal descendance, except that now we do not require collective acceptance over and above that specified by (iii) and only partial causation need be at stake. We might require causal necessity: for all i, g_i would not be a group with ethos E_i if the previous group g_{i-1} would not have been a group with ethos E_{i-1}. Partial causation in this sense of causal necessity need not be transitive. Thus it need not be the case that the relation holds between g and g'. An example of dynamic sameness in the above sense is given by the Glenn Miller Orchestra. The orchestra was started by Glenn Miller in the 1930s and survived his death in 1944. Without much, if any, change in its ethos (the type of jazz and the kind of playing together it exemplifies) it has survived under different leaders until today, when Wil Salden is its leader.

As Mathiesen also emphasizes, a group can divide into two; that is, branching is possible. As noted, transitivity also may fail. These observations show—correct as they are—that collective identity is not an identity notion in the standard sense that satisfies transitivity and the linearity condition that prohibits branching. Note that if and when g' and g'' fuse into the sum g' + g'', it may well happen—although there is no necessity—that (iii) and (iv) become satisfied and that the fusion group is collectively identical with g.

7

COOPERATION

1 Cooperativeness

It is often said that human beings are social and are disposed to cooperate. This seems right, but the exact content of the statement is not very clear.[1] We have learned from biology and ethology that such factors as "kin-altruism" and "reciprocal altruism" can ground cooperative behavior in animals. In the case of human beings, we think—somewhat similarly, but in more general terms—that people are social: people are also disposed to cooperate within large groups where direct reciprocity is not generally possible, and they often cooperate with strangers. Compatibly with this, it will be argued in chapter 9 that the disposition to cooperate may well be a culture-gene-based coevolutionary adaptation in humans.

Generally speaking, human sociality is a many-faceted thing, which involves at least that people on the whole need, and enjoy, the company of other human beings. This kind of dependence can be intrinsic (sociality as an irreducible basic want or need) or instrumental (related to features such as self-respect, honor, pride, and so on or to various things that they want to achieve but cannot achieve alone). One central fact is that people in their thinking and acting tend conformistically to take into account what others think and do (recall the discussion of we-attitudes in chapter 3 and see chapter 9). Accordingly, others' approval and disapproval of one's ways of thinking and acting form an important motivational element—over and above one's judgments based on instrumental or nonsocial considerations. More support for sociality comes from the fact that human beings are de facto communicative symbol users (and indeed language users) and that communication is based on shared meanings and shared uses and indeed is normally cooperative. At least within ingroups, this cooperation-involving sociality assumption is a general initial presupposition underlying any person's thinking and action.

The above considerations, of course, induce a strong element of conformity and cooperativeness into normal social life. Thus, even if human beings often

149

have differing private goals, they are still disposed to behave cooperatively, at least toward their kin and, perhaps by analogical extension, toward their friends and other close group members and to some extent with all human beings. Furthermore, people often have interlocking goals and tend to cooperate in terms of reciprocal exchange even with strangers in certain contexts (e.g., in business). Generally speaking, the ability and disposition of human beings to cooperate (at least conditionally, if the partners do) is a central element in the success of the human species.[2]

Cooperation seems to be innate, a coevolutionary adaptation based on group selection, the basic reason for this being that human beings have evolved in a group context.[3] In the case of primitive human tribes, cooperation became a disposition that was regarded as favorable and one that, accordingly, was imitated in such groups. The cultural environment accordingly selected in favor of dispositions adapted for life in cooperative groups, and this kind of cultural evolution led to more cooperation in the course of time. (See chapter 9 for discussion.)

Yet it is not easy to specify under what conditions people actually cooperate (and conform) rather than defect, act competitively, or even act aggressively. The latter kinds of behavior are all in their different ways opposite to cooperation, and people also seem to be disposed to such behaviors. Recent theoretical and experimental investigations have shown that mere reciprocity (be it direct or indirect) does not suffice for sustained cooperation especially in large groups. What is needed is so-called strong reciprocity, which is a predisposition to cooperate with others, and to punish (at personal cost, if necessary) those who violate the norms of cooperation, even when it is implausible to expect that these costs will be recovered at a later date.[4] Accordingly, strong reciprocators are conditional cooperators who cooperate as long as others are cooperating, but they are also "altruistic" punishers who apply sanctions to violators (including those who fail to punish when they should).[5] Interestingly, the we-mode approach of this book entails strong reciprocity, and it also shows that group reasons and acting as a group member are needed for sustained cooperation among people (group members).[6] Here the proximal "reason" for cooperation is normally that it is simply a presupposition in the group. Thus a member can normally expect some amount of cooperation from any group member.

The focus below will be on *rational* cooperation rather than its factual motivational grounds, although appendix 1 gives a brief survey of extant motivational accounts of cooperation in the full sense.[7] The account of this chapter argues that cooperative joint action forms the core of full cooperative action.[8] This kind of cooperation will be called *we-mode cooperation*. There is also *I-mode cooperation*, which is based on the participants' private (I-mode) preferences and goals. Both kinds of cooperation are important and worthwhile objects of study in their own ways. While most current theories and empirical studies concern cooperation in the I-mode sense, I here emphasize full, we-mode cooperation.[9]

Cooperation will rather easily come about in situations in which it is intrinsically rewarding and does not involve an incentive to free-ride. Simple coordination situations are of this kind. In contrast, there are collective action dilemma cases in which collective and individual rationality conflict (see below). In such cases, cooperation will be costly and defection will give a higher payoff, and rationally achieving cooperation will be difficult. Nevertheless, people typically cooperate more than individualistic accounts based on selfishness suggest. One central reason for such abundance of cooperation seems to be that people often think and act in the we-mode or at least in terms of a shared we-perspective (be it in the I-mode or we-mode). People tend to act as group members, respecting the cooperative requirements of the group, and this results in cooperation that is for the use and benefit of their group ("we" for them).[10] The group members accordingly see to it that defectors are noticed and corrected (punished or at least properly instructed, depending on the case). This view can also explain why acting as a private person tends to lead to defection in dilemma situations but not when acting as a group member.[11] In order to explain cooperation in large societies, a much wider or more extended "we" is needed.

I-mode cooperation involves no proper collective goal ("*our*" goal). Rather it is often (but not necessarily) based on reciprocity and compatible private goals, often only type-identical goals. This may also be called cooperation in the sense of *coordination*. A central distinction is that between *plain* I-mode cooperation and *progroup* I-mode cooperation, one involving a thin we-perspective (and privately had group reason).[12] Note that a person may be prosocial, for example, and altruistic, and may cooperate on that basis with other people. This is not yet a group reason. On the other hand, she may strive to maximize the benefit of a group in some kind of egalitarian and fair way. This is often an I-mode progroup reason. A stronger kind of group reason is based on a person's identification with the group and her adopting the full group perspective (we-perspective) and acting as a group member. This gives the thick we-mode reason that we-mode cooperation intrinsically requires.

In this chapter I will compare I-mode and we-mode cooperation by discussing some action situations in which cooperative order can be created, alternatively, in the I-mode way or in the we-mode way. It will be argued that we-mode decision-making may lead to beneficial cooperation also in situations where I-mode and progroup I-mode decision-making fails. In addition, we-mode cooperation may be more persistent, because it is based on the group members' shared collective commitment to cooperate. Both types of decision-making, or more generally thinking and acting, are needed for capturing the essential features of social life.

2   I-Mode Cooperative Action

Arguably, one cannot cooperate nonintentionally; for instance, I cannot nonintentionally cooperate to paint a house with you. In cooperation, the participants must *intend to cooperate*, respectively, in the I-mode or in the we-mode sense, possibly under their own conceptualizations of these kinds of cooperation. The intention to cooperate entails some willingness to cooperate, and it excludes strong coercion. In this section, I will discuss I-mode action. In such collective cooperative action, the actors cooperate individually but not collectively (i.e., jointly) intentionally.

Cooperation has two central dimensions: (1) its *teleological content* (i.e., its end or telos, what the participants intentionally strive to achieve), and (2) its *social content*, that is, interaction with some other agents relative to the content in question. Dimension (1) gives *teleological intentionality* ("directedness" intentionality). This dimension must always exist, even in cases in which the agents act with no further goal except cooperation itself (e.g., I perform an action with no further goal but still by means of this action purport to adjust my action to your action and thus to cooperate with you). In dimension (2), we can speak of *intentionality in the social connectedness* sense. This case deals with social "aboutness" intentionality and contrasts with the "directedness" intentionality of (1), and it consists in the agent's relevant epistemic and normative relationships to the participants. This involves not only treating the other participants as "intelligent parts" of one's environment but also each participant's intention to cooperate (at least in the reciprocity or "adjustment of action" sense—see below).

In collective cooperative I-mode action, the actors cooperate individually intentionally but not jointly intentionally. In this case, a participant must believe that he is cooperating with somebody or some others and that they are cooperating with him, although he might not know who the participants are. There can be knowledge of the social connectedness relating the participants—the agent must at least have a belief to the effect that there are other cooperating participants.

I will now give a stylized account of I-mode cooperation in a simple two-person case where each participant performs one or more actions and has one central goal in the situation in question. The participants' intentions to cooperate entail that both their intentions (goals) and means actions (i.e., their actions that they use as the means to achieve their goals) are either naturally or institutionally interdependent in the situation in question, or that they simply are voluntarily made interdependent by the participants due to their forming the intention to cooperate. If rational, the participants must mutually believe that they are so dependent.

I-mode cooperation essentially involves adjusting one's means actions and goal (assuming only one is at stake here) to the other participant's actions and goal so as to further both the other's goal (i.e., goal satisfaction) and one's own goal, the latter possibly only through the other's furthering it by his actions. (See clause (2) of (CIM) below.) As indicated, the means actions may be naturally or institutionally dependent prior to action (think of carrying a table jointly or playing chess), but in some cases, the agents' connected goals will make them dependent even when there is no prior action dependence. Thus, for instance, we may cooperate in the I-mode so that my goal to go to Paris to take care of my business is connected to your goal to go to Rome to take care of your business by my adding to my antecedent goal my promotion of your business while in Paris, and analogously for you. Even if there is no behavioral dependence between the means actions, the latter still have become dependent—your means action will further the satisfaction of my goal, and vice versa.[13] (If the agents here formed a joint intention to perform the cooperative joint action to satisfy the joint goal made up of each agent's goal, the same example can be adapted also to the we-mode case— see section 5. Then each agent performs his part of the joint action as his part.)

The participants need not cooperate in a group context; thus they may just cooperate in the degenerate sense of the I-mode that was called the purely private I-mode in the previous section. Here is the proposal, the *analysans* of which entails other-regarding (and in group context, progroup) I-mode action:[14]

(CIM) A_1 and A_2 *(intentionally) cooperate in the I-mode* to achieve their goals G_1 and G_2

if and only if

(1) A_1 and A_2 have the goals G_1 and G_2, respectively, as their intended private goals (namely, goals had as private persons in contrast to goals had as full-blown members of a social group);

(2) they willingly perform respective interdependent means actions x_1 and x_2 believed by them to be conducive (at least indirectly, via the other's action) to their respective goals so that each takes himself thereby to have adjusted his acting and goal to the other's action and goal with the purported result that the other's achievement of the other's (possibly adjusted) goal is furthered and that, by the other's analogous acting, also the achievement of his own (possibly adjusted) goal is furthered.

Note that each participant need not know what the other's goal is, although he must believe that the other has one in this context. To get a notion of (functionally) rational I-mode cooperation from the above conceptually minimal notion, we add two clauses saying that the information in clauses (1) and (2) must be mutually believed (clause (3)) such that the mutual belief is not idle (clause (4)):

(3) A_1 and A_2 rationally mutually believe that (1) and (2).

(4) (2) in part because of (3).

In addition, full rationality can be taken to require that the beliefs in (2) be true—to achieve epistemic coherence between the participants. I will comment on the clauses of (CIM) below.

According to (2), the participants are assumed to be disposed willingly to perform relevant contributory actions that their own goals may not strictly require. Thus the participants are disposed to incur extra costs (this being rational as long as the costs of performing them are less than the gross gains accruing from their performance).[15]

Some comments on the variety of dependencies that might be involved in (2) are now due. First we note that G_1 and G_2 may—for example, in cases of spontaneous cooperation with no further individual goals—be just the proximate goals conceptually inherent in intentional actions, namely, the so-called result-events of x_1 and x_2, respectively. I already noted that action dependence might be due to antecedent goal dependence (although, conversely, some amount of indirect goal dependence anyhow comes about due to means action dependence). For example, we might have $G_1 = G_2$ such that these goals can only be satisfied by the same state token. Then the means actions cannot rationally conflict, and A_1's action must contribute to A_2's goal, and vice versa. A case in point is where two drivers coming from opposite directions get out of their cars to remove a fallen tree from the road; their shared goal is $G_1 = G_2 =$ the log is removed from the road. The removal of the log might take place in terms of I-mode cooperation in the sense of (CIM).

However, sharper and stronger formulations of action dependence may be used for some situations. Thus, thinking of a game-theoretic interaction case, one may require optimal satisfaction of a participant's goal, entailing that he has to choose his action x_i so that it is optimal for his goal (in the sense of maximization of expected utility or something weaker) while at the same time facilitating the other's reaching his goal. A still stronger dependence requirement is that, relative to goal satisfaction, x_1 is (optimally) performed if and only if x_2 is performed. Here the goals may be only parallel (be they the same or different) and satisfied by different event (or state) tokens, or they may be the same in the stronger sense of being satisfiable only by the same token, in a sense divided by the participants through their actions. An example of the parallel (but dependent) goal case is offered by a block world case where A_1 is not able to move one of his blocks to his goal location unless A_2 first suitably moves one of his blocks, and vice versa.[16]

My account can make room for both altruistic and selfish cooperation. In the case of altruism, a participant, by taking "costs" that exceed his gain from achieving his antecedent goal, acts in order to further the other's goal and, indeed, in effect makes it his goal to satisfy the other's goal and takes the existence of his "new" goal to depend on the existence of the other's goal. Altruistic cooperation involves helping the partner (and it might also be taken to include sanctioning defection and thus collectively helping the partners of cooperation). In the case of selfish cooperation, the participant performs his action by which he furthers the other's goal as a means of furthering his own goal, and the more selfish the cooperation, the more he is using the partner for his purposes. Depending on the goal correlation, his performance of his means action may already directly further his own goal, but at least the other's action performance will further his goal.[17] Because of the latter, in-built feature, each cooperative means action will at least in that indirect sense further one's own goal. In general, if mutual cooperation furthers the participants' present goals—or some of their other goals—better (or at least not worse) than what their acting alone would (think of rational exchange where the participants reward each other), then cooperation is rational.

Above the agents perform the token actions x_1 and x_2. We may now call their set $\{x_1,x_2\}$, or in the n-person case $\{x_1, \ldots x_n\}$, an *individually intentional cooperative collective action* or, using our technical terminology, an *intentional cooperative collective action in the I-mode*.

The intentionality of cooperation in our account depends on the intention to cooperate, possibly under the participants' own descriptions of cooperation involving the main elements of (CIM). This intention thus basically has the content to perform means actions of the kind specified by clause (2), given the information in clause (1). The intention to (willingly) cooperate, accordingly, does not entail that the participants need to have a separate goal to cooperate over and above their intended goals and intended actions as specified in (1) and (2) of (CIM); rather, it can be an unreflected intention-in-cooperation. Note that cooperation does not, of course, guarantee that G_1 and G_2 actually are achieved.

When people act together in the I-mode (in the sense of (CIM)) they do not act as a group, which they can be said to do when they act in the we-mode. In the I-mode case, they act collectively in an "aggregative" sense that possibly involves interdependent means actions. In the I-mode case, a person's private intended goal is achieved only when she has achieved it by his action in the context of collective action. In contrast, in the we-mode case, the Collectivity Condition (of chapter 2) is satisfied.[18]

Account (CIM) allows for I-mode cooperative action in a group context. We arrive at such a context, in a rudimentary sense at least, by assuming that $G_1 = G_2$ and these goals form the ethos of the simple I-mode group that the participants here form. In more interesting cases, there is a preexisting group that the goals G_1 and G_2 serve (e.g., the ethos could be the goal of cleaning a yard, and A_i's goal would be to do what he reasonably can to help the ethos goal being achieved). The end result of successful cooperation would be the achievement of the privately shared goal.

As to rational cooperation, in clause (3) the agents are required to have a mutual belief concerning the relevant pieces of information. Here is an argument for clauses (3) and (4): Suppose that the participants' goals and actions are dependent in the sense of clause (2), be the dependence antecedent or voluntarily created on the spot. Then the participants will rationally need the other's performance, at least for an optimal result (namely, goal achievement) for themselves. This rationally requires that each agent A_i, i =1, 2, believes and trusts that the other one will adjust her goal and perform her means action as required by clause (2). In addition, A_1 must of course believe that A_2 believes that A_1 will similarly participate, for otherwise A_2 would not have a good reason to participate; and similarly for A_2. Furthermore, they must lack the belief that the relevant negated higher order belief contents are true.[19] To justify clause (4), we note that the resulting mutual belief cannot be idle; it must serve as the participants' (partial) reason for participation.

Clause (3) serves to make cooperation to some extent social and rational, because it gives a reason to say that everyone believes that all the participants are cooperating and that their goals are promoted by the others' promoting their goals. The cooperation thus is socially intentional. For instance, a person may act to achieve her goal of doing all she can to further her aim to make the town more beautiful, believing that everyone has the same goal and the same or shared ethos and is acting in a parallel way and that there is mutual belief about all this. The actions form a cooperative collective action, as the agents share a goal that they promote by their intentional actions. This is still an I-mode collective action, which is not jointly intentional. Here the participants have the shared intended we-goal in the I-mode as their partial reason for acting. Given (3) and (4), we are dealing with a reason-based we-goal in the I-mode. The participants' actions are indirectly interdependent due to their goals having been voluntarily made interdependent.

A promise-based I-mode collective cooperative action is the strongest case with regard to the intentionality of the cooperation and the social ties between the actors. Here the participants are (only) privately committed to take part. The private commitment is a social normative commitment based on mutual promises. Each person has normatively committed himself not only to himself but also to the others to do what he has promised. If a participant wants to pull out from the cooperation, he is accountable to the others. To use an analogy, he is the captain of his boat, and he views the situation from his own point of view and not necessarily from the point of view of the group's interest. He is steering his boat in the same direction as the others as long as he deems it worthwhile. In contrast to the we-mode case, he is not a cocaptain sharing authority with the others on the same ship in view of the group's interest. The Collectivity Condition will not be satisfied (cf. ch.2 sec.1). The social aspects in this case contain mutual promise and mutual knowledge about others' intentions in addition to the ones in previous categories, and there is a "strong" I-mode we-attitude and action on it.

To end this section, I will briefly consider how (CIM) functions, and we start by giving a simple example to illustrate it in the case of a *coordination* situation. Agents A_1 and A_2 have as their shared private goal to meet (thinly conceived: to arrive at the same place). Let the equally good respective means actions be going to the station (s_1, s_2, respectively) and going to the church (c_1, c_2). Their actions leading them to meet (namely, the pairs s_1, s_2 and c_1, c_2) achieve coordination and lead to the satisfaction of their goals. The two other action pairs do not satisfy their goals. There is no conflict in this situation. Both agents are assumed to act individually ("privately") rationally to successfully achieve their goals. This entails that they must have selected one of the action pairs leading to coordination. Here the participants are dependent on each other in a potentially regress-creating way—recall the discussion in chapter 3.

Note that we have the same regress also when there is difference in the positive payoffs and we have what has been called a "Hi-Lo" situation. Here the coordination problem can be solved in the I-mode, for example, if one participant commits himself to choose Hi and signals this to the other one. Then it is rational for the latter agent to choose Hi as well, and this fact makes the former agent's action rational. Another way to go would be to assume that it is mutual knowledge among the agents that each unconditionally acts on the basis of payoff dominance. This is, however, an extra assumption even if plausible. It is a kind of collective principle, as it concerns the players considered together.[20]

Conflict can be introduced into a coordination situation by assuming that the agents have different preferences concerning where to meet, although they still prefer to meet rather than not. Here the conflict is not disturbingly big, and this modified coordination case (a "battle of the sexes" situation) usually qualifies as I-mode cooperation in the sense explicated by (CIM).

As seen, cooperation requires that agents not, at least unconditionally, maximize their own benefit (preferences involving goals) but contribute to the joint effort, which usually involves a cost to them. Problematic cases occur when successful joint effort increases the utility of all of the agents but free-riding agents gain more because they get the benefit without paying the cost. In such collective action dilemmas, there often are two distinct and incompatible actions C and D such that D is the individually rational action and C is the collectively rational action. Individual rationality and collective rationality can be defined in various ways, but the former is usually taken to involve (private) utility maximization and the latter, Pareto efficiency or maximization of group's benefit (often just regarded as the sum of individual utilities). As a typical example of a collective action dilemma, consider a two-choice PD with the choice alternatives C ("cooperation") and D ("defection").[21] In this case, D dominates because choosing D is always more rewarding to the agent than choosing C, regardless of the choices made by the others. However, the agents would nevertheless be better off both individually and collectively if they both chose C instead of D. In a PD, D is the dominating strategy and DD is the only equilibrium, so according to standard game theory, rational agents will always choose D in a single-shot case. Thus, in general a PD cannot rationally be solved cooperatively in the single-shot case in the sense of (CIM) without changing the game.[22] However, as recent experimental results and also anecdotal common-sense evidence indicate, normal socialized agents in fact tend to cooperate much more both in single-shot and long-term situations than what most available accounts of rational cooperation (and they are typically I-mode-based accounts), such as that given by standard game theory, would predict.[23] One recent solution to this puzzle comes from the experimentally backed view—commented on above— that people are *strong* reciprocators who conditionally cooperate when others do but are also disposed to punish defectors, including those who fail to punish.[24]

In contrast, cooperation in the full, we-mode sense is acting together as a group or as one agent to achieve a shared collective goal (see section 5). This is acting for a we-mode reason and is thus we-mode cooperation. In the PD, this entails acting collectively rationally as a group, and this leads to the group's choice of CC over DD.[25] We can say that it is the group that makes the choice here, not the individual group members—and then it is not a PD for group members qua group members.

3 Cooperation and Transformation of Utilities

As to modeling the kinds of effects on agents' goals and preferences, a more systematic account than that involved in (2) of (CIM) goes via utility transformation functions that turn "given" utilities into "final" utilities. The final utilities often significantly change the original interaction situation. The given utilities represent the mutually known valuations of the action sequences in question, and the final utilities are those on whose basis the agents form their intentions and act.[26] The final utilities arise from the agents' deliberation using social information (especially the others' utilities) from the new interaction situation in question, while the given utilities are those with which they, so to speak, enter the situation. Both experimental evidence and theoretical psychological reasons speak for such utility transformations.

We can illuminate these utility transformations by concentrating on cases where the transformation is linear. How can some given utilities u_{ijh} be transformed into final utilities, say, u'_{ijh}, in a situation of interaction? We consider the two-person case where the participants (1 and 2) affect each other's utilities. There are interesting empirical situations or types of cases where a linear transformation seems approximately appropriate.[27] To discuss some central cases of "attitudinal orientation," we start with the linear assumption of transformation:[28]

$$(LT) \qquad u'_{ij1} = au_{ij1} + bu_{ij2},$$

where a and b are parameters taking values between -1 and 1. For the sake of simplicity and to gain conceptual illumination, we only concern some ideal, pure cases below in which the parameters can have the values -1, 0, and 1, and assume that the participants' utilities are interconnected as required by (LT). Of the nine possible cases, the following are the most interesting in this context (agent 1 is used as the reference individual).

(i) $u'_{ij1} = u_{ij1}$; a = 1, b = o (own gain, "selfishness")
(ii) $u'_{ij1} = u_{ij2}$; a = 0, b = 1 (others gain, "altruism")
(iii) $u'_{ij1} = u_{ij1} + u_{ij2}$; a = 1, b = 1 (joint gain, "cooperation")[29]
(iv) $u'_{ij1} = u_{ij1} + u_{ij2}$; a = 1, b = −1 (relative gain, "competition")

Formula (i) indicates that player 1 will make no utility transformation due to the social situation but will operate on the basis of his given utilities (selfish relative to participant 2). Transformation (ii) involves a person's complete identification with his partner's utilities. This is prima facie a cooperative transformation, but the matter depends on the other's transformation. The joint utility approach defined by (iii) is clearly cooperative and fits the progroup I-mode. Formula (iv) defines a particularly competitive kind of utility transformation: What matters is how much you are ahead. Some amount of competition can be involved in cooperation (think of competing salesmen in a business organization).

Supposing that both participants indeed share (LT) (at least on the level of their mutual beliefs) concerning the available payoff, let us consider the effects of transformation in terms of the two-choice PD (with C and D standing, respectively, for cooperation and defection), as follows.

	C	D
C	3, 3	1, 4
D	4, 1	2, 2

A mutual joint gain transformation will turn this into the following coordination game.

	C	
D		
C	6, 6	5, 5
D	5, 5	4, 4

Now CC is the only Nash equilibrium and also a Pareto-optimal solution.[30]

Clearly then, the player's attitude toward the interaction situation may have a radical effect on the outcome. In a study of cooperation, the joint gain transformation is the most interesting one, because when applied mutually it will always result in perfect correlation of preferences. This is similar to Harsanyi's social welfare function that is supposed to represent "ethical" preferences.[31]

However, it must be emphasized that transformations are not always helpful. In a coordination game, for instance, they do not help. Consider, for instance, a coordination situation:

1, 1	0, 0
0, 0	1, 1

The jointness transformation would clearly not lead to a rational solution (the pair (1, 1) is replaced by (2, 2), without strategic gain). Here the participants are dependent on each other in a regress-creating way, as emphasized in the literature and discussed in chapter 3. This shows that while the kind of progroup I-mode approach to cooperation expressed by the joint sum transformation often works in the direction of enhancing cooperation, in the case of a coordination dilemma of the above kind, it does not work. Instead, if the participants choose in the we-mode, namely, as a group, they can solve the coordination game in favor of cooperation by selecting one of the pairs (2, 2) as their shared group goal.

In general, the type of the transformation may depend on several factors, like the characteristics of the agents, the relationship among the agents, and the nature of the interaction situation at hand. It could also be allowed that the type of function used may be shaped by experience, enabling learning from previous interactions.[32]

Preference transformations enhancing similarity are important, because cooperation is more likely to occur if the agents' preferences are positively correlated (see note 17 on *corr*). In the I-mode case, this involves that the shifting or adjusting of goals and means actions required by (CIM) will be easier in the case of high preference correlation. Accordingly, in a PD, preference transformations will occur and change the game into a "milder" collective dilemma situation, such as a coordination dilemma of the kind that the assurance game (where, in the case of the first player, the CC joint outcome is preferred) involves (see appendix 2 for discussion). Another possibility is the kind of cooperative game that joint transformations in the above sense (iii) yield.

Also the possibilities for we-mode cooperation may improve with high preference correlation, since highly correlated preferences can more easily lead to a goal (or an action alternative) becoming collectively accepted as the group's goal. This contrasts with the I-mode case in which the agents base their decisions on their private utility functions (even if perhaps progroup ones).

4   Group Preferences

Group members' functioning in the we-mode requires functioning on group reasons and thus it requires the attribution of attitudes (representational mental states) to groups, although in my account they do not in an ontological "super-agent" sense have them. Furthermore, we must be able to speak of the cooperation between groups (e.g., between the states in the European Union) and thus to speak of preferences, intentions, beliefs, actions, and interrelations between groups.

Accordingly, when discussing we-mode preferences underlying group intentions and joint intentions, we need a notion of group preference that a group, g, has as a group. This is because individual group members' we-mode preferences derive from the preferences of the group; or at least from what they prefer as a group (see below). Indeed, the group members' we-mode preferences can in general be taken to derive from the group's constitutive goals and standards, its ethos. However, as the ethos consists only of the constitutive goals, beliefs, standards, and so on of the group, we must also allow that nonconstitutive goals, beliefs, standards, and so on can be involved and can be a source of we-mode preferences, with the rationality provision that the ethos is not violated. In general, the ethos of g will determine how group-relevant states in the world are to be ordered in terms of preference.

Note that the ethos in general expresses the values of the group, and values are, as such, normative. However, here it suffices to discuss values merely in a "descriptively normative" sense, that is, the sense of describing what values a group has. Furthermore, I will below concentrate on preferences, partly because they are more proximate determinants of group action and cooperative joint action.[33]

I take the group preferences to be analogous to other group attitudes, as discussed in chapter 6. Group preferences (and utilities) thus are to be based on collective acceptance and not on aggregation of I-mode preferences. They are artifacts due to the group and must be based on the members' acceptances when functioning as group members. Such acceptance may be preceded by group discussion, negotiation, bargaining, and so on. Group preferences in the meant sense thus are preferences that we-mode groups have. Note that both we-mode and I-mode groups can have aggregated preferences, respectively aggregated on the basis of we-mode or I-mode preferences. In such aggregation the members share a suitable procedure (e.g. majority voting) and endorse (respectively in the we-mode or in the I-mode) whatever will be the result of the aggregation.

In the manner of chapter 6, I assume that there are "operative" members for the group (possibly consisting of all its members) who have the authority from all the group members to accept preferences and possibly other contents for the group. (The preferences here may concern relevant action-goal sequences.) The "positional account" of chapter 6 now gives us this (recall (GATT)):

> (GP) Group g *prefers* X *to* Y *as a group* if and only if there are operative members of g such that
> (1) these agents acting as group members in the we-mode (and accordingly performing their positional tasks due to their exercising the relevant decision-making system of g) intentionally collectively accept as a group with collective commitment that X is preferable to Y for g;
> (2) there is mutual knowledge among the operative members to the effect that (1);
> (3) because of (1), the (full-fledged and adequately informed) nonoperative members qua members of g tend to tacitly accept with collective commitment—or at least ought so to accept—that their group g prefers X over Y;
> (4) there is mutual belief or knowledge in g to the effect that (3).[34]

Considering the case in which all the group members are operative ones (think of informal egalitarian groups, for instance), clauses (3) and (4) become emptily satisfied. Thus, we can say that in conditions of mutual knowledge, such a group prefers X over Y as a group if and only if its members collectively (or jointly) accept that X is preferred to Y in group contexts—and if and only if the group members as a group prefer X to Y. Thus we can here speak about preference attributions to a group and speak about the members jointly or as a group preferring X over Y.[35] Note that group preferences may be subject to the discursive dilemma in the sense in which Pettit has discussed it. Thus either a premise-driven or a conclusion-driven way is possible, and additional considerations are needed if the most rational solution is to be obtained.[36]

In (2) and (4), the mutual knowledge requirement can in some cases be relaxed to the requirement of mutual *knowability* (which still entails group-publicity), for it may not always be important that all members actually know about group acceptance but rather that they can obtain such knowledge.

Account (GP) does not require that any one of the group members prefers X to Y in the I-mode; group preferences might be, for example, emergent compromises made on the basis of I-mode preferences. In groups where the decision-making is based on argumentation or informal discussion, this may happen on a case-by-case basis, but especially in large groups, the use of suitable institutional mechanism with formal rules and procedures is typical (think of the majority voting procedure). Such an institutionalized and codified method may replace the specially authorized operative members, as the collectively accepted and authorized procedure will yield group decisions as its output.[37] In general, the results of the procedure may significantly differ from the agents' original opinions—both as group members and as private persons. Thus (rational) group preferences need not directly reflect the individual members' private preferences, except perhaps in the long run.

We may speak of group utilities qua the group's utilities, too. They can be based on group preferences analogously with how individual utilities are represented on the basis of an individual's preferences and thus, in view of clause (1) of (GP), come to represent the (operative) members' collective preferences. Aggregation can sometimes be used when it happens to be feasible. We might in the case of our earlier PD in section 3 take the group utility to be simply the average of private utilities, and thus the group can come to transform the earlier PD situation in terms of the joint utility transformation to yield this:

3	2.5
2.5	2

The group will here choose as its collective goal the outcome maximizing the group utility (here the outcome CC), and the group members can then use the matrix to infer their required part actions. Recall that in the we-mode case, the group is the basic agent, and it chooses from joint outcomes (that are valued in the above matrix) and the group members acting properly as group members choose a corresponding action (here C). In this particular case, it would mean that both agents rationally choose C.

However, this kind of idealized situation might not come about, and the members might still retain their private preferences to the contrary and only act as group members because the group so requires and perhaps even coerces. If their private preferences dominate, the original collective action dilemma will be there, at least in the members' thoughts. A tenable solution may require either more permanently changing the group members' preferences by socializing them suitably or using sanctions to achieve the right kind of cooperative action (which then might not be based on a wholehearted desire for it).

Note that in a PD, the we-mode preference (of CC over DD) happens to coincide with the I-mode preference, since both players' I-mode utilities are larger in CC than in DD (CC is Pareto-preferred to DD). Note that a participant might prefer CC over DD not merely because of his self-regarding reasons, but because he other-regardingly, but in the I-mode, prefers CC to DD—say, for the reason that the sum or product of the participants' utilities from CC is greater than that from DD. In a way, shared collective goals thus yield the same result as the mutual joint gain transformations leading to the maximization of utility sums as presented above. However, in the case of the joint gain transformations, the utilities are still I-mode utilities instead of we-mode utilities, unless collectively accepted as what is to be maximized. Speaking generally, we-mode utilities (and thus group utilities) need not be functionally dependent on the corresponding I-mode utilities, and the group can equally well adopt a different view (say the Rawlsian view equating group utility with the smallest individual utility).

A group's preferences (namely, what the group members have collectively formed and accepted to be the group's preferences) can be attributed to group members when they are functioning as group members. Thus if the group has G as its intended goal, its members will be disposed to accept and endorse "We intend to achieve G" as expressing their we-mode joint intention. This kind of distribution principle seems valid for all group preferences. Thus we can discuss group preferences in our PD in terms of stylized practical inferences, as follows.[38]

(1) We intend to achieve collective goal G.
(2) We mutually believe that to achieve G we must bring about CC by our collective action.
Therefore:
(3) We intend to bring about CC by our collective action.

A group member may (and will, when in a "reflective mood") reason in the following manner.

(a) We intend to bring about CC by our collective action.
Therefore:
(b) I intend to perform my part of our bringing about CC by our collective action.

Note that even in clause (b) we are dealing with a we-mode intention, because, as discussed in chapter 4, the participation intention that it concerns is conceptually dependent on the we-mode joint intention expressed by (a). The above principles are assumed to involve that the group members indeed function as group members in the standard, we-mode sense of chapter 1. Thus, in contrast to the I-mode case, rational acting as a group member in the we-mode sense entails rational cooperation in a situation viewable as a single-shot collective action dilemma.[39]

There are two basic ways to act when taking other agents into account. One can operate on the basis of one's I-mode goals or on the basis of a full-blown collective goal. These considerations, corresponding to the two (namely, the weak and the standard) kinds of acting as a group member, can also be combined. Discussing the two kinds of preferences quantitatively in terms of utilities, an agent A_j will have I-mode utilities of the kind $u_{ij}(X)$, i representing I-mode, and we-mode utilities of the kind $u_{gj}(X)$ concerning an action-goal sequence X, namely, an action-process starting with an effective intending and ending up with the result event of action X. (We can here alternatively use $u_{gj}(X)$ for A_j's quantitative I-mode evaluation of g's preference, which would mean that both utilities here would be I-mode utilities.) Rational action can be based on one of these or on some kind of optimal way of taking both kinds of utilities into account. Recall here the self-interested, altruistic, jointness (or cooperative), and competitive transformations, where the self is now contrasted with the group rather than with another group member.

Let us suppose that X is an action in a group context but in general not one that our agent is preemptively obligated by the group to perform when acting as a group member.[40] In such a case, a linear combination corresponding to our earlier I-mode case may be a feasible way to define a combined resultant utility that the agent will maximize or "satisfice" when rationally deciding which action X to perform:

$$u_{tj}(X) = w_i u_{ij}(X) + w_g u_{gj}(X)$$

Understood in this way, I-mode and we-mode utilities (or more generally group utilities including the I-mode group utility as specified above) can be linearly combined to yield agent A_j's total utility $u_{tj}(X)$ concerning an action X. The factors in u_{ij} are supposed to be viewed from an individual's perspective, whereas those involved in u_{gj} are factors viewed from the group's perspective but as evaluated by A_j. The same factors may have an effect on both, but they are viewed from different perspectives. Intersubjective differences can be allowed with respect to not only individual reasons but also (evaluated) group reasons.

To consider some special cases, when $w_i = 0$ and $w_g = 1$, unconditional progroup cooperation is entailed, and when $w_i = 1$ and $w_g = 0$, we get action on mere private preferences or goals (which may be other-regarding, of course). When the unconditional progroup condition holds in the case of all members, they share and are committed to the goal G (here: the ethos) and can be said to have at least a nonnormative agreement to cooperate (namely, to act together toward G). However, a member may take group reasons into account in a weaker sense, while also respecting individual reasons. This may happen, for instance, if he has not fully committed himself to a collective goal. Basically, the weights are determined by the interaction situation and the individual's dispositions to value individual and group reasons. They are not usually up to the individual to strategically choose.

In a PD situation, if the group (dyad) has selected CC as its goal (or takes it to be entailed by its goal), then $w_i = 0$ for both players, and thus the expected utility of C will exceed that of D for all probability assignments.

In this setup, we can accordingly get a kind of solution to a collective action dilemma without having to consider external mechanisms (e.g., sanctions) that change the game-defining individual preferences. In some other cases, however, the above kind of linear combination account does not work well, if at all. Section 6 discusses this matter.

5   We-Mode Cooperation

In we-mode thinking, in contrast to the I-mode case, an agent is supposed to view herself as part of a social group or collective and act as a full-fledged member of the group. The group here can be even a temporary task group consisting of some agents who face the task of carrying a heavy table upstairs. Having formed a joint intention (goal) to do it, they already form a group in a we-mode sense. Such a group is capable of action. The adoption of the group's point of view in general requires cooperation between the members to facilitate the group's action as a group (recall the practical inferences discussed in section 4).

On conceptual grounds, we-mode action indeed is inherently cooperative, as the satisfaction of the Collectivity Condition already shows. Full-blown cooperation involves joint action. However, there is the additional psychological fact that one can cooperate willingly (i.e., out of a cooperative attitude) or reluctantly.[41] Taking this factor into account, a joint action performed out of a cooperative attitude can be said to be more cooperative than one performed reluctantly (but still as a full-blown joint action). All joint action types (irrespective of how the part-preferences correlate) thus can have both willingly and reluctantly performed tokens. If all the participants of cooperation participate out of a cooperative attitude, we have a case of full-blown cooperation. A person having a cooperative attitude toward a joint action X must be disposed to reason and act willingly in ways contributing to X. Let us distinguish between the actions that a joint action conceptually and functionally requires for its performance and actions that further it but are not strictly required. A cooperative (or willing) participant of full-blown cooperation must be disposed willingly to perform his part of X and must also willingly accept a share—reasonable for him relative to his capacities and skills—of a required extra action. In addition, he must be disposed to perform unrequired extra actions related to X—at least as long as they are not too costly in relation to the gains achieved. A cooperative attitude can be based on various kinds of motivation, but in typical cases, it will involve goodwill not only toward performing X (which I invariably require) but also goodwill and faithfulness toward the other participants and acting in part for their personal sake. (This much cannot be required when we-mode cooperation involves some coercion or sanctions or involves an order-giving authority.)

Allowing that less than a maximal amount of cooperative willingness be present, collective cooperative action is equivalent to acting together (jointly) toward a shared intended collective goal.[42] Joint action is constitutively cooperative activity, where the shared collective goal in joint action serves to make the participants' part actions cooperatively connected. While there can be some conflict between the parts (as in a game of tennis) and, in this sense, some difference in cooperativeness built into various joint action types, the basic setup is that of cooperative harmony. Thus, when the persons involved act as a group, they act as one agent, cooperative harmony must exist between their actions (and action intentions), and they must trust that the others will not let them down in the process.

Intended shared collective goals satisfy the Collectivity Condition, and—as goals can be regarded as contents of intentions (more precisely, "aim-intentions," in the sense of chapter 4)—I am actually saying that we-mode cooperation amounts to acting jointly (or together) on the basis of a relevant joint intention (recall (AT*) of chapter 5, section 4). There is no need to require an antecedently existing group here, because a joint intention already defines one, a social group capable of action.

Recall from chapter 6 that such a joint intention will be a group reason that also may be preemptive. In such a case, the joint intention (amounting to a group intention in view of $(GINT)$ of chapter 4) is an authoritative group reason.

Below is a stylized summary of a simple "egalitarian" two-person case (the case with operative members for coordinating the activity will be commented on later).[43]

(CWM) A_1 and A_2 (*successfully*) *cooperate with each other in the we-mode* in bringing about goal G if and only if

(1) G is a collective goal type, namely, an "achievement-whole" the achievement of which can be divided—either *ex ante actu* or *ex post actu*—into A_1's and A_2's parts;

(2) A_1 and A_2 jointly intend to achieve G by acting jointly in the sense of (AT^*), and they achieve G jointly in accordance with and partly because of this joint intention of theirs to achieve G together.

To go from the above conceptually minimal notion to a notion of (weakly) *rational* we-mode cooperation, we add two clauses saying that the information in clauses (1) and (2) must be mutually believed (clause (3)) such that the mutual belief is not idle (clause (4)):

(3) A_1 and A_2 rationally mutually believe that (1), (2);

(4) (2) in part because of (3).

Clauses (3) and (4) can be justified as in the I-mode case, mutatis mutandis, and I will not here comment on this matter.[44]

Account (CWM) relies on the notion of jointly intentional joint action (see (AT^*)), that is, collective action based on the participants' joint intention, and indeed makes cooperative joint action and (plain) joint action equivalent. To present two qualifying remarks, we note, in accordance with (CWM), that each joint action *type* is cooperative. However, some action types (those in which the inbuilt part preferences correlate perfectly, e.g., lifting a table) are more cooperative than some others (e.g., playing tennis, where the part preferences do not correlate perfectly). In addition, recall that in the fullest kind of we-mode cooperation the parties truly *willingly* (as opposed to reluctantly) perform their parts.[45] Thus, acting out of a cooperative attitude makes a *token* of joint action (and a token of a participant's part action) more cooperative than if it were performed unwillingly (reluctantly). Account (CWM) is not directly concerned with whether token actions are performed out of a cooperative attitude or not.[46]

The we-mode group that is involved here (already on the basis of the members' joint intention) is assumed to be both externally and internally autonomous (see chapters 1 and 10). The participants need not be in a fully symmetric position; there might be, for example, power relations specifying a task division, and there often is an operative-nonoperative member distinction. Still (CWM) applies, as the asymmetries are due to the participants' collective acceptance due to my assumption of external and internal autonomy—and then at least strong coercion is prohibited.

In cooperative joint action, the participants' joint telos in the part performances is to participate in acting together to achieve G, although not all the participants in many-person cooperation need to have this end, as long as the cooperative action functionally works (recall chapter 5, section 5).

In this case of collectively intentional collective cooperative action, the group members, in effect, have a collective intention expressible by "We will cooperate to achieve goal G." This contrasts with I-mode cases, in which the intentions are private and have the form "I intend to contribute toward goal G," where G is a goal shared in the I-mode (recall chapter 3). In this context, the group is taken to be capable of action and in effect to be a we-mode group. The group will at least try to bring it about that G is satisfied or promoted in accordance with its ethos. When the members intentionally together see to it (*stit*) that G is promoted, every group member can be said to have a part or "slice" in this joint *stit*-ing, and this part is in principle irreducible to actions described without reference to the joint *stit*-ing. The parts here may also involve helping, advising, or sanctioning others—when needed (recall schema (W2) of chapter 4). The totality of the members' part actions, based on their jointly *stit*-ing G, when successful, collectively taken, amounts to a we-mode cooperative collective (or joint) action toward G. The account (CWM) will be satisfied in this type of general case, although perhaps without the presence of a cooperative attitude.

As we are dealing with a we-mode case, the participants are collectively committed to the joint goal involved (in our earlier example, to bringing about that the town is beautiful).[47] The collective commitment entailed by the participants' collective intention has the content that the members, qua group members, collectively promote the shared collective goal (be it the group's ethos or something else). In the case of rational agents, collective commitment, of course, presupposes that the persons believe or know that there are others who are analogously committed. As seen, collective commitment enables a group to act as a group and thus to perform we-mode collective cooperative actions. Thus, in principle, for persons acting fully on the ground of the group-perspective, there will be no collective action dilemmas, for there can be no conflict between individual and collective rationality in the group: the group rationally prescribes mutual cooperation for its members. The group conceptualizes a preanalytic action situation in its we-mode terms and does not—as such and as long as a pragmatically adequate account is not required—make use of the participants' private preferences. (The group members may still be tempted to act on the latter—see section 6 and also chapter 8, section 4, for similar remarks related to the PD.)

When matters thus are seen from the group's point of view, private conflicting interests are laid aside, and the group is regarded as the basic agent. In I-mode cooperation, people are only privately bound to cooperate. Even if there is a mutual promise to cooperate, they may yet decide to withdraw when the project becomes costly and pay the fines for breaking a promise. In contrast, in we-mode cooperation, the persons, being collectively committed, participate in a joint project with shared authority. Shared authority presupposes that one person is not allowed to act as he chooses. His actions are open for all to criticize. As seen in chapter 1, the collective commitment involves social commitment, due to the fact that the committed persons are coauthors of the action. Thus they are committed not only to themselves but to each other to perform their actions promoting the group's ethos. People will act as proper group members if they are consistent with their collective commitment. As a consequence of all the above, much more *persistence* and *stability* concerning the fulfillment of tasks can be expected in a we-mode group. It is an inbuilt presupposition that the others will perform their parts of the joint project and that the project will be given up only on mutual agreement. And more *flexibility* in action will often be involved: the group members will be disposed to help (or correct or pressure) each other when needed, while in an I-mode group helping and pursuing "emergency" tasks will in general have to be negotiated. Both I-mode and we-mode cooperation presuppose trust in the others' participation, and in the we-mode case, a strong kind of *respect-based trust* will have to be involved.[48] (See the concluding section for additional remarks.)

Even if on the group level the members are jointly seeing to it that G, they may, compatibly with (CWM), use whatever "tools" (e.g., hiring agents to do something) that are believed to be useful. Here the members' part actions simply are actions qua a group member in the standard sense, and by these actions they represent the group. In internally autonomous groups, the members either all are operatives functioning in equal positions or have internally appointed some operatives for various tasks, resulting in a (normatively) structured group with power-involving positions. In the latter case, operative members with authority may give directives with the purpose of coordinating the participants' activities optimally with respect to the joint task at hand. An example would be a symphony orchestra in which the conductor's task is to coordinate the players' activities in a "musical" way (for instance, choice of tempi and phrasing is central here). Some mild coercion may be present, and the participants (here players) may not be allowed to help each other extensively if that happens at the expense of the quality of the total performance. Joint action here may involve the participants' relevantly sanctioning, and exerting pressure on, others. Cases with external authorization as such may well involve exercises of authority that do not lead to cooperation at all. An army unit's orderly behavior based on its commander's orders need not be more than minimally cooperative (but it could also be highly cooperative).[49]

This concludes my treatment of intentional cooperative collective action. As seen, all cooperative I-mode and we-mode cases can be regarded as collective actions based on a shared we-attitude. In this sense, cooperative collective action is conformative action, which should not be a surprise. However, there can be conflicts in all these cases. For instance, some group members may compete (think of competing salesmen in a business organization) and be in partial conflict. But their positions in the group are still consistent, or, if some competitiveness is normatively built into the positions, at least there is much shared common ground ensuing from the shared ethos (basic goals, etc.) of the group to which they are collectively committed.

6 Cooperation and Acting as a Group Member

In this section, acting as group member will be assumed of the participants of cooperation. This is actually an obvious assumption in a group context. This is because the following equivalence almost trivially holds, given our earlier discussion.

(*) A group member acts as a group member (in the core sense, namely, either the standard or the weak sense) if and only if she intentionally cooperates with respect to the group's ethos with the group members.

There is thus both the I-mode version and the we-mode version of this general thesis, which, among other things, covers the important case of cooperation in a democratic state. Action in a group context respecting the ethos of the group can be regarded as institutional action, at least in a we-mode group (see chapter 8 for discussion). Accordingly, our thesis tightly connects cooperation and institutional action, at least in the we-mode case. The we-mode thesis is rather trivially true, because the concepts of acting as a group member and cooperation with respect to the ethos of the group are closely related. The we-mode thesis says that a group member acts as a group member in the standard sense if and only if he cooperates in the we-mode with the group members (in the sense of (CWM)) with respect to the ethos. (A cooperative psychological attitude need not be assumed to be present in all cases.) We will not need the I-mode thesis in this section. Appendix 3 gives a proof of (*) and its two subtheses. Note that the general situation in actual life is probably going to be that both we-mode and I-mode cooperation are involved in institutional cases, with a certain percentage of each.

When acting as a group member, some of the actions thus may be hierarchically ordered, in the sense that first come obligatory actions, after which decision is made about which of the permissible actions to perform. In the case of action that the group with preemptive authority obligates, a member is normatively required to act on the group utility and to try to maximize or "satisfice" it. (However, as claimed in section 2 of chapter 6, we-mode group reasons may be taken by the group members to be, *pro tanto* rather than preemptive—and *pro tanto* reasons can be weighed against other reasons in contrast to properly obeyed normative requirements.)

In the case of strictly obeyed normative requirements (concerning what one ought to do) I-mode utilities have no place. In addition to obligatory actions there are permitted actions, but here also individual tastes (I-mode utilities) can properly step in, as long as the group utilities will lead our agent to promote the ethos and not to violate it. In the I-mode case of acting weakly as a group member, no we-mode utilities are present, but group utilities are. Group utilities need not always be we-mode utilities (representing preferences expressible by "We as a group prefer X to Y") but can be I-mode ones representing preferences of the kind often expressed by "I prefer X to Y for the benefit of the group" without the latter being based on the former. Recall from chapter 4 that in the we-mode case the conceptual order is that the we-mode we-preference precedes the we-mode I-preference, irrespective of how the latter precisely relates to I-mode I-preferences.

I will next consider in terms of a simple example under what circumstances it is rational to act cooperatively as a group member and thereby promote the ethos (the identity-conferring constitutive goals, etc.) of group g. There are two ways of viewing the situation. The first view is to take a group member to be well socialized, so that the we-mode goals, preferences, and utilities will overwhelmingly be dominant reasons for his action. His social identity is fully *fixed*, we may say. This view fits well with our analysis of group preferences and the related practical inferences. The other possibility is that the group member has a *flexible* social identity, so to speak, and is trying to make his decisions on the basis of both his I-mode utilities and his group utilities. He may use group-beneficial transformations to arrive either at I-mode progroup utilities or—much better from the group's point of view—at we-mode utilities. In this second case, we are, generally speaking, dealing with a kind of *switch problem*, that is, a switch from (dominantly) thinking, including preferring, and acting as a private person (or, for that matter, as a member of another group) to (dominantly) thinking and acting as a member of g. The switch need not involve direct intentional action but may be action that can indirectly be brought about by the agent or by his social environment, including educators; in other, more dramatic cases, one can even speak of the "group taking over" the agent. Note, too, that the group may conceptualize an action situation directly in its terms. Then, if the group members indeed are functioning fully as group members, no switch is needed, as the member's private preferences do not get in the group's way.

In section 3, utility transformations concerned only one kind of social information, namely, the others' utilities. To make my analysis more realistic, I will now consider agents acting in a group context and indeed acting at least weakly as group members. In this section, the groups, at least initially, will be I-mode groups (recall chapter 1). Acting as a group member can accordingly here be regarded as acting toward the same ethos that the participants have privately accepted and are only privately committed to. When acting in a group context, there will be several new motivational factors affecting action. These factors can be conceptually built into the social group situation and thus taken to reflect what a group member will have to take into account in her action. These factors lead to transformations that go beyond those discussed in section 3. They change the participants' utilities into the kind of final utilities that acting in a group context ultimately requires.

Let us start by considering I-mode utilities relevant to "single-shot" situations that de facto occur only once but in which the factual possibility of a repetition of the situation is not ruled out.[50] Assume there is a collective step good, E, in group g. (E might represent its ethos.) Assume first that E is an "indivisible" and nonexcludable collective good, that is, a good whose use or consumption does not reduce the amount available to others and that is made available to all the members of the collective in question. Also assume, for simplicity's sake, that there are only two participants with two possible choices (C and D), that E can be produced even alone, and that there is a fixed total collective cost, the individual cost of producing it alone being higher than when it is produced together.

Let u be the gross reward (utility) each participant receives when E is produced. I will assume that utilities are intersubjectively comparable and that objectively existing processes are being evaluated here. When E is produced by the participants' action, there will be a jointness effect, say, j, that can be negative in some cases. The jointness or social effect can basically be of two kinds, either an effect concerning functionality or efficiency or an effect concerning social capital. In general, j is a function of the costs and a net jointness effect. Let the jointness or interaction effect of this kind of material efficiency and achievement be reflected in a parameter i. The social capital component, e, included in the jointness effect measures the increase in trust, networking, skills, and knowledge gained from cooperative action (here: action as a member of the group). Below e can thus be taken to reflect also the effect of the ethos. This is the typical "dual structure" feature of structural social properties. The agents both produce and reproduce the system when complying, but such production and reproduction on the other hand relies on the proper working of the system. Their contributions tend to provide the group with new knowledge and ideas as well as new ways of acting and new skills. All of this is a collective good, thus available to all group members once brought about.[51]

I will denote by j the increase in social capital due to collective action and will simplifyingly assume that j is a sum of the kind $i + e - c/2$. Thus, when both participants contribute, they will each receive the payoff $u + i + e - c/2$, and this is the same as $u + j$. Next, we consider the possibility that one of the agents defects. Supposing that E can be brought about alone and that the other participant's contribution here amounts to bringing about E alone; the free-rider will then gain a certain amount f by his defection, namely, by switching from C to D. Alternatively, f can be regarded as a free-rider incentive.[52] If one agent, B, defects, then the other one, A, has to produce E alone. This will cost him c (rather than $c/2$), and he may lose more due to the fact that he (correctly believes he) is a "sucker." The total loss (namely, the extra effort plus the sucker effect) accruing to A from his being the sole contributor will be denoted by s. In principle, factor s can also have a positive value, in that the sole contributor may view herself as a morally good person or something of the kind. There might also be other, higher order effects: While A's utility may be affected by his thought that he is being cheated by B, this fact may in turn affect B's utility, and so on.

Assume also that there is a social norm in force barring free-riding.[53] Thus, there is a negative normative sanction effect, a quasi-moral one, from defection, given that there was an obligation or at least a normative expectation to contribute. I will denote the effect of social sanctions (and the related psychological consequences of shame as well as guilt) as m. In the case of mutual defection, this social sanction may be nonexistent or, at any rate, may have a different value. Let the mutual defection utility, including the social sanction effect, be m^*.

What we now have is the following, assuming that the participants are in a symmetrical position with respect to their payoffs and writing out only participant A's (the row player's) payoffs.

	C	D
C	$u + j$	$u + s$
D	$u + f + m$	m^*

Here E can be taken to amount to the joint outcome CC, or at least E is taken to entail CC.

When should a rational agent A contribute (cooperate, choose C) rather than defect? This question can be answered by comparing the expected payoffs for C and D accruing to A:

$$EU(C) = p(C_B/C_A)(u + j) + p(D_B/C_A)(u + s)$$
$$EU(D) = p(C_B/D_A)(u + f + m) + p(D_B/D_A)(m^*)$$

If A acts on his preferences, he will cooperate rationally (in an instrumental sense of rationality) in the production of E by choosing C if and only if EU(C) > EU(D). If both players view the situation in similar terms, we get mutual cooperation, and it is plausible to regard the analysans of (CIM) of section 2 to be satisfied. This is because, other things being equal, the jointness factor j then will have to be sufficiently large and the sucker effect will have to be sufficiently small as compared with the case in which the agents had not yet entered the interaction situation and reasoned about taking action.

Consider now a PD defined by the preference ordering DC, CC, DD, CD for the row player A and by CD, CC, DD, DC for column player B. For the purpose of illustration, we assign the following numerical values to the participants' preferences (utilities).

	C	D
C	2.50, 2.50	−1, 3
D	3, −1	0, 0

Our parameters might now get the following values: $u = 2, j = 0.50$ (using $e = 0$ in $j = i + e − c/2$), $s = −3, f = 1, m = 0, m^* = 0$. Then, under full uncertainty, EU(C) = 0.75, and EU(D) = 1.50. Hence the rational thing to do for both participants is to defect. The situation can be changed, for example, by changing the values of m and m^*. Thus we may assume that $m = −1$ and $m^* = −1$. Then EU(D) = 0.50. Thus EU(C) > EU(D), and cooperation is rational. Note, however, that the transformations have changed the preferences and we do not have a PD any more. Thus this solution to the dilemma is "external" rather than "internal." The transformations in our illustration are basically linear transformations of the kind studied in section 3, except that the several parameters make the situation more complex.

Our above parameters represent reasons for rational intention formation and action in cases involving a conflict between collective and individual rationality. In terms of them, it is also possible to formulate decision-making criteria for when to rationally comply (cooperate) with the ethos and when not.

Let E be an ethos goal or ethos-related goal, a collective good. In our first case, the goal state E is assumed to be wanted and intended in the I-mode by the agents. I will concentrate on the second of the discussed views related to the switch problem and assume that our group members need not be fully socialized. The main question here is to compare group-related, namely, ethos-promoting behavior with I-mode behavior (and especially I-mode behavior that is ethos-promoting only if it suits the individual's preferences or utilities). The harder problem is to show that we-mode ethos-promoting behavior rationally wins over ethos-promoting I-mode (namely, progroup I-mode) behavior.

The group members' assumed I-mode preferences about the situation will now be contrasted with we-mode preferences related to their group. These we-mode preferences, which amount to g's preferences, are to be understood as in section 4. We will now consider under what conditions the switch from I-mode to progroup I-mode (involving the group stance, albeit in the I-mode) is rational in our simple situation. In the earlier plain I-mode case, we used e = 0 to reflect the fact that the agent may not have acted for the group at all. In the progroup I-mode case, we have $e > 0$, and the agent acts in part for the reason that the group requires it or that it is to the benefit of the group—and accordingly cooperates. Earlier the joint outcome CC was valued by our agent as $u + j$. With $e > 0$, a suitable positive value may result in $EU(C) > EU(D)$, and we have a case of the progroup I-mode that also can "solve" the collective action problem (here PD) at hand.

In this simple example, we now let $e = 1$ in $j = i + e - c/2$ instead of $e = 0$ and, using the earlier values for the other parameters in the first case (thus $m = 0, m^* = 0$), we arrive at an assurance game (see appendix 2) with the following expected utilities.

$$EU(C) = \frac{1}{2}(2 + 1.50) + \frac{1}{2}(2 - 3) = 1.25$$
$$EU(D) = \frac{1}{2}(2 + 1 - 0) + \frac{1}{2}(0) = 1.50$$

and thus $EU(C) < EU(D)$. It suffices now to assume that mutual defection is sanctioned with the value $m^* = -1$ to make cooperation more rational than defection, for then $EU(D) = 1$ and $EU(C) > EU(D)$. Thus in the progroup I-mode case, less sanctioning is needed than in the earlier pure, possibly fully selfish I-mode case.

Next consider the we-mode in this context.[54] In a collective dilemma situation such as the PD above, the group prefers the joint outcome CC to DD, and its members choose C over D. If the members here think collectively rationally, they will think in the we-mode. The we-mode depends on the collective acceptance by the group of E (hence CC) as the group's goal, collective commitment to E and CC, as well as for-groupness (in the full sense satisfying the Collectivity Condition). The important thing to emphasize here is that we basically are dealing with the change of agency from individual group members to the group. If we view the matter of achieving E from the group's point of view, we can say simply that here the group prefers to achieve E to not achieving it: E is better for the group than –E. Thus if the costs for achieving E are such as to make the expected utility of E higher than that of –E, a rational group will try to achieve E. There is in general no PD or any other collective action dilemma here.[55] The I-mode account concerned an individual's decision making, whereas here we are dealing with the group's decision-making.

However, while the above situation is what we in principle have, we may still make the educated guess that in actual social life, things are not so smooth. Group members must be supposed to follow the group's directives and recommendations for the theory to work, but that is a strong requirement, especially in the case of large groups where the members may not fully identify with the group. Thus, through the back door, as it were, we are back in a dilemma situation (be it a PD or some other collective action dilemma). Were the group members to be fully collectively committed to the idea that they necessarily stand or fall together (as expressed by the Collectivity Condition) and thus to group preferences, they would have to give up the original PD. But here we are dealing with the possibility that some of the members give up that idea. Not only is this the case, but we must face situations where our group is in conflict with some other group or groups. For instance, there may be another group competing for the same good (the other group may want to graze their cattle in the same area we want to use). In such a situation, the chance of ingroup cooperation often increases, based on the old idea that a common enemy unites. Still, individual group members will have an incentive to free-ride if their we-mode commitment to the group is not firm enough, so that their group-goal-based we-mode preferences do not preempt I-mode preferences from having motivating force.[56]

To deal with this kind of real life situation, we must again consider the earlier parameters. What happens to them in the we-mode case? Here the agents act together in the we-mode on the basis of their joint intention (or at least the operative members in the group are supposed to share the intention). This provides the participants with at least a minimal group-social reason to participate in the production of E and makes them satisfy the Collectivity Condition.[57] Related to this factor unique to the we-mode, one may make the educated empirical guess that forming such a we-mode intention and group-social reason will increase the value of the jointness parameter j, which can happen, for example, by increasing the amount of trust and social capital in the group, as compared with the (progroup) I-mode situation. Furthermore, this shared intention rationally entails collective commitment (which can be taken to entail for-groupness) to E; and we-mode for-groupness, in contrast to I-mode progroupness, involves the quasi-conceptually necessary "standing or falling together" idea expressed by the Collectivity Condition.

Collective commitment will do much work in the we-mode case, although in real life, where a group seldom is fully homogenous concerning the collective commitment and its strength, the group will have to monitor the situation and use positive and negative sanctions. What does collective commitment do in particular? Suppose our agent A is switching from progroup I-mode to we-mode. In our earlier setup, m and m^* will then have bigger (negative) values in the we-mode case.[58] Here m derives from social sanctions and the possible accompaniments of the agent's feeling of guilt ("I should really have done C") or shame ("others think I should have done C and I would indeed have liked to conform"). Shame may come about due to (overt) social disapproval and perhaps threats of dismissal from the group. Furthermore, there may be objective sanctions (e.g., fines). If all participants defect, there will be no overt social sanction, and m^* will have a smaller value than m.[59]

In the we-mode case, the sucker effect s will either be zero or it will have a positive value ("I am proud to be the sole person to act for the group"), and in any case s will here have a bigger value than in the I-mode case. Furthermore, the jointness effect j will or at least may be larger in the we-mode case due to the social commitment involved in collective commitment. For instance, helping and encouraging may occur and bring about a net increase in j, and there will be an increase in social capital. Furthermore, the group members may now act in a more disciplined and orderly way (due to social commitment), and this may bring about a larger jointness effect than in the (progroup) I-mode case.

As seen, the we-mode case entails a strengthened version of strong reciprocity: the group members are disposed to cooperate if the others do and to correct, sanction, and punish those who do not cooperate. Thus, for a group reason, the members are conditionally cooperative and prepared to sanction defectors (including those who fail to sanction and punish) to the effect that rational cooperation can take place. The second-order collective action dilemma (that generally affects the I-mode case) arising from the costs of punishing or correcting defectors tends to get solved. At least in groups with voluntary membership, it is plausible to assume that there exist committed members for whom the cost of punishing (e.g., socially criticizing) defectors is not unreasonably high. They might be able to construct an impersonal system ("the police") for this and persuade others to participate in the costs. This would suffice to block the emergence of higher order collective dilemmas of punishment.[60]

In this section it has been argued that we-mode action will in many dilemma cases win over progroup I-mode action, and the latter will win over the pure I-mode case, which better fits selfishness and "for-me-ness." These effects are likelier to happen when the agents are sensitive to what others think of them and their action. Mainly because of the shared social reason for joint action and the ensuing collective commitment and the social sanctions involved, it is harder to defect in the we-mode case than in the I-mode case and even in the progroup I-mode case. Furthermore, properly socialized group members do not even have an incentive to defect at all, as they act with the full group-perspective. (See the summary section for additional points.)

7 Summary

This chapter has studied cooperation by distinguishing between two kinds of cooperation. The weaker kind of cooperation was called I-mode cooperation and was analyzed by (CIM). The basic idea in it is that the participants function on the basis of their private goals and commitments but are disposed to shift their goals and means actions toward the other participants' goals and means actions so as to further the others' as well as their own goals, expecting the others to act similarly. The stronger kind of cooperation is called we-mode cooperation. As analyzed by (CWM), it is basically equivalent to joint action as a group (in the sense of chapter 5) and thus, in contrast to the plain I-mode case, involves the group perspective and acting as a group member. Accordingly, practical reasoning based on the group's preferences was shown to be central. However, the additional feature of cooperativeness, namely, a "willing" attitude toward the joint action, is required. This basically excludes strong coercion. In some cases of cooperation, special operative members authorized to coordinate activities may be present. Cooperation (possibly with only a small amount of willingness) and acting as a group member were argued to be truth-functionally equivalent.

This chapter also studied various functional aspects of cooperation. Thus it was shown, in terms of a simple example about public good provision in a group, that in some cases progroup I-mode cooperation can rationally win over plain I-mode cooperation and that, in turn, we-mode cooperation can in some cases be instrumentally more rational than progroup I-mode cooperation.

To conclude with some general remarks, we-mode reasoning leads more easily to cooperation simply because the we-mode, in contrast to the I-mode, constitutively is cooperative, hence cooperation also will be more persistent, ceteris paribus, and involve less need of sanctioning (recall (CWM)). The participants' private motivations do not matter. They view the situation as a case of the group acting, and they function as "cogs in a machine" or "limbs in a body" (the Collectivity Condition being at work). In contrast, in the I-mode case, their (private) motivations may more easily change (even if they share a joint plan to act together). This is because the group is not backing those motivations and because the participants view the situation merely as themselves acting in a social context of interacting persons rather than being a part of an acting group. It was shown that we-mode acting will often be more (instrumentally) rational for an individual than I-mode acting (including progroup I-mode action). However, it is to be kept in mind that the progroup I-mode theorist can simulate the we-mode by means of making extra assumptions, for example, by allowing agreements for each step in question, so to speak. Yet this kind of continuous agreement-making often is not possible in practice and is bound to need sanctioning to guard against free-riding. The we-mode, in contrast, allows for more speed, creativity, and flexibility because of the group-perspective involved.[61] Furthermore, in the we-mode case— which is based on an atmosphere of trust—there is less need to regard people as "knaves," assuming here the common-sense wisdom that if people are treated as knaves they also tend to act as knaves.

As argued in section 6, in some cases the we-mode approach is rationally better than the I-mode in a functional sense. But could the participants somehow have taken other I-mode features into their decision-making and rationally fared better in that way? First, are they somehow better off when acting in the I-mode than in the we-mode? The problem is complex. The agents' basic valuations of the situation (and which factors they thus regard as important) may differ in the case of we-mode and I-mode agents. This matter is partly culture-relative: in collectivist cultures we-mode valuations are prevalent, while in individualist cultures I-mode valuations are more central. Education and environmental influences seem to matter here, even if people might be genetically disposed to group thinking. (Recall also that group thinking can be either I-mode or we-mode.)

People thus might in fact act, and indeed act subjectively rationally, either prevalently in the we-mode or prevalently in the I-mode in accordance with their cultural valuations and standards. Yet there are objective elements involved here. For one thing, all cultures that we know about have groups and institutions, for instance, and those group items are to be conceptualized as we-mode notions (see chapter 8). The we-mode is the presupposed mode of acting in groups, even if people may (weakly) act as group members and follow rules also in the I-mode sense.[62] These group notions represent at least epistemically objective features of the social world.

Understanding the social world fully requires the use of full-blown group notions, hence the we-mode. The we-mode is not reducible to the I-mode—primarily because of its necessary dependence on the group's view of the situation and of the members regarding a group as an authority for their thinking and acting. In contrast, the I-mode is not dependent on group reasons, except perhaps in a contingent sense. In all, it is plausible to think that the we-mode is conceptually, explanatorily, and—at least to an extent—ontologically indispensable.[63] Explanation depends on understanding, and understanding here requires the we-mode we-perspective. This means also that in the study of social action, for example, cooperative action, we-mode accounts may well supersede I-mode accounts, which of course tallies with what was said earlier in this book.

Finally, here is a brief reminder of the basic distinctive benefits of we-mode cooperation as contrasted with I-mode (including progroup I-mode) cooperation. The we-mode

- Is central for understanding the core concept of cooperation;
- Gives ("implies or implicates") a uniform motivating group reason for all participants;
- Creates order both on the group level and the member level that is better than the I-mode (mainly because of collective commitment);
- Gives more stability, persistence, and often also more flexibility;
- Is based on and entails shared social capital involving respect-based trust;.
- Is sometimes more rewarding even in a utility-maximizing sense;
- Involves relevantly monitoring and controlling other group members and sanctioning, if need be, and thus entails strong reciprocity;
- Guarantees the group's responsibility for its members' actions as group members—independently of their individuality (new and future members as well as nonoperative members are thus covered), as will be shown in chapter 10;
- In principle, avoids collective action dilemmas (e.g., PD) at the ingroup level; however, the real dilemma here rather is whether to be a "we-moder" or an "I-moder";
- Because it is based on group authority, allows better for change and crisis management, for example, in the case of natural catastrophes, intergroup conflicts, and so on (see chapter 8);
- Works much better in the case of large groups, as no pairwise contacts and relationships between individuals are needed; indeed the we-mode provides for more generality, for instance, by covering, in principle, also future members and by tending to treat the group members as interchangeable (recall the earlier comments on depersonalization in chapters 1 and 2).

Appendix 1: Theories of Cooperation

Let me list what Boyd and Richerson take to be the main competing theories to account for cooperation with strangers even beyond one's society:[64]

1. The "heart on your sleeve" hypothesis claims that humans are cooperative because they can truthfully signal their cooperative intentions.
2. "Big mistake" hypotheses propose that contemporary human cooperation results from psychological predispositions that were adaptive when humans lived in small groups of relatives. From the genes' point of view, cooperation is a big mistake.
3. Manipulation hypotheses propose that people are either tricked or coerced into cooperating in the interests of others.
4. Moralistic reciprocity hypotheses hold that greater human cognitive abilities and language allow humans to manage larger networks of reciprocity,

which account for the extent of human cooperation. Especially central in this approach is strong reciprocity, which involves conditional cooperativeness and disposition to punish or correct defectors.[65]

5. Cultural group selection hypotheses argue that the importance of culture in determining human behavior causes selection among groups to be more important for humans than for other animals.

Let me add this to the above list:

6. The "meme" theory.[66] According to the meme theory, people aim at spreading their ideas (memes) in a maximal way. Memes are defined to be what is transmitted when people imitate each other's behavior. The assumption of people being disposed to imitate each other in ways leading to maximal meme-spreading is central. Cooperative behavior is taken to be a feature that is being imitated precisely because of its leading to extensive meme-spreading. Thus, if we suppose that (1) people have the capacity and disposition to imitate each other's behavior or certain kinds of behaviors, and that (2) (the idea of) cooperative behavior is something that is generally being imitated (or is more often imitated than is noncooperative behavior) because it leads to extensive spreading of one's (other) memes (namely, ideas) among people, then we have an argument for cooperativeness. (see chapter 9.) Collective action dilemmas still seem to pose a problem for meme explanations.

While there seems to me to be some truth in all of these theories, I agree with Boyd and Richerson that views 1–3 are, at least, one-sided and as such not plausible. Theories 4 and 5 are close to my view, and so is theory 6, suitably construed (see chapter 9).

Appendix 2: Note on the Assurance Game

In our example in section 6, our transformations resulted in an assurance game. In addition to the coordination game commented on earlier, this is the second cooperation-friendly transformation of a PD. In a coordination game, there are various—both bilateral and unilateral—ways of rationally arriving at a solution yielding equilibrium, which obtains when the agents both choose CC or both choose DD. Once such an agreement or quasi agreement (to mutually choose one of the alternatives) has been arrived at, there are no more problems for rationality, as an equilibrium will be reached. However, an assurance game is not quite as cooperation-friendly, for there the participants may need assurance from the other partner to choose C, the Pareto-preferable equilibrium-yielding choice.

Let us consider the matter briefly in terms of the following assurance game.

		B	
		C	D
A	C	4,4	1,3
	D	3,1	2,2

The preference orderings thus are CC, DC, DD, CD for A and CC, CD, DD, DC for B.

If the players are minimaxers, that is, if they maximize their security, then they both choose D. Note that CC and DD are Nash equilibria but CC is also Pareto-optimal.

Why should a player then choose C? If (a) he wants to maximize his utilities (here: arrive at four utiles) and if (b) he trusts that the other person is thinking similarly. When is (b) the case? Basically when the participants are not lone security maximizers or ill-willed persons but cooperative social persons relying on others' similar sociality. What is required, furthermore, is that (a) and (b) be mutually believed by the players. Thus A must believe that B is a rational and trustworthy cooperator and that B believes the same of himself, and belief iterations are possible if needed.

Summing up, we have:

(1) It is rational (in the utility-maximizing sense) for a player to choose C if it is a mutual belief among the players that they are both rational and trustworthy cooperators.

(2) It is rational (in the security-maximizing sense) for a player to choose D if it is a mutual belief among the players that they are both security maximizers.

(3) Rationality in the utility-maximizing sense does not entail rationality in the security-maximizing sense, nor does the converse hold. These kinds of rationality are, but not always, in conflict with each other.

What (1) and (2) involve is that even in an assurance game, cooperation does not come about without further ado, so to speak, but many things must be believed or assumed by the players. Thus, even if the players have started their interaction by being in PD (involving the preference orderings A: DC, CC, DD, CD and B: CD, CC, DD, DC) and have by some means, for example, transformed or had been forced (e.g., due to institutional arrangements or coercion) to change the game into an assurance game, the above problems still remain to be solved.

I claim that the we-mode with its conceptually in-built presupposition of trust in others' participation provides a solution for an assurance game, as follows.

(4) Suppose that the players (i) act for the mutually accepted reason that their action will promote the group's goal (here the goal that CC represents or is conducive to), and (ii) are collectively committed to the goal (the CC-related goal) that they have accepted for their group and thus act in the we-mode; then rationally (and also group-socially, for that matter) they ought to choose C.

In (4), it is not required that the players communicate about the particular situation at hand. They are only required to mutually know what the situation is like, namely, that it is an assurance game situation in which the group's mutually accepted goal is one to which only the joint outcome CC is conducive.

Transformation of "nasty" collective action dilemmas like the PD often results in an assurance game.[67] Of course, there are plenty of other game-theoretic possibilities as well. Besides the assurance game, at least the imitation game, the threat game, and the cooperation game, are other relevantly similar games for which my we-mode thesis (5) applies.[68]

Note that corresponding to the four joint outcomes in a PD there are obviously $4 \times 3 \times 2 \times 1 = 24$ ways for a player to order the outcomes. Assuming that players are in symmetric position, the two players also face the same amount of combination (as the total number $24 \times 24 = 576$ then reduces to 24). Of these 24 possibilities, 12 are rational in that they do not lead to conflicts between the players. Julian Nida-Rümelin has systematically discussed all the symmetric and individually rational 12 cases into which a PD can be transformed. In addition to the assurance game, also cases involving justice (in the sense of equality) and altruism turn out to be factors that lead to the mutual cooperation outcome being rationally chosen.[69]

Appendix 3: Cooperation as Equivalent to Acting as a Group Member

It will be shown below that acting as a group member in the core sense and cooperative collective action are equivalent on the basis of our analyses (CIM) and (CWM) and the definitions (a) and (b) of chapter 1, section 4, defining acting as a member in the core sense. The thesis is thus:

(*) A group member acts as a group member (in the core sense) if and only if he intentionally cooperates with the group members with respect to the group's ethos.

I will discuss both the I-mode version and the we-mode version of this general thesis about the equivalence of acting as a group member in the core sense and cooperation toward the ethos.

We-mode Thesis: A group member acts as a group member in the standard sense (AGMS) if and only if he cooperates in the we-mode (in the sense of (CWM)) with respect to the ethos with the group members (given that they cooperate).

I-mode Thesis: A group member acts as a group member in the weak sense (AGMW) if and only if he cooperates in the I-mode (in the sense of (CIM)) with respect to the ethos with the group members (given that they cooperate).

The we-mode version is trivial, although not completely circular. Acting as group member in the standard sense entails that the acting members are collectively committed to promoting the ethos. We-mode cooperation is cooperating together toward a collectively accepted goal (here: the ethos). Cooperating together here is collective we-mode cooperative action in the sense of (CWM), possibly only with action tokens with a low degree of cooperative attitude. Roughly, we have cooperation from acting as a group member, as the group members are supposed to do their share of the group members' collective action of promoting the ethos with collective commitment in conditions of mutual belief. Collective commitment to the ethos in this context entails that the ethos is the members' we-mode collective goal, thus a jointly intended goal. Analysis (CWM) therefore applies to this case.

As to the converse entailment, we-mode cooperation toward the ethos trivially gives us collective acceptance of the ethos, because the group's jointly intended goal required by (CWM) is plainly assumed to be the ethos and because joint intention entails collective commitment (and conversely, which we needed above). Thus the collective action considered will involve these elements, and the participants are acting as group members in the standard sense.

In the case of the I-mode thesis, we first consider the implication from left to right by assuming action toward the ethos with private commitment to the ethos. The simple proof is that we have parallel action toward the same goal, and this is minimally cooperative action if there is some mutual adjustment of action toward the others' goal. Acting as a group member in the weak sense (a) entails that the agents are acting toward the same goal in terms of the actions in classes (1)–(4) discussed in section 3 of chapter 1. Action toward the ethos must by the nature of these actions be consistent and based on this "harmonious shared bottom." The required adjustment toward the others' activities will be there to some extent because the actions in (1)–(4) by their characterization promote the ethos, which here can be regarded as a privately shared goal. A member's so acting toward the shared ethos will thus make its satisfaction likelier both for him and the others. Hence at least minimal cooperation in the sense of (CIM) is obtained.

To get the entailment from right to left, we apply (CIM) to the ethos and consider the group members' adjusting their actions toward the others in the sense of clause (2) of (CIM), assuming private commitment toward the shared ethos. Then the definition (a) of acting as a group member immediately applies, and we have the entailment from right to left.

Appendix 4: The Basic Theses on Cooperation

In this chapter, only some of the central questions of cooperation have been dealt with. A comprehensive theory will have to cover much more. The account given in my work on cooperation presents and defends the following main theses.[70]

> *Basic Thesis of Cooperation*: Two or more actors cooperate in the full, we-mode sense if and only if they share a collective (or joint) goal and act together to achieve the goal.
>
> *Commonality Thesis*: Ceteris paribus, the more commonality of interest (preferences) there is in a situation, the more likely cooperation is to be initiated and carried out successfully and—speaking of rational coopera-tive situations—to give the expected individual rewards, understanding this to mean rewards from acting together (relative to not acting so).
>
> *Closeness of Given and Final Preferences Thesis*: Ceteris paribus, the closer (and the higher) an actor's given and final preferences, namely, prefer-ences$_g$ and preferences$_f$, are, the more likely he is to rationally cooperate in the long run (in a sense respecting his given preferences).
>
> *Reward Thesis*: Ceteris paribus, all intentionally and knowingly under-taken cooperation by normal ("normally rational") and normally acting

human agents is expected by the participants to be more rewarding to them than noncooperation, at least in circumstances favorable to carrying out the activity.

Plain Cooperation Thesis: People can cooperate in the we-mode by just adopting a joint goal, whose joint achievement need not be a actually rewarding for the agents or even expected to be rewarding (even in favorable conditions).

Motivation Thesis: One may cooperate for one's private (purely personal) reasons (which are allowed to be selfish or other-regarding as well as short-term or long-term) or for one's collective reasons; these two reasons, namely, the collective reason and the private reason, may be in conflict with each other, serving to create collective action dilemmas.

Institutional Thesis: Cooperative structures, including we-mode ones, are central for the existence and maintenance of social institutions and hence society.[71]

8

SOCIAL INSTITUTIONS

1 Collective Construction of Social Items

Many social and collective properties and notions are collectively man-made. There are two important features of the collective creation of some central aspects of the social world that have previously been emphasized in the literature.[1] The first feature of conceptual relevance and import is that of the (collectively) *performative* and *constructive* character of many social notions such as that of an institution. Example: The collective acceptance of squirrel pelt as money by medieval Finns can be understood to have entailed that for them squirrel pelt has the institutional status of money. The second is the *reflexive* nature of many social concepts. Example: Squirrel pelt is not money unless collectively accepted to be money. My account adds a third feature, the collective availability or "*for-groupness*" (satisfying the Collectivity Condition) of collective social items (chapter 1). It will actually be shown in this chapter that the we-mode is equivalent to the Collectivity Condition and that thus my present third feature amounts to adding the we-mode into the account. For-groupness entails that the members of the group in question (recurrently) *act as group members* and hence tend to respect and promote the ethos and are thus acting for the group and for a group reason. I will argue that for-groupness shows that a social institution is a *group-level*, we-mode matter rather than an *individual-level*, I-mode matter. Indeed, if institutionality is understood in a wide sense, it can be taken to amount to the we-mode. Given this, institutional reality can be regarded as basically generated (and also as largely constituted) by we-mode groups and acting as a group member in them (although also I-mode activities take place in institutional contexts, but only in a nonconstitutive sense).

There are also other features of social institutions that will be mentioned below. They are to be seen more as contingent preconditions or consequences of social institutions than conceptually involved elements. Thus, typically institutions are "collective responses" to human need satisfaction in a group, where disorder and collective action dilemmas would otherwise threaten the functioning of the collective in question. Social institutions, accordingly, tend to offer cooperative solutions to collective action dilemmas and to create order both on the collective and the individual level (the latter by offering group reasons—we-mode reasons—for action). They also make new kinds of behaviors conceptually possible relative to the preinstitutional situation (e.g., functioning as a professor).

I will below discuss what I term the collective acceptance account of (collective and constructed) sociality. It emphasizes the "cultural" nature of social institutions, that is, the fact that they are collective artifacts that in principle could have been formed in other ways (consider the trivial institutional case of left-hand versus right-hand traffic). While collective acceptance thus in principle involves freedom of choice, in actual practice there may be strong practical constraints of choice (e.g., what can be used as money must be psychologically and physically feasible for humans).

According to the collective acceptance account, we-mode collective acceptance creates, and is required for, institutional entities and practices. As for money—for example, in the medieval case of squirrel pelt being money—collective acceptance can be taken to have created it and to have been required. However, the group members must of course have had some understanding of what money in general is (that it is a medium of exchange and storage of value). While money might have come about due to a trial-and-error learning process, ultimately "performative" collective acceptance must have been in place for squirrel pelt to become money (*our* money for the group members, including also future members). As soon as the members ceased to collectively accept squirrel pelt as money, it lost its status and function as money. Squirrel pelt as money is a "token" institution depending on the "generic" institution money (see section 5). Also money in the generic sense (money as an institutional predicate) is based on collective acceptance and thus construction.

This approach concentrates on, and takes as its default value, *intentional achievement actions*. However, neither coming to hold a we-attitude nor holding a we-attitude need always be intentional actions.[2] Thus, in principle, an agent can *nonintentionally* acquire a belief (a belief as a content) and, for instance, accept that there is a tree in front of him. I will below concentrate on "acceptance" beliefs, which in this context are states of acceptance of a content (sentence, proposition) as correct (or true), while "experiential" believing is a state in which the agent experiences something as true or real.[3] Typically, a state of acceptance is produced by the intentional (and voluntary) mental action of acceptance and is, furthermore, based on the agent's reflection of what is being accepted and often also on relevant evidential considerations—for example, other group members' acceptances. While (individual) acceptance of something as true (and giving up such acceptance) can be or could have been intentional, it need not always be. But there must still be an intentional or voluntary element in such acceptance, involving that the action was up to the agent to perform (e.g., when realizing that she was deceived by a trick, the agent may intentionally give up the claim that she saw a tree in our example).[4]

As seen in chapter 6, collective acceptance amounts to group members' coming to hold and holding a relevant we-attitude and acting on it, and thus acceptances as states (namely, as states resulting from acceptance action) are basically dispositions to act appropriately in accordance with the contents of those states.[5] The account of acceptance in the sense of holding a we-attitude of a relevant kind can here concentrate on intentions and beliefs, because the concept of action is based on the idea of doing something at will under the guidance of beliefs. Thus intentions and beliefs always accompany wants, wishes, fears, and whatever can motivate (intentional) action.

The account of collective acceptance given in section 1 of chapter 6 ended up with the view that group g accepts p as (correctly) premisible for g if and only if the members of g come to share a joint attitude with content p either with the world-to-mind direction of fit (wmdf), in relation to the intention family of attitudes, or with mind-to-world direction of fit (mwdf), in relation to the belief family. Here the having of the joint attitude entails the satisfaction of the relevant Collectivity Condition, and the members are collectively committed to seeing to it that p is premisible, in conditions of shared we-knowledge what the df of p is. The we-acceptance and the attitude it generates is either an intention or a belief, or more precisely an attitude with wmdf or mwdf.[6] The group's acceptance of p serves as a reason for a group member to hold p and for his p-based actions. This account, then, does not speak of any specific mental state but only says that the members qua members of g are assumed to be collectively committed to seeing to it in the right way (in terms of action obeying the direction of fit associated with p on that occasion) that p is premisible, given the mutual understanding and knowledge about p and its direction of fit. This is basically what the "construction" or "creation" of a collective idea or thought amounts to.[7]

As an illustration, we consider a collective social action performed for a joint group reason (a we-mode reason). In a group there might be a we-mode goal to oppose a tax increase by voting against it, and the group may express this goal or intention by asserting "Our group opposes tax increase." This is an assertion concerning what the group intends, and it is also a performative declaration by the group that it has the intention. Furthermore, it issues a directive to the members to function appropriately—opposing tax increase ought to be the members' we-mode goal. In situations like this, collective acceptance amounts to acceptance in the sense of conative commitment to a proposition s (intention to make s true or to uphold s, e.g., s = The tax increase is to be prevented).[8]

Generally, at least some amount of we-mode collective acceptance is needed in the case of social institutions and institutional facts, because institutions are basically full-blown group phenomena: The participants share a "common fate," and the Collectivity Condition must be satisfied. A distinction will be drawn here between full-blown content-constitutive and plain constitutive we-mode collective acceptance (construction). What will be called fully *content-constitutive* collective acceptance or construction is we-mode collective acceptance wherein also the *content* of collective acceptance is fully collectively constituted or constructed—this applies to purely institutional cases, like the squirrel pelt example in which the group members correctly take it to be entirely up to them to make squirrel pelt their money. Such full-blown constitutive we-mode collective acceptance of a content always has the wmdf. In the squirrel pelt case, the belief content is fully and correctly constituted by the group, and the belief is made true simply by the group members treating squirrel pelt as money in their thoughts and activities. No input from the group-external world is relevant to the truth of the belief. It is the group members' own activities that socially "validate" the belief and make it true for the group. This is what is meant by saying that group beliefs based on constitutive construction in the purely institutional case (where the content is being created) have the world-to-mind direction of fit—but, given the model of performative declarations, they also have the mind-to-world direction of fit (for instance, the belief that squirrel pelt is money also represents the group fact that squirrel pelt is money). While the group members can fully validate the belief in the purely institutional case, this is not (at least fully) possible in the case of *stereotypic* and *dogmatic* group beliefs that at least partly concern the natural world but are still constitutive or the group's mental state. An example is given by the belief that stars determine people's fate. Here the group members incorrectly believe or take it to be the case that it is up to them to construct (the truth or satisfaction of) a content, as here (in contrast to the purely institutional case) there is an objective truth in the matter: stars do not determine people's fate. Yet the group members can by their activities partly (but only partly) validate the belief—for example, by interpreting the horoscopes in a suitable way that seemingly concurs with reality. Here we are not dealing with content-constitutive construction, although the fact that the group believes a certain thing does get constituted here (see section 2).

The general form of content-constitutive collective acceptance thus is this: a group collectively accepts and constructs in a truth-determining way a content for g with collective commitment. This kind of thick, group-level collective acceptance (or construction) is not available in the corresponding I-mode cases, where only a kind of aggregative private acceptance of a content by the participants in suitable interdependence and knowledge conditions is possible. However, social institutions require collectively constructed contents with a special group status. To put the matter bluntly, social institutions in the full sense are a group-level rather than a private, individual-level matter. They can only be constructed by we-mode collective acceptance (construction).[9] Group members' appropriate we-mode functioning can adequately take the group level into account. Functioning as group member in the we-mode is the operative force here: it brings about the changes on the group level. We-mode in principle involves *generality* and *interchangeability*. Generality means here that what is created for the group level holds for all members, including future ones, and interchangeability involves relevant disregard of individuality (hence possibly depersonalization and anonymity). The I-mode, private level operating in terms of interpersonal I-mode agreements and the like cannot reach to the group level encompassing the above for-groupness features of generality and interchangeability.

The group belief (content) that squirrel pelt is money can be taken to express a *constitutive* rule (an analytic meaning rule enabling, and on some occasions requiring, a "new" kind of action—namely, the *use* of squirrel pelt as money.

This belief can also be viewed as an ordinary descriptive belief, and then it has the mind-to-world direction of fit. At least newcomers in the group can rationally view it also in the latter way when learning what the institutions of the group are.

Constitution is conventional, in the sense that the group members could in principle have made something else their money, but here they did not. Due to this, we are here at bottom dealing with a case of pretending and make-believe (that something is the case), but as the pretense is socially shared, it will work.[10] The performative element in this kind of institutional pretending can be highlighted by saying that here collective acceptance theoretically *could* have taken place by the members of the group declaring (in chorus, if you like): *We, qua group members, hereby take squirrel pelt to be money in our group, with the understanding that money is a medium of exchange and storage of value.* That squirrel pelt thus comes to count as money is a constitutive belief content (with wmdf and also mwdf) in the group applying to all possible contexts in the group's realm of concern. This kind of collective performative speech act is my central theoretical model for explicating the *conceptually* central features of the social construction and maintenance of those parts of the social world that are taken by the participants to be up to them correctly to "decide" on and create.[11] The "hereby" in the above italicized sentence indicates the performative character of the involved speech act. The performative sentence is reflexive (as seen from the entailed "by *this very* declarative utterance") and self-validating for them, as discussed above. Of course, it is essential here that the group members follow up by the right kind of action (e.g., exchange involving squirrel pelts as money).

However, the above conceptual model does not require that institutions are created in terms of suitable speech acts. Indeed they hardly ever are, but I am still claiming that even in historically accurate cases, the relevant conceptual features of the collective acceptance model must ultimately be present. Thus, if the participants indeed act in the right way based on the right we-mode beliefs and/or intentions, which need not be well articulated and reflective, we still have a case of the required kind of collective acceptance (even without a performative speech act). In addition to this sufficient condition, there is the following necessary condition: A substantive number of the participants have to think and act, at least more or less, *as if* the above kind of rule that squirrel pelt has to be treated as money had been authoritatively issued for the group (by the group members or their authorized representatives). Functionality is a desideratum (e.g., you have to get your daily bread by your squirrel pelts or whatever your money is), even if many old institutions are not very functional today.

I have spoken above as if the group in question were an unstructured, egalitarian group. However, many groups are normatively structured and have special operative members who decide and/or act for the group (recall chapter 6). The above account of collective acceptance as such applies only to operative members—and I am here assuming that in unstructured groups, all members are operative ones. The nonoperative members need not in actual fact be committed to what the group has collectively accepted. However, they *ought* to be so committed, and they are at any rate assumed to go along with what the operative members have done for the group (recall chapter 6).

Section 2 will present my basic thesis of sociality or institutionality, while sections 3 and 4 give an account of social institutions proper, section 5 gives an account of the special group status that instituted items have, and section 6 is about norm obedience.

2 Collective Acceptance Thesis of Sociality

In this section I will discuss the collective acceptance account of sociality that centrally relates to constitutive collective construction in a group (that was seen always to result in group-relative wmdf acceptance) and to institutionality (in a broad sense).[12] What the group members may—correctly or not—take to be up to them to construct includes cases of collective artifacts such as pure institutions (e.g., the squirrel pelt case with full content construction) but also such group-reflected facts as that the group has certain stereotypes and dogmas about the natural world—in these latter kinds of cases the world of course will have the ultimate say as to what is the case "out there" although the "sociological" group fact about the group's normatively binding belief state itself still is something constituted by the group. The account to be given states a necessary and sufficient criterion for something being (or having been) actually accepted by the group in question from among the propositions that the group takes to be entirely up to it to correctly accept as true or correctly assertable.[13] In the purely institutional case, the account to be given makes the content collectively social, whereas in the case of "natural" group beliefs, only the belief state qua a kind of quasi-mental group state (but not its content as such) is made collectively social. The groups that will be concerned are groups that can act, in effect we-mode groups in the sense of chapter 1.

The collective acceptance account in the constitutive case that covers social institutional contents such as the belief content that squirrel pelt is money and also some other constituted social facts (like facts concerning what attitudes a group has) is based on the following general and important thesis elucidating collective sociality—equivalently, group-sociality—that a group constructs or creates.

> Collective acceptance thesis (CAT): Proposition s is collectively social (or group-social) and expresses a collectively social or institutional state of affairs) in a primary sense in a group g if and only if (a) the members of group g collectively accept s for the group, and (b) necessarily, they collectively accept s for g if and only if s is correctly assertable for the members of g functioning as group members.

According to clause (a), we have collective acceptance of s that involves for-groupness and, assuming here also collective commitment, is in the we-mode. If it were not in the we-mode, the central Collectivity Condition would not hold (see below and appendix 1 for the precise connection.) The Collectivity Condition is a cornerstone of this book, as it unifies certain important group themes as expressible by slogans such as "All for one and one for all," "We stand or fall together," "We share a common fate." For realistic cases, the requirement may be that a (functionally) substantial number of the group members are assumed to accept s in the we-mode sense. In the case of structured groups, the members who actually are required to be involved in collective acceptance are the operative members.[14] The kind of *constitutive* collective acceptance that we are dealing with here, according to (b), entails premisibility and correct assertability of s for the group members when they act as group members; the necessary equivalence "if and only if" expresses both conceptual and metaphysical necessity. It is conceptual, as we are speaking of collectively constructed and constituted parts of reality, and it is metaphysical in a group-relative sense because the construction is basically "self-validating" if obeyed. What is thus constituted necessarily exists as a practice-involving fact for the group.

Clause (b) entails that a collectively social s is reflexive: for example, squirrel pelt is not money unless it is collectively accepted as money (the converse also holds). Thus collective sociality is intrinsically based on collective acceptance. The ethos of g is obviously something that is collectively constructed by the members of the group, although perhaps not by its current members; and of course many other things belonging to the realm of concern of g are collectively constructed by it.

It can be argued that collective sociality as characterized by the (CAT) thesis amounts to institutionality: s is collectively social (or group-social) if and only if s is *institutional* (in a *broad* sense).[15] The institutionality interpretation is based on the features that s is performatively constructed and constituted by the group for its use, that s applies precisely to group contexts, and that s is reflexive. As will soon be seen, (CAT) also applies to the fact that a group believes thus and so (this can be expressed by s here). When the group reflects on this matter it becomes institutional in the present sense. (Institutions still require more than what instituting in the above sense involves, especially that group members largely obey what has been constituted in terms of the (CAT) thesis—see section 4.)

The above "constructivist" account elucidates the distinction between what, according to their view, is and what is not up to the members of g correctly to make true or correctly assertable, and thus premisible, for the group members qua group members. Those and only those propositions that satisfy the analysans of (CAT) are in a constitutive sense social and express social (broadly institutional) artifacts. The thesis (CAT) applies both to generic institutions (e.g., to what money is) and to token institutions such as what is money in a group (recall the squirrel pelt example). In our example, the proposition "Squirrel pelt is money" (= s) qualifies as a possibly idealized actual case of a collectively social proposition among medieval Finns. It was collectively accepted for the group. Had it not been, it would at best have expressed a social state of affairs among some subgroup. Next, s satisfies the criteria that (a) it is necessarily collectively made and upheld, and (b) its collective acceptance entails its correct assertability or premisibility for g, and conversely. Thus s is premisible for the group members when acting as group members, and this kind of premisibility for g on metaphysical (and group-dependent) grounds entails collective acceptance in the case of any constructivistically social proposition s.

In our example, the connection between an object's being a squirrel pelt and its being money can be regarded as ontologically significant, part of the ontology of the institution of money.[16] It is the sociality (or institutionality) of s here that makes (CAT) satisfied. The thesis (CAT) elucidates the elements that go into collective construction and shows how exactly the sociality element functions in a group. Had s been a true "natural" statement such as "Grass is green," it would potentially have been correctly assertable and premisible as such, but by itself such an s would not have entailed collective acceptance for the group and (CAT) would not have become satisfied. Notice that an irrational group might accept a stereotype independently of its objective truth value. For instance, it might accept the proposition "Stars determine our fate" (s). Here s by itself does not satisfy (CAT). However, group beliefs as collective mental acceptance states expressed by s do satisfy (CAT). Such propositions about a group's mental states—and not directly the contents of those states—are deemed collectively social according to (CAT). In general, in propositions of the kind "We collectively accept that s," the iteration of the collective acceptance does not logically give new entailments, as $CA(CA(s)) \leftrightarrow CA(s)$, but the reflective collective acceptance involved here makes the fact expressed by $CA(s)$ collectively constructed and institutional. (CAT) will be satisfied, given that the other required conditions are in place. Now we have obtained the result that both purely institutional propositions (those contents that are completely up to the group) and social stereotypes and dogmas viewed as mental states rather than as contents of mental states qualify as collectively social. The distinction between these two cases in terms of our account is interesting and reflects the intuitive distinction between the cases at hand: In the case of the mentioned kinds of stereotypes and dogmas, in contrast to the purely institutional beliefs, it is not up to the group correctly to decide about the truth of the contents.

The above account holds true equally well of leadership, marriage, property, financial, educational, and religious institutions (thus banks, universities, and churches as institutional systems), and so on. We can also speak of derived sociality. Roughly, a sentence is collective-social (or broadly institutional) in a derived sense if it is not social in the above primary sense but presupposes for its truth (for the group) that there are some relevant true (for the group) sentences that are collective-social in the primary sense. For instance, sentences using "power," "unemployment," or "wealth" are, at least in some cases, candidates for constructively social sentences in the derived sense.

Notice that many (nonconstructive) social propositions fail to satisfy (CAT) and may even fail to be social in the derived sense. Thus sentences expressing latent or unilateral social influence are social features of the social world that would not—and correctly so—be cases of even derivatively social features in the constructivist sense (not even when many agents are concerned). The same holds for "naturally" social emotions such as envy often is (e.g. Tom envies John his new car). Furthermore, there are several kinds of shared we-attitudes that are not socially constructed either (for instance, shared fear may be a "natural" or "non-constructed" social phenomenon).

The following important property holds true for a group attitude held by a normatively unstructured group g toward a content p (namely, ATT(g, p)).

(*CollTh*) ATT(g, p) is collective-social (or, equivalently, broadly institutional) in the sense of (*CAT*) if and only if ATT(g, p) satisfies the Collectivity Condition (GCC) (of chapter 2).

See appendix 1 for precise proof of this theorem. Given the connection expressed in (*CollTh*), it can be claimed that *all the collectivity that the collectively constituted parts of the social world include is covered by and specified by the Collectivity Condition.* I will only consider in precise terms (in appendix 1) the case of the collectivity of group attitudes and actions and accordingly concentrate on the generalized version (GCC) that applies to the satisfaction of any attitude and action. Let us consider the following formulation of this principle.

(GCC) It is necessarily true (on quasi-conceptual grounds, thus on analytic a posteriori grounds) that the participants' shared we-attitude toward p, namely, ATT(g, p), is satisfied for a member A_i of g (qua a member of g) if and only if it is satisfied for every other member of g (qua a member of g).

Version (GCC) can be applied to actions (action descriptions) by speaking of we-actions instead of we-attitudes. This and even more general formulations were briefly discussed in chapter 2, but here we will operate with this simple version.

As will be shown in appendix 1, (*CollTh*) amounts to saying that an attitude satisfying the Collectivity Condition (GCC) is collectively accepted for the group with collective commitment. This is basically because collective acceptance with collective commitment is built into the notion of quasi-conceptual grounds and thus group-constitutive grounds (recall chapter 1). We thus arrive at the following important claim conjectured to hold generally (and not only in the attitude-action satisfaction case) but that will be proved in precise terms for the attitude-action case in appendix 1.

We-mode ↔ collectivity ↔ collective sociality ↔ (broad) institutionality.

That is, these four notions are equivalent basically on conceptual grounds. There is a clear intuitive, preanalytic basis for these equivalences in the fully general case. First, the we-mode has earlier been argued preanalytically to involve, thus entail, the Collectivity Condition (consider, for instance, "we stand or fall together"), but, as seen from (GCC) and the discussion in chapter 2, the meant quasi-conceptual construction involves collective acceptance for the group with collective commitment. Thus, the converse also holds in the analytical developments of this book. That we-mode entails collective sociality is intuitively based on the idea that only we-mode groups can be involved in full-blown reflexive collective acceptance. In the analytical context of (CAT), collective acceptance in its analysans was assumed to be in the we-mode. Accordingly, the converse entailment is true on the basis of the technical analysis. Finally, as argued above, collective sociality can be said to amount to institutionality, in the sense of something being collectively instituted. Thus I have indicated why the four concepts, which are cooperative already in virtue of the cooperativeness of the we-mode (recall chapter 7), can be regarded as equivalent.

3   Introducing Institutions

A social institution in the broad or general sense (e.g., money, language) can be regarded as a specific type of norm-based—and in some cases aim-based—social practice in a group (often a society).[17] I will below focus on these kinds of general institutions. Roughly speaking, social institutions give or "define" the ground rules for how to act or for what counts as a collective item with a signified symbolic and social status in a society (or other collective). In this sense, they are *collective goods* available to all in the group (recall (*CollTh*) of section 2). We can view institutions in terms of the ethos of a social group. The ethos normatively directs the functioning of the group members, some of the norms being constitutive. Assuming that we are dealing with a "nonfleeting" group, actions as a group member are recurrent actions. In view of the discussion in section 3 of chapter 4 and section 4 of chapter 6 these actions are actions based on a shared we-attitude. Thus we arrive at the result that acting as a group member in a nonfleeting group is a "core" social practice (as defined in chapter 5).[18] More generally, a we-mode group's normatively governed social practices will be institutional even if they are not directly ethos-based. When a we-mode group thus has conferred a special status to a social practice by its we-mode (hence constitutive, with wmdf) collective acceptance, a social institution is created. This constitution makes the institutional practice normative: It ought to be the case in the group that squirrel pelt is treated as money in it; and this ought-to-be norm entails the appropriate ought-to-do norms for the group members. An institution is a group phenomenon involving two key elements, norms and collective activity, and the norms must constitutively confer a special "institutional"—namely, symbolic, social, and normative—status to the activity or to an item involved in the activity.

The notion of a social institution is used in several different senses in the literature. In different disciplines there are various ingrained usages, and theorists often have different things in mind when speaking of institutions; and even when they have the same thing in mind, they often emphasize different features of their shared *analysandum*. First, a social institution is often regarded as a kind of recurrent, norm-based collective activity. A version of this view says that institutions (specifically, institutional norms) define "the rules of the game in society."[19] A second, narrower idea restricts social institutions to those collective activities in which the normative frame is given by a hierarchically structured system of positions and roles, along with the accompanying exertion of power or influence. This is the organization sense of institution. Notice that my above view of institutions as norm-governed acting as a group member fits this organization sense, if the group in question is an organization. According to a third idea, adopted by game theorists, a social institution is an equilibrium point in a repeated game. This does not involve social norms but only rationality features, and it applies only to activities that can be modeled as games in the sense of game theory. Furthermore, it requires equilibrium behavior. However, no matter how good the order-creating equilibrium idea may be, many extant social institutions seem not to be in equilibrium in the "self-policing" sense normally required by game theorists. According to a fourth approach (which I find congenial), social institutions may be characterized by their social functions. This approach can also include accounts in terms of invisible hand processes and the like.[20]

Social institutions can, accordingly, be viewed on partly contingent grounds to have collectively—but not necessarily intentionally—arisen and to be in typical cases "ossified" devices that create *collective order* and *individual guidance* (*thus order*) in a human community and thus help people to satisfy their basic needs, such as needs related to food and shelter, sexual relations and reproduction, sociality, and social power. As a functional result from collective need satisfaction, institutions in different areas of social life tend to arise: *familial, educational, religious, political,* and *economic* institutions. These are institutions—social systems—that social scientists generally deal with, but only their organized forms can be institutions in the sense of the CAT-based account (*SI**) of section 4. The above kinds of theories do not, at least, emphasize that a social institution involves a new, group-constructed status of any kind, while that is what, for example, Searle's and my present account do.[21]

Basic needs are in many cases difficult to satisfy for all—there often is a scarcity problem related to their satisfaction. Furthermore, their instituted satisfaction is typically a public good, as the good is meant to be for everyone in the group. This makes for the possibility of free-riding concerning the institutionalized provision process that the members are required to participate in. Here individual interests or preferences conflict with collective ones. In game-theoretic terms, we are dealing with such collective action problems as coordination dilemmas (e.g., on which side of the road people should drive), full-blown collective action dilemmas, for example, the PD and Chicken, in which there is partial conflict between collective and individual interests and preferences, and situations of full conflict (zero-sum situations in game-theoretic terms). The institutional solution to these situations creates sanctioned norms that guide people to behave in one way rather than another so that free-riderism is avoided and order both in a collective and an individual sense is increased.[22] The order aspect obviously involves that people will obey the norms, which typically are supposed to serve basic human needs and interests.

As an additional bonus, institutions tend to *facilitate, economize,* and *"routinize"* activities and thinking about those activities. They create order both on the individual level by providing group-level reasons and hence also on the collective or macro level. People do not need to engage in decision-making each particular time a norm-governed situation is at hand, and this tends to make the relevant actions routine. So both thinking and acting tend to get more routine, we can say, and this leaves room for the new kinds of activities that institutions make possible by creating new "territories" in the social world. (The other side of the coin is that routines may psychologically restrict the new avenues available.)

A social institution can be assumed to give a new institutional (conceptual or symbolic, social, and normative) status to some social practice or some object involved in such practice (for instance, consider squirrel fur as money). This involves the mentioned *enabling* function of social institutions as their conceptually in-built feature: new kinds of actions are made possible by social institutions. I will below apply (CAT) to social institutions. It helps to distinguish those normative practices that are institutional from those that are not. The platitude that social institutions and other related notions are collectively manmade, accordingly, is explicated in terms of we-mode collective acceptance (amounting to relevant shared we-attitudes with wmdf).[23] Collective acceptance in this context is compatible with different accounts of the rise of institutions. It is compatible not only with the possibility that institutions are formed by external *decree* or by the members' *agreement making* but also with their creation being a gradual involuntary *evolutionary* or *invisible-hand* process. However, eventually there must be collective acceptance of the institution (see (*SI*) in section 4). There is also the issue of the legitimacy of social institutions (recall section 2 of chapter 6). It concerns the justification and the bindingness of the institutional norms. The justification will vary depending on the institution at hand. In any case, in order to be rationally legitimate, an institution should, in principle and ideally, be individually and collectively rewarding and tend to solve relevant collective action dilemmas. Furthermore, if an institution is grossly unfair, for instance, and thus lacks legitimacy, the target people may not act as the institutional norms require; and so on. The analysis of institutions in force below will implicitly take into account the motivational impact of the legitimacy of social institutions. Obviously, physical force and sanctions will in general not suffice for the upholding of social institutions. For instance, if almost all people were criminals violating institutions, there would not in general be enough resources (e.g., police, military) for maintaining the institutions. Social institutions accordingly rely to a great extent on (group-social) normativity, trust, and a widespread disposition to act as a group member.

Let me next consider some principles for classifying social institutions, starting with the *generality* aspect. Thus, (1) *language* can be regarded as the most fundamental social institution underlying all other social institutions. This claim applies to language as both a generic and a token institution. Language is "self-identifyingly" institutional because it is intrinsically based on collective acceptance in the reflexive sense of the collective acceptance account: linguistic symbols refer by being collectively represented as referring. The rule-conception of language makes meanings of linguistic items depend on (conventional) constitutive rules, which people satisfy by their linguistic practices.[24] All human social institutions involve language or at least symbolic elements (see the discussion of institutional status predicates in section 5). Language users must rely on the correct use of concepts in all their other institutional and conceptual activities. Concepts can be regarded as rules to be mastered by people as skills even if they need not have explicit knowledge of rules.[25] A simple example is the skill of being able to classify things correctly, for example, to apply "red" correctly in the sense that red objects are included and nonred things are excluded. Such institutional linguistic abilities and skills are presupposed in institutional acting of the kind that, for instance, using money involves. (2) *Money, marriage*, and *property* are examples of social institutions that typically are general, namely, society-wide. In their generic sense, they are not specific to any "within-society" institutions such as some organizations are. The truth of (2) presupposes (1). (3) *Organizations* involve specific positions and "task-right systems." They typically presuppose the existence of various political, economic, and other (perhaps cultural and religious, etc.) institutions, and they presuppose language. Thus (3) presupposes (2) and (1). In this context, the terms "language," "money," "marriage," and "property" should be taken as abbreviations for the norm-governed practices that are involved—for example, the use of coins in economic exchange, and so on. In a more comprehensive account, one should deal with the social systems of communication, economies, systems of law, family systems, and so on in various societies.

Only group items that are represented as existing by the group are institutional. Thus an organization-expressing proposition must be reflexively collectively accepted for the use of the group (as (CAT) specifies). This entails that, at least ideally, the for-groupness and collective commitment aspects, based on collective acceptance, must be involved and that thus the members of the organization ought to function as group members in the we-mode in it (see section 4). "Public good" organizations are prime examples of social institutions. They have been constituted to serve some relevant goals (needs, interests, what have you) of the members of the collective in a public good fashion (based on for-groupness). The collective need not be a society, but it seems that it must be a community that can relatively independently satisfy its relevant goals and interests. Accordingly, a (public or private) postal service established for a community will at least typically satisfy for-groupness, collective commitment, and collective acceptance and thus be the meant kind of social institution. But a business company need not satisfy for-groupness and the (CAT) formula and thus may not be an institution even for its employees (and still less for the larger community within which it operates).

According to colloquial talk, a social institution can be of various *ontological* kinds. As examples from literature and common parlance witness, there are at least the following possibilities for what ontological kind of entity a social institution prima facie is: (a) social practice—for example, the old practice of sauna bathing on Saturdays in Finland; (b) object—for example, money; (c) property of an individual—for example, ownership; (d) linguistic entity—for example, natural language; (e) interpersonal state—for example, marriage (when not treated as a case of (b)); (f) social organization—for example, the national postal system, a university. Of these, (a)–(e) are often general, society-wide, although they do not have to be so, while (f) is typically not. While social institutions can be conceptualized in these various ways, they are all related to and in my analysis amount to norm-governed social practices—namely, group practices involving the group members' functioning as group members.

In relation to (b), we consider marriage as an example showing that it need not be construed as an abstract entity, basically because marriage in the generic sense can be seen as a relation between persons (case (f)). The following rough and sketchy account of marriage in Western societies can be proposed: for all persons x, y, R(x, y) is a marriage relation that (to an extent) governs the life of two persons if and only if R contains the duties and rights prescribed in the state law (or whatever) and entering R requires a special procedure (wedding) where an authorized person imposes the relevant duties and rights onto x and y. Marriage is a normative relationship, and the spouses are assumed to obey the norms in question. Marriage is not an abstract social entity, something outside space and time. What I just said about marriage applies, mutatis mutandis, to, for example, debts and obligations in general and also to groups such as corporations (recall chapter 6). They involve normative relationships between persons, and such relationships can be given a naturalistically acceptable, even if nonreductive analysis in terms of norm-related activities and dispositions. Notice that an obtaining normative relationship has duration, and it "lives" in people's minds or brains and actions, in records, and so on, and is not outside of space and time.[26] Social institutions (in the sense of normative institutional practices) can be taken to supervene on the we-mode jointness level (the level of singular, noninstitutional agents, actions, and attitudes, as well as actions and joint attitudes, and the like): Change the institution, and something in the mentioned base must change.[27]

Some degree of social *"functionality"* is necessary for an institution, no matter how old and "ossified" it is. For instance, when we take money to be a social institution, we imply that the use of money (e.g., in contexts of exchange) is an institutional social practice. A person who owns a house, for instance, can engage in the social practice of selling and buying and in the social practice of prosecuting people who violate his rights by trying to damage his house. The other cases are analogous. Thus there are linguistic practices (case (d)) and business practices, teaching practices, religious practices, and so on that are related to business companies, the school, and the church, respectively. The social practice often is not a recurrent joint action but, rather, a recurrent individual action performed partly because the others participate.

4 Institutions More Precisely Analyzed

In this account, a social institution is a collective creation involving repeated normatively governed collective acting as a group member, thus at least to some extent in an ethos-respecting sense.[28] The normative element may be entailed by the ethos, or it may be based on separate collective acceptance by the group members. The we-perspective and sufficient collective commitment (on the group level) to the collectively constructed ethos of the group will thus be involved.[29] At least some institutional action must be in the we-mode—this will be argued for later. While social institutions need not be entified, the term "institution" is a convenient shorthand—I will therefore continue to speak of social institutions as if they were entities.

My account relies on social norms of two different kinds: (i) formal or informal rule-norms that are based, directly or indirectly, on group-authorized agreement making (resulting in, e.g., laws, charters, informal rules), and (ii) "proper social norms" that are either society-wide or group-specific norms based on normative collective expectations and that require action in response to them. Rule-norms are basically norms that an authority, such as a government or governing board, imposes on the members of the collective in question (e.g., a professor must teach a certain amount of classes each year). These norms are explicitly stated, as in the paradigm cases of state laws, and they can "exist" in a weak sense even when people do not pay much attention to them. The other kind of norm is one based on mutual normative behavior expectations in the group (e.g., the members of the press are to sit on the left side of the conference hall). In general, people learn to obey these norms during socialization. They are often not codified and perhaps not even verbalized. There are generally sanctions associated with social norms. They are, respectively, either "official" authority-imposed sanctions or group sanctions consisting of social approval and disapproval. (See appendix 2 for more details.)

In the case of general institutions like language, money, marriage, and property, society-wide norms are involved, and thus the institutions concern everyone in the society. In the case of institutions connected to a social organization (e.g., the school system in a community), both kinds of norms may generate task-right systems involving relationships of social power.[30] There can be task-right systems utilizing either or both kinds of norms. For instance, marriage is primarily based on rule-norms, while mutual gift-giving is based on expectation-based norms. Language is a mixed case.

While language can be regarded as a general institution, there are also more specific institutions involving special language local to some group in the language community. Thus certain recurrent events may be referred to in specific linguistic ways that are not as such known to nonmembers. Thus in a certain village a football match played on Sundays or sauna bathing on Saturday nights may get a special status that also gets a specific name or description. It may be necessary to use this description to give the factually correct description of the social practice. Similarly, the collective use in a group of a system of musical notation will be institutions in the sense meant here. We may speak of a "concept institution" in these cases, where no normative obligations need to be involved except norms concerning the use of language.[31]

Somewhat loosely, a social institution in the full sense ontologically amounts to group-based normative social practices, which consist of recurrent, ethos-respecting activities as a group member, thus based on a relevant shared we-attitude (see section 4 of chapter 6 for my argument of the latter feature). We may also say that a social institution is a reflexive social system consisting of norm-governed social practices accepted by the group for the group. A social institution, at least typically, involves a collective good because it deals with shared group affairs. Furthermore, it purports to solve a collective action dilemma or coordination dilemma, and in any case, a social institution is meant to achieve collective coordination and order. As the institutional norms are collectively created and constituted, this gives a reason to think that the collective acceptance account and its (CAT) formula expressing attitudinal reflexivity applies to all institutions. Speaking of primary social institutions, namely, institutions that do not themselves consist of institutions, the following classification of social institutions can be proposed.

(a) institution as a norm-governed social practice;
(b) institution conferring a new conceptual (and social) status to some entity (e.g., person, object, or activity);

(c) institution conferring not only a new conceptual and social but also a new deontic status and status functions to go with it to the members of the collective in question;

(d) institution as an organization involving specific social positions and a task-right system.

In view of what will be said below, (a)–(d) can be taken to represent increasingly stronger kinds of social institutions. The strongest case (d) has already been commented on. Case (c) is the case that fits, for example, money, marriage, and property. This case is what John Searle takes as the object of his analysis. It is a merit of his account that it emphasizes the notion of a (deontic) institutional status.[32]

In my account also, case (b) is central. This "concept" notion of institution is taken to satisfy the (CAT) formula, which makes it "attitudinally reflexive" and thus gives the institutional practice its special status.[33] Reflexivity applies to cases (b), (c), and (d) but need not apply to (a), the view of institution as a suitable regularity (in the I-mode).[34] What can be called the "standard" cases of social institutions are cases (b), (c), and (d), which all involve a special institutional status of a constituted item. In contrast to (a), the standard concept of a social institution is basically a we-mode concept, but some amount of I-mode norm-obedience is still possible—how much is a *contingent* fact dependent on functionality. My analysis of standard institutions will be given in terms of the (CAT) formula.[35] A standard social institution is one that is constituted and represented by the group as a social institution, as the group's specific norm-governed social practice. The group will be or become a we-mode group, and the resulting institution concept is a we-mode notion.

In weak cases, the collective acceptances creating institutional practices are only mutual acceptance beliefs (with a performative function entailing wmdf), but the important institutions are based on agreement making and the resulting rule-norms. Thus property rights, for instance, and other law-based notions in general require group-authorized agreement making. Roughly speaking, agreement making amounts to the shared acceptance of a norm-entailing, nonsingular proposition, say, s, accompanied by the joint intention and commitment to carry out (or, as the case may be, maintain) what s says. Generally speaking, s expresses one or more ought-to-do, ought-to-be, may-do, or may-be norms, including some constitutive norm. To enable appropriate action for a shared social reason, mutual belief must in general also be required, and it is taken care of by the requirement that the members share a we-attitude toward the content expressed by the sentence s. The agreement making that created the institution may have taken place generations ago, but the institutional norms may still apply. If current acceptance is not sufficiently widespread, specific control and sanctioning systems (involving, e.g., the police and the army) may have to be employed.

To proceed to my more precise account, I will abstract from "area-specific" institutional notions and give a rather general summary account or theory of standard social institutions (at least cases (b)–(d)). The account below relies strongly on the analysis (CAT) and assumes that the collective in question is an "egalitarian" one (in contrast to the later account (SI*)) and that it is the same one that collectively accepts the institution-expressing proposition. This proposition, s, can be a complex and compound one, and it is assumed to include at least one constitutive norm, such as is "Squirrel pelt is money," among the norms it expresses.[36] My somewhat idealized and stylized account for a social institution that is socially in force is as follows.

> (SI) Proposition s expresses a *social institution* (*in the standard sense*) for group g if and only if
>
> (1) s expresses or entails the existence of a g-based social practice (or a system of interconnected social practices) and a norm or a system of interconnected norms (including some constitutive norms) in force in g, such that the social practice obeys the norm (or norm system);
>
> (2) the members of g rationally collectively accept s for g with collective commitment; here it is assumed that collective acceptance for the group entails and is entailed by the correct assertability of s.

In this analysis, I take an institution to be a system of social practices (e.g., exchange, and so on, activities in the case of money) governed by a system of norms that are in force in g. That the social practices are g-based means that they amount to recurrent acting as a group member. Collective acceptance constitutes the institution-expressing proposition s as true for the group, and in this sense it constitutes a social institution for the group. Some of the norms are specifically constituted as meaning-conferring norms, namely, constitutive norms. As collective acceptance is a we-mode concept in this context, our account makes a social institution concept a we-mode concept. Moreover, clause (2) serves to make it reflexive.[37] Thus, the slogan "What is money is not money unless taken to be money" becomes clarified. As the basic elements of (SI) have already been discussed at length, I will here only make some additional, qualifying remarks.

According to (SI), an institution is one for the use of the group and typically for the benefit of its interests. Let me note that in a more general analysis than given by (SI), it may be necessary to deal with two groups, say g and g', such that the institution creates a collective good for g' and g is the group maintaining the institution. The institution could be a non-profit organization that, as collectively accepted by g, provides goods for g' (say poor people in a certain corner of the globe, although here we may consider the possibility that g = g' = mankind).

An institution that is socially in force must involve an actually existing practice of the kind (SI) refers to. (If there is only a norm system without the relevant activities or even dispositions to act relevantly, it is not yet—or anymore—socially in force.) The institution, namely, the norm-governed social practice or some special aspect of it in some cases, need not yet be functionally successful when it satisfies (SI). While it purports to create order and to solve one or more collective action dilemmas (which need not be more than coordination dilemmas), whether it succeeds in that is a different matter. The analysans of (SI) will often contain institutional terms like "money" or "lawyer," and it is nonreductive. Rather, its nature is ontological, because it basically goes from institutions as entities to actions.

While clause (1) makes all institutions *normative* in a group-social sense, what is this sense in the b-case, the "concept" sense of an institution? The social practices that the institution involves and that the institution concept presupposes or entails may be normative, in that they involve obligations and rights for the members participating in the social practices, but the institution need not be normative in this strong sense (which sense would indeed make it a case of (c)). But there will be collective commitment to the "social" existence of the concept and its use in the group.

The system of norms governing the social practices may be directly entailed by the ethos of the group, or they may have been separately accepted. Social institutions basically being we-mode constructions, the social practices (ideally) should be we-mode practices (see section 6). However, I-mode practices respecting the ethos and even practices in a behavioral sense satisfying the norms (without the right group reason) also will help to make the institution do its job and create the required kind of collective order in the group. The social practices are regarded as social practices in the *core* sense, namely, performed because of a shared we-attitude (see section 5 of chapter 5). Institutional action, then, is seen to be action as a group member, and, as shown in chapter 7, such action is cooperative action (either in the I-mode or in the we-mode). In the case of a state-wide institution, institutional action will be cooperative action relative to the constitution of the state, its ethos.

As will be seen in section 5, the institutional status that standard institutions confer on the involved social practices, or some of their constituent parts, is based on the constitutive norms in (1) and on the reflexivity feature of (CAT) and hence (2). A constitutive norm serves to at least partially define a concept. In some cases, it has the Searlean form "X counts as Y in context C."[38] Briefly put, it requires a group perspective that supersedes the interpersonal I-perspective.

Account (SI) is still lacking in realism, in that it does not explicitly account for power relations between group members (or, for that matter, between the group in consideration and other groups). In structured collectives where the operative-nonoperative distinction is in place, the nonoperative members need only accept the institution in a tacit sense involving the possibility of at least some degree of dissent and opposition—at least if the collective is based on nonvoluntary membership as in a nation. To give a stylized account of a simple case, here is an obvious way to generalize (SI) for a "two-layer" case with the operative-nonoperative distinction where the operatives have received their power from the group members (recall the discussion in chapter 6):

> (SI*) A proposition s expresses a *social institution* (*in the standard sense*) *for a normatively structured group* g if and only if
> (1a) the operative members of g, say, $A_1, \ldots, A_m$, when performing their (we-mode) tasks in their respective positions and due to their exercising the relevant authority system ("decision-making" system) of g, collectively accept s, and because of this exercise of the authority system they ought to continue to accept it, at least until (new) reasons not to accept it emerge;
> (1b) collective acceptance for the group entails and is entailed by (the correct assertability of) s;
> (2) there is a mutual belief among the operative members $A_1, \ldots, A_m$ to the effect that (1a);
> (3) s expresses or entails the existence of a g-based social practice (or a system of interconnected social practices) and a system of interconnected norms (including

one or more constitutive norms) in force for g, such that the social practice generally is performed at least in part because of these norms;

(4) because of (1), the (full-fledged and adequately informed) nonoperative members of g tend to tacitly accept—or at least ought to accept—obeying the normative content of s, as members of g;

(5) there is generally a mutual belief in g to the effect that (4).

In this summary outline, (4) allows for the possibility that the nonoperative members disagree, at least in their thoughts, with what s expresses, and it also allows for some amount of coercion organized by the group concerning the institutional norms.

When discussing the organized forms of functionally motivated social and societal institutions such as the economy, education, religion, or the family, it has to be kept in mind that most, if not all, people are involved in all of these systems. They have roles and positions related to these systems, and these roles and positions may be related to different groups. For instance, an employee of the university such as a professor participates not only in the education of students but also in the economy of the university. At home, he or she as a spouse gives economic and other support to the family. Examples can easily be multiplied. While the economy is also an institutional system in the sense of (SI), it contains actions and practices pertinent to different groups in the broader group, society, to which it basically pertains.

While (SI) or (SI*) in effect only apply to we-mode groups, the converse also holds in the following sense: any nonfleeting we-mode group with established practices can be taken to be an institution-carrying group. Basically, there is a social practice that involves acting together toward the ethos, and there are constitutive norms, for example, that the ethos ought to be furthered and satisfied by the members' activities. Furthermore, there is the special institutional status of the ethos that involves reflexivity (e.g., that this club is *our* special running club requires that we take it to be so—in analogy with squirrel pelt money getting its special status by being taken to be squirrel pelt money in *our* group).

5   The Special Status of Institutionalized Items

I will start the discussion of institutional status by considering what a scientific study of social institutions can be taken to involve. It of course involves building theories that adequately describe and explain institutions (e.g., economic, religious, or educational institutions). Each such theory is bound to be very complex and to be based on a rich social vocabulary where several kinds of institutional concepts also occur. In the realm of education, for instance, lower and higher kinds of educational institutes will be involved as well as various positions related to teaching, learning, and administration in them. As to economy, it is concerned with the production, distribution, and consumption of goods and services. When discussing economy, what has to be considered in the macro theory (as indeed macroeconomic theory does) are notions related to the use of money like economic exchange in the market, storage of value, demand and supply of money, credit, and the connection of money to notions like inflation and unemployment.[39]

In standard cases, we are initially dealing with a situation in which there is a regularity type of account, a behavioral-observational account of institutional acting. Call this account or theory T(O), where the set O of predicates represents the extralogical concepts of the theory. Now consider the case where institutional predicates, consisting of, or at least including, predicates with a new status, are added to the theory. Let their set be M. Money could be represented by one of those predicates. Connecting this new set of predicates M with the original set O, we arrive at a new, enriched theory T'(O + M). This theory may contain a simple meaning-related constitutive rule that has the form of a conceptually necessary implication (see the rule S → M below).

As to T', it may not be easy to grind out its analytic or meaning component, which would constitute the semantic content of the M-predicates, the new institutional predicates introduced by this theory. I assume that we are dealing with a social theory where modal concepts do not occur explicitly (but may occur implicitly as in the prescriptive interpretation of "Squirrel pelt is money"). I also assume that the theory can be given a formalization in first-order predicate logic.[40] One simple possibility is to use the so-called Carnap sentence of T' to do the job.[41] The Carnap sentence (T'^C) is defined as follows: $T'^C = T'^R \rightarrow T'$, where T'^R is the Ramsey sentence of T'. The total theory T' amounts to the conjunction of its Ramsey sentence and its Carnap sentence, and the Carnap sentence has no deductive consequences with respect to the set O.[42] I wish to point out here that my account (SI) does not take a stand on the specific nature of the meaning-postulates or constitutive norms. The institution-expressing sentence s corresponds to the theory T'(O + M).[43] Constitutive meaning postulates can be handled in the way just sketched, without commitment to the specific forms that meaning postulates may have. The Carnap sentence might thus well be collectively accepted as a general *constitutive* principle of a social institution with the normative status (comparable to what "Squirrel pelt is money" was above taken to have).

I will next present some new observations and results related to the notion of an institutional predicate with a special institutional status and use my paradigm case of squirrel pelt being money as a simple example. This case contains the constitutive norm that we may express by "S is constituted by us as M" or at least occasionally by the constitutive norm "S counts as M in group g," where S stands for squirrel pelt and M for the "antecedently understood" notion of money.[44] Here M must be a meaningful, interpreted predicate so that the above constitutive sentence makes sense. It is, however, central to keep in mind that M might also be created in the same process—based on collective acceptance—by which the above constitutive norm is created. (For instance, the system of norms in clause (1) of (SI) might implicitly define M, and in the social theory T' of institutions envisioned above, the same goes for the M-predicates.) The Sunday soccer match case discussed earlier is also a case in point.[45]

As to money, the norms in (SI) might specify, roughly, that "money" refers to a medium of exchange and storage of value, and so on, and that the owner of money has various deontic powers. The predicate "money" will be applied to certain conventionally selected (namely, by collective acceptance) hardware items (e.g., squirrel pelt, coins, notes, or even electronic imprints of suitable kinds). In the case of marriage, to discuss another example, we may think that marriage is a legally defined (but basically moral) concept. For instance, the parliament of a country accepts certain norms (laws) for marriage, thus at least partially defining the predicate "marriage." These norms may say that marriage is a relationship between a man and a woman and that a couple to be married must undergo a certain process (e.g., wedding process) after which they acquire such and such obligations and rights vis-à-vis each other and the surrounding society. The practices obeying these norms will be formed out of the various couples acting in appropriate ways, as the norms require or allow.

We must distinguish between a *generic institution* (such as marriage or money in general) and *tokens* of it. As said, the parliament might issue laws that characterize marriage and say what it amounts to from a legal point of view. This is to be distinguished from "token" institutional facts such as that John and Jane are a married couple. The priest wedded them, and in doing that she applied the institution to create an institutional fact. In the money case, we assume that the institutional predicate "money" is understood: There is the generic institution saying that money involves exchange activities of such and such kinds, and so on, and that the possession of money gives such and such powers to the owners of money. Next we construct the token institution saying that squirrel pelt is money. Furthermore, there is the *concrete squirrel pelt token* that also is money. But this last thing is only an institutional fact. So there are three things here: (a) the generic institution of money; (b) the applied (or token) institution of money (e.g., that squirrel pelt is money); and (c) the institutional fact that this particular token of squirrel pelt is money.

An item's institutional status is constituted by its conceptual, group-social, and normative status. We can clarify the *conceptual* status of an item O as M in terms of the inner structure of s: Squirrel pelt represents (symbolizes) money, and this fact is respected by actions in the right way.[46] The new *group-social* status of O is simply that O is M in a constitutive sense in the group: On the basis of group acceptance, it is necessarily so that O is M. Finally, a constitutive norm is an *ought-to-be* norm in the first place: It ought to be the case that squirrel pelt is treated as money in the group. Therefore, the members ought to treat squirrel pelt as money. This is what the new normative status of the instituted squirrel pelt involves.

To add some precision to this account of institutional status, we continue with our above example. Squirrel pelt (O) is constituted by collective acceptance to be money (M) in g:

(1) $N((x)(O(x) \rightarrow M(x)))$,

thus for a token squirrel pelt a, we can trivially infer that it is money. In our treatment, the institution expressing proposition s of (*SI*) will be assumed to entail (1). The predicate O is a noninstitutional predicate in the philosophically interesting cases, and we may concentrate on such cases here. The necessary implication in (1) expresses "quasi-conceptual" necessity, namely, necessity governing the use of predicates in g as based on collective acceptance. Thus it governs the semantic relations of symbolizing and representing, as well as conceptual constitution in the group. Thus we have: "O constitutively is M." (1) thus constitutes O as M conceptually, socially, and for the group (the for-groupness feature follows from (CAT)—recall section 2).

From the pragmatic point of view of the members of g, (1) gives a normative counterpart:

(2) Ought$_{be}$ (N(x)(O(x) → M(x))),

with the deontic ought-to-be operator Ought$_{be}$. The constitutive ought-to-be norm (2) is the normative counterpart of (1), because (1) has the wm direction of fit and because the satisfaction of (2) is reinforced by collective commitment. Hence it at least in ingrained cases gets the above normative interpretation that, furthermore, entails that under appropriate conditions the members of g ought to treat squirrel pelt as money. Thus (2) serves to define part of he *normative status* of M, and the other interconnected norms spoken about in (SI) do the rest of the work.

Above M was regarded as a *previously understood* predicate: "Money" is a predicate whose meaning is clear enough for our present purposes, perhaps because it is antecedently so or because the norms in the first clause of (SI) implicitly define it (e.g., "marriage" qualifies as an example or a relational institutional predicate). In contrast, in some conceivable case, M might be a new predicate the meaning of which is currently being defined in terms of collective acceptance. In the more general setting related to the theory T′ considered above, we can say that the O-predicates ground the M-predicates, and the O-predicates may be noninstitutional. What the precise relationship between these two kinds of predicates is cannot be fully specified a priori, but it seems possible to defend the view that the M-predicates supervene on the O-predicates. In general, there is multiple realizability (there are many possible kinds of hardware for token money).

We can now precisely define the notions of (a new) conceptual status and social status in g:

(CS) O has the *conceptual status* of being M in g if and only if O constitutively represents ("symbolizes" or even simply "is" in the predicative sense of "is") M in g.
(SS) O has the *group-social status* of being M in g if and only if s = O →$_N$ M is collectively accepted in g as explicated by the CAT formula.[47]

The notion of institutional status gets the following definition.

(IS) O has the *institutional status* of being M in g if and only if (i) O has the conceptual status and (ii) the group-social status of being M in g, and (iii) O is governed by a relevant constitutive ought-to-be norm connecting O and M (e.g., (2)) and thus has a specific normative status in g.[48]

Feature (iii) is in fact a consequence of (i) and (ii). Norm governance should be understood broadly enough to cover the concept sense of institutions, thus to cover the use of the term "M" in connection to O (namely, that "M" ought to be used to characterize O in the context in question).

Note that Searlean deontic status can be reinterpreted to be a subcase of (SI), one in which the group-social status is defined by a "deontic sentence," namely, a sentence s that ascribes deontic powers to a person or a class of persons.[49] In this case, group-social status could also be called "political status," as the institution gives powers to certain group members concerning (shared) group goods. Searle's constitutive rule "X counts as Y" is supposed to govern activities, but he does not say much about this and indeed gives only one detailed example. This example and the accompanying discussion are only concerned with powers assigned to persons mentioned inside the content expressed by s (e.g., s = S has the power (S does A)). Searle's example, "X, this piece of paper, counts as Y, a five-dollar bill," can be taken to entail "We accept (S, the bearer of X, is enabled (S buys with X up to the value of five dollars))."[50] Thus, to put the matter in a simplified way, the Searlean account may be compared with my account by taking the institution-expressing sentence to be something like "Certain kinds of pieces of paper count as dollar bills," and we can take it to entail the above statement "S, the bearer of X, is enabled (S buys with X up to the value of five dollars)" and in the more general case to entail the proposition s (= S has the power (S does A)). Here s is a deontic proposition, and it guarantees that the social status of money as dollars entails deontic powers to the owners of money (dollars).

In general, in cases in which the institutional status conferred on a normative practice—or certain elements in such a practice that satisfies my analysis (SI)—involves a deontic status element, we require this: The institution-expressing sentence s in conjunction with sentences expressing circumstantial factors, such as the participants in a particular social practice and perhaps some relevant aspects in the practice, will give deontic powers to the participants in the practice. Thus, if "Squirrel pelt is money" is the collectively accepted institution-expressing sentence in g, then every participant in the institutional social practice in question possessing at least one squirrel pelt has the deontic power to buy something (x) with the squirrel pelt in question.[51]

Conceptual status goes beyond the (antecedent) physical properties of the instituted item (but rather supervenes on its physical basis). Thus, squirrel pelt symbolizes or counts as money, and in this constitutive semantical relation, money is a predicate that applies—in virtue of the conceptual symbolizing or counting as relation—to squirrel pelt not on the basis of the physical features of squirrel pelt but because the group has collectively accepted that "money" is to apply to squirrel pelts. Thus, the requirement that M not be applicable to O merely on the basis of the physical features of O should actually be formulated by saying that the applicability of M depends on a conventional and artifactual element, and that element is here taken to be collective acceptance.

Both in the case of social institutions and artifacts used as tools (e.g., stones used as hammers), one alternative out of several "in-principle" alternatives gets picked out as the "right" one. This is a "cultural" feature of collective artifacts. The central conventional element on which social institutions are based, accordingly, is collective acceptance in the strong sense of the (CAT) thesis.[52] To give one more illustration, consider Searle's nice example of a border made of stones.[53] When the stones constitute a border in a mere physical sense (e.g., by forming a "sufficiently" high wall), no collective acceptance is required. But when the border is only somehow physically marked or indicated, collective acceptance is needed—and the CAT model has a place here. It follows that "attitudinal" reflexivity will then obtain.

To sum up, our detailed and sometimes tedious and obvious-looking analysis has yielded the following "theorem" (relative to a certain group).

> If s is a social institution-expressing proposition with "O counts as M" as the constitutive norm involved in it, then
> (a) s is reflexively collectively accepted for the group with at least some substantial amount of collective commitment (in the sense of (CAT)),
> (b) the collectively accepted constitutive norm "O counts as M" gives a specific institutional (namely, conceptual and group-social) status to the fact of O-things having the feature M,
> (c) M does not apply to O merely on the basis of O's physical features or features not related to collective acceptance, and
> (d) it is up to the members of g ("us") to determine the truth of s, and once collectively accepted, s is indeed true or correctly assertable; a social institution hence is a collective artifact that has been collectively created by "us."

In addition, the converse of the above summary statement is true basically because of (a).

6 Obeying Norms

In this section, the problem of why to obey the norms of social institutions will be discussed. I will start with a discussion of norm obedience in general and then proceed specifically to the institutional case. Clearly, there can be many kinds of reasons for obedience, and I will only highlight the topic below by considering some motivational factors that group members may plausibly be taken to have and act on. First, moral and group-based quasi-moral reasons obviously can play a central role. There are also relevant underlying factors such as the motive to achieve gains and results, the sociality motive, and the power motive that may be reasons for the agents.[54] I will not enter a systematic discussion here but concentrate on the sociality motive, in the sense of the desire to achieve social approval (and possibly derivatively social power) and to avoid disapproval and loss of cooperation partners. I will assume that this motive can be strong enough to lead to norm obedience.

We will below be concerned with a simple norm saying that a member of group g ought to do X in circumstances C. A norm of this kind can be either an authority-based norm or a norm that is based on the group members' implicit collective acceptance of it as "their norm" ("One ought to do X in C in our group") (see appendix 2 for social norms). This is a group norm and offers the members a group reason for doing X in C. The very notion of a group norm is a we-mode notion. However, a group norm allows for obedience on private or I-mode grounds, for example, from the motive of getting social approval or avoiding disapproval. A norm allows for some disobedience without becoming dysfunctional.

We first consider how a member of g can plausibly be taken to reason in the I-mode when acting out of the motive of sociality, here approval-seeking. We assume that the members mutually believe that X is collectively beneficial for the group in the circumstances, but that $-X$ (namely, not-X) is (or possibly is) privately individually better than X. I propose the following stylized schema of practical inference for a member (here "I") who does not participate in the group's operative members' acceptance of the norm as such and thus does not function as a group member in the standard, or we-mode, sense.

(1) g accepts (via most of its members', or via its operative members' collective acceptance) the norm to do X in C (that every group member ought to do X in C), because a situation where everyone does X in C is collectively better than the other choice alternatives (e.g., that everyone does $-X$ or that p percent do $-X$).[55]

(2) I value what the other group members think of me or expect me to do.[56]

(3) The members of g mutually expect (normatively and factually) that any member will do X in C.[57]

(4) I value doing X more than doing anything else, $-X$, in these circumstances (involving (1), (2), and (3) applied to me), although doing $-X$ would be more valuable to me than doing X if no social expectations were involved.

(5) I act on my valuations and thus intend to do X in C.

(6) C obtains.

Therefore:

(7) I do X.

Here the conclusion (7) is that that the person in question is conforming to the norm, but not necessarily obeying it, namely, acting for the right group reason: "Doing X in C is our norm."[58] Rather she acts for the approval-seeking motive, although also instrumental rationality is involved (e.g., in (4)).

A typical case with this kind of problem is a collective action dilemma such as the PD. In such a situation, there is a free-rider effect ($-X$ is better than X if the others do X) but here a member nevertheless gains more by doing X if all members do X than by doing $-X$ in a case where all do $-X$. The above schema shows how this kind of case is transformed to a different, milder case by the conformity assumption. To illustrate this in terms of a simple two-person, two-choice PD with C and D as the choices, in the original PD we have the ranking DC, CC, DD, CD. After the introduction of the conformity assumption (2), the PD is transformed into a cooperative situation where CC gets the highest value and CD is ranked second, whereas the other two other joint outcomes are ordered as DC, DD by the valuation assumption.

Other sources of motivation may be present as well or take the place of social approval. Thus in (2) and (4), for instance, rational nonsocial gains, in the sense of maximization of expected utility, might be spoken of. I will not here formulate this more explicitly but will later in this section consider the rational choice approach to norm obedience on a somewhat more general level.

Next we consider obeying a norm in the we-mode sense. Here the overt structure of the situation is simple. A group takes the view that for some reason one of the action alternatives, say, X, is better than the other ones. A group member then ought to do X or participate in doing it if indeed he acts properly as a group member. So the following pattern of practical reasoning can be proposed.

(1) We, the members of group g, collectively accept the norm expressible by "Every group member ought to do X in C" for g.
Therefore:
(2) I intend to act as a full-blown group member and believe that this requires me to do X in C.
(3) C obtains.
Therefore:
(4) I do X (or participate in our doing X either by doing X or something Y that amounts to my part of X).

Here collective acceptance in the strict we-mode sense entails that the participants have as their joint intention to do X in C and are collectively committed to this. Thus, clause (2) can be regarded as a consequence of (1). Clause (2) basically expresses an intention that does not or need not depend on what the other members think of me.

However, we may think of real-life situations in which the group members are to varying degrees committed to doing X. Thus the we-mode group reason that one ought to do X in C (the "right" reason for obedience) would not be a preemptive reason but a *pro tanto* reason (yet a reason that alone would be rationally sufficient for X) that allows for an I-mode reason to come to play a role. The latter can be precisely of the conformative kind that we have considered above in the I-mode case. Thus a person may perform X in the we-mode case in part because the others expect that.

One further point to note is that the others' sufficiently extensive participation is an underlying *conceptual presupposition* for a member's participation. However, it is a contingent matter whether they act as group members should. Therefore, *rationality* requires a member to check that the conceptual presupposition indeed is satisfied and that the others indeed do participate—and this is another, rationality reason for taking the others' expectations into account.

In the we-mode case, it holds that when the group thinks and acts in a certain way, the group members qua group members also think and act so. Thus, as default, I qua a group member act for the group reason, here that X is collectively better (better for the group) than the other alternatives. In the I-mode case, in contrast, that the others expect a member to participate in doing X is an extra contingent assumption that, given our sociality assumption, will motivate her to act. There need be no group reason to motivate her, but rather her calculations in this situation and her being conformative lead to participation.

Note that in the case of a collective action dilemma such as PD, the group's view is that we should do X because it is collectively better than −X. For the group there is no collective action dilemma of this kind, as, in principle, the group members do not act strategically with respect to each other but do as the group reason specifies. Here it says that X is better for the group than −X, hence the group's choice is X.

Next I will consider some further points that favor the requirement that the members in a group obey *institutional* norms in the we-mode sense.[59] Arguments based on "we-ness," social identity, change of institution, and (instrumentally) rational gain will be considered. They can all become involved in the members' practical reasoning for functioning in the we-mode, for example, by suitably incorporating them into premises (2) and (4) in the above we-mode pattern of reasoning to obedience. (I will not here go into detail.)

We-ness and Collective Construction

As seen, (SI) and (SI*) make the institution-carrying group a we-mode group, and this already guarantees some amount of we-mode acting. The new conceptual status of what has been instituted is one for the group in question and assumes that the group members are committed to using the concept in their thinking and acting. The Collectivity Condition will be satisfied, and this makes the institution a necessary part of the group members' "common fate." Accordingly, a fully justified reason for institutional action from a group's point of view must refer to the fact that the group members collectively accept the instituted item for group use and for their action as group members in group contexts (see (CAT)). For instance, if certain pieces of metal are to count as money in the group, there must be a group belief—a we-mode we-belief—to the effect that those items indeed are money for their group. The group takes those pieces of metal to be money, hence a person functioning in the group context can expect that the others will take the pieces of metal to be money. Most centrally, this is not only an interpersonal matter of the members' beliefs about who takes those pieces to be money and who does not, but is a group matter concerned with all actual and potential group members and others (e.g., visitors) functioning in that group. The group members are supposed to act for a desire-independent group reason ("these coins are money in our group") to be trustworthy partners. This (we-mode) case contrasts with the situation (an I-mode case) where the members only we-believe individually that they, without reference to a group reason, can use the pieces of metal in their everyday commerce. But even in the I-mode case, the general I-mode we-belief that those coins are money in the group is required on pain of financial loss.[60]

Social Identity

A general reason for requiring we-mode acceptance and action is that institutional activity essentially involves a social group or collective, in the sense that the social identity (or partial identity) of the participants involves the group in question. They take themselves to be part of the "we" that the group for them is or involves. In order to preserve and promote their integrity (based on their identity involving this social element), the participants will, or at least should, obey the institutional norms and the group's ethos in general.[61] The group members are to respect their ethos-based social identity and to be disposed to act, and normally also do act, as group members in the we-mode sense. Furthermore, a substantial amount of we-mode thinking and action is required to avoid alienation from the group and the loss of social identity involved. The participants acting on social identity thus act on what the group requires or on what is good for the group.[62]

Change

Changing and modifying an institution requires functioning in the we-mode. For instance, if money gets new functions or if the metal coins are made of somehow is exhausted, we-mode group-level decision making is required to *constitutively* renew the institution (recall section 1).[63]

Instrumental Rationality

There are functional reasons for the we-mode that are based on rational choice.[64] Given the view that social institutions are solutions to collective action dilemmas (e.g., PD-type cases or at least coordination dilemmas), cooperative solutions cannot rationally be arrived at without substantial amounts of we-mode action toward shared collective goals. We consider a simple two-person PD. In the single-shot case the dyad ("we" for the two members) rationally ought to choose C when the dyad acts as a group. Strictly speaking, a group does not see any external situation as a PD for its members: There is no intragroup PD for members acting as group members, and an outcome that is the group's goal ("our goal") need not be its members' private goal. In a situation that is from the private or I-mode point of view a PD, C (or, from the individuals' point of view, the joint outcome CC) dominates over D (or the joint outcome DD). Free-riding is excluded in the group, because the group members are supposed to act as full-blown group members. How the action as a group comes about is another matter—sometimes the participants have voluntarily adopted the we-ness approach and thus operate as a group, while in some other cases they need to be monitored and controlled with sanctions to do that. (Then the higher order sanctioning problem must be solved—recall the comments in chapter 7.) Obviously, in the iterated, long-run case the group will continue to choose the alternative C, as there is no dilemma situation for it (we are assuming that the group, in turn, is not in a collective dilemma situation with another group) and as C, of course, continues to dominate over D in the group agency case.

Now consider the I-mode. In the single-shot case, the individuals individually rationally choose D.[65] What about the institutional case, which represents an iterated case? Standard game theory argues on the basis of backward induction that when the game is known to have only a certain finite number of iterations, the participants should defect on all rounds. (A rational person will defect in the last round, as this is like the single-shot case; but then what was the next-to-last round becomes the last round, and defection is again rationally recommended, and so the regress is on.) On the other hand, if the game is taken by the participants to have some chance of going on and does not have a finite stopping round, then the "folk theorem" applies.[66] According to it, any joint outcome of the game can become an equilibrium under a suitable choice of strategies. Thus, even if the mutual cooperation outcome is one of the possible equilibria (that, e.g., tit-for-tat and tat-for-tit yield), there still is a multiple equilibrium problem. The conclusion is that in the iterated case also, the we-mode wins over the I-mode, as the we-mode guarantees cooperation but the I-mode does not—it only gives cooperation as an individually rational possibility. Even if a change of game to a coordination type of game (e.g., assurance game—see chapter 7) would be allowed, one can argue that the we-mode solution is more stable and also more flexible, for example, in cases of the environment causing relevant preference changes in the situation. The overall conclusion is that in the central case of collective action dilemmas, the we-mode is functionally better than the I-mode on the whole, given the assumption that the participants (group members) indeed act as a group.[67]

7 Summary

The account of social institutions given in this chapter takes social institutions basically to be normative social practices in a group with a special conceptual, social, and normative (in one word, "institutional") status. Collective acceptance by the members of the group in question is taken to be central. Not only is such collective acceptance we-mode acceptance but also it must be constructive (or performative) collective acceptance having the world-to-mind direction of fit and being capable of conferring a special institutional status to the institutional practices (or at least some of their elements). The required kind of collective acceptance is reflexive collective acceptance as analyzed by (CAT) in section 2. Simplified and applied to the case of squirrel pelt being money (or the predicate "money" being correctly applicable to squirrel pelts), it entails for group g that squirrel pelt is money in g if and only if it is collectively accepted and constituted by the group members to be money. In order to do what it is supposed to do, collective acceptance here must be we-mode acceptance, hence also collective commitment to squirrel pelt's being money is involved. In all, the we-mode group g here constructs a monetary institution for itself. (See section 1 for constitutive versus non-constitutive collective acceptance or construction.)

The basic account (SI) in section 4 summarizes the above ideas in general terms. Section 5 discusses in more detail the notion of an institutional status of an item, and section 6 is concerned with obeying norms, especially with the we-mode obedience of institution-based norms.

According to the collective acceptance account, social institutions, qua collections of position-involving normative structures, can be causally effective ultimately only via the group members' minds and actions (including nonintentional ones). Accordingly, we need not assume that they ontically include other, more "holistic" elements (although the social institution concepts are irreducible holistic primitives). Thus, when "money" is taken to indicate an institution, it at bottom must be intimately connected to normative exchange practices in which "objects" to which the predicate "money" is predicable are being employed and that most centrally involve, for example, the owners' powers related to the use of money.

On functional grounds, the group members typically need to have more or less correct beliefs about, for example, money and school, and so on, when they act, but they need not think that by so acting they contribute to the maintenance and renewal of the institutions involved, although that is what objectively is taking place here.[68] Considering the group-dependent part of the social world, in order to be intelligible (in the sense of being correctly explainable) at least this part of the social world must be conceptualized largely as its inhabitants conceptualize it. This is because otherwise the contents of the created social facts here do not depend on the group members' thoughts and cannot be made sense of as facts with social meaning to the participants. For instance, understanding that squirrel pelt is money in g requires taking the point of view of a member of g.

Social institutions are, of course, not the only collectively constructed items in the social world. Thus, physical social artifacts such as church buildings, cars, chairs, books, and generally much of, at least, a city-dweller's environment and "public social space" and "social geography" can be cited as examples of such causally effective entities. They can enter causal connections not only qua having suitable physical features but also, and in this context in an important sense, qua being artifacts expressing normative or nonnormative collective practices and affecting the underlying mental states. Various unintended and unanticipated consequences (e.g., high inflation and unemployment, pollution of the environment) also belong to social artifacts broadly understood (see section 2 for other kinds of social items).

To summarize the perhaps most central claim in this chapter, if not this book, we recall that this chapter has argued for the following equivalences, arrived at in section 2:

> We-mode $\leftrightarrow$ collectivity $\leftrightarrow$ collective sociality $\leftrightarrow$ (broad) institutionality.

Appendix 1: Collectivity and Sociality

In logical terms, the (CAT) formula of section 2 can be rendered as follows.[69]

> (CAT*) p is social (in a primary constructivist sense) in g if and only if
> FG(CA(g, p)) & FG(N(CA(g, p) $\leftrightarrow$ p)).

Here N stands for artifactual conceptual and metaphysical necessity (recall the above comment); FG(CA(g, p)) means that group g collectively accepts p for the group. Thus, if p is social, it will satisfy what comes after "if and only if" in (CAT*), and conversely. Condition FG(p) entails that p is correctly assertable (thus premisible) in g with a certain direction of fit based on its meaning or interpretation. CA must be a performative achievement-expressing notion, and "acceptance" is general enough to cover both the creation and upholding of s and has achievement conceptually built into it. Thus the equivalence in (CAT*) expresses a kind of conceptually necessary, and thus constitutive, connection. I will assume that FG distributes over necessary equivalence, equivalence that holds in all situations within the group's realm of concern (recall chapter 1).

In order to discuss the important notion of collectivity in view of (CAT*), we consider it as applied to sentences about a group's having a propositional attitude (intention, goal, belief, wish, etc.). We assume that the sentence or proposition can be formally rendered in the form ATT(g, p), assuming that g is "we" for the participants and that (CAT*) expresses an analytic truth about collectivity in the constructivist (thus CA-dependent) sense:

> (CAT**) ATT(g, p) is collective-social (group-social) in g if and only if
> FG(CA(g, ATT(g, p)) & FG(N(ATT(g, p)) $\leftrightarrow$ ATT(g, p)))

Next we recall the general Collectivity Condition from chapter 2 and section 2 above and formulate it in a slightly more precise form, as follows.

(GCC) Supposing that ATT(g, p) expresses a collective attitude that an egalitarian (namely, normatively unstructured) group g has, it is true on quasi-conceptual grounds (hence necessarily) that this collective attitude is satisfied for a member A_i of g qua a member of g if and only if it is satisfied for every other member of g qua a member of g.

We can now show that the following thesis is true.

(CollTh) ATT(g, p) is collectively social in the sense of (CAT*) if and only if ATT(g, p) satisfies the Collectivity Condition (GCC).

We assume here that a kind of distributivity principle, we could term it the "chorus principle," for ATT holds. On the ground that the group has ATT(p), the members of g can in principle collectively and individually express (e.g., say in chorus) that they have the collective attitude: "We have ATT that p" (or "ATT(g, p)"). Here are some possible instances of this collective attitude claim: "We will achieve our goal p," "We will bring about p," "We believe that p," "We wish that p were the case."

The proof of (CollTh) is sketched as follows, using "CA-reason" to entail the "quasi-conceptual grounds" of (GCC).

(1) FG(ATT(g, p)). (From FG(CA(g, ATT(g, p))) and the distributiveness of FG)

(2) ATT(g, p) is collectively available, namely, the fact that ATT(g, p) is the case is collectively available for the use (e.g., in practical inference an action) of all members of g acting as group members. (From the intended meaning of the for-group-operator incorporating the chorus principle)

(3) The satisfaction conditions of ATT(g, p) are based on the CA-reason, namely, the reason that g has accepted ATT(g, p) as expressing, for example, the group's goal and that thus (1) is the case. (From the fact that FG(CA(g, ATT(g, p))))

(4) For the CA-reason, it is true that ATT(g, p) is satisfied for group g if and only if it is satisfied for every member, that is, if and only if the inferred, and thus we-mode proposition, ATT(j, p) is satisfied for every member j. (Group-reason-based distributiveness of common goal, namely, the chorus principle, and (3) as to the satisfaction aspect)

(5) For the CA-reason, it is true that if ATT(x, p), x representing a group member, is satisfied for x = j (i.e., the proposition ATT(j, p) is satisfied), then ATT(x, p) is satisfied for any group member k (i.e., ATT(k, p) is satisfied). (From (4))
Therefore,

(6) ATT(g, p) satisfies the Collectivity Condition (GCC).

Thus, given the tenability of this proof, it can be safely assumed, as was already done, that collective acceptance in (CAT) is in the we-mode, the Collectivity Condition being the core of the we-mode. The converse entailment of (CAT*) by (GCC) is seen to be true on the basis of obvious entailment of (5) by (6), and the conditions (2)–(4) which are not dependent on the main premise (6) and hold in this case as well as in the earlier case. Note that (CC) also gives the following analytically true "chorus" principle for egalitarian groups and their members qua group members.

(*Chorus Principle*) ATT(g, p) if and only if (i in g) ATT(i, p).

The thesis (*CollTh*) is central, as it connects the we-mode with collectivity. Basically, we-mode and collectivity in the meant social sense go together and are central and indispensable for the description of the social world.

As for the case of mutual belief (MB), collective acceptance (for the group) and the central formula (CAT) entails the truth of the sentence "MB(p) ↔ p" for the group. Taking belief here as performative acceptance belief, as before, this says that for the group it holds that p if and only if p is mutually accepted as true for the group. (Note, however, that there can also be mutual beliefs that are not acceptances-for-the-group.)

Indeed, the above argumentation indicates that (CAT) is applicable to all basic collective attitudes, namely, to the belief-family and the proattitude-family of concepts, which are directly relevant to constructivist collectivity. To put it as a slogan: *The only (full-blown) notion of collectivity in the social world that a theorist needs is that provided by (CAT) and, in the attitude-based case, equivalently by (GCC) in view of the above (CollTh).*

As already shown in the text, (GCC) basically amounts to the same as saying that the attitude ATT above is in the we-mode. Thus we arrive at the central result that (CAT) and (GCC) are equivalent not only to each other but also to the we-mode of the attitude or action in question. All this basically comes about from the idea that institutionality (collective sociality) is a group phenomenon based on functioning as a full-blown group member in a group context.

Appendix 2: Social Norms

My account of social norms divides them into two basic kinds, authority-based norms and "proper," mutual-belief-based norms. As elsewhere in this book, assume, partly for simplicity, that we are dealing with a case of internal authorization by the group members of some operatives (authority) to accept rules for the group. Authorized norms are basically group-social we-mode norms ("*our*" norms). However, such norms can also be obeyed on an I-mode basis, but not all members can on all occasions obey in the I-mode if the norm indeed is in force. Both authority-based and proper social norms are collectively constructed by collective acceptance and thus involve a conventional element. My noncontingently true (but stylized) analysis of simple social ought-to-do authority-based norms, summarizing the central aspects, is as follows (see the only slightly different accounts in Tuomela, 1995, chap. 1, as well as Tuomela and Bonnevier-Tuomela, 1992, 1998; also see Tuomela, 2000c, chap. 6).

(RN) A norm N expressible by "Everyone in g ought to perform X when in circumstances C" is a *social ought-to-do rule in the authority-based sense* (or is an *ought-to-do r-norm*) motivationally in force in social group g if and only if

(1i) N (or at least a prescription whose logical or conceptual consequence N is) has been explicitly accepted, formulated, and issued for g by an (internally authorized) authority (namely, operatives);

(1ii) the members of g can acquire the mutual belief that they ought to perform X always when in C—on the ground of their (possibly only tacit) acceptance of (1i)—from linguistic information made publicly available by the aforementioned authority to the members of g;

(2i) many members of g perform X in C (or at least are so disposed), and

(2ii) at least some of them sometimes perform X because of their believing, in part due to the factors specified in clauses (1) and (3), that they ought to perform X in C is a group norm in g and that they are (normatively and factually) expected by at least the operatives to perform X when in C;

(3) there is in g some group-social (hence group-authorized) pressure—mutually believed to exist by at least those members referred to in clause (2ii)—that is, at least in part, due to group-social rule-sanctions (e.g., fines) against deviating from performing X in C (and this may in part account for both (2i) and (2ii)).

My analysis of "proper" social ought-to-do norms is as follows.

(SN) A norm N expressible by "Everyone in g ought to perform task X when in circumstances C" is a *proper social ought-to-do norm* (or an *ought-to-do s-norm*) motivationally in force in social group g if and only if

(1) the members of g implicitly collectively accept or tend so to accept—and are disposed to mutually believe to the effect—that the members of g ought to perform X in C;

(2i) many members of g perform X when in C (or at least are so disposed), and

(2ii) at least some of them sometimes perform X, at least in part, because of their believing that they ought to perform X in C, because it is their group's norm and also in part because they are, in accordance with (1), normatively and factually expected by other members of g to perform X in C; and

(2iii) there is a mutual belief approximately to the effect that (2i) and (2ii) in g;

(3) there is in g some group-social pressure, at least in part due to social sanctions (members' disapproval for deviation and approval for obedience), against deviating from performing X in C; and there is a mutual belief to this effect in g (and this mutually recognized pressure may in part account for both (2i) and (2ii)).

A proper social norm in this sense is a we-mode norm, due to the fact of having been collectively accepted by the members (or at least a substantive part of them) as their norm. Collective acceptance here (and also in (RN)) is assumed to be reflexive and to involve collective commitment to satisfying and maintaining the norm. The relevant group reason for the members' doing X in C in the case of both kinds of norms is that it is a group-social norm in g ("our norm") to act so. The most central differences between rule-norms (RN) and proper social norms (SN) are that the former but not the latter are based on special operative members' collective acceptance (although also in (RN) all group members might be operatives in some cases) and that collective acceptance is public, explicit, and articulated in the former but only implicit and unarticulated in the latter kinds of norms that are based on mutual beliefs.

9

CULTURAL EVOLUTION OF COOPERATIVE
SOCIAL ACTIVITIES

1 Cultural Evolution and Collective Intentionality

In this chapter some aspects of the evolution of cooperative social activities (and group properties more generally) will be discussed. Evolution is here taken to concern both biological and cultural evolution. As a working hypothesis, cultural evolution is below assumed to be based on group selection (at least concerning the central problems under study). What a study of evolution, especially cultural group-based evolution, gives is a dynamic picture of group life and therefore of, for example, the evolution of social institutions. While my discussion below does not attempt to create a detailed dynamic theory of institutional change, it will give some tools for doing it and take up some problems related to the transmission of group culture from one point of time to another. In particular, I will apply the group-based notions that have been developed earlier in this book. In this section I will give a survey of what can be regarded as the evolutionary underpinnings of the we-perspective (be it in the progroup I-mode or we-mode). After it, I will discuss cultural evolution generally and outline a simple mathematical account of group change—or, rather, of the change of group properties (section 2).

In Darwinian biological evolution, the central processes are driven by differential replication. We recall that Darwin's theory is based on the three postulates of the struggle for existence, variation in fitness, and the inheritance of variation.[1] In certain circumstances of scarcity (exemplifying "struggle for existence") some individuals fare better than others due to their genes ("variation in fitness"), and the variations resulting from that adaptation process are genetically transmitted to the next generation ("inheritance of variation"). Mutation and recombination, qua variation-producers, are central innovative elements in biological evolution. Generally speaking, gene-based inheritance is pivotal in biological evolution, while learning-based transmission of social and cultural elements ("memes" or whatever they are taken to be) is supposed to take its role in cultural evolution, below regarded as being based on group selection.

Cultural variation (variation not due to genes or nonsocial environment) seems common in nature (e.g., among birds and apes). However, it is mainly only of the *local enhancement* type, in which individuals learn on their own without social learning. In contrast, cumulative cultural evolution seems rare.[2] Such population-level cultural evolution leads to behaviors that no single individual is likely to invent on her own. It seems to require special capacities, adaptations, which only higher animals have. The ability to acquire new kinds of behaviors by observing others' action, or *imitation*, has been argued to be essential for cumulative cultural change in general.[3] Due to imitation (or, more broadly, observational teaching and learning), culturally preservable skills emerge. This is *cumulative cultural evolution*. Mere conformist transmission obviously cannot do all the work in cultural evolution, because it is not innovative. At least in the human case, learning and creative, "lucky" errors often create new cultural knowledge, practices, and skills.

Speaking in general terms, cultural activities in a (modern) human group are shared intentional activities (including the intended and foreseen products of these activities). Using the terminology of this book, it can be proposed that culture consists basically of collectively accepted and, typically, culturally inherited shared forms of thinking and acting.[4] Shared thinking can be taken to amount to we-attitude-based thinking: a person has an attitude in part because the others in the group have it (or because the operative members or leading persons of the group have it). Normative expectations have a special and important role here. Thus, human beings can collectively assign new institutional (symbolic, social, and normative) statuses to activities and create artifacts out of physical things and properties. Thus institutions and organizations find a place here, in the sense that the thoughts can be the thoughts governing institutions and organizations, which again have dynamic impact on people's beliefs and other thoughts (think, e.g., of the creation of new institutional beliefs).[5]

Recent research on cultural evolution gives reasons to claim that collective intentionality is a product of coevolution, indeed an adaptation (i.e., a stable evolution-based disposition). Coevolution in this sense is based on two processes or mechanisms of inheritance, a gene-based mechanism and a culture-based one.[6] For our present purposes, it is not important on which level (the gene level, the level of the individual, or the group level) the gene-based system of inheritance operates. The central thing is that it is Darwinian and thus based on natural selection. However, the culture-based system operates on the level of the population (or "group"). This system operates on cultural variation on the basis of cultural transmission ("inheritance") of cultural items—basically contents of attitudes and actions, in my account. When these two systems interact in concert, we speak of coevolution. Roughly, in successful coevolution, a cultural factor makes a group having that cultural feature survive, and the assumption is that the cultural factor has a genetic counterpart, and thus we have a connection to gene-based evolution. The best documented case is that of a gene for lactose tolerance becoming prevalent in dairy farming societies. Analogously, the we-mode and, more generally, living in groups also cause pressure for the genetic side.[7]

People are generally disposed to act as members of the "natural" social groups (families, ethnic groups, etc.) to which they belong and have belonged to a great part of their lives. The members of kin-based groups, especially, are strongly disposed to function and act together, presumably, at least, in rudimentary we-mode.[8] But the same applies also to larger groups. While a great many animal species live in small groups, humans live in larger groups. Our human ancestors started forming groups larger than kin-based groups at least tens of thousands of years ago. These larger groups, which could consist of up to hundreds of members, have been called "tribes." They consisted of smaller, coresidential groups. A tribe is characterized by the fact that its members typically speak the same (possibly rudimentary) language, have the same culture (e.g., in the sense of shared myths and social rituals), intermarry, and tend to cooperate with each other. Such cooperation appears to have been based on rudimentary symbolic communication and to have involved collective intentionality (at least rudimentary joint intentions); this contrasts with, for example, the "cooperation" of lions when hunting.[9]

In contrast to other higher animals, humans not only live in large groups and act as group members, intentionally cooperating (and also competing) with each other, but also often cooperate with members of other large groups.[10] Let us call this kind of cooperation—that is not explainable by kin or (direct or even indirect) reciprocity—"general" cooperation. This kind of cooperativeness is unique to humans and is probably due to coevolution. It seems that chimpanzees do not spontaneously cooperate (cooperate in a sense based on even rudimentary joint intentions) in their natural environments, not even with close kin; and even human-reared chimpanzees cannot be adequately socialized.[11] This is a reason for thinking that cooperativeness and indeed the we-mode that full-blown cooperation requires are coevolved adaptations in humans.[12]

To give a detailed coevolutionary explanation of cooperativeness and the we-mode is, however, a hard task in the present state of knowledge. To be sure, there are correlated underlying factors that can be mentioned. One is that, in comparison with chimpanzees, humans have a much larger brain (especially cortex) and there is the fact (possibly a consequence or a coevolved fact) that humans have the capacity to live in larger groups and to cooperate with unknown members. Living in larger groups relates to our ancestors living in savannah-type conditions (think of foraging, defense, etc.) and to the length of the child-rearing and socializing period. Furthermore, living in large groups and general cooperativeness seem to require language for the purpose of communication.[13] While I will not here try to sort out the exact connections, I would like to mention an interesting piece of work by Michael Tomasello and his colleagues. They have recently argued, compatibly with what was said above, that *the capacity for collective intentionality is required to account for language capacity and cooperativeness in humans.* They accordingly discuss and, to an extent, defend the *phylogenetic* hypothesis, according to which, based on group selection, humans evolved skills and motivations not only for competing but also for collaborating with each other in activities involving shared goals and joint intention and attention. In the same article they also argue, in part on the basis of their experimental work, that selection for good collaborators requires capacity for intention reading and motivation for sharing psychological states with others.

Their *ontogenetic* hypothesis is that the mentioned two capacities of intention reading and motivation toward collective intentionality interact during the first year of life to create the normal human developmental pathway leading to participation in cooperative cultural practices.[14]

There are other related ways of arriving at the same conclusion about cooperativeness and collective intentionality. One argument says that cooperative hunting and defending the ancestral group, especially in the case of large groups, was more successful than functioning alone or in very small groups.[15] This gave selective advantage to cooperation and functioning as a group member, and here we have again a phylogenetic argument for collective intentionality. Richerson and Boyd belong to those who claim this, and to explain cooperation also in large groups they postulate that humans are characterized by two sets of social "instincts."[16] There are "ancient" instincts that humans share with their primate ancestors, and there are "tribal" instincts that allow people to interact cooperatively with a larger set of people, the tribe. The ancient instincts may sometimes conflict with the tribal instincts. Cooperation based on the former either is kin cooperation or reciprocity cooperation rather than cooperation in large groups, which is what tribal instincts help to explain. The tribal instincts are argued to have coevolved with genes so that eventually they became genetically based. Indeed, these authors suggest more concretely that by the late Pleistocene, humans had evolved the social instincts necessary to create societies on the tribal scale. The tribal social instincts must have involved capacities for collective intentionality, because that is what proper cooperation involves.

The rudimentary "we" used for speaking of one's family and accounting for group life will in the above coevolutionary scenario be accompanied by a tribal "we," sometimes conflicting with the rudimentary "we." While kin cooperation can be accounted for by Hamilton's rule (related to closeness of kin) and while cooperation in a coresidential group can be accounted for by (direct) reciprocity and to some extent by kin, the tribal "we" involves the idea of togetherness with people who may be personally unknown to the agent in question. The togetherness that the tribal "we," being an adaptation at the tribal level, involves is still different from the "we" that cooperation in large-scale societies requires, not to mention the largest possible "we" that universal morality is often taken to require.[17]

The tribal instincts (and the genes they are based on) may both promote large-scale cooperation and, on other occasions, be against it. Richerson and Boyd suggest that a combination of punishment and conformist cultural group selection can solve that problem and can lead to a dynamic equilibrium: They argue that as human genes coevolved with primitive prosocial cultural norms, the cultural environment selected in favor of dispositions adapted for life in cooperative groups; and as the old social instincts became better adapted to life in culturally cooperative groups, cultural evolution could produce still more cooperation. Punishment of primary behaviors is not enough, punishment of those who fail to punish when they should is also needed, and so on.[18] I would like to add that also softer factors may be needed—that is, factors based on educating and teaching children and group members "to behave properly," to cooperate to the extent that promotion of the ethos of the group in question and the underlying more general cultural norms and standards require (recall chapter 7). This seems to require that coevolution produced (quasi-)moral emotions such as shame and the capacities to learn and internalize local practices and norms. Such (quasi-)moral emotions made people sensitive to arguments and sanctions, and their learning capacities enabled them to modify their behaviors appropriately.

As a result of all the above, people came to be equipped with capacities for cooperation with distantly related people, for emotional attachments to symbolically marked groups, and for willingness to punish others for transgression of group rules. Group emotions such as group shame, pride, and honor also found a place in this process. Eventually, cooperation became the default value, as is the case mostly in current modern societies. Only if things go badly wrong with respect to people's selfish interests do they give up cooperation. Finally, cultural evolution led to more sophisticated institutions that, in turn, enlarged the scale of cooperation.[19] In all this, the we-perspective has to win over the I-perspective, and the best result comes from organizing the group into a we-mode group.[20]

In this kind of coevolution leading to cooperativeness, the use of symbols, for example, to mark groups was available and probably was used, at least, some forty thousand years ago. This factor supported life in large tribes (where the members did not know one another) and the development of social institutions. Symbolic marking makes it clear, for instance, that the right kinds of group members are being imitated.[21]

We recall from chapter 3 that conformism (as explicated in terms of shared we-attitudes) is a central, partly cooperative feature in humans. Such conformism (based, e.g., on testimony or observational learning from others) is in many cases a "cheap" (economical and quick) way of gathering information and learning new skills, in comparison with learning from scratch, so to speak. It helps people collectively to accumulate knowledge, enabling them to "stand on the shoulders of giants." We will see later that there are two major kinds of conformism that are relevant in this connection: conforming to what the majority thinks and does (or to some other features it has) and conforming to what successful individuals think and do (including experts, individuals in power, cooperative individuals, idols, etc.). Of course, nonconformist individual or joint learning is central, too, because there are completely new things to be learned and because reliance on the majority may lead to disaster in some cases.

The above is compatible with the emphasis of the difference between ingroups (or, in my terminology, "we-groups") and outgroups ("they-groups") that the social psychological identity theory and self-categorization theory discuss. Cultural group selection shows—on the basis of the conformism involved—how the cohesion and ethnocentricity that are supposed generally to characterize the ingroup and negative attitudes toward outgroups tend to arise.[22] In the case of a large amount of conformist transmission, cultural selection typically results in intragroup variation getting smaller (more cohesion results) while there are various possibilities as to what happens to the intergroup variation. It will get larger if there is a tendency in the ingroup to conform to traits different from those prevalent in the outgroup (and this may of course be mutual). Competition between the groups may then increase, and thus perhaps hostilities arise. On the other hand, the original ingroup may culturally invade the outgroup and maybe fuse it into itself. In such a case, intergroup variation becomes smaller.

To summarize and structure part of the above discussion and to relate it better to the general concerns of this book, I propose the following simplified and stylized evolutionary argument for we-mode collective intentionality and cooperation.

(1) Culture-gene coevolutionary group selection selects for groups that function well.

(2) A well-functioning group requires that the members function on the basis of the shared group perspective (either I-mode or we-mode we-perspective) and thus collective intentionality.

(3) Functioning on the basis of the group perspective requires functioning as a group member toward the ethos of the group and toward fellow group members. Therefore,

(4) The members' functioning as group members requires that they cooperate with each other, that is, it requires intragroup cooperation.

(5) The fullest sense of a well-functioning group requires we-mode intragroup cooperation (and relevant collective intentionality as well as acting as a group member).

Therefore,

(6) Coevolutionary group selection optimally tends to require we-mode collective intentionality.

Functioning well is a quasi-quantitative notion and concerns at least the group's achievement of its basic goals, and so on. Given this and given that well-functioning groups are produced as premise (1) says, we can say that the better a group functions, the more we-mode functioning (collective intentionality and cooperation) it must involve. This is the less strict formulation of (5). As to the tenability of the premises of the above argument, (1) relies on what various researchers—especially Boyd and Richerson—have presented evidence for in the literature. Premise (2) relies on what has been argued in several chapters of this book; especially chapters 1, 2, 7, and 8 are relevant for the required functionality of the we-perspective and present both conceptual and contingent factual arguments and evidence. Premise (3) is noncontingent and just amounts to an analysis of what acting on a group perspective amounts to. The intermediary conclusion (4) was argued for in chapter 7. Premise (5) relates to (2) and is largely based on the evidence given for it earlier (see especially chapter 7). Premise (1) entails the conclusion of (4), and (5) requires the additional specification that (1) indeed also produces groups functioning well in the fullest sense. The entailed conclusion (6) connects coevolution in groups to we-mode collective intentionality in optimal cases.[23] In support of (6), it can still be said that when comparing the we-mode and the I-mode from an evolutionary point of view, the we-mode would seem to involve a more reliable mechanism to account for fitness-increasing behavior in groups than the progroup I-mode, but without involving fitness-diminishing features. Thus the we-mode would seem to be the (co)evolutionary winner, at least concerning central group contexts.

This evolutionary argument connects to the theory of Boyd and Richerson not only through the assumption of coevolutionary group selection but also in that these authors' tribal instinct hypothesis concurs with the idea of acting on the basis of the group perspective and gives an underlying explanatory mechanism for it. Tribal instincts are coevolutionary products of group selection, and they pertain to groups roughly the size of tribes—ranging from a handful of members to several hundreds or even more members who still sometimes are likely to be in face-to-face interaction. By making use of suitable "work-arounds," people get close to tribal conditions and, partly because of that, are also able to function and cooperate in large-scale groups.[24]

This argument is highly stylized, but it indicates the general line of evolutionary argumentation of a kind that supports (although is not strictly required for) the theory of this book. Supposing that the argument is tenable, the argued coevolved genetic basis ontically grounds acting as a group member and collective intentionality (at least in the I-mode).[25] We would thus have a kind of conceptual "discussion stopper" here: Collectively intentional mental states need not be grounded in any underlying mental states, as the jointness level would be based on physical entities.[26] (This only holds for their "form," not contents, which are culturally and socially determined.)[27]

Our above discussion of coevolutionary considerations supports the idea that collective intentionality and we-thinking is a fundamental and probably a coevolved stable disposition, something crucial to being a person.

2   Social Groups and Cultural Evolution

In this section, some dynamic aspects of group practices and change of group properties will be studied. By such dynamics I mean the rise, maintenance, and change of group practices in a context where they receive feedback both directly from their performance ("internal" feedback) and from the surrounding social and physical environment ("external" feedback). The complex issue of dynamics mostly depends on contingent causal happenings in the world, and therefore such a study, having an a posteriori character, must be mainly the task of a sociologist. However, a philosopher can also do something: He can try to find the central conceptual elements of cultural evolution and to find some general features of change.[28]

I will below take for granted that cultural group evolution is a real phenomenon and will rely largely on the theoretical and empirical evidence for this provided by Boyd and Richerson and others working on the topic.[29] I will be interested in the theoretical aspects of the maintenance and change of collective activities such as social practices. However, I will also to some extent consider the cultural evolution of collective activities (and relevant features like social attitudes).

As a first step toward a precise account of social dynamics, let us consider a simple scheme from systems theory that operates on the macro level of groups, their collective states and actions. Social groups, rather than mere populations (as sets of individuals), will be central elements in my account, but the mathematical treatment does not distinguish between I-mode and we-mode groups.[30] Social groups are thus suitable sets of individuals, and we will focus on one such group. All other individuals in the system are lumped together to form the "society," R, external to the group, g, made up of individuals. The total system dealt with here thus consists of the couple {g, R}. (The system need not comprise all of society.) We assume that sets and states can be partitioned as follows. The relevant motivational (mental and/or physical) total state $x(X, t)$ of each set or group X of individuals in g is divided into an "internal" part $x^{int}(X,t)$, which is in part the causal result of X's own collective action and an "external" part $x^{ext}(X,t)$ resulting from the actions of the other set of individuals. In the case of g, we may also put the effects of "nature" into $x^{ext}(g,t)$, so that R is really society plus nature. These states are coupled in the sense that they influence each other causally. However, it is often possible to separate these influences so that a group's (set's) collective internal state is only affected by the causal effects produced by that very set.[31]

The mathematical model is basically a group-level model. It attributes mental states and actions to groups. However, as groups will here be taken to consist just of a set of individuals suitably related to each other, we can also alternatively think that the mental states and actions are attributed collectively to the group members. Thus, instead of the group-level interpretation, we can adopt a "jointness-level" interpretation, in which the mental states and actions are attributed to the m group members of the social group g, for example, $ATT(A_1,\ldots,A_m)$, where ATT is the attitude or action and $A_1,\ldots,A_m$ are the members in question.

At time t, the whole system is in state $x(R, t) + x(g, t)$ (using + here for set-theoretic sum), which causally leads to a certain causal result at $t + 1$ deterministically or with some probability.[32] This result is taken as the system's new input at $t + 1$. This new input similarly produces a new causal result at $t + 2$, and so on. The input always has both a group-internal and an environmental part. Thus each new causal output is a function of both the group's internal state and the effect of the environment. This function may be probabilistic—it is a factual scientific problem what its precise nature is. As the system is dynamic, it can implement learning. The group members act on the basis of their total state and produce actions (joint and/or separate actions) that give feedback to the group's total state at the next moment of time. The total state might be or include a shared we-attitude, for example, a joint intention—either in the I-mode or in the we-mode.

The possibility of incorporating a kind of replicator dynamics into this account will be considered below. When doing it, the main move is to use probabilistic functions connecting inputs to outputs and those representing the feedback from outputs back to the inputs. Both intentional and nonintentional actions are, in principle, dealt with here.[33]

As indicated, the group's total state $x(g, t)$ can either be one single mental state (e.g., a group intention together with whatever beliefs, and so on, it requires), or it can be further divided into components representing different kinds of collective or joint attitudes and causing different kinds of collective actions. Thus, there is anyhow a collective attitude—conceptualized in the participants' conceptual framework for action—that accounts for collective action, which can be one of several kinds. There is, or can be, standard *causal action* such as is involved in jointly building a house or having a swim together. But there also is, or can be, symbolically creative *collective acceptance* action that functions in analogy with linguistic performatives and that is central for the creation of social institutions (recall chapter 8). The participants may collectively come to accept that some physical goods (say, squirrel pelts or pieces of gold) have the special institutional status of qualifying as money, thus creating new symbolic and social status for those entities and in many cases giving the participants relevant deontic powers concerning the institutionalized items.[34] Here we have the symbolizing and make-believe capacities at work.

A we-mode collective attitude is prone to yield group action, namely, a group's performance of an action as a group, whereas an I-mode shared attitude results in "coaction" (a weak kind of acting in concert, see chapter 5), provided there is at least a common goal. The collective attitude that is of prime interest here is joint intention. For instance, it could be the joint intention with the goal content "A table is to be built in way w." This joint intention can be merely a shared weak we-intention in the I-mode: The group members all have the intention to build a table in the way w, and they have this intention in part because they believe also the others in the group have this same intention and because they also believe that there is the mutual belief in the group that the members have this intention. Speaking in terms of cultural evolution we can say that the basis here typically is conformist transmission: the members come to share their intentions, and indeed we-intentions, on the basis of cultural transmission that often is conformist, that is, based on imitation and perhaps on teaching or other forms of social learning.

In we-mode groups, basically all members both teach others and learn from others and, when need be, are collectively committed to such teaching and attempts to learn—recall that in we-mode groups the members, figuratively speaking, are in the same ethos-driven boat. Thus, in a we-mode group, parents and other teachers (intentionally) teach and thus come to transmit cultural information to others and to the next generation. The basic thing here is that a we-mode group (that has been assumed to be capable of acting as a group) can be taken to see to it that such cultural transmission takes place—reliably and to an adequate extent. That is why the institutional system of education exists in typical large we-mode groups (e.g., states). In modern societies, teaching and learning often takes place through suitable symbolic means such as texts (for instance, knowledge by "testimony" is a case in point). Much of the learning is nonintentional, especially in the case of younger people, who may—intentionally or nonintentionally—acquire views, knowledge, and skills from other youngsters, idols, sometimes because of pressure to conformity.[35] Such learning need not be purely conformist; the learners may also empirically check the truth of what their social surroundings offer to them. Social learning involving conformist elements will lead to some sharing of information. Such sharedness can vary in degrees, and what cultural evolution does, in the case of both we-mode groups and I-mode groups, is to spread the information so that sharedness becomes more extensive. If an extensively shared we-intention is successfully realized, then the social practice—based on conformistically acquired shared we-attitudes—is reinforced. When it is not successful, it is weakened. There may, however, be new influences coming from either the ingroup or the external environment (e.g., outgroups) that also affect the situation. These influences may be based on individual learning.

To elaborate on conformist transmission of information in a group, I will below consider the case where there is not yet enough sharing of that attitude and where, especially, conformist learning will bring about the amount of sharing that collective action requires in the case at hand. Consider a simple case of a group g where only one attitude, say, ATT, is under discussion. It could be having some goal, G, or it could even be having or adopting the ethos of g. (Recall that every group has an ethos, however minimal.) I will speak of ATT as a goal G (which technically could be just a group ethos with the world-to-mind direction of fit).[36] We assume that at a certain point of time, p percent of the members of g have the attitude ATT (e.g., preference or goal) with content q, while the other 1–p percent have the attitude ATT with content s, where q and s are mutually exclusive contents and (to simplify considerably) jointly exhaustive. (Note that from now on the term "p" stands for probability, not content.) Let us use the notation $ATT_1 = ATT(q)$ and $ATT_2 = ATT(s)$ and assume that ATT_1 entails $-ATT_2$.

We may now ask under what conditions ATT_1 (e.g., intention) may spread in the group so that the great majority of the group members acquire ATT_1 and are prone to cooperate. Cultural evolution (especially in large, lasting groups) seems to solve the problem under certain conditions. We ask what the value, p', of ATT_1-havers will be at the next round. We let r_1 and r_2 be the "replicatory propensities" of ATT_1 and ATT_2, respectively. These replicatory propensities are to be compared with utilities. We can now compare the expected replicatory propensity of ATT_1 with that of ATT_2 relative to the probability of an individual changing from having one of these attitudes to the other one. This relative probability, given our mutual exclusiveness assumption, is $p(1-p)$. Thus comparing the "betterness" of the respective quantities $p(1-p)r_1$ and $p(1-p)r_2$ in terms of their differences, we arrive at the new probability (relative frequency) p' for ATT_1 relative to ATT_2 (namely, $p' = p(ATT_1/ATT_2)$) by means of the following simple difference equation that Joe Henrich makes use of.[37]

$$(RD) \qquad p' = p + p(1-p)(r_1 - r_2)$$

This difference equation is a simple version of the difference equations used in replicator dynamics in which the "fitness" or replicative power of an item such as ATT_1 here is compared with the average fitness of the other items under discussion (here: the set of other relevant attitudes). The corresponding differential equation gives a generalization to the continuous case.

In (RD) the replicative fitness r_i (i = 1,2) may be physical (or nonsocial). In such a case we can speak of the success of ATT_i in terms of the results that its realization leads to. Acquiring ATT_i is a matter of environmental learning. In other cases, r_i may have social (especially conformist) content. By conformism I here mean that the individuals conform either to the majority's attitude or to the operative members' or leaders' (including opinion leaders') attitudes. I will below take (RD) as the basic formula representing cultural or group change ("evolution") in this kind of simplified context. This formula will be refined below and given more social (especially conformist) content, so to speak.

In accordance with this, Henrich derives the following, more detailed formula for the change (or probability) in the case of cultural learning and evolution.

(HRD) $p' = p + (1 - p)p(r_1 - r_2) = p + p(1 - p)B$
$= p + p(1 - p)(b(1 - a) + a(2p - 1))$

Here the difference $B(= r_1 - r_2)$, varying between -1 and $+1$, is given cultural content in terms of (statistical) "biases." In this newly interpreted difference, the second component $a(2p - 1)$ represents the "conformist transmission" component (with $a =$ the degree of reliance on conformist transmission relative to other forms of cultural transmission) while its first component $b(1 - a)$ represents other—statistically speaking—"biases" (the cultural "direct" and "prestige" biases), and where b stands for constant bias. Henrich also includes in this parameter the biases due to individual learning (and keeps the physical interpretation of (RD) for unbiased transition). However, I will not do this below when applying the present ideas to the dynamic action framework summarized above.

Conformist transmission is basically imitating others (all of the others, their majority, or some other subset of them, such as the operative members or leaders), and it can lead to a similarity of preferences (and other attitudes, in principle) through an S-shaped change curve. As can be seen from (HRD), a decisive factor here is how much bigger the replicatory potential of ATT_1 is than that of ATT_2, and this again depends strongly on conformist transmission and on other "biases" that I will not here study in detail.[38] While, in general, there will be several equilibria, one reachable equilibrium will indeed be that where p is maximal. In such a case, when preferences are being concerned, full similarity of preferences will thus be achieved. The similarity of preferences (namely, high corr) strongly facilitates cooperation.[39]

Henrich shows that (HRD), in the case of cultural bias being present, leads to S-shaped evolution curves, while evolution without cultural bias (involving a substantial second component $a(2p - 1)$) never yields S-shaped curves. An S-shaped curve is one where the trait, for example, attitude, in question is slowly adopted in the beginning (i.e., the relative frequency then is low, and the process has a "long tail") but quickly picks up later when a "critical mass" of people have adopted it. An S-curve can lead to the probability $p' = 1$, but that in general is not the only equilibrium in the process. Long-tailed S-curves abound in the real world, and this fact gives support to this account of cultural evolution. Unbiased (social) learning (including purely individual learning based on rational choice) that Henrich calls "environmental learning" results in R-shaped curves, where the new trait is adopted quickly at the beginning.[40]

What happens now in the case of the dynamic systems-theoretic account outlined above? We assumed earlier in our interpretation of the situation in question that there already is a collective attitude such as a shared we-intention. But in the evolutionary account, we have not yet arrived at that as only a fraction of the members of g have the attitude, let us call it ATT_1 again. Leaving detail aside, the mentioned "probabilification" will yield a probability measure that—concerning one single attitude ATT_1—says how its probability (relative frequency in the group) at a point of time $t + i + 1$ depends on its probability at $t + i$. Let us here assume this much (which is quite much). Then we have obtained the conditional probability of the new internal state $x^{int}(g, t + i + 1)$ of g, given its earlier state $x^{int}(g, t + i)$, and the same for the external states $x^{ext}(g, t + i + 1)$ and

$x^{ext}(g, t + i)$. The former represents (a) $p^{int}(ATT_1)$ at $t + i + 1$, and the latter (b) $p^{ext}(ATT_1)$ at $t + i + 1$.

Combining these will yield $p'(ATT_1)$ (the updated probability value at $t + i + 1$). I suggest the following way of combining them. We take the environment R here to consist merely of the nonsocial surroundings of the group, or more precisely, of the environment that is not socially copied by the members of g. Given this, we can take (b) to express environmental learning when the difference equation for it corresponding to (RD) is formulated. (This difference equation, we recall, compares ATT_1 with ATT_2.) In contrast, the probability (a) is central in the cultural, conformist type of evolution concerning the spreading of ATT_1. One way to combine (a) and (b) would be to assume that some individuals rely merely on (a) while the others rely solely on (b). This is what Henrich does.[41] While the matter does depend on the application of the formalism that one has in mind, I propose rather that in a typical or average individual, both forces, the one reflecting environmental individual learning and the one concerned with conformist adoption in the group, are at work at any time—in principle at least. It is compatible with my idea to combine (a) and (b) linearly with appropriate weights,

$(Comb)$ $p(ATT_1) = EXT(p^{ext}(ATT_1)) + INT(p^{int}(ATT_1))$,

where $EXT + INT = 1$

and take the updated value of $p(ATT_1)$ to be, omitting reference to ATT_1,

$(CombRD)$ $p' = EXT(p^{ext} + (1 - p^{ext})p^{ext}B_{env})$

$+ INT(p^{int} + p^{int}(1 - p^{int})B_{int})$

where EXT is a parameter representing nonconformist environmental learning and INT a parameter representing conformist and other "biased" social influence, and $EXT + INT = 1$. (I will focus on conformism—with respect to the majority or the elite of the group—below, as it seems to be the most central single element.)[42] The parameter B_{env} represents the difference in the nonconformist replicative potentials of ATT_1 and ATT_2; and we can write it as $B_{env} = r_{1env} - r_{2env}$. (In the terminology of Boyd and Richerson, this parameter deals with "guided variation.") The parameter B_{int} ($= r_{1int} - r_{2int}$) analogously reflects the difference in the conformist replicative potential of ATT_1 versus ATT_2 and includes not only majority conformism but conformism to leaders' views and prestige imitation and conformity to socially appreciated ideas and activities. Here, B_{int} might be defined as $b(1 - a) + a(2p - 1)$, following Henrich, but remember that, so defined, other biased social influence than conformism would also be included.

Speaking in terms of the whole population of people consisting of the holders of either ATT_1 or ATT_2, we can say this: p' and $1 - p'$ now reflect the expected replicatory power of ATT_1 relative to ATT_2. If $p' >> p$, the subpopulation with the former attitude is on the winning side as to its cultural adaptivity concerning ATT_1 relative to ATT_2, and recall that these attitudes may be complex, constitutive ones expressing the respective ethoses of two social groups. That need not be the case, though, and not more than one of the subpopulations need to be a social group with a constitutive ethos (goals, values, standards, beliefs, etc.). But if both are, which might well happen, at least if the evolutionary process takes decades or centuries, we can see how this framework can be related to cultural evolution of groups relative to each other.

The criterion of adaptive fitness need not be the extinction of the group (meaning that the group members die out or leave the group) but simply the low value of p'. If it is sufficiently low, the group is a "loser," but if it is high, it is a "winner." (It is unnecessary here to speculate about numerical values.)

Account (*CombRD*) by itself serves as a simple replicator dynamics, but it seems not to have easily findable analytic solutions. As it is rather closely related to what Henrich arrives at, similar results seem to be forthcoming, although I will not here study the details.[43] Note that, as a limiting case, institutional attitudes, for instance, are based solely on the internal, conformist component, and thus INT = 1, which results in an S-shaped growth curve. Purely individual learning ("guided variation") is without a conformist component and relies on EXT = 1 (consider learning on one's own how to best fell a tree or finding out by looking whether it is snowing outside). As Henrich shows, this tends to result in an R-type curve—one with quick initial learning—if analyzed in nonsocial terms by means of (*RD*). Account (*CombRD*) should be investigated in terms of simulation, which I must leave for others to do.

Above I have been figuring a process in a group g—without further structure or "groupness" features—that starts with less similar member views and preferences but, partly due to conformist transmission, leads to similarity of preferences and beliefs. Thus it presupposes that there are individuals who are prone to conform to others or selected others with respect to some characteristics. This premise was in effect discussed in section 1 and argued to have genetic support. That is, partly on coevolutionary grounds, people tend to be conformative (a feature inherent in cooperativeness) relative to their "central" groups and disposed to act as group members. As seen, these groups may be not only minimal kin groups (families, clans, etc.) but also larger tribes to which our ancestors belonged.[44]

As seen, Boyd and Richerson claim that humans are cooperative also in large-scale societies. In such modern societies, people are "ultrasocial."[45] This ultrasociality involves cognitive cooperativeness in addition to mere conformity (such as unintentional imitation with little cognitive content). I take cooperativeness, in the cognitive sense meant here, to involve the capacity to deal cooperatively with, for example, collective action dilemmas. These dilemmas can be solved cooperatively by means of institutions and systems of control (requiring people to cooperate and educating and punishing those who do not cooperate and also those who fail to punish when they should). This is precisely what we-mode groups do or are supposed to do.

We recall that the most elementary unit in our dynamical analysis has been a population of individuals, a social "macro entity." On the basis of our discussion, we can distinguish between three kinds of evolution or change:

(1) individual (or aggregate) level change related to the statistical distribution of attributes of individuals in a population (regardless of the social groups to which they belong);

(2) formation of a social group, capable of action, on the basis of some cultural content (here primarily, an ethos) winning over other ones;

(3) group change and evolution in a comparative context relative to other groups also capable of action. Only this third type of case involves group selection in the sense that a group is assumed to get selected.

Let me next clarify these cases in some detail.

(1) We have spoken of one or more group members' attitudes or features gaining or losing in popularity. The criterion on this level is simply the change in the statistical distribution of the attitude in the population. This change can come about due to different factors, as seen, and in fact an individual's belonging to a certain social group (a certain subpopulation defined on the basis of some other feature), rather than another group or subpopulation, may be one of those factors. The criterion of the success of evolution here is how widely a cultural item is capable of spreading itself and, if there is competition, how well it competes with its rivals.[46]

(2) When group members acquire relevantly similar preferences, the above individual-level type of evolution can result in the formation of a social group, perhaps only an I-mode group (recall chapter 1). More precisely, similar I-mode preferences are, as such, not sufficient for the formation of a social group, but similar preferences make the emergence of a group likelier. Note that similar goals entail similar preferences, in the trivial sense that if, for example, the individuals have committed themselves to a goal G, they prefer G to −G; thus we can continue to speak of the similarity of preferences. Ceteris paribus, the similarity of preferences (the high correlation case) leads to cooperation with a higher probability than the low correlation case.[47] (The similarity of preferences is defined over the totality of joint outcomes—as for single outcomes there might be cases of conflict with similar preferences (e.g., we may all prefer to have the same loaf of bread).)

A proper we-mode group capable of thinking and acting as a group requires that the individuals have come to accept the same ethos-related preferences with collective commitment. The leap from an I-mode group to a we-mode group is a qualitative one, and it is also something that simple "conformist transmission" on the level of individuals may not be capable of generating and explaining.

Anyhow, even when g has become a full-blown we-mode group, our present kind of replicator dynamics can be applied to it. We can still speak of the group members' attitudes and changes in them due to social learning. However, now the group's ethos and other group features (such as its other goals and norms) that are not present in a mere, "nongroup" population will play a role. This suggests that group influence at the single-member level might be taken into account, at least partly, in terms of a special group parameter, a conformity-inducing factor, to be added to the replicatory fitness of the members of g (now assumed to be more or less similar in their relevant attributes, such as ATT_1 above). A group can of course change, and while at a point of time it may have arrived at similar preferences concerning something (e.g., a goal state, or ethos), the situation may change as a function of the success of its actions and the resulting change in probabilities such as $p'(ATT_1)$. The changes may happen either way. When the similarity between the members gets smaller (e.g., the amount of people adopting ATT_1 gets smaller), the group may eventually disintegrate (e.g., if ATT_1 represents the ethos) and new (sub)groups get formed; or the group members may decide to change the ethos and start anew.

In this kind of group change, we are dealing with change (or cultural evolution) in the sense of the social group "waxing and waning" in terms of how successful it has been in its social activities. In general, a group cannot be taken to prosper if it is not successful in satisfying its ethos and its nonconstitutive goals (generally: attitudes with the world-to-mind direction of fit). Thus if a group purports to get food and shelter for its members, the satisfaction of those goals is central for group success. The goals of the group thus must be satisfied for it to prosper, but of course different groups with the same goals may differ greatly in their abilities to bring about the goals.

In this context, we are typically dealing with we-mode groups. This presupposes that relevant we-preferences and other we-attitudes (such as we-intentions and we-beliefs, as well as plain attitudes) are conformed to and shared to a sufficiently large, if not maximal, degree. Indeed, the group has bound itself to its central interests and preferences, and its members have collectively committed themselves to them. These commitments include the members' social commitments to each other to accept those preferences as their we-mode preferences and respect them in their action. The group—by means of its educational system—checks and controls that the relevant cultural information gets adequately transmitted. In sophisticated groups, there will be objective sanctions for misbehavior and an institutional system of control to monitor the members and to enforce the sanctions.

(3) The third kind of group change (here proper group evolution) concerns the relationship between a certain, typically we-mode, group (its ethos in particular) and some other group or groups. Thus it ultimately concerns which groups get selected (or may get selected). This present kind of change is an explicit intergroup case. Accounts of cultural evolution and hence replicator dynamics also become applicable in this wider context. Accounts (RD), (HRD), and (CombRD) clearly seem applicable here.

A group's being able to satisfy its ethos and other goals may not be enough for group success, because other groups may do better. Thus, at least in situations of scarcity (thus inversely dependent goal satisfaction), the ablest groups tend to win. Winning here may include not only survival of group members but also change of membership to the advantage of the winners. The criterion of success is not only how well a group satisfies its ethos but is in part also how well its ethos is able to attract other groups or group members. For instance, the members of a losing group may become members of the winning group, or the losing group may start changing its ethos "toward" the ethos of the more powerful winning group, and so on. The criteria of comparison here are of the intergroup kind, but not yet purely objective—think here of Kuhnian paradigm-preserving scientific communities and the creation and construction of scientific information in them.

I will not here discuss objective criteria of evolution in detail, but let me mention some simple examples. The life and death (and related matters) of group members is an obvious objective criterion of success (e.g., if the members of the group losing out get killed, seriously ill, or weak). It is also an objective matter if the group loses all its members due to their giving up their membership so that the group at least temporarily dies out. A somewhat more indirect criterion is the deterioration of the environment that the group needs for food, shelter, health, and other vital needs. A group that does not spoil its environment will fare better than a group that does. Furthermore, it can be noted that, by some external observer's standards, one group may fare better than another due to unintended consequences—for example, it may indirectly bring about food, security, or wealth to other groups or people by means of its actions.

When we speak of social learning and other cultural effects, we must account for them in terms of the individual (or micro) level or the "jointness level" (or meso level) while the basic situation in our mathematical model is described on the group level (or macro level). Thus, for instance, a group may believe something (e.g., that p), and this belief may evolve to something else. This is still to be cashed out basically in terms of the group members' (or the group's operative members') we-beliefs (or we-acceptances) that p and their coming to change this we-belief to something else due to conformist transmission or some other kind of social influence (and in some cases on the basis of individual learning, to account for new knowledge). Note that several kinds of jointness effect may be involved here. Thus some group members might come up with something new in their discussion and other interaction (e.g., experiments that could not be performed alone). The group members may accordingly come to accept new beliefs (views) and goals for the group. Such views can be about natural things, for example, "$E = mc^2$" or "Stars determine our fate." Or they can concern institutional artifacts, for example, "Squirrel pelt is money." These group beliefs can in some cases be formed testimonially, primarily on the basis of reliance on other group members' sayings and judgments. In the institutional case, which does not rely on the external contribution of the world at all, the accepted views and ideas are institutionalized in a normatively governed sense.[48]

As Boyd and Richerson emphasize in their work cited above, cultural selection on the population level is likely to happen if there are relevant differences (say, concerning cooperativeness) among populations, if these differences affect the "fitness" (persistence or proliferation) of populations, and if these differences are transmitted through time. If all these conditions hold, then, other things being equal, cultural attributes that enhance the persistence or proliferation of social populations will tend to spread. If the population happens to be a social group (or a collection of social groups), as is the case in my approach, this statement applies, too.

The above discussion gives support to the following claims. Conformism is a coevolved psychological disposition, with mirror neurons as part of its neural basis; conformism tends to lead to the similarity of views and ideas, such as the similarity of preferences (or highly correlated preferences); both shared I-mode (or "private") and we-mode preferences shared to a high degree are likely to yield shared we-intentions, resulting in in-group cooperation concerning matters central for group life. (The we-intentions here need only be we-intentions-in-action—instead of being conceptually demanding and psychologically formed we-intentions.) On this coevolutionarily adapted cooperative basis, social institutions and other social structures can be created in we-mode groups—in terms of collective acceptance.[49] While the disposition to conform may be common to many species, the cognitively more demanding activity of cooperation seems to depend in part on specifically human genes (note that even human-reared chimpanzees do not cooperate to the same extent as humans). The replicatory dynamics of this section shows how these various elements can be thought to change in time as a function of what is going on in a social group and its environment. Cooperation and we-acting and the accompanying we-thinking (thus even we-mode thinking) is probably based on a co-evolved disposition: Cultural evolution and genetic evolution can be taken to coevolve in the fundamental matters of conformism and cooperation and what can conceptually and factually be built on them—ultimately our modern societies. Finally, reliable and qualitatively adequate cultural transmission of information can best take place in we-mode groups in terms of the group's seeing to it by means of its governing and monitoring apparatus that that happens. In I-mode groups in which the cultural transmission of information takes place only on an interpersonal basis, the reliability of cultural transmission is lower, and the preservation of group culture may not be as successful.

As seen, in effect, my serious use of group concepts is one central factor that distinguishes my account from that of others. One of my central critical points against the account by Boyd and Richerson is that, at least in their mathematical model, they operate with too thin a conception of culture and social cultural transmission. For one thing, cultural evolution contains much more than simple cultural transmission. I have especially in mind the creation of cultural and social institutions by means of performative collective acceptance. When a kind of item (some precious stone, squirrel pelt, etc.) is given the new institutional status of money, something new is created. The creation and maintenance of institutions is a group matter, and their maintenance and revision, at least, cannot take place without some we-mode thinking and acting (chapter 8). All this requires the use of the performative powers that humans have and that have partly been built into natural languages. This kind of new, collectively created social construct with a special institutional status so far has not been properly accounted for in Boyd's and Richerson's otherwise highly impressive work on cultural evolution.

3 Summary

This chapter has presented and discussed (co)evolutionary arguments for the claim that the disposition to form collective intentional states (and having a shared perspective) as well as to cooperate is a coevolutionary adaptation in humans. Indeed, I find plausible the view, recently argued for especially by Tomasello and his collaborators, according to which the capacity and motivation for sharing intentional states is an evolved central aspect of being a person.

The chapter gives an account of some central dynamic aspects of social activities, with special reference to cooperation. As the driving forces of such activities typically are, at least in part, social and conformist, cultural evolution is involved here. My account relies on some conformist evolutionary assumptions built into the probabilities of forming shared we-attitudes (say shared preferences and shared we-intentions) to account for changes in a group's attitudes and activities. The we-perspective and social groups are thus seriously involved in my account. The following cases of change were investigated: (1) individual (or aggregate) -level change related to the statistical distribution of attributes of individuals in a population (be it a social group or not); (2) formation of a social group on the basis of some cultural content (here: ethos) winning over other ones; and (3) group change and evolution in a comparative context relative to other social groups.

I have earlier (e.g., in chapters 3 and 8) emphasized the following two things: (1) people frequently tend to adopt their attitudes and actions in a conformist way and thus form shared we-attitudes and act on them, and (2) when speaking in particular of cooperative action, the high correlation of preferences (over joint outcomes) can be argued to be central facilitating elements for all cooperation. These features were seen to come together in the dynamic situation when the Boyd-Richerson-Henrich-type account of cultural evolution is adopted. I proposed a—basically compatible—technical version of this type of view and discussed the relevant cultural elements.

My account of cultural evolution relies on collective intentionality and employs the theory of propositional attitudes (and action based on them). Social institutions present a good example of cultural elements that are not created merely by imitation or by individual learning but that my account can handle. While my starting point is the macro level, I have a detailed jointness-level account to implement and enrich the macro-level account. Group attitudes, collective intentionality, and propositional attitudes are features that are not at least explicitly involved (although the first two of these, at least, are discursively present) in the Boyd-Richerson-Henrich I-mode theory of cultural evolution.[50]

10

GROUP RESPONSIBILITY

1   Introducing Group Responsibility

Under what conditions is a social group responsible for what it does and causes? This is the basic question that will be considered and answered in this chapter.[1]

This account will concentrate on retrospective (rather than prospective) responsibility for actions performed by externally and internally autonomous groups. When we hold a group retrospectively responsible for some action, we take the members of the group, qua members of the group, to be praiseworthy or blameworthy for what the group has done in light of some normative (e.g., prudential, moral, legal) standard. My main task is to analyze and elucidate normative responsibility.[2]

My account builds on the assumption that there is a group-social obligation for the group members to promote the ethos.[3] To see this, we note that any group has a goal-like ethos with the world-to-mind direction of fit of satisfaction that it is committed to satisfy. Given this, the group members, collectively taken, are prima facie (or *pro tanto*) obligated to contribute to the satisfaction of the ethos. I will here assume that every member is so obligated, and this will in fact generally suffice for my treatment. A group-social obligation need not be *properly* normative, but I will still include it in my account of normative responsibility. In typical cases the obligation will be a properly normative, basically either moral or group-social ("institutional"), obligation. In groups that can be voluntarily entered (and exited) this assumption can be satisfied through group membership, for when signing up for membership a person thereby accepts the obligation to respect the ethos of the group. This need not be assumed below, but some kind of obligation to promote the ethos must be there.

Except for the end of the chapter, I will concentrate on we-mode groups (recall chapter 1). Sections 2–5 deal solely with them, thus groups that are constructed by their members as groups capable of action as groups. I will, accordingly, concentrate on groups that are autonomous, in the sense that the group in its decision-making (e.g., concerning its choice of an ethos) and acting is free from coercion, be the coercion due to group-external sources or sources internal to the group. In addition, the group members are in principle free to exit the group. Recall from chapter 1 that a we-mode group is a group in which a substantial part of the group members are collectively committed to the ethos and in which all members ought to accept it and thus to be collectively committed to it as group members. Due to the collective commitment toward the ethos, a we-mode group is capable of action as a group, because the collective commitment here is shared collective commitment qua group members that is based on and entailed by the participants' joint intention to promote the ethos (consider "We together as a group intend to see to it that the ethos will be promoted"). As the ethos has the world-to-mind direction of fit of satisfaction, it can be satisfied only by goal-directed collective action, namely, joint action in a broad sense (see section 4 of chapter 1). In contrast, in an I-mode group (also characterized in chapter 1), the members are assumed to be only privately committed to the ethos, or at least they ought to be so committed (consider "I as a private person intend to help starving people"). Accordingly, an I-mode group is not, or need not be, capable of acting as a group, although the members may act toward a shared goal. (for instance, some people going to Alfonzo's for lunch on the basis of their private intentions with the same content—these people form an I-mode group.)

The account of normative responsibility to be developed needs an analysis of what a group's action qua a group is and of what acting as a dissident group member involves. Group action was analyzed in chapter 6, and that account will be slightly revised below to account for dissidents. Note that group action is evaluated with respect to its ethos, but in that account the ethos, while it may be normative as such, is viewed descriptively. Thus, what a group as an agent causes can be viewed in a nonnormative way. Recall, however, that if we speak of the group members' actions, then we are dealing with group-social normativity (in the sense of chapter 1). It is normativity regulating the group members' relations to the ethos and their ethos-based interrelations: A member ought to promote the ethos and do it in part on instrumental-rational grounds and in part because he cannot let down his fellow group members. The normativity that is directly relevant to our present discussion is in general given by moral, legal, or prudential standards.

When a group acts, there can be dissidents. Intuitively, their actions correspond in the individual case to the agent's actions that are somehow faulty although still qualifying as its intentional actions. Thus a dissident must not violate all of the criteria for acting as a group member. A member can be a dissident to a certain degree if she violates some part of the ethos and the actions required for ethos promotion. I claim that the group is partly responsible for its members' actions as group members, and this also includes dissidents' actions. In analogy with the single-agent case, the group is responsible for its members' actions even when they are to some extent dysfunctional.[4] Normative *control* group responsibility will be the focus below. Thus only what the group can, or reasonably ought to be able to, control is relevant, not all the myriads of outcomes that group action produces.

As said, my approach is meant to apply primarily to externally and internally autonomous groups with voluntary exit possibility.[5] Group responsibility for an action performed by the group can be accounted for in terms of the joint responsibility of the group members acting qua members of the group—at least in the dissident-allowing sense of section 2. This sense entails the criterion that a member at least ought to be committed to the ethos of the group and to what the group accepts as its goals, beliefs, and normative principles. He ought to act in the group context as the ethos and other group directives require, but if he does not, the other members ought to intervene. The main idea in the dissident-allowing responsibility case is that the group is normatively responsible for their ethos-violating actions: the group ought to have controlled the dissidents better.[6]

2   Acting as a Group Member in the Dissident-Allowing Sense

The basic we-mode and I-mode notions of acting as a group member were analyzed in chapter 1 in terms of (AGMS) and (AGMW); here I will concentrate on another, somewhat nonstandard notion, namely, acting as a group member in the "dissidence" sense. My focus will be the we-mode group.

One can obviously act within the realm of the group's concern but fail to obey the ethos of the group. One can even perform treasonable acts against the group and its ethos. In such cases, one is acting as a group member in the dissidence sense to be discussed next. I will now consider adding to the analysis of the standard notion a disjunctive clause that allows for intentional violation of the ethos. This liberalization can be made in view of the fact that the group is collectively committed to satisfying and maintaining the ethos and the ethos-spanned sphere of actions. In terms of the members' commitments, it is thus required on conceptual grounds that every group member ought to be collectively (namely, we-mode) committed to the group's collectively accepted ethos and that at least a substantial number of the members in fact so have bound themselves (this is a functional requirement). Thus the group members are obligated to act as group members in the standard sense and thus to perform actions within the classes (1)–(4) of section 3 of chapter 1.

Because of its commitment, the group is, at least to some extent, responsible for any wrongdoings by its members when they function as group members (possibly only as dissidents). What we thus arrive at is the dissidence sense of acting as a group member. The dissidence category is defined by adding the following disjunct to the analysis of the standard sense to complement the action classes (1)–(4):

> (5) A group member's intentional action that belongs to the realm of concern of g but that violates the ethos, E, possibly with the purpose of violating it, in a context where at least some of the member's actions still respect E

Class (5) thus allows for revolutionary action that aims to overthrow or change E, based, for example, on the agent's desire to improve it. Alternatively, such action can have the violation of E as its anticipated consequence rather than as its aim. This type of action fails to be action as a group member in the full we-mode sense (and, for that matter, also in the I-mode sense), and it is necessarily exceptional (not all group members can at the same time satisfy (5)). As defined, a dissident can violate the ethos but still consistently be a group member in a diluted sense, and of course a dissident can unsuccessfully act in the standard sense as long as he intends to promote the ethos but does not succeed in that. In general, a dissident (or violator) in this sense must be connected to the ethos in one way or other; he may obey part of it or he may act in reference to the ethos in order to modify it.

We now have the following analysis to be added to the we-mode sense (AGMS) of functioning as a group member discussed in section 3 of chapter 1. Assuming a substantial amount of collective acceptance in the group of the ethos, and by implication of the action classes (1)–(4), with collective commitment to maintaining the ethos and thus to performing the actions in these classes, I propose:

(AGMD) A member of g performed an action Z in the *dissident-allowing* sense of acting as a group member if and only if Z belongs to one of the classes (1)–(4), being thus action as a group member in the standard (namely, we-mode) sense, or belongs to class (5).[7]

As will be seen later, in case (5), g bears some (but not full) responsibility for the violator's action Z, depending largely on how much it has tried to control the violator's activities. The group's responsibility for Z is based on the simple idea that it is acting as a unity, trying to perform a task, say, X, which it has accepted for itself. X could be its ethos or a task compatible with the ethos. If Z indeed violates the group's attempt to achieve X, it (rationally) must try to control its members' actions. If, however, it fails to do that, for example, due to negligence it will bear some responsibility for the occurrence of Z. It did not prevent Z while it reasonably could have done so.[8] The primary (prospective) responsibility of a group is to control its members so that unitary group action in the intended sense comes about. If the group fails in that, it is directly (retrospectively) responsible for its failures to control and indirectly responsible, to an extent, for the dissident's action Z.

3   Group Action and Dissidents

The discussion of group responsibility in this chapter focuses on group action and its consequences. It should be noted that there are conceptually different kinds of actions both in the case where a single agent does something or some agents jointly do something and in the case where a social group is the agent. An agent can *perform* an action, it can *do* something, it can *bring about* something or *cause* something to happen, or it can *see to it* that something is the case.[9] I will below operate with basically two notions, *bringing about* something and *seeing to it that* (stit-ing) something is the case. Stit-ing Y can be taken to entail bringing about Y, where Y is an action or a state or event, in circumstances where $-Y$ initially obtains. Notice that stit-ing Y is necessarily intentional, namely, stit(g, Y) is necessarily intentional, supposing g is the agent here. Bringing about something, on the other hand, can be nonintentional and can be regarded as equivalent to causing something to happen or to come about.

My account concerns internally authorized groups.[10] The notion of group action that I will here discuss is the earlier we-mode notion considered in chapter 6. Now a remark on dissidents is added to it, and thus group action qua a group can be analyzed basically as follows, assuming that—on conceptual grounds—acting for the group is a task rather than only a right of the operative members.[11]

> (IGA*) Group g *brought about an action or state*, Y, *intentionally* (or, alternatively, *saw to it that Y was the case*) *as a group* in the social and normative circumstances C, if and only if in C there were operative agents $A_1, \ldots, A_m$ of g, such that
>
> (1) $A_1, \ldots, A_m$, acting qua group members either in the we-mode sense (and performing their positional tasks due to their exercising the relevant decision-making system of g) or in the dissident-allowing sense (AGMD), intentionally together brought about Y in the sense of (AT*) (i.e., there was an action X such that the operative agents intentionally together brought about X, and this performance of X generated, and was correctly believed and purported by the operative members to generate, Y), or, respectively, these operative agents saw to it that Y;
>
> (2) because of (1), the (full-fledged and adequately informed) nonoperative members of g, as members of g, tacitly accepted the operative agents' intentional bringing about (or seeing to it that) Y—or at least ought to have accepted it;
>
> (3) there was a mutual belief in g to the effect that there was at least a chance that (1) and to the effect that (2).

Account (IGA*) is an analysis of proper group action, namely, of action where the group acts as a group. When the operative members $A_1, \ldots, A_m$ (where $m \geq 1$) acted as group members in the we-mode sense, they shared the we-intention to bring about (or *stit*) Y (which in our group context may be the ethos E). In this case, they freely acted together, at least in a wide sense.[12] Here a group action can be said to be *constituted* of these we-mode actions by the members and authorized representatives of a group. Some amount of dissident action among the members (both operatives and nonoperatives) can be tolerated—as long as Y comes about. Account (IGA*) analyzes group action as involving the group as a whole. Indeed, the exercise of the decision-making system was claimed to involve internal authorization, authorization by the whole group. Note that in (IGA*) the nonoperative members are assumed to have the *pro tanto* obligation to (tacitly) accept what the operative ones brought about (or *stit*-ed), and, as will be seen, this fact will make even the nonoperative members take part in group responsibility (they may be dissidents refusing to obey the obligation).

The phrase "intentionally together brought about Y" means, roughly, that the operative members were acting on the basis of their shared we-intention expressible by "We will bring about (or *stit*) Y," which actually accounts for their collective commitment to Y. In the group case, Y can be E, or at least it must not contradict E. Notice (concerning especially the case Y = E) that the members' actions need not have been joint in a stronger sense than that they did what their group positions (or, simply, the ethos) required or allowed them to do as their parts of the group's bringing about Y. When the members act as group members in the standard (we-mode) sense (AGMS), Y is an ethos-compatible and ethos-promoting action. It should be noted that, at least in the case of accounting for moral responsibility, it must be assumed that the operative group members acted freely.

In our present context, we can accept the special wide interpretation of clause (1) according to which some operative members can violate the ethos. In such cases, they are acting in their positions, but they are performing actions that are not ethos-compatible. Thus also the resulting group action might contradict the ethos. However, on pain of changing the group into another one or into competing subgroups, the violating operatives are assumed by the analysans of (IGA*) not to succeed in "essentially" changing the ethos-promoting intentions and actions of the group. When the violators do succeed in changing the group's action, the group, when acting intentionally to produce an ethos-compatible action, may still have brought about the blamable result, say, Z, as a group. The group intentionally did something less than Y, say, Y' (e.g., an initial part of Y, so to speak, in a sense analyzable by means of (IGA*)). In any case, Z was different from Y—the group thus missed its original target. Due to the violators' activities, Z might not be ethos-compatible. This can happen if it did not control the violators to a sufficient degree. If it was capable of such control, it can be blamed for the result. The group as a whole (and not only some of its members) can be said to have brought about the action or outcome Z, and it is thus partly responsible for it.

4 Introduction to Normative Group Responsibility

While the group ethos provides an internal normative standard for judging the group's functioning as a group in terms of its members' activities (and hence for judging whether the group is responsible for an action as a group), proper group responsibility involves a group-external normative standard that in general relates to things like what the group-external social environment (e.g., humankind, society, or the more proximate social environment) normatively (e.g., morally) expects or can be taken normatively to expect. In the normative case, we make the usual distinction between prospective and retrospective responsibility, to be commented on in the next section. Group responsibility also involves the praiseworthiness-blameworthiness distinction. Basically, when group g has as its task to *stit* Y (an action or outcome), it is praiseworthy if it succeeds in so doing. If it does not succeed, it is blameworthy (see (RNGB) in section 5 for qualifications). Allowing for degrees of praiseworthiness and blameworthiness, it seems that all cases of "control-related" responsibility become covered.

Let us consider the case of group action in some more detail to see the various possibilities involved. We first consider the logical possibilities (or truth conditions) related to *stit*-ing a state Y. In our scenario, there are the following four exhaustive and mutually incompatible logical possibilities at two successive points of time: (1) YY, (2) Y$-$Y, (3) $-$YY, (4) $-$Y$-$Y. These combinations mean the following. In (1), state Y first obtains and will continue to obtain unless some agent interferes and changes it into $-$Y, and analogously for the other cases. Formulated more exactly, we can say that (intentional) *stit*(g, Y) can be made true by the following mutually incompatible and exhaustive logical possibilities.

(i) YY involves omitting bringing about −Y and preventing any other party (nature and agents) from doing it;

(ii) Y−Y requires preventing Y from changing into −Y (against other parties, nature's, or agents' "attempts" to do so), thus it involves sustaining Y;

(iii) −YY involves not preventing −Y from changing into Y and thus also counteracting other parties' "attempts" to sustain −Y;

(iv) −Y−Y involves (positively) bringing about Y.

In all of the cases (i)–(iv), the group g can be the "agent" (i.e., all its members or all its operative members form it), or simply some member or members of g acting qua group members can in principle make the condition in question satisfied. While stit-ing is necessarily intentional, the above possibilities also apply to the nonintentional counterpart of stit-ing, namely, acting so, or bringing it about, that a state obtains, comes about, or is prevented. The above classification of outcomes applies both to we-mode groups and I-mode groups. In all the above cases, we can speak of group causation in a broad sense, if we allow omissions also to be causal events.

Notice that the group's nonintentional action and its nonintentionally causing something necessarily involves that it must have been intentionally trying to do something compatible with the ethos. One interesting consequence of this can be illustrated as follows. Suppose A, B, and C are the sole members of g. Assume that they at least initially accept the joint intention to bring about state Y (required by a normative standard S), and that Y here is best brought about by only one person, say, A. Accordingly, A tries to bring about Y, but the outcome yet is another state X. This may have happened by mistake, recklessness, or negligence, or due to a noncooperative environment; or perhaps A actually decided to become a violator in the course of acting and brought about X instead of Y. We assume that B actually does nothing relevant to Y but is "in reserve." C is newly turned dissident, despite his original we-intention to realize Y, and he now opposes Y. It may indeed be due to his action that X rather than Y comes about. The result here is (using causation in a suitably general sense that takes into account so-called conventional generation) that (a) group g, acting (nonintentionally) against its ethos, caused X, even if B did not act at all; (b) g is internally normatively responsible for X (relative to S); and (c) B, qua functioning as a group member, is also partially responsible for X. Had g been an I-mode group, none of (a)–(c) would be true. Instead it could only be said that X came about due to the causal interaction of A's and C's activities.

More complex cases also fit this pattern. Thus, in a larger group there could be members who try to bring about an ethos-required or at least ethos-compatible action, while there are also dissidents who try to bring about a different outcome Z. The final result might be that neither subgroup is successful in its attempt but that the group (specifically, the group members when acting as group members in either the standard sense or as violator-members) ends up (collectively nonintentionally) causing something X, different from both Y and Z, as the group members' activities in the standard, we-mode sense do not, at least fully, succeed in controlling the dissidents' behavior.

In the we-mode group, the agents are intentionally and normatively connected, and this fact underlies the truth of (a)–(c). As to (a), the intentional connection that also B shared the we-intention to bring about Y—or if he lacked it, at least that he ought to have shared it, because of his membership in g—makes for the case that the whole group was involved in the action. The members of g are in the "same boat" with respect not only to Y but also to X (relative to S). In the case where X comes about due to A's and C's action and interaction, A and B ought to have monitored and controlled C's action better to ensure that the outcome of the group's action is the intended Y and not X. The group can thus be regarded as (normatively) responsible for what kind of members it accepts, and a person is responsible for what groups he takes up membership in. Clause (b) is true because a group can be taken to be responsible for its failures. Note that there is the weaker, I-mode sense of causal bringing about that we already used for the I-mode group. According to it, only A and C causally produced X; the intentional and normative connections do not matter for this notion (and could not matter if there was no joint intention, as has been assumed of the I-mode case). Observation (c) is true basically because of (b) and the fact that B is a member of g.

Consider a situation where a group g, due to the demand of its ethos or due to an external demand, accepts as its task to *stit* Y. This entails that it ought to *stit* Y, where the "ought" will be the group-social "ought" discussed in chapter 1. The goal could be the (here "group-internal") standard, S, with respect to which group responsibility is judged. More interestingly for our present purposes, the "ought" may be properly normative and based on prudence (what is prudent for it to do), morality (what it morally ought to do), or legality (what the law demands or licenses), and so on. A typical example of a moral ought would be the case of the group's having promised to some party to do something Y (that is not immoral). I assume that the group's task as accepted by it must be compatible with the ethos. Of course, there may be standards applicable to the situation that would require the group to *stit*($-Y$), but if that is incompatible with its ethos it cannot—at the risk of changing its identity—accept *stit*-ing Y as its task, although it might be required by, say, a social convention.

Given a deontically relevant normative standard, we are dealing with full-blown *normative responsibility*. For instance, the group may have as its task to *stit* Y and be *prospectively* normatively responsible for Y, in the sense that it, as required by S, should see to it that Y and thus see to it that, when appropriate, the activities required for that by our earlier cases (i)–(iv) in section 4 will be performed by it or by its members.

Group g is *retrospectively* internally, and possibly also externally, normatively responsible in the (rational) praiseworthiness sense for having seen to it that Y, if indeed the group successfully intentionally saw to it that the state Y obtained, given that *stit*-ing Y was its task. If Y came about only due to g's nonintentional action, this action is not praiseworthy. If $-Y$ obtained at the later time point, then, ceteris paribus, g is retrospectively normatively responsible in the *blameworthiness* sense for the occurrence or obtaining of $-Y$, given that the task of the group was to see to it that Y. The blameworthiness cases, of course, contain all the "negative" possibilities in (i)–(iv) above. To go through these cases, in case (i), g will have failed to ("negatively") sustain Y, in the sense of preventing its change, and it is responsible for that. In (ii), positive sustaining of Y is at stake, and g is responsible for failing to do that. In (iii), g must counteract "attempts" to sustain—and is responsible for failing to do that. Finally, in (iv), g is responsible in the blameworthiness sense for failing to bring about Y. When speaking of g's actions here, it must be emphasized that they need not be "positive" intentional actions of the group as a group; nonintentional omission suffices. Thus, because of the dissident's action, the group causally ends up producing a result that was against its ethos and against its operative members' intention. Then the dissident is at least partly responsible for the action, while the group bears direct responsibility for failing to control his activities and indirect responsibility for the violating action.

Note, too, that often the group is responsible *to some party* (or, if you prefer, "*before*" some party) that endorses or perhaps even creates the standards in question. For instance, if a group g (a group of Boy Scouts) promises a farmer not to damage his forest when camping, the farmer permits the group to camp on his land. Here g has made a promise to an external party, P, and thus is responsible to P. P is assumed to be justified and perhaps required to ascribe praise or blame. More generally, the target P that the group is responsible to can be of several kinds, for instance P = g (the group is responsible to itself, to its ethos, relative to its internal standard), P = a particular agent (e.g., the farmer in the example), P = the surrounding society, or P = the class of rational human beings or humankind (e.g., a terrorist group might be morally responsible to humankind for destroying an important art museum). When the party P is something other than g, it will be, or at least may be, the source of the normative standard. (However, I will not usually consider this aspect explicitly below.)

5   An Analysis of Normative Group Responsibility

To discuss normative responsibility in more detail, let us consider the logically possible cases related to Y and apply a normative standard, S, entailing that the group ought to *stit* Y (or bring about or maintain Y). We will here speak of bringing about Y, as Y might just be a consequence of g's doing (e.g., *stit*-ing) something else. *Stit*-ing something Y relates primarily to prospective responsibility and for setting the group task, while the notion of bringing about is the right one for discussing retrospective normative responsibility (and especially what the group is blameworthy for). Basically, we now have to go through the cases that are in the discussed truth conditions (i)–(iv) of *stit*-ing Y and also the cases in the set of causal consequences that the group brought about when trying to *stit* Y and when operating in the Y-spanned group context.

Let me now consider what praiseworthiness amounts to. The standard S can basically be of two kinds. First, it can stand for what the ethos of the group requires or licenses for the action situation at hand. It is assumed to entail that g ought to *stit* Y. This case is the group-internal case, and the ethos-based standard is necessarily present in all group action as a group. For instance, if g is a Mafia group, its ethos may require certain criminal acts to be performed in the situation at hand, but such criminal acts would be, for example, morally and legally prohibited. Such prudential, moral, legal, and so on, standards generally represent what the external society or social environment is disposed to apply to the situation. This kind of normative standard may contain the requirement that the group ought not to do anything that harms other people or that it is simply irrational. Here the source of normativity, as related to the impact of g's action, would be, respectively, morality or rationality. Note that in the Mafia case, the normative standard would entail that g ought to $stit(-Y)$, if its ethos entails that is should, on the contrary, see to it that Y; and if it does the latter, it is of course to blame for its action. This much we can even say a priori. Below I will mainly be concerned with an external standard, S. (The group-internal, ethos-based standard is here viewed only descriptively in relation to assessing what the group does, and is responsible for, as a group.)

It must be assumed that the normative standard S is *deontically relevant* to Y and that the group understands this and is "*deontically sensitive*" to this fact. In general, S can be taken to specify whether Y is required (in terms of *stit*, ($O(stit(g,$ $Y)))$, permitted ($P(stit(g, Y))$), or forbidden ($F(stit(g, Y))$) or whether another kind of deontic relationship obtains. Whatever task g adopts for itself, it will be regarded as *prospectively responsible* for it relative to S.

Let us now consider *retrospective* normative group responsibility in the case of a we-mode group. Here is my proposal for elucidating praiseworthiness where success is evaluated with respect to *stit* or bringing about activity:

> (NRGP) Group g is *normatively retrospectively responsible in the praiseworthiness sense* for Y relative to deontically relevant normative standard S where Y is a group action (performable by g in the sense of (*IGA**)) or an individual group member's (or members') we-mode action as a member of g (in a sense allowing dissidents) or an outcome of either kind of action
>
> if and only if (or to the extent that)
>
> (0) it was the case prior to action that, compatibly with the normative standard S, group g ought to have seen to it that Y or brought about Y; and they knew that or, because of the rationality standards related to S, they ought to have known that, and
>
> (1) g intentionally *stit*-ed Y or, respectively, brought about Y (in the sense of (*IGA**)).

The phrase "to the extent that" will cover vague cases where a strict assessment of the truth of a condition is not possible.

What about (rational) blameworthiness? Here is my proposal for the group's being at least to an extent blameworthy:[13]

> (NRGB) Group g is *normatively retrospectively responsible in the blameworthiness sense* for X relative to a deontically relevant normative standard S, where X is a group action (performable by g in the sense of (*IGA**)) or an individual group member's (or members') we-mode action as a member of g or an outcome of either kind of action
>
> if and only if (or to the extent that)
>
> (0) it was the case prior to action that, compatibly with the normative standard S, group g ought to have seen to it that Y or brought about Y, where Y is an action or outcome of action that is incompatible with X and is to be performed in the group

context in which the members are acting in the we-mode as members of g (in a sense allowing dissidents); and they knew that or, because of the rationality or reasonability standards related to S, they ought to have known that, and

(1) g intentionally brought about X, or stit-ed X, or intentionally let X happen;

or

(2) g intentionally omitted preventing X (outcome) from coming about or from obtaining or continuing to obtain;

or

(3) g brought about X (or let it happen) as a foreseen but perhaps not an intended consequence of its intentional action (in contrast to (1));

or

(4) g brought about X as a consequence of its intentional action, or it let X happen while it did not foresee X happening but reasonably ought to have foreseen it;

or

(5) g brought about X, or let it happen, by mistake when intentionally trying to bring about Y as a group, and there was either recklessness or negligence involved in its so acting;

or

(6)(a) when intentionally trying to bring about Y, g ended up bringing about X, or it ended up letting X happen, because of its (dissident) members' action that it ought to have prevented but did not, although it was capable of it or it reasonably ought to have been capable of it, or (b) the group members had by their attitudes violating S and favoring actions of kind X (perhaps indirectly) facilitated the dissidents' action that served to bring about X.

In this account, the first clause (0) is thus assumed to hold true no matter which of the disjuncts (1)–(6) are satisfied. Notice that, assuming that Y entails $-$ X, the bringing about action and the letting happen action in our phrasing of (1) correspond, respectively, to the cases $Y-Y$ and $-Y-Y$ discussed earlier in the context of the truth conditions of $stit(Y)$, while the cases YY and $-YY$, respectively, correspond to (2), and thus all the four logically possible cases become covered here. Note that stit and bringing about cover the intentional and non-intentional causality involved (accepting also omissions as causal), and the deontic requirements ("oughts") give the normative aspect of group responsibility.

Clause (3) gives the standard rationality condition for responsibility that foreseen outcomes of an agent's action are something the agent is in general responsible for. Here X was not intentionally brought about, but the group acted in the situation and therefore did something or other intentionally. (This contrasts with case (1), where X is at least weakly intended as it is intentionally performed or brought about.) In (4), this requirement is strengthened, again in the standard fashion of the literature of single-agent (legal) responsibility, to cover what the agent should have foreseen but did not.[14] This is an epistemic rationality requirement concerning the agent's knowledge, and it gets its concrete content from what is normally rational in the group in question or in the case of the surrounding society. Clause (5) is also based on an idea that is standard in the literature, although it applies the idea to the group case. (Recall that we are dealing with we-mode groups here—they are assumed to be capable of acting as one agent.)

In (6), there is no assumption of recklessness or negligence. The group is taken to be responsible for all activities of its members qua group members that it could and should have controlled. This applies especially well to the case of S. Consider the case of the farmer who accuses the group of camping Boy Scouts for setting part of her forest on fire, as one boy mistakenly started the fire. (Perhaps he did it due to a temporary memory lapse and without really acting out of negligence or recklessness.) The group still gets at least part of the blame: it is primarily blamed for not having controlled the boy, and indirectly it can thus be blamed also for the fire.

Generally speaking, clause (6)(a) is based on the idea that there may be dissidents who on purpose try to block the group's activity. Such a dissident, of course, is not acting in the standard sense as a group member, but he is still acting in a group context, maybe purporting to achieve a change in the group's ethos. When a group has committed itself to its ethos it is responsible for satisfying and maintaining it, ceteris paribus. Hence, it ought to have controlled its members better in a case where the members functioning as group members are violating a group norm. The group is exempted from responsibility in cases in which it lacks the capacity to control interferences to its ethos-compatible activities, unless it reasonably ought to have had such capacity (the group should only take on tasks that it reasonably can be expected to be able to handle). For instance, external circumstances, such as stormy weather or a terrorist attack, may qualify as such uncontrollable circumstances. The uncontrollable interferences might be group-internal as well. For instance, some group members might have become dissidents and started to use terrorist methods, a situation that could not reasonably have been foreseen and thus prevented by expelling those members beforehand (see (6)(a)). I am assuming that a rational group is capable and ought to be capable of keeping itself informed about the nature of the persons it admits and keeps as its members. However, there will be borderline cases and therefore the above analysis makes use of the weakening "to the extent that." Clause (6)(b) concerns the kind of cases that Larry May has emphasized: The group is to a degree responsible for X if its members' relevant harmful attitudes favoring S-violating actions (of which X is a representative) affected the dissidents' attitudes and resulting actions (here X).[15]

This account claims that clauses (1)–(6) are each sufficient for group responsibility, given (0). I do not have a strict proof to show the necessity of (0) & (1) or . . . or (6), but I have at least taken into account all the truth conditions related to *stit*(Y). Understanding causality broadly, it can be said that (*NRGB*) also involves nonnormative causal control in a sense of expressing the kind of causal control that *stit* involves.

6 A Group's Responsibility for Its Members' Activities

The discussion below will make use of the principle that a we-mode group, according to (*NRGB*), is normatively responsible for some actions that do not amount to actions as strict group actions—thus generally for what its members do when acting as group members (be that in the standard, we-mode sense or in the dissident-allowing sense). The latter possibility is considered explicitly in (6) of (*NRGB*). The mentioned responsibility principle can be justified roughly by the intuitive idea that a group can be seen as a person that is normatively responsible for much of what it causally produces. As a "group person" basically consists of, and is constituted by, its members, it is also (partly) responsible for what its members qua members produce. Or, put in terms of joint action, the basic idea is that the members share a we-intention expressible by "We will do Y together" and, when the intention is satisfied, "We did Y together." The agent of the intention is "we," and its content is joint action as a group, and thus we, the group members, are (partly) responsible for what everyone in the group does when we do Y together.

In this account, the requirement of collective commitment for groups plays a central role (recall section 1). In a we-mode group acting as a group, the members, at least the operative ones, thus ought to be we-mode committed to the group's ethos and relevant (ethos-congruent) intentions, and a (substantial) part of them are assumed to be so committed in order for the group to be functional (see chapter 1). (Recall that this may come about by the members' having signed up as members or by their showing by their actions that they are in fact members.) The collective commitment in question is a component of the joint intention they have in view of their having collectively accepted the ethos (with a world-to-mind direction of fit of satisfaction). Given collective commitment, with the entailed disposition and obligation to cooperate and to correct or punish noncooperators (in accordance with, for example, schema (W2) of chapter 4 concerning we-intenders), we arrive at this: Each member's action represents the group, at least to an extent, and the group is to some extent normatively responsible for what each group member intentionally does as a group member. Indeed, the group is responsible in the control-related sense for all the cases of a member's acting as a group member that fall under the clauses (1)–(6) of (*NRGB*), namely, all the ways in which acting as a group member (in the wide dissidence-allowing sense (*AGMD*)) can take place when the disjunctive analysans (1)–(6) is satisfied.

At least in the case of externally and internally autonomous we-mode groups, member responsibility (in the normative sense) is a collective notion satisfying the Collectivity Condition (recall chapters 2 and 8): Necessarily, if the group is responsible for doing something, then every member when functioning as group member (and not as a private person) is (partly) responsible for what the group does; and conversely, necessarily, if a member is responsible for an action or omission, then the group is (partly) responsible for it. I am here taking a view of normative group responsibility according to which group responsibility in a we-mode group makes all members responsible, at least to some degree, even in normatively structured groups. The fact that the members think and act in the we-mode makes the group responsible for its action, hence for the members' actions constituting it.

If a group is responsible, there must always be some individual(s) who are or were directly responsible for the action or consequence in question in the control sense of responsibility (section 5): The group is not an extra superagent over and above the members. David Copp has recently argued that a group can be responsible without any of its members being responsible.[16] Copp's argument can be illustrated by cases of the discursive dilemma of group decision-making. The dilemma concerns the conclusion-driven versus the premise-driven way of making group decisions (recall chapter 4). To illustrate, we consider the following case of the decision-making of a tenure committee (here assumed to be a we-mode group). A decision has to be made on whether a candidate exhibits excellence in teaching, research, and service. Excellence in all three is required for tenure. Committee members A and B judge a candidate to have achieved excellence in teaching, while C does not. A and C think that the candidate has achieved excellence in research, while B does not. B and C think the candidate has achieved excellence in service, while A does not. If they vote on all issues, the result is, supposing majority voting is used, that the candidate has achieved excellence in teaching, research, and service, but each member votes against recommending tenure, since none think the candidate has achieved excellence in all three. Suppose the committee then goes for separate voting on teaching, research, and service and as a result decides to recommend tenure. If the result is bad, the committee is to blame. But the individual members cannot be blamed because none were in favor of tenure. Yet the committee intentionally recommended tenure against the best judgment of each of its members. It may seem that the committee is a group agent with independent intentional states and can be blamed when its members cannot. For it was the group, thus the members qua members, who decided upon the method to be used in making their decision; they chose between the use of the premise-driven and the conclusion-driven method in favor of the former. Thus they, collectively considered, are responsible in the we-mode for the bad result, even if they might not be responsible in the I-mode (for instance, because all had private excuses). My overall conclusion concerning Copp's thesis in view of my account can be concisely formulated as follows: His thesis is incompatible with my account, because according to my account a group is normatively responsible, for example, for a wrongdoing if and only if its members, when thinking and acting in the we-mode, are responsible for it as a group. In other words, the existence of group responsibility requires member responsibility, which furthermore must be of the we-mode kind. However, if Copp were only claiming that group responsibility is compatible with the absence of private or I-mode responsibility (although this does not seem to be his basic idea), then our accounts would of course be compatible.

When the item that responsibility concerns is an outcome of a group action rather than an action, the above discussion needs to be complemented by the standard points about action consequence as in (NRGB): It must be either an intended consequence of intentional group action or an antecedently foreseen or foreseeable consequence of it or of some controllable but uncontrolled dissidents' action. Here "foreseeable" means that the agent ought to have been able to form the expectation, and "controllable" stands in part also for those cases where the group should have checked what kind of persons they admit as members.

A case can be made for excluding, at least from full responsibility, those members who explicitly have spoken out and are against the group's blameworthy action. How the degrees of responsibility are to be determined depends not only on the degree and kind of contribution to the action or outcome X in question but also on the normative standard applied to the case at hand. Detailed discussion of degrees of responsibility must be left for another context.

It might be claimed that groups should see to it that dissidents either dissociate themselves from the group, for example, by giving up their membership (although that should happen prior to the violation in question occurs to relieve the group from responsibility), or accept their fair share of the responsibility for the group's action. This claim is not acceptable, at least in all cases, because from an external point of view, a dissident should rather stay in an immoral group and try to change it.

The central thing in assessing a group's responsibility for its intentional action is to have a criterion for when a group acted as a group and when not. Basically the analysis (IGA*) performs the task. When a group intentionally acts as a group, it must intend to do something related, if not the very action in question; and even the stronger claim can be made that any group action (action by a group, and its members' joint action as a group) must "under some description" be intentional and thus involve group intention. These are important assumptions. Some (or all) group members may (nonintentionally or intentionally) "jointly" cause or causally bring about something X that is not compatible with the group intention and do this when functioning qua group members (thus being bound by their collective commitment to perform an ethos-compatible action). This is not group action qua a group, because the members are not jointly intending to do anything related to X, and perhaps the group did not here act as a group at all. Nevertheless, the we-mode group will be normatively responsible for many things that it caused and especially for what all or some of the members acting as group members in the dissidence sense caused (recall clause (6) of (NRGB)). While full-blown intentional group action is a proper subclass of the activities that the group is causally and normatively responsible for, here we are dealing with what the group members privately intentionally (or at any rate not jointly intentionally in congruence with the ethos) or nonintentionally causally produce. This can be attributed to the group in the causal sense that the dissident members were acting in a group context and they collectively (and perhaps jointly) caused X. Thus the group qua a group nonintentionally caused X partly because the other members, functioning in the we-mode sense as group members, neglected their task to control the dissidents. According to clause (6) of (NRGB), the group is then at least partly responsible for X in this case.

As said, when we allow the use of the dissidence sense in clause (1) of (IGA*), we cover the possibility that some operative members are violators of the ethos and act against their mandate from other group members. Here the correctly acting operative members serve to create the ethos-congruent group intention that gives the purported meaning to the group's action, even if the ethos is violated.

Obviously, it does not follow that if a group is responsible for a violator's action, then it as a group intentionally did as a group what the violator did. If the group surrounded a house, all group members ought to have participated in doing their parts of this group action. However, suppose one member violated the group goal and did nothing relevant or even tried to prevent the others from doing their parts. Whether or not the violator (dissident) successfully blocked the group's meant action, still the group's action as a group here depended on its intention to surround the house that it attempted to realize as a group. This justifies the fact that it is retrospectively responsible for the violator's action—it was an action that ought to have been part of the group's action (thus the members' joint action) and ought to have been controlled and brought into line with the group's intention (see clause (6) of (NRGB)). The actual world must cope with unfulfilled obligations, and as a result explicitly normative requirements such as (4) of (NRGB) are needed. The analogous remark applies to the psychological imperfections dealt with by clauses (5) and, in part, (6).

While a violator's action might not be attributable to the group to yield the group's action as a group, other group actions are entailed or quasi-entailed on the basis of group responsibility: Because the violator acted as a group member within a group context, the group ought to have better controlled the violator's acting. Thus, it omitted doing something it ought to have done. The group may have to impose sanctions on the violator (suppose the group was formed by firefighters who did not succeed in saving the burning house because of the violator's action). Finally, the violator's action is something the group is responsible for, as he did something that involves the group and as he was acting in the wide dissidence-allowing sense as a group member. To consider an example, a criminal group (e.g., a terrorist group) might have in its ethos the principle that capitalistic institutions ought to be opposed and terrorized. Here we have an ethos-related obligation relative to which group responsibility in the sense of (NRGB) can be discussed. Depending on the values of the variable S, (NRGB) will make (possibly) different actions normatively required. In order to be able to judge whether a terrorist group is blameworthy for an action or event, (NRGB) should first be applied—of course with a specific interpretation of S. If only the group's own ethos is normatively taken as a standard and the group is a terrorist group, blameworthiness might not result. If Y is the act of murdering a central bank director, it might be a required action. But if S is taken to be a group-external standard, $stit(-Y)$ will generally be the requirement.

Let me illustrate this account in the case of a business corporation, here assumed to be a we-mode group (recall chapter 1, section 7). It basically consists of owners (shareholders), the governing board, executive officers, and subordinate executive personnel. The executive personnel are hired by the corporation (and the same may apply to its governing board). The owners in a sense form an independent group that can in principle externally and internally freely decide about its ethos—that will be the ethos of the corporation or its central part. The owners authorize the governing board and the executive personnel to decide and act for the corporation within certain limits. We may speak of the executive part as a group that is dependent on the owners' group. The executive part of the corporation has only a limited freedom in deciding about how to promote the ethos of the corporation. Nevertheless, being hired, this personnel has the freedom to give up the membership in the organization. In it those higher up in the hierarchy are responsible for those lower in the hierarchy. The latter are lower operatives (for decision-making) and, in a sense, "nonoperatives" (a misnomer here) relative to the next higher level in the hierarchy. This kind of responsibility structure obtains because authorization flows downward in the hierarchy. In contrast, in the owners' group, everyone is an operative member and is self-authorized.

The "dependent group" of executives differs from a group with full external and internal autonomy concerning the members' responsibility. Being without internal autonomy, they cannot be taken to be responsible for the actions and decisions of the members higher up in the hierarchy (They cannot affect the internal power structure or remove inefficient position-holders above their own position.) In the case of a corporation, the lack of internal autonomy is due to the lack of external autonomy. The lack of external autonomy gives the members of the dependent group no chance to decide about its ethos, and this restricts their possibilities to fully function in the we-mode. Note, however, that any member is responsible for agreeing to work, for example, in a criminal or race-discriminating company.

I have above accounted for a we-mode group's responsibility for its actions and "bringings about" (in terms of (NRGP), (NRGB), and (IGA*)) and also for the group's (prospective and retrospective) responsibility for its members' actions, and I have connected the two issues through (IGA*) and my above remarks. All this concerns the we-mode case where the group acts as a group and the members ought to be collectively committed to the group ethos and, if we have the operative-nonoperative distinction in function, to the operative members' decisions and actions for the group. As before, the we-mode groups are taken to include both single-ethos and multiethos groups. In the multiethos case, the external standard S_e may be a standard that is part of a subethos that is not in the nuclear ethos.

Note that groups lacking external and/or internal autonomy do not fit my scheme without modifications. Coercion, whether external or internal, makes the coercers rather than the operatives (when they are different agents) responsible, at least if there is no exit possibility. Externally autonomous groups can function in accordance with this scheme if they can decide about the central aspects of their ethoses and appoint the position holders in the group.

7   Group Responsibility and I-Mode Groups

Let us next consider group responsibility in the case of I-mode groups and I-mode collective action (recall chapter 1 for I-mode groups). Does aggregated private commitment give group action in a strong enough sense to yield group responsibility? I-mode joint action (for instance, in the sense of (AT#) in chapter 5) by the members of an I-mode group can be regarded as a weak kind of group action. The group members can all act toward the same goal in terms of their private commitments. In many cases, no behavioral interaction is needed for a group to act, and thus no requirements for cooperativeness concerning such interaction need to be imposed. For instance, the people of a village might dump garbage in the commons and do it in the I-mode. The group perhaps may end up with a ruined commons, and this was I-mode group action. In this kind of case, one may speak of a weak kind of I-mode shared group responsibility. The members collectively caused the commons to become ruined. The I-mode group here can be taken to consist of a conglomeration or aggregate of members privately committed to the ethos.

While there can be a kind of unitary acting in the sense of the members striving to achieve the same privately shared goal, this kind of group action is not action as a group in the full sense, basically because there is no proper joint intention to be realized. If the group members' actions jointly caused a certain result, whether known to them or not, they were jointly causally responsible for the result, however without being responsible for others' actions (recall the garbage dumping case). The I-mode group is not morally responsible *as a group* in the sense of (NRGP) or (NRGB). What is more, it cannot be normatively responsible for anything *as a group*—because it cannot properly act as a group.

The result collectively brought about might be good for all members or bad for all members. If the result harmed the members, it still was not a "group harm" (harm caused by, or to, the group as a group), and no moral group responsibility ensues, only (shared) individual moral responsibility. This is the case also when group responsibility is based on genuine (and not overdetermined) joint causation, for the individuals who participated in the joint causation of the bad outcome still have a share not only in joint causation but also in responsibility.[17] The members might be jointly fined for the morally bad causal result, and they then have to figure out between themselves how to pay. This does not entail or indicate the existence of proper group harm. The I-mode group in question is not a group that could be responsible as a group for any individual group member's action. There is only collective individual responsibility. Neither is there a social group that is harmed as a group.

Typical public good (and public bad) cases are I-mode cases. If the group members jointly brought about the good or the bad, they may be jointly responsible if they knew and intended (etc.) that the good or bad would causally come about because of their joint action. The group is not responsible as a group, but rather, these individual group members are responsible, collectively considered. The group is just an aggregate here, a collection of individuals who happen to share an interest.

An alleged case of collective responsibility is the Kitty Genovese case (and other similar cases). A woman is being killed in the street while the bystanders do nothing to help her. Here we have interdependent private responsibility of the kind "I ought to call for help unless nobody else does" and collective responsibility in a weak sense.

There can be more complex I-mode cases. In an I-mode group, the members might agree—in the I-mode—to perform a task such as build a bridge together and also make an I-mode agreement concerning the members' parts and contributions. The group's task is performed (and, we may assume, its ethos satisfied) when the bridge has been built. All this can have taken place in the I-mode with private commitments, and thus the members would be responsible basically for their own part performances and what those performances jointly cause.

My general conclusion is that in the I-mode case, there is no such thing as proper group action as a group and that the group as a group is not responsible for its members' actions. There is only private, although possibly interdependent and joint, shared responsibility of individuals.[18] In many such cases—resembling the Kitty Genovese case—it may be required that the members of the I-mode group are obligated to organize themselves to become a we-mode group. This responsibility (obligation) as such is still only shared I-mode responsibility. But in the resulting organized group that can act as a group we have (at least almost) a we-mode group. The members may agree that they will necessarily be "in the same boat" (i.e., in effect accept the Collectivity Condition) and accept that they will all participate in having a share in group responsibility. Thus they will have constructed a we-mode group that is normatively responsible for its activities as shown by (NRGB). In all, it has been argued that group responsibility can only be accounted for in we-mode terms, and the truth of this claim gives a strong argument for the importance of the we-mode.

8 Summary

My central assumptions and theses on control-involving group responsibility in this chapter have been as follows.

(0) A group, even a we-mode group, is not literally an agent (person) and thus in the strict ontological sense cannot be responsible for anything. However, as seen in Chapter 6, a we-mode group can be taken ontologically to consist basically of its members, functioning in the we-mode as group members relative to its ethos, and this justifies treating the group as an agent, because it can be taken to think and act as a unity (or as a group, if you like). Thus, as shorthand, we-mode groups can be said to be capable of having attitudes and acting.

(1) A we-mode group can be (prospectively and retrospectively) normatively responsible as a group for its actions and outcomes of its actions under certain circumstances; recall especially (NRGP) and (NRGB) of section 5. A we-mode group is basically a group in which the members, under conditions of mutual belief or knowledge, are obligated to promote the ethos of the group and in which a substantial number of them in fact are collectively committed to such ethos promotion (recall chapter 1).

(2) When a we-mode group acts, there are operative members who act for the group (all the members might be operatives). To put the matter in terms of joint action, the basic idea is that the members share a (we-mode) we-intention expressible by "We will do Y together" and, when the intention is satisfied, "We did Y together." The intentional agent of the intention is "we" (the group members as a "we"), and its content is joint action as a group; thus the group members ("we") are responsible for what everyone in the group does when they do Y together. As the we-mode joint intention and the joint action are irreducible to I-mode and private intentions and actions (chapter 4), the same holds true of the relationship between group responsibility (and the we-mode collective responsibility explicating group responsibility) and the corresponding kind of I-mode private responsibility. There are cases of group responsibility where some members bear no private (e.g., moral) responsibility for what the group has produced although they are to an extent responsible as group members (e.g., the members might be "in reserve" only). All the group members are, or ought to be, collectively committed to the group's action, and they accordingly bear responsibility for

what the group did, and this includes mistaken actions and dissidents' actions (see (NRGB)).

In all, responsibility for performing an action X as a group member is conceptually different from responsibility for performing X as a private person: Private responsibility, of course, does not entail responsibility as a group member, and responsibility as a group member does not entail at least full responsibility for X as a private person (although in this case the person is privately responsible at least for being a member of the group).[19]

(3) An I-mode group cannot be normatively responsible as a group for its actions, for it cannot even act as a group, although it can to an extent mimic such action, for example, through its members' promises. An I-mode group can be collectively responsible in an aggregative sense, possibly involving interdependence, for outcomes (possibly jointly) causally produced by the members' actions. This entails that the members are privately responsible.

(4) If a many-person we-mode group with external and internal autonomy is normatively responsible for something X, then no one of its members is *solely* normatively responsible for X as a group member.

This clause speaks of a member's *responsibility as a group member*, thus in a group context, but totally bypasses the question of his *private personal responsibility*. To take an example of an internally nonautonomous hierarchical group with a dictator, for example, an army unit closely simulates this case. The members cannot voluntarily leave the group (or can only do it on pain of extreme sanctions). The dictator's power can be enforced by strong punishment, even death, if the order is disobeyed. In such a group, the dictator will be solely responsible for X as a group member, as the other members do not act freely and as they blindly obey the dictator's orders, being coerced to do what they do as group members. Even so, they would bear at least some private individual responsibility for their actions.

The following partial analogue of (4) holds also for I-mode groups.

(4*) The members of an I-mode group can jointly cause X and be jointly privately responsible for it, even when none of the members is *solely* responsible for X. However, this group cannot be normatively responsible for anything as a group (although its members can share private responsibility).

(5) In some but not all cases where a we-mode group brings about an action or outcome X, it is also normatively responsible for X (see (NRGB) and the discussion commenting on its clauses).

As I-mode groups can never be normatively responsible for any X, we do not have an analogue of (5) for I-mode groups.

(6) When a we-mode group is normatively responsible for an X (in the sense of (NRGB)), some of its members must have appropriately acted as group members with the result of X coming about (and here acting involves also omission).

(7) A member of a we-mode group can to a large extent (but not completely, on pain of free-riding on responsibility) escape attribution of responsibility qua a group member in a case where the group is responsible for a blameworthy action X if she was not involved in the causal production of X and if she explicitly publicly disassociates herself from the production of X (e.g., by explicitly publicly speaking

against the production of X before its occurrence and perhaps even by disclaiming her membership in the group).

This chapter has been focused on "*control-based*" group responsibility, primarily in the case of we-mode groups. My account has concerned *stit* and bringing about and related achievement actions. The group is supposed to exercise control over its relevant environment and to be responsible at least in suitable cases. We have noticed that only some group members need to directly do (and control) something when, say, the group *stit*-s something. The others are in reserve and only indirectly involved, one can say. Of them it holds true to say that they might have been directly involved (in the production of some event) but perhaps weren't needed on this occasion. In all, while the group is here supposed to control the situation relative to its task to *stit* Y, say, and hence prevent X from coming about, translated into group-member level, this involves in typical cases that some members are directly involved and are directly controlling the process supposed to lead to Y. The others are only indirectly involved and in indirect control of the process (but might have to step in). In principle, all group members ought to take part in the group's *stit*-ing Y and do what they can to bring Y about, but in actual practice a division of tasks may be more practical.

A group can, nevertheless, be responsible in a kind of "accountability" sense even when it is not responsible in the control-related sense (especially the blameworthiness sense (NRGB)) analyzed in section 5.[20] Although I will not here properly discuss the matter, let me make some remarks. A relevant case in point is provided by groups that have changed at least their membership and possibly the group ethos. Still there may be some kind of group responsibility. As in the case of an individual agent, there is at least an accountability requirement in the group case. Thus, at a certain time point, we have directly and indirectly control-responsible members if the group is collectively control-responsible. At a later point of time when the group members may have changed, there is no control-related responsibility, but—because of group continuity—there is still a kind of *accountability responsibility*, an obligation to be subject to and to answer criticisms and to accept shame, at least in a cognitive sense. The group members qua group members (although not perhaps qua private persons) must in typical cases be prepared to make amends and compensations if they have gained from the immoral acts of the predecessor group. A case in point is the sense of accountability that the Germany of today (which has a new ethos) must face concerning the atrocities of the Nazi era.[21]

NOTES

INTRODUCTION

1. Collective acceptance and construction relevant to our goal example will be discussed in chapter 8 in terms of the reflexivity-involving collective acceptance thesis (CAT) that is shown to amount to a general form of the Collectivity Condition. While one can perhaps speak of construction of goals and so on also in the progroup I-mode case, there is no group construction but only aggregated private construction.

2. See Tomasello and Rakoczy (2003) and Tomasello et al. (2005).

3. See Richerson and Boyd (2005), Tomasello et al. (2005), and the investigations referred to in these articles; also see chapter 9.

4. The American author Jeremy Rifkin (2004) distinguishes between the "American Dream" and the "European Dream"; these partly correspond to and go together with the I-mode and the we-mode, respectively. Here is how Rifkin summarizes the European Dream: "The European Dream emphasizes community relationships over individual autonomy, cultural diversity over assimilation, quality of life over the accumulation of wealth, sustainable development over unlimited material growth, deep play over unrelenting toil, universal human rights and the rights of nature over property rights, and global cooperation over the unilateral exercise of power" (p. 3). He defends the European Dream against the American Dream. In this book I do not defend any particular view or program in social and political philosophy—but note the connection to republicanism and communitarianism made in the text.

5. See Richerson and Boyd (2005).

6. We-attitudes and we-actions can be partly based on nonintentional imitation and "pattern-governed" activities—in general on subpersonal level activities; compare to mirror neuron research.

7. See Tuomela (2002b), chap. 7, for the model.

CHAPTER 1

1. The Collectivity Condition was mentioned in the introduction and will be discussed below and especially in chapter 2.

2. As to collective commitment, see, e.g., Castelfranchi (1995), Cohen et al. (1997), Gilbert (1989, 2000), and Tuomela (2000c, 2002b).

3. See Tuomela (1984, 1995, 2002a, 2002b) for my earlier, less elaborate views of the we-mode or group mode.

4. Some sections in this chapter draw on the article by R. Tuomela and M. Tuomela (2003). I gratefully acknowledge Maj Tuomela's permission to use that material (in revised form).

5. To give a simple example, our group might have as its topic of concern round (P) objects and their color, assuming for simplicity's sake that red (Q) is the only color that can be involved. The group might believe that there are only round and red objects (x) and nonround and nonred objects but that there are no mixed cases. The intentional horizon in this linguistic setup consists of those stated descriptions in the set $\{+ -P(x)\ \&\ + -Q(x)\}$ that the group has attitudes about (namely, $P(x)\ \&\ Q(x)$ and $-P(x)\ \&\ -Q(x)$). The intentional horizon is a subset of topics of the realm of concern of g (which allows all the four logically possible state descriptions).

6. My notion of ethos is partly—but only partly—technical. Thus, the first meaning given to the word "ethos" in Webster's *Third International Dictionary* is this: "the guiding beliefs, standards, or ideals that characterize or pervade a group, a community, a people, or an ideology." In a somewhat stylized way, I will assume below that the group members interpret and understand the content of the ethos in about the same way, although perhaps in terms of their own conceptualizations. In practical life, this may not always be a true assumption, but here I cannot consider this matter. I will not either discuss the underlying, typically implicit cultural values, norms, and standards that are not group specific.

7. A nuclear ethos might conceivably contain a disjunction of elements from the subethoses (e.g., the allowed religious beliefs could be listed disjunctively or, my mundane example, the kinds of stamps that are to be collected might be given disjunctively in an obvious way when a Swedish and a Finnish club merge together). A problem I do not directly discuss here is the dynamics of group integration, especially in the case when some groups merge into one group. Basically, however, what is said in the text about the relationship between the full group ethos and the various subethoses still holds, although other aspects will also become involved.

8. The notion of something being for the group intrinsically means public availability to the group members, in this book. However, it is a contingent but important additional assumption that what is for the group generally means its being for the benefit of the group, perhaps only in the sense of satisfying a group goal or want, etc.—even if such satisfaction might not in another, consequentialist sense be good for it. In we-mode cases, for-groupness is assumed to involve the satisfaction of the Collectivity Condition, to be discussed in detail later.

9. The ethos has the world-to-mind satisfaction of fit—or, more precisely, the beliefs in it have the world-to-mind direction of fit—of semantic satisfaction, as will be seen in chapters 6 and 8 (see, e.g., Searle, 1983, for the notion of direction of fit).

10. Collective acceptance basically is voluntary and intentional acceptance, but some of a group's and a group member's values may be ingrained and may even be based on a less than fully intentional learning process (e.g., because of having been taught by parents or other individuals) leading to suitable "pattern-governed behaviors" exhibiting the values, beliefs, and so on in question (see Tuomela, 2002b, chap. 3). Thus, although collective acceptance basically is intentional, in some cases it is not intentional under the right description, so to speak, as a child may learn some of its values and beliefs under other, more concrete descriptions. In this book I will focus on we-mode collective acceptance. (See chapters 6 and 8.)

11. From a logical and ontological point of view, the notion of "we" is a predicate that applies to several individuals, a thick "we" of course involving various togetherness properties that a thin "we" does not.

12. A group reason is obviously a "desire-independent" reason in Searle's (2001) sense (see chapter 6 and Tuomela, 2005a).

13. This characterization also applies to the beliefs in the ethos. The Flat Earth Society has as its constitutive belief that the earth is flat. How does a group member act on the belief content that the earth is flat? He makes appropriate inferences and acts in the right way (e.g., refrains from sailing around the globe, etc.). Here the constitutive belief that yet fails to fully constitute its very content (in the sense of chapter 8) has the world-to-mind direction of fit.

14. See the bulletin board view of chapter 4.

15. There are higher order groups such as organizations that can be regarded as collections of interrelated groups and societies that are collections of organizations (see Bates and Harvey, 1975; also see my related discussion in Tuomela, 1984). In this book I will, however, keep things simple and, except for a few remarks on higher order groups, will deal only with the most basic case of first order groups.

16. This is a version of the (CAT), to be discussed in chapter 8. It is not required that the members of g cognitively and reflectively function on the truth of the (CAT), although their activities should not contradict it.

17. My account seems compatible with the view that Preyer (2006) advocates, namely, that social systems are collections of member-roles. He also emphasizes the members' commitment to some basic group values, and so on, as does this book.

18. Some cases of ethos-acceptance concern a group belief rather than collective intention, but even here the belief as something constitutive of the group involves a general joint intention. Acceptance as a group member will be analyzed in chapter 6. The ontology of social groups will be discussed there. (This account of we-mode groups derives in part from the account of "functional" groups in Tuomela, 1995, chap. 4; also see Tuomela, 1984, chap. 8.)

19. I here identify a group with its ethos shared by the members and say that the ethos is not the ethos of a we-mode group unless it is collectively accepted (constructed) to be its ethos, and collective acceptance is taken to satisfy the (CAT) thesis of chapter 8, section 2, and will thus be constitutive acceptance.

20. See Tuomela (2002b), chap. 5, for this.

21. There is no mutual belief requirement concerning the theoretical requirement (3). Perhaps it could be required for the sophisticated members of g but hardly all the members, especially not in the case of large groups.

22. There may be partial circularity here, but notice that often the group ethos has been accepted earlier, and that even when it is currently accepted, not all members need at least initially participate in the acceptance (see chapter 6). Even in those cases where the members' acceptances constitute the group's acceptance, each member's acceptance will have to be reason-based on the other members' acceptances qua group members.

23. The ontological aspects of social groups are discussed in the appendix to chapter 6.

24. My present account is somewhat idealized. In a more realistic account—especially in the case of large groups such as nations—it seems plausible to think that there may be complementary knowledge of the ethos and, in general, of the culture of the group (e.g., "You know a part of it while I know another part of it," etc.).

25 See Tuomela (2002b, 2003a).

26. This class of actions in a group context and especially the notion of the right circumstances is discussed in Tuomela (1995), chap. 5, in detail. There the phrase "the right social and normative circumstances" for positional action is analyzed in detail. While space does not here permit a fuller discussion, let us draw on an example used in that context. Consider the signing by Finland's president Risto Ryti of the so-called Ryti-Ribbentrop Pact

with Germany in 1944. Ryti acted in part as a private person and did not satisfy all the position rules concerning a president. He seemingly made a pact with Germany acting as a representative of Finland. While he seems to have made the pact with the approval of the government, this pact was on purpose never taken to the Parliament to be ratified by it, and so all the position rules were not satisfied. The Finns did not consider this to be a pact between the two countries, while the Germans did. Here we have a real-life example of the difficulties involved.

I wish to note that, in principle, role behavior related to positions can also be included in class (1). What I called "position-related role" actions in Tuomela (1995), chap. 8, thus come to be included here. (For instance, giving public lectures might thus be such an extraduty action related to a professor's position.) Furthermore, it can be noted that class (4), to be defined below, in addition can be taken to include "role" actions also investigated in my aforementioned work (think of the role actions of a "mother-type").

27. The norms involved here can be rule norms and/or proper social norms—see Tuomela (1995), chap. 1.

28. See Tuomela (2002b), chap. 4, for presupposition reasons and routines.

29. See Tuomela (2002b) for this kind of intentional pattern-governed action as distinct from nonintentional Sellarsian pattern-governed action. In addition, case (iii) may be regarded as a strong kind of pattern-governed action.

30. See chapters 4 and 6 as well as Tuomela (1992, 2000c).

31. Technical normativity involves only linguistic forms like "ought," but neither moral nor legal nor other substantive normativity is entailed. One may speak of "proper" normativity in these latter cases. When technical normativity involves performing speech acts, it also comes to involve linguistic quasi-normativity that is socially sanctionable. This still falls short of proper normativity.

32. Even performing a speech act publicly involves technical normativity of the linguistic kind, because, e.g., the speech act of assertion (e.g., "The weather is fine today") involves a linguistic-social "ought" for the speaker to be prepared to defend the content of the assertion.

33. Let me note that a group-social ought involves group concepts in a general sense, sometimes independently of their specific factual and extralogical content. For instance, in a chess game or in an organization or, more generally, institution, there are some "oughts" and "mays" serving to define the game or organization, and this applies even to jointly carrying a table upstairs, and so on. These constitutive "oughts" can be regarded as institutional. The central point here is that they presuppose the purely conceptually grounded group-social "oughts" in our present focus. In the context of a group acting rationally as a group, the members ought, on group-rational grounds, to perform their parts. These group-rational "oughts" also presuppose the conceptual ones. Moral group "oughts," generally speaking, concern the good of the group. They also presuppose the constitutive group-social group norms.

34. See the CAT formula in chapter 8 and in Tuomela (2002b) as expressing we-mode collective acceptance.

35. Margaret Gilbert has in her 1989 book and later works similarly emphasized the role of "joint commitment" in contexts of joint action and related contexts. Her notion of joint commitment entails performance obligations to the joint action and to other participants. This contrasts with my we-mode notion of collective commitment, which as such is intention-relative and entails only a group-social "ought." Thus my treatment covers more ground than hers. Christopher McMahon (2005) has compared Gilbert's notion of collective commitment, which involves that a decision to rescind must be a joint one, with what I would call I-mode collective commitment or "aggregated private" commitment. Such I-mode commitment is weaker, in that a single participant can himself make the judgment

that it is feasible for him to leave the joint action or that it would be reasonable for the group of participants to leave the project. In agreement with Gilbert, I also require of collective commitment that it cannot be rescinded without the "permission" of the group (recall the intuitive phrase "standing or falling together").

36. See, e.g., Tuomela (2002b), chap. 2.

37. The general view expressed in this book bears similarity to the social psychological "social identity" theory and its refinement the "self-categorization" theory, in spite of conceptual and terminological differences. The main concern in social identity theory is the social identity of persons (see Turner, 1987). This theory defines social identity as those aspects of an individual's self-concept that are based on social group or category membership together with emotional, evaluative and other psychological correlates, e.g., the self defined as male, European, Londoner, and so on. In addition to this intergroup sense, one may also speak of intragroup social identity on the basis of one's position in a group. The most distinctive theoretical feature of the self-categorization analysis of group formation and group cohesion is the idea that these depend on the perception of self and others as a cognitive unit (in contrast to nonmembers) within the psychological frame of reference, and not on mutual interpersonal attraction and need satisfaction (see Turner, 1987, p. 64).

The central hypotheses of this theory (according to Turner, 1987, p. 36) are as follows. First, people are motivated to establish a positively valued distinctiveness for groups with which they identify in contrast to relevant outgroups. Second, when social identity in terms of some group membership is unsatisfactory, members will attempt to leave that group (psychologically or in reality) to join some more positively distinct group and/or make their existing group more positively distinct. Third, the group members are dependent on each other for acquiring information about the world (see chapters 3 and 9).

According to the self-categorization theory, the group has psychological reality in the sense that there is a specific psychological process, namely, self-categorization or self-grouping, that corresponds to and underlies the distinctive features of group behavior (see Turner, 1987, p. 66). Acting and functioning as a group member (in the sense discussed in this book) is closely related to a person's taking herself to have a certain kind of group-based identity in the sense of the self-categorization theory. Identification with the group under suitable conditions of salience leads group members to act as group members. Turner argues that the cognitive process of depersonalization enables the shift from personal to collective identity: One's unique characteristics fade from awareness, and one defines oneself in terms of stereotypical group characteristics (see Turner, 1987, chap. 3, but see also the criticism by Brewer, 2001). Depersonalization in turn produces acting as a group member (in my terminology). Group cooperation and positive sentiments toward the group and other members occur because identifying with others leads to a "perceived similarity of interests and goals" (shared ethos, in my approach). There will also be conformity because of the resulting adoption of shared group norms regulating action (recall the function of collective commitment, in my approach). Thus it can be said that it is a consequence of depersonalization that group members come to see themselves as parts of a group, "we." For recent critical discussions of the social identity and the self-categorization theories, see, e.g., Hogg and Abrams (1988, 2001), Capozza and Brown (2000), Brewer (2001, 2003), Hogg and Tindale (2002), Turner and Reynolds (2003), and, for an evolutionary perspective, Kurzban and Neuberg (2005); see also chapter 2, section 3 of this book.

38. See Tuomela (1995), pp. 234–41, for a discussion of this notion under the label "right social and normative circumstances" for action.

39. Acting in a group context may also involve subconscious acting—for example, on the basis of ingrained subconscious group beliefs. Yet the acting must be performed intentionally, although its belief-related reason remains unconscious at the time of acting. Thus

when asked, the agent in question is taken to be disposed to admit that he meant to do what he did (successfully or not) or at least that it was not something he did unintentionally.

40. Promoting the ethos can take place in a weak sense; see my earlier discussion. Furthermore, the reason in question can be a "presuppositional reason" in the sense to be discussed in section 5.

41. See chapter 4, section 3; chapter 5, section 5; and chapter 6, section 2; as well as Tuomela (1989) and (1995), chap. 5.

42. Baltzer (2003) discusses the important features of anonymity and interchangeability of members in the case of large groups. He also emphasizes that in such groups every member represents the group and every other group member. I agree with his main points. Nevertheless, I wish to emphasize that the notion of acting as a group member of course applies equally well to large as to small groups. Furthermore, the point about representation also applies to small groups.

In contrast to large groups, in small groups, members tend to have many more private social relations with each other than in large groups. For instance, in the case of a family, these private social relationships are so strong and important that they may be taken to partially define the notion of family (or at least are typically central in the case of particular families).

43. The collective commitment related to beliefs in E concerns seeing to it that they are not violated, and the world-to-mind direction of fit is understood so in their case, not in the sense that the world somehow has to be changed.

44. Accordingly, for any action X that is required by the ethos, the group, ceteris paribus, is not "as it ought to be" unless it performs X. Here one cannot strictly formally deduce, by modus ponens, the conclusion "g ought to do X" from the premises "If g has ethos E, then it ought to do X" and "g has E." Here the "ought" must be taken to cover the if-then statement: it ought to be the case that if g has E, then x ought to do X. The conclusion is premise-dependent and logically nondetachable, although it is "practically" detachable (i.e., the group is not as it should be unless it performs X). (See Broome's discussion, 2000.) In the case of *pro tanto* obligations and norm conflicts, it seems that the normative requirement can still be viewed as a *pro tanto* reason, contrary to Broome's claim.

45. I thank Kaarlo Miller for emphasizing the change-obedience combination. Miller also made several other good points concerning this section.

46. Using O for ought-to-be, CA for group acceptance, and R for reasons for group acceptance, we note that the obligation can be taken to have the form O(if R then CA). Here plain obligation to accept E, namely, O(CA), cannot be detached, if R is true. This is an acceptable claim of deontic logic (indeed, basically the same logical point that was made in an earlier note). However, the group is not functioning rationally properly unless (it continues to maintain E supposing it originally accepted E rationally on the basis of R. See section 2 of chapter 6 for a point that makes it possible to combine normative requirements (in the case when group reasons are such requirements) with I-mode reasons, but on pain of excluding full functioning as a group member.

47. In stronger cases with public multilateral intention expression (nonnormative case) we get a better doxastic ground for group action, and in the case of the participants' having made an agreement to act in a certain way (this includes the case of normative acceptance of a joint plan) we get even a group-binding obligation. Even in this last case we might not get normal "positive" group action but only omission action. In this sense we might not have full group action based on a joint intention or a shared collective goal.

48. Collective pattern-governed behavior in the sense of chapter 3 of Tuomela (2002b) is a case in point.

49. Collective rituals such as dancing and singing together are central. For the centrality of shared melodic singing and rhythmic moving of one's body, see, e.g., Storr

(1993), especially chap. 1. Richman (1987) argues that music is the 'language' of emotional and physiological arousal. Specifically, a culturally agreed-upon pattern of rhythm and melody, that is, song, that is sung together, provides a shared form of emotion that carries along the participants so that they experience their bodies responding emotionally in very similar ways. This Richman takes to be the source of the feeling of solidarity and good will that comes with choral singing: people's physiological arousals are in synchrony and in harmony, at least for a brief period. The emotion here could indeed be a we-feeling of solidarity construed as a we-attitude in the sense of chapter 3 ("I am proud of this group and believe that others also are and that this is mutual belief in the group"). It seems that a we-feeling can basically be of at least three kinds: (1) we-feeling as a we-attitude in the already-mentioned sense; (2) we-feeling (e.g., with the cognitive content "Our group is great") could arise in interaction between people where feelings are expressed and expressions communicated (e.g., football fans watching a match and interacting emotionally); (3) we-feeling (2), with the addition that there is a collective cause of the feeling (e.g. "Hurrah, our team won the match!").

Similar considerations but with greater force and in more detail are presented in the recent article by Steven Brown (2000)—see the relevant note in chap. 9 of this book.

50. See Brewer (2003), esp. pp. 30–31, for a review of relevant research; see also chapter 2, section 3 below.

51. Note that mutual belief about collective commitment suffices for actual collective commitment, assuming commitment to be a persistent intention to participate: If there is mutual belief among a substantial part of (the operative) group members to the effect that the whole group as a group is committed in the world-to-mind fashion to ethos E, then there is shared we-mode commitment (intention) to contribute to E by those members, and hence, assuming successful execution of intention, collective action results. This result requires the additional, but highly reasonable, assumption in its antecedent that each member who believes that she is committed also actually is committed.

52. As for trust, see the discussion by Maj Tuomela (2003).

53. A social commitment notion is also discussed by Gilbert (1989, 2000) and Castelfranchi (1995), although their notion is based on (directed) obligation and seems thus to be properly normative. Furthermore, my notion of collective commitment is attitude-dependent, in contrast at least to Gilbert's notion. However, from a functional point of view, my approach still resembles these accounts.

54. Another social aspect about a collective commitment is that it is a we-commitment involving the mutual belief that the others are similarly committed; more exactly, each participant is committed to the item and believes that the others are and that there is a mutual belief concerning this among them (see chapter 3 for we-attitudes).

55. See Castelfranchi (1995) as well as Conte and Castelfranchi (1995) for related distinctions and points.

56. Commitment to oneself and to the others has already been discussed, but let me here make a point about the social sources of commitment related to how violations are sanctioned:

(a) Nonnormative case: For instance, if A and B have formed a joint intention to paint a house together, it might happen that A has overestimated his skills and is not able to adequately fulfill his subplan. Then he may just inform B about the situation and is not subject to more sanctioning than perhaps a charge of overestimation.

(b) Normative case: Here the reaction to violation has the form "Violating behavior is socially inappropriate or incorrect." There are three subcases here:

(i) The violating behavior breaches the ethos of the group.

(ii) The violation concerns the general conventions and customs of the society.

(iii) The violation concerns the moral norms and principles of the society (or at least against what is felt or believed to be morally right or socially appropriate in the society).

In all of the (b) cases, there is also (technical) social commitment (case (a)) involved. This is because the very nature of joint activities in general involves only shared control over the outcome.

57. Castelfranchi (1995) speaks of a "witness" where I speak of the "audience."

CHAPTER 2

1. The history of the we-mode and the I-mode is a matter that cannot be discussed in this book. Let me, however, make some sweeping remarks, or should I say research hypotheses, without properly presenting evidence on the matter. The general picture about some important philosophers in the last century seems to be this (and here I am indebted to Mulligan, 2001, and Hans Bernhard Schmid, 2005): Heidegger (1980/1928) and Sartre (1966/1943) are individualists. What is missing in Heidegger's account is what can be called *Gemeinsames Dasein* ("jointly existing people"). Heidegger has his social notions *Mitsein* ("being together") and *Fürsorge* ("care"), but these are more like social psychological notions than properly social notions. Thus the concern is with reciprocity between individuals, not with the relations between a group member and a group. Similarly Weber (1968/1921) is a well-known individualist. Durkheim (1965/1912) is more of a holist and takes society as a whole to have an impact on the members (individuals). He seems to operate with a kind of we-mode idea. Of recent American philosophers of course Wilfrid Sellars (1968) should be mentioned as a champion of the we-mode/I-mode distinction in ethical contexts. (As to my own earlier contributions, see Tuomela (1984, 1995, 2000c, 2002b.)

2. A longer discussion of the matter will be found in chapter 4, section 5.

3. Collective acceptance must be assumed to satisfy the "(CAT) thesis" mentioned in chapter 1 (see Tuomela, 2002b, Tuomela and Balzer, 1999, and especially chapter 8 here).

4. One may also take a broader view of the notion of collective content. Thus, Miller and Tuomela (2001) define collective content as follows. Goal P of an agent X has *collective content* if and only if (X believes that there is a mutual belief that) P is satisfied for X if and only if it has to be satisfied for a plurality of X's group members sharing P. In the sense of this definition, the satisfaction of a collective attitude (here goal) necessarily involves collective content. Note that the action bringing about the satisfaction of the attitude can be a singular action or state rather than a joint action. In the we-mode case, we have action realizing the collective commitment involved in the we-mode attitude, that is, an action by which the participants try to see to it that the goal comes about (or is maintained, as the case may be). Let us call this a c-action, and distinguish it clearly from the actual concrete means-action (m-action) that serves (normally causally) to bring about the goal-state. Such c-action, which is we-mode acting together understood in a broad sense, is needed in the case of full-blown we-mode collective attitudes. If the above collectivity account is taken to refer to m-action, it does not provide more than a sufficient condition of collectivity.

Let me note that the satisfaction of the (CAT) formula of chapter 8 basically gives both a necessary and sufficient condition for collectivity in its central artifactual sense (see appendix 1 to chapter 8). The (CAT) formula (implicitly) deals with c-actions rather than m-actions in the above sense and thus succeeds in capturing collectivity.

5. It can be noted that from a logical point of view the Collectivity Condition amounts to a special, group-relative version of the golden rule, using a consistency formulation of the latter. I will not here discuss the matter. See Gensler (1996) for the logic of the golden rule.

6. This treatment of the general Collectivity Condition was prompted by critical remarks on a previous version by Kaarlo Miller.

7. I am here speaking of structuration (social position structure) in terms of social norms, which serve to create (normative) *task-right systems* attributable to group positions—see the account of social norms as rule-norms or proper social norms in chapter 8. I will below often consider structured (thus nonegalitarian) groups and regard unstructured ones as special cases of them, that is, special cases with "empty" or "nil" structure.

8. My point about the feasibility of I-mode acting also applies to norm following and even to fulfilling an agreement, as long as there is some amount of we-mode acting in the group. Considering the latter example, one may take an instrumental attitude toward agreements and only contribute to their fulfillment as long as such activity is not too costly or has more overall utility than not obeying the agreement. An agreement in its proper sense is in the we-mode. Thus you and I can make the agreement to paint a house together, this agreement being *our* agreement (i.e. one in the we-mode), but even here each of us must personally (although in the we-mode sense) accept the plan as his part of the agreement.

9. When one is committed to the belief that p, one is committed to act in ways compatible with the truth of p, acting in part for the reason that one believes that p. Such commitment to a belief has the world-to-mind direction of fit of semantic satisfaction, as will be explained in more detail in chapter 6.

10. We may also say that the group members here in effect are collectively committed to the appropriate employment in their inference and overt action of the Sellarsian (1968, 1969) dot-quoted sentence .s., which has the logical form B(we, .p.), A dot-quoted sentence .s. is one which plays the same role in a given language or representational system as s plays in our base language, here English. B represents acceptance belief (here B is assumed to apply both to collective agents such as "we" and to single agents such as group members).

11. For-groupness here involves collective premisibility and availability in the sense of chapter 6 of a content, here respectively E or p, and acting on its truth in group contexts. As to the benefit aspect, recall chapter 1.

12. The members of the group in consideration must at least typically mutually believe (either in a *de dicto* sense, that is, under a certain description, or in a *de re* sense, that is, in the sense of direct "acquaintance") that they are its members, and they are assumed to have at least approximate mutual knowledge of its ethos (its constitutive features). The group is "we" for them, but it need not be a "conative" we, one leading to collective activities.

Alfred Schutz has considered a "nonconative we," one relating to commonly experiencing things of common concern. According to him, "the face-to-face relationship in which the partners are aware of each other and sympathetically participate in each other's lives for however short a time we shall call the 'pure We-relationship'" (Schutz, 1967/1932, p. 164). The pure we-relationship is to be distinguished from "living in the We-relationship": "Moreover, while I am living in the We-relationship, I am really living in our common stream of consciousness" (p. 167). "The pure We-relationship involves our awareness of each other's presence and also the knowledge of each that the other is aware of him" (p. 168). In his later work he gives an example: "Among those objects which we experience in the vivid present are other people's behavior and thoughts. In listening to a lecturer, for instance, we seem to participate immediately in the development of his stream of thought. But—and this point is obviously a decisive one—our attitude in doing so is quite different from that we adopt in turning to our stream of thought by reflection. We catch the

Other's thought in its vivid presence and not *modo praeterito*; that is, we catch it as a 'Now' and not as a 'Just Now'" (1962, p. 173). Reflection is always "one step" behind vividly present experience. Schutz's account is somewhat marred by a lack of a proper account of (propositional) mental states and their conditions of satisfaction. For a modern reader, terms like "stream of consciousness" require further analysis.

As a rough account of the above idea, consider this: A and B function in an "experiential" we-mode relation and form a "we" (however temporarily) if and only if there is an attitude ATT and a content p such that they actively share ATT toward the same content p and are collectively ATT-committed (ATT-bound) to p, and they are in addition disposed to express their attitudes, in effect, as "We share WATT(p)." Active sharing of WATT(p) entails that both agents have ATT(p) and focus attentively to their having it, and believe that the other has ATT(p) and also that they both mutually believe that.

13. In Tuomela (2003a) and R. Tuomela and M. Tuomela (2003), essentially these and also some other notions are defined and discussed.

14. As shorthand, presupposing the satisfaction of the Collectivity Condition, we-mode WM amounts to the conjunction CA&FG&Cocom, where CA means reflexive collective acceptance, FG means for-groupness, and Cocom means collective commitment to satisfy or maintain the attitude in the appropriate way.

15. In Tuomela (2003a) yet another I-mode notion, termed *instrumental* I-mode, is discussed. According to this, A, a member of group g, has ATT(p) in the *instrumental I-mode* relative to group g in situation C if and only if A has ATT(p) in part because she is functioning in the group context related to g (but might not be acting as a group member) and hence is privately committed, in the ATT-way, to content p at least in part for herself in C. Thus, acting as a group member is not required here.

16. See Tuomela (2000d, forthcoming a) and Searle (2001) for this kind of view; see (WMR) and (IMR) in chapter 1.

17. See Tuomela (2003a) and R. Tuomela and M. Tuomela (2003) for discussion.

18. Note that the progroup I-mode (*IM2*) does not satisfy the Collectivity Condition, in contrast to the we-mode. If you and I share the progroup I-mode intention to go to Alfonzo's for lunch, that joint action is of course our shared goal, but it is not collectively accepted as our group's goal, there is thus no for-groupness, and we are not collectively committed to satisfying this goal together. In the we-mode case, the Collectivity Condition is meant to apply to "collective acceptance for the group with collective commitment" and accordingly to all the three involved aspects. These are not present in the I-mode case, and as the Collectivity Condition does not apply to other than we-mode cases, in an I-mode situation it must fail to apply.

19. Note that in the we-mode, an agent's thinking and acting must be of the "right groupish" kind, but it may still be the case that his private motives partly coincide with his we-mode attitudes and actions, which possibly are means toward his private goals.

20. See Tuomela (2003a) for an irreducibility argument concerned with (*ii*) and (*iii*) that relates to action identification.

21. Of course also a we-mode agent can in actual practice rationally evaluate his gains and losses. The point made here is the idealized one in which he does not do it. In real life he is willing to "pay" more than the I-mode agent, but there is a limit to that. Even in such cases there is a difference in degree concerning the threshold of quitting.

22. Two points can be made here. First, speculating about the primacy of the we-mode over the I-mode in early infancy, the baby and the mother seem to form a "we" that the baby somehow recognizes before it is able to experience its own self as separate from that of its mother. See Tomasello et al. (2005), although this interpretation is strictly my own speculation. Second, as Walther et al. (2004) show by means of a functional magnetic resonance

264 NOTES TO PAGES 59-61

image (fMRI) investigation, social intentions indeed have neural correlates that nonsocial intentions do not have. However, these authors' experiments do not yet clearly distinguish between the correlates of I-mode and we-mode collective intentionality. See also the related points in Adenzato et al. (2005).

23. See chapter 6 and Tuomela (1995), chaps. 5–7, for discussion of such group attitudes as contrasted with mere aggregates of shared we-attitudes.

24. Especially in large groups there will be authorized operative members for belief formation (see chapter 6).

25. In addition to my own work, at least Margaret Gilbert's and Philip Pettit's work on group beliefs should be mentioned. The central references are: Tuomela (1992) and (1995), Gilbert (1987, 1989), and Pettit (2001). In Tuomela (1995), chap. 7, I compare Gilbert's and my own accounts in detail.

26. To concisely illustrate the discrepancy between we-mode group beliefs and private, I-mode beliefs (shared we-beliefs in the sense of chapter 3), consider a dyad g consisting of members a and b. We first assume $B_a(p)$ and $B_b(p)$ (or possibly even $B_b(-p)$), where the beliefs ($B(p)$) are I-mode beliefs (possibly acceptance beliefs). In the group-binding case, a and b jointly accept p; this is a we-mode joint acceptance belief. Assuming that the group's collective decision-making system is at work, we get $B_g(p)$, which says that the group has the normative, group-binding belief that p. The nonbinding I-mode case is construed here as aggregative, shared we-beliefs that p, in the sense that the group members believe that p, and believe that others believe that p and that this is mutually believed by them. This I-mode account need not always agree with the belief $B_g(p)$ (see chapter 6 for further points).

27. See, e.g., Pettit (2001), p. 112. In Tuomela (2003a) I have pointed out some problems with his account (also see Miller, 2003). Basically the problems have to do with Pettit's questionably applying the majority vote principle to the single premises of a deductive inference structure to get his discrepancy result. When correctly applied to the conjunction of the premises, the majority principle does not give the claimed discrepancy result. Nevertheless, some of Pettit's examples work correctly and show that there indeed can be "discursive dilemmas" in collective reasoning.

28. See Pettit (2003).

29. See McMahon (2001) for an interesting approach arguing for what I call progroup I-mode solutions to cooperative dilemmas. See my review in Tuomela (2005a), where I also defend the we-mode.

30. This matter is discussed in chapter 7. Notice that standard game theory operates only with I-mode notions (although some features of the we-mode are available in cooperative game theory), and the same can basically be said of theorizing in economics, which indeed does make extensive use of standard game theory. The social identity and self-categorization theories in social psychology are "in spirit" we-mode theories, or largely so. I would also like to mention here that the so-called team game theory, originally started by Bacharach, does make use of the we-perspective and appears to represent pro-group I-mode theorizing (see Sugden and Gold, 2004).

31. For Rawls's liberalism, see his 1993 book, and see the comments in Tuomela (2000c), chap. 13. My claims concerning Rawls are tentative and do require further substantiation. What is clear, anyhow, is that collective intentionality (even if it only be of the progoup I-mode variety) plays a central role in his and some other political theorist's views.

32. The reader is referred to chapter 8 and to Tuomela (2002b).

33. For my previous treatments, see Tuomela (1995), chap. 4, and especially the long discussion in Tuomela (2000c), chaps. 11–13. See R. Brown (2000), chap. 5, for recent social psychological discussion. Let me here present the conclusion arrived at in the study by Worchel et al. (1998). In their experiments, the subjects were making paper chains either

alone or as group members. The results were clear-cut (R. Brown, 2000, p. 190): The subjects worked consistently harder when there was an outgroup present, and they worked hardest of all when they were all wearing a uniform different from the one worn by the outgroup members.

34. See, e.g., van Vugt et al. (2000); see also the various relevant evolutionary points made in Sober and Wilson (1998) and Katz (2002).

35. Brewer (2003), p. 31. For discussion of these and other relevant experiments, see Brewer (2003), Insko and Schopler (1987), Insko et al. (1992), and Kollock (1998), to mention some sources.

36. See Tomasello et al. (2005).

37. See Richerson and Boyd (2005) and Wrangham (1980).

38. The basic text is Triandis (1995), which I will discuss here.

39. Also see Triandis and Trafimow (2003) as well as Hofstede (1994) for relevant empirical research.

CHAPTER 3

1. See Searle (1983) for direction of fit and relevant discussion in the single-agent case.

2. There is of course much nonconformative behavior in social life. I will not say much about such cases, nor will I say much about the nonsocial reasons that people have for conforming.

3. Symbolically: $WATT_x(p) \leftrightarrow ATT_x(p)$ & $B_x((y)ATT_y((p)$ & $MB_g((y)ATT_y(p)))$. Here B stands for belief and MB for mutual belief, and ATT represents some attitude. Verbally, this account says that a member x of group g has the we-attitude WATT(p) by definition if and only if x has ATT(p) and believes that all the members, y, of g have ATT(p) and also believes that it is mutually believed in the group that all the members have ATT(p).

4. Using the locution "for the reason that" to cover the weaker case "in part for the reason that" and moving directly to the account with ATT, one possibility to analyze reason-based we-attitudes (WATTR) in precise terms is as follows.

(i) $WATTR_x(p) \leftrightarrow ATT_x(p)$ for the reason that $B_x((y)ATT_y(p(y))$ & $MB((y)ATT_y(y)))$.

The other possibility is as follows.

(ii) $WATTR_x(p) \leftrightarrow ATT_x(p)$ for the reason that $(y)ATT_y(p(y))$ & $MB((y)ATT_y(p(y)))$.

The latter formulation fits an "externalist" account of reasons better. But if the right-hand side of the reason statement is false, that is, if the social aspect is objectively nonexistent, then (i) represents the fallback position, perhaps. I take the analysans of (ii) to entail that the agent believes that $(y)ATT_y(p(y))$ & $MB((y)ATT_y(p(y)))$. (As to my recent account of reasons for action, see Tuomela (forthcoming a).)

5. For the reason to be in the agent's control (which case is our main concern here), we must require that the formation of ATT is intentional action. Given this, the reason in question is her reason for action.

6. See Durkheim (1982/1901), p. 59: "A social fact is any way of acting, whether fixed or not, capable of exerting over the individual an external constraint; or which is general over the whole of a given society whilst having an existence of its own, independent of its individual manifestations. Social facts are things." Durkheim's idea of a social fact has some connections to my account of we-attitudes. An in-built feature of a we-attitude is that "the

others" think and act in certain ways and the reference point agent takes that social information into account in either a causal or intentional way. My "reason" can thus also be a cause, and at least in that special case it resembles Durkheim's external social constraint—perhaps Durkheim's account also could involve reasons. (However, my account does not speak of social facts as "things" in the sense Durkheim speaks of them.)

Let me note that in the preface to the second edition to his book, Durkheim somewhat liberalizes his above characterization when responding to his critics. Consider this (1982/1901, p. 45): "But in order for a social fact to exist, several individuals at the very least must have interacted together and the resulting combination must have given rise to some new product. As this synthesis occurs outside each one of us (since a plurality of consciousnesses is involved) it has necessarily the effect of crystallizing, of instituting outside ourselves, certain modes of action and certain ways of judging which are independent of the particular individual will considered separately." This seems even closer to my we-attitude account.

Another theoretician whose theorizing also seems to involve the idea of a shared reason-based attitude is Max Weber (1968/1921). According to his famous idea, in social action the subjective meaning given by the participants to a situation involves their being mutually concerned with each other and oriented by virtue of this fact.

7. In my account, I have omitted one factor that must be required. It is that intentions are reflexive: x is assumed to intend to do something as intended. I will not put this reflexivity feature in the content of the intention but rather regard it as a requirement that intention involves (see Tuomela, 1995, chap. 3). In saying this, I am assuming, in contrast, that what is in the content of the intention is something that the agent is "actively engaged with" and that her intention to bring about by her actions that p cannot be satisfied unless p indeed is satisfied because of her action. In this sense, the action-relativity of an intention is involved in the full content of the intention.

8. I will not here discuss these problems; see Tuomela (2000c), chap. 11; nor will I consider the matter of "statistics" related to under what conditions people indeed conformatively adopt attitudes and act on shared we-attitudes.

9. Recall note 49 in chapter 1 on music.

10. The reader is referred to the paradigmatic research by Asch (1987/1952) to the survey by Moscovici (1985), and to the textbooks by Stangor (2004) and Aronson et al. (2005), for newer conformity research.

To make a point concerning the empirical explanatory power of conformism, let me mention recent research by Bardsley and Sausgruber (2004). These authors argue that in the investigation of public good acquisition, the "crowding-in" phenomenon, in at least some cases, needs conformity (rather than altruism or the economists' favorite, reciprocity) as its explanans. Crowding-in means that there is positive correlation between the amount people contribute to the public good and expected contributions from the others. For instance, altruism predicts crowding-out (contributing the less the more others contribute) and thus conflicts with conformism. Empirical experiments seem to favor conformism. This also holds for conformism contra reciprocity. Reciprocity in the economists' sense requires that others' behavior matters through its effect on the individual's welfare. This assumption need not be satisfied in public good cases.

11. See, e.g., Gallese (2001) and Stamenov and Gallese (2002).

12. See Tuomela (2000c), chap. 5.

13. See the detailed proof for the mutual belief requirement in the context of joint action given in Tuomela and Miller (1988).

14. See Tuomela, (2002b), chap. 4, for a discussion of various weaker cases.

15. See Boyd and Richerson (1985) and Richerson and Boyd (2001, 2005).

16. We can technically account for the case of idols as follows.

$$WATTR_x(p) \leftrightarrow ATT_x(p)/_r(y)(M(y) \to ATT^*_y(p)) \& MB_g((y)(M(y) \to ATT^*_y(p)),$$

where M means being a valued person in the subject's opinion and where, to avoid logical paradoxes, the arrow is taken to express a "strict" implication. There might, for example, be only one such model in the group. Yet another possibility is that M is extended to cover also successful persons, persons who need not be valued but still are suitable objects of imitation because of their success in the group.

17. To make a point about the reasons involved: Consider an example where a person has the we-goal that G in part because another person has that goal. This is just a social attitude based on a social reason. First, on the lowest level, this might represent a case of nonintentional imitation and adoption of a goal. Second, the goal may be adopted on the basis of intentional imitation. This is the level of intentionally making the other's goal the reason for one's having the goal. This contrasts with the first case, because in that case there was only a cause, whereas here we have both a cause (a purposive or intentional cause) and a reason. In a third kind of case, a person may intentionally adopt the other's goal and do it not only because she has it (social reason, level 2) but also because it is mutually known in the group that almost everyone has G (or ought to have G). For instance, if we are to carry a table jointly or paint a house jointly, it will have to take place in part on the basis of our mutual belief that we all will participate. I could not rationally do my part unless I believed that you will participate and that you believe the same of me (see the account in the text). Notice that what was said about goals above applies to belief, too, mutatis mutandis. Epistemological testimony would fit in here either in the second or the third kind of case, although one may claim that even the strongest, third type of case does not always yield good epistemic grounds.

18. I-mode we-intentions may also be for the group (progroup) but not in the full sense satisfying the Collectivity Condition.

19. However, in the case of an I-mode we-intention, there can still be a necessary connection between the participatory intention and the social reason on the basis of *rationality*, while this does not make the connection a *conceptually* necessary one. Thus, rationality might require that the agent intentionally brings about p (e.g., makes the house habitable if he plans to stay there).

Note that a *we-mode* we-intention may of course have other kinds of reasons that are contingently connected to it, and an I-mode we-intention may have reasons or conditions that are based on other than strictly conceptual connections; these include connections based on rationality.

20. See chapter 6 section 1.

21. In the case of an I-mode (weak) we-intention, one may technically build in the social condition (the reason fact that the others intend to participate) but that would still not make it a we-mode we-intention but only a progroup I-mode intention (recall the weak sense (a) of acting as a group member from chapter 1).

22. See Bratman (1999).

23. I argue in Tuomela (2000c), chap. 3, app., in effect that the rationality involved here is based on the rationality of functioning as a group member and being collectively committed to performing the joint action in question. This collective commitment is part and parcel of having a joint intention in the we-mode. Collective commitment entails that the participants must at least believe that they are able to perform the joint action (with some probability). This again requires meshing subplans.

24. See Bratman (1999), p. 114.

25. See chapter 4, section 5, for this and other related points.

26. A more relaxed kind of coordination can also amount to a connection technically expressible by a correlation or correspondence less than maximal. Thus, it can have the

form *corr*(ATT(I), ATT(you)) > k, where *corr* is a measure of correspondence and k is a suitable constant. (See Tuomela, 1985, 2000c, and chapter 7 here for the *corr* measure.)

27. See the discussion in Tuomela (2002b), chap. 3.

28. See Lewis (1969).

29. Sugden (1993) takes up this circularity problem and claims that it can be solved in terms of a shared collective goal. I agree, provided that not much is built into the notion of a shared goal (see below). My discussion below of the circularity problem makes use of Tuomela (2002a), with some improvements.

30. Think of a child's "accepting" moral norms and values in a nonintentional sense—as a kind of pattern-governed behavior—and partly even against her will; see Tuomela (2002b), chap. 3, on this.

31. In the latter case one might, for example, argue that a fully rational agent would at least try to avoid regress problems from the very start.

32. In the general case of coordination of attitudes (ATT, including actions) the following formulation can be used in terms of wide acceptance (recall my earlier remarks).

(P_{gen}) I will accept p given that you will accept p, but you will accept p given that I will accept p, but I will accept p given that you will accept p, but you ... ad infinitum.

Here p can describe, for example, intention, belief, or moral judgment (e.g., in the belief case p = We believe that the earth is flat). A further factor that can be taken into account is the case where a person has a reason-based we-attitude that depends on another person's reason-dependent attitude. We have to enrich the general formulation (P_{gen}) slightly to capture this. Thus, where p = G is a goal and q = the members of the group have G and this is mutually believed in the group, the enriched formula now is:

(P'_{gen}) I will accept p given that you will accept p, q being the case, but you will accept p given that I will accept p, q being the case, but I will accept p given that you will accept p, q being the case, but you ... ad infinitum.

33. On the basis of schema (RC) we may formulate the following action instructions to A (and respectively to B).

(a) commit yourself to one of the alternatives, given that you know that B (respectively A) has not committed himself to the other alternative.

(b) see to it that B (respectively A) learns about your commitment.

(c) secure for yourself that B (respectively A) is "relevantly" rational.

34. See Lewis (1969), Tuomela (2002b), chap. 6, and chapter 7 here.

35. Furthermore, if we are to believe recent claims by neurophysiologists, there is also the less rational and less intentional, subpersonal way out provided by "mirror neurons": we are disposed to think and act similarly (see Gallese, 2001). Thus if I see you doing X I am—in suitable circumstances—disposed also to do X, period. No loops, no circularity here. However, it seems that mirror neurons only provide a necessary condition for some bodily actions, and they may not dispose people to act in a very strong sense. Thus the mirror neuron system alone will not solve coordination problems.

36. Below I draw on Tuomela (2002b), chap. 2.

37. See Schelling (1960), Scheff (1967), Lewis (1969), and Schiffer (1972).

38. For discussion and arguments, see Lewis (1969), Ruben (1985), Lagerspetz (1995), and Tuomela (1995, 2001).

39. See Schiffer (1972) and Grice (1989).

40. See Scheff (1967) for discussion of the above points.

41. See Lewis (1969), chap. 2, and, for the weaker account in terms of dispositions to come to believe, Tuomela (1995), chap. 1.

42. This is the approach I advocate in Tuomela (1995), chap. 1.

43. See the discussion in Tuomela (1995), chap. 7.

44. See Halpern and Moses (1992) and, for a more general account, Balzer and Tuomela (1997a).

CHAPTER 4

1. Recall that in the I-mode case there may be a kind of group reason involved, but it is had privately and does not satisfy the Collectivity Condition. There are the following three possibilities for intending in the I-mode: (1) the person functions solely as a private person; (2) the person is a member of an I-mode group (recall chapter 1); or (3) the person is a member of a we-mode group but only functions as a group member in the weak, I-mode sense rather than in the standard sense.

2. See Tuomela (1984, 1995, 2000c, 2000d) and Tuomela and Miller (1988).

3. See Sandu and Tuomela (1996) and Belnap et al. (2001) for *stit* and *jstit*.

4. The logic of the joint intention to see to it jointly that X will take place or obtain is studied in Sandu and Tuomela (1996). The central notion in that study is a joint strategy that binds the participants into a group with respect to their choices.

5. A linguistic formulation that typically seems apt for aim-intentions is "intending that something be the case," taken with the understanding, however, that an aim-intending agent is still required actively to contribute to the coming about of the state in question (and this conceptual condition is in general independent of whether realizing it is rational for him or not).

6. In this sense my account sides with Michael Bratman and Seumas Miller against Margaret Gilbert. See Bratman (1999), pp. 125–129, Miller (1995), p. 64, and Gilbert (1990), pp. 6–9.

7. In the general case, each agent can be taken to accept "We together will jointly see to it that X" (or its equivalent) and "I will participate in, or contribute to, our jointly seeing to it that X," while in the case of directly performable joint action, the ("variable") content of a we-intention can accordingly be taken to be "to perform X together," entailing a participation intention for each participant.

Recall that the collective acceptance of an intention as the group's intention entails the satisfaction of the Collectivity Condition discussed in chapter 2. Applied to satisfaction, this condition says, roughly: Necessarily, if the joint intention (goal) is (semantically) satisfied for one of the participants, then it is satisfied for all participants.

8. See Tuomela (1995), chap. 2, and Tuomela (2002a), on which I will draw below.

9. By speaking of interdependent private acceptance in this paragraph the creation of I-mode joint intention (in the sense defined in chapter 3) can be accounted for, provided the regress problem discussed there has been circumvented.

10. In the exchange between Gilbert (1993) and Bach (1995), the latter presents an "offer-acceptance" model of agreement making. My BBV account can also be taken to cover Bach's (asymmetric) cases. (See Tuomela, 2002a, for discussion.)

11. See Tuomela (1995), chap. 5, for some qualification, and see Balzer and Tuomela (1997) for an early account of the "buildup" of joint intention.

12. For instance, the account in Tuomela and Miller (1988) allows for this possibility.

13. See the discussion in Tuomela (2000c, 2002b).

14. This case requires the analysans of the "bridge principle" of Tuomela (1995), chap. 3, to hold true and the acceptance to be *normative, thick acceptance*. A revised and improved

270 NOTES TO PAGES 91–94

summary account follows of the bridge principle of Tuomela (1995), chap. 3, which purports to connect plan-language with agreement language in the case of joint intention.

(JIP^*) Some agents (say, $A_1, \ldots, A_m$) have formed the *(agreement-based) joint intention to perform* X if and only if (a) each of them has accepted a plan to perform X jointly, (b) each of them has communicated this acceptance to the others, and (c) it is a true mutual belief among $A_1, \ldots, A_m$ that they are collectively committed (in a normatively group-binding sense involving an obligation) to performing X and that there is or will be a part or share (requiring at least potential contribution) of X for each agent to perform that he accordingly is or will be committed to performing. Here the agents' reason for their aforementioned mutual belief is (a) and (b).

On the right-hand side of the analysis, acceptance must be understood in a normatively group-binding sense involving an obligation. While this bridge principle then is not very informative from the normative point of view, it still shows how strongly the "plan language" must be understood to give equivalence. Of course, if acceptance is understood in a weaker sense—which is perhaps the more normal sense—then the agreement account remains the stronger of the two.

15. Cf. Scanlon's "Principle F" (1998, p. 304).

16. The collective acceptance model, developed in Tuomela (2002b), is presented and further refined in chapters 6 and 8 here.

17. I discussed we-intentions as shared we-attitudes in the 1980s and later more generally as applicable to all kinds of attitudes (see, e.g., Tuomela, 1984, 1995, 2002b, 2005b, and also see Tuomela and Miller, 1988, sharpening the account given in my 1984 book). In Tuomela and Bonnevier-Tuomela, 1997, shared we-attitudes are discussed in more general terms.

18. However, note that in my account, "we" can be represented by a predicate, WE, applying to m individuals for some m (see note 20). Thus no ontologically significant plural subject is literally postulated here, seemingly contrary to, e.g., the view of Gilbert (1989).

19. This account is a slightly modified version of the one in Tuomela and Miller (1988).

20. From the point of view of the logical form of joint intentions, we-intentions, and group intentions, the following rather trivial point is central to keep in mind. A joint intention can be expressed by an $(m + 1)$-place predicate $JI(A_1, \ldots, A_m, X)$ standing for "the agents $A_1, \ldots, A_m$ jointly, as a group, intend to perform the action X jointly." Here "as a group" can be symbolized by assuming that the agents function as proper group members thus as members of a "we," and we have $WE(A_1, \ldots, A_m, X)$. The agents thus form a thick "we," at least concerning X. This thick "we" can be cashed out by saying that the agents have collectively accepted joint action X as the agents' "goal" or as what they are to perform together for the group they form, being collectively committed to performing X jointly. In this context, each member A_i has the we-intention to perform X (that is, each A_i intends to perform X together with the others, as expressed by "We will do X"). This is symbolized by $WI(A_i, \ldots, A_m, X)$. The account (WI) in the text gives an analysis of what this involves. Finally, we can speak of a group's intention to perform an action, such as X, here. This is symbolized by $I(g, X)$. In our simple case, g consists of $A_1, \ldots, A_m$. In this case $JI(A_1, \ldots, A_m, X)$ and $I(g, X)$ are truth equivalent, the two sides of one and the same coin, so to speak. In more interesting cases, where the group involves the distinction between authorized operative and nonoperative members, the account (GINT), to be stated below, gives the connection.

21. The joint intention can be based on a joint decision or agreement making or can just be what a collective acceptance of a joint plan involves. As such, the formation of a joint intention (that amounts to the group's intention) need not be based on a group reason. This point resembles that involved in saying that agreement making need not be based on agreement making.

22. Recall that I have characterized the we-mode in terms of three features: (1) the attitude or action must be collectively accepted as the group's attitude or action; (2) it must be for the use and, typically, benefit of the group's interests; and (3) the participants must be collectively committed to the attitude or action.

23. See the references mentioned, especially Tuomela and Miller (1988), for justification.

24. See the account in Tuomela (1995), chap. 3.

25. This is argued in Tuomela (1991). See also Tuomela (1995).

26. For two different logical formalizations of we-intentions in the sense of (WI) and joint intentions in the sense of (JI), see Sandu and Tuomela (1996) and Balzer and Tuomela (1997b).

27. Within my account it holds true that jointly intending and thus we-intending agents must intend that (also) the others intend to perform their parts. Here is an argument, concisely put:

(1) We will, by acting jointly, bring about X, e.g., a state or joint action.

(2) I we-intend X and hence intend to perform my part of our bringing about X.

(3) I presuppose, and partly therefore we-intend, that you (or the others, more generally) intentionally participate in our bringing about X.

(4) I we-intend to see to it that you (appropriately continue to) we-intend X.

(5) I we-intend to see to it that that you intend to perform your part of our bringing about X.

Here clause (1) is to be regarded as an expression of joint intention, and a joint intention is taken to consist of we-intentions (see (JI)). Clause (2) connects a we-intention to an intention to perform one's part (see (WI)). Clause (3) repeats part of clause (ii) of (WI), and (4) makes use of the assumption that joint intention entails collective commitment. Finally, conclusion (5) connects my we-intention to your intention to perform your part (see (WI)). It is thus seen that joint intention in my sense involves both collective (hence social) commitment and joint persistence. Note that also schema (W2) in effect leads to (5).

28. This account, presented earlier in Tuomela (1995), is my explicate for the "general will" Rousseau speaks of. The general will is contrasted with the will of all (Rousseau, 1960/ 1762, p. 193): "There is often a great difference between the will of all and the general will; the latter studies only the common interest, while the former considers private interest, and is only the sum of individual desires. If we take away from these same wills the pluses and minuses which cancel each other out, the remaining sum of the difference is the general will." It is not clear what the "remaining sum of the difference" really amounts to. In any case, while the general will appears to be similar to a group's intention (thus to the operatives' shared we-intention), in my account there need be no such connection to I-mode intentions (aggregated wills) and their "sums of differences" as we have in Rousseau's account.

29. Christopher Kutz has recently argued that in a "minimal" joint action, the participants need not share a collective end but need only have a "participatory intention," that is, an intention to do one's part in joint action (accompanied by the belief that the part action indeed will contribute to the collective end or goal). As just seen, I accept this for the case of actions performed by structured groups (which actions Kutz also includes among joint actions), for in the case of group action in my account, there need not be even such a participatory intention in the case of all participants. However, I claim, seemingly contrary to Kutz, that in the case of many-person joint action, a relevant joint intention is required for jointly intentional performance (except perhaps in the case of some kinds of defective joint actions). I generally require collective commitment for joint intentionality, but Kutz's

account does not require it or even shared private commitment. This feature makes his minimal joint actions to some extent functionally deficient.

To go into some detail about Kutz's (2000) account, let me indicate where I think his analysis faces a problem. His argument for the need of only participatory intentions goes in terms of the following two conditionals where G is the end or "result" involved in the joint action in question and P is the agent's ("my") part (p. 101).

(1) If I did not believe that P was a way of contributing to G in such circumstances, I wouldn't do P but would do P'.

(2) If I did not believe that P was a way of contributing to G's occurrence in such circumstances and I did not believe G could be realized in these circumstances, I wouldn't do P (but would do P' or might call the whole thing off).

According to Kutz, both conditionals have to be true in the case of full-blown joint action, but in the case of minimal joint action, (2) may be false. I claim that these conditions are rationality conditions rather than conceptual conditions for joint action. Condition (1) might not be satisfied in the case of an irrational agent. Condition (1) appears to be compatible with all the agents believing or even mutually believing that g is not achievable. This seems problematic in most cases. Counterfactual (2) is too strong. Even a minimally rational agent might just hope that P together with the other participants' contributions might lead to G but not really believe it. But on conceptual grounds, he could still intend the end G. So (2) is not needed for intended ends. On the other hand, the participant in this kind of case, expressing minimal joint action, does not satisfy the requirement that he be (collectively or even privately) committed to G. This is basically because he may even believe that G might not be attainable.

As will be seen in chapter 5, there are also weaker kinds of collective actions in which not even a participatory intention in the above sense is needed. These collective actions are actions based on shared we-attitudes, where the shared we-attitude, e.g., a shared I-mode we-goal or we-belief or we-fear, serves as the participants' reason for action (in the typical case of conformative we-attitudes for harmony-inducing action).

30. See Tuomela (1995), chap. 9, on the interrelationistic version of individualism, which has the feature that groups as agents are viewed merely in an instrumental sense.

31. This is what Searle (1990), p. 405, says: "We are tempted to construe 'doing his part' to mean doing his part toward achieving the collective goal. But if we adopt that move, then we have included the notion of a collective intention in the notion of 'doing his part.' We are thus faced with a dilemma: if we include the notion of collective intention in the notion of 'doing his part,' the analysis fails because of circularity; we would now be defining we-intentions in terms of we-intentions. If we don't so construe 'doing his part,' then the analysis fails because of inadequacy." (see also Miller, 2001, pp. 71–73.) In Tuomela (2005b) I respond to this charge and claim that while there is some circularity, it is not vicious. On the whole, Searle's discussion of the Tuomela-Miller (1988) article is based on misunderstandings, as I have shown elsewhere (e.g., in Tuomela, 1995).

32. For my earlier weak notion of joint action see Tuomela (1984), pp. 130–33, where rudimentary joint action is analyzed functionally and causally in terms of we-attitudes in a weak functionalist sense argued to cover social "pattern-governed behaviors" in Sellars's sense. Furthermore, the discussion in Tuomela (2002b), chaps. 3 and 4, of collective pattern-governed behavior, generalizing Sellars's relevant notion to the collective case, may be consulted as giving justification to the claims in the previous and this paragraph.

Let me point out that this way of answering the charge of circularity is somewhat different from the long answer I give in Tuomela (2005b).

33. For instance, Seumas Miller's theory is concerned with such interpersonal action directed toward an individualistically conceived "collective end," and similarly Michael Bratman's account belongs to the I-mode realm. See Miller (2001) and Bratman (1999).

34. One can also list other features of the we-mode that are different from the features of the I-mode. One feature still worth emphasizing is that the notion of a part of a joint action X is not conceptually reducible to individual actions, as, e.g., Seumas Miller's theory assumes. One's part depends crucially on X and may not be antecedently fixable. Think of the practical inference schema (W2), which may generate new elements into one's part during the course of the performance of the joint action. This shows that there are, in principle, indefinitely many factors that may enter the situation during action. The part cannot be fully specified beforehand. However, this critical point seems not to apply to Bratman's theory, as he only speaks about "our J-ing" in his account.

35. See Miller's and Bratman's accounts.

36. See Miller (2001), chap. 5.

37. Gilbert's (1989, 2000) account is not specific about the jointly intending participants' attitudes. What happens in their personal minds when they participate in a joint intention? As seen, my elaborate answer is framed in terms of we-intention and intention to perform one's part.

38. Searle claims that collective intentions are irreducible to individual intentions and mutual beliefs. However, when he actually tries to spell this out, he does not succeed in showing that collective intentions are different kinds of intentions, and leaves collectivity almost unanalyzed; cf. Zaibert (2003). Furthermore, as argued by Meijers (2003), Searle's account is atomistic and does not account for interpersonal relations and in particular not for the social commitments that the participants are taken to have in relation to each other.

39. One can also make the critical point against Bratman's account that it seems unrealistic in the case of large groups. The members of a large organization cannot realistically be expected to form their intentions in the way Bratman's account requires (try to mesh your action plans with hundreds or millions of other people having first based your intending on theirs!).

40. The conceptual interdependence of joint intention and joint action is also commented on in chapter 5, section 3.

41. In addition, Bratman's example of "unhelpful singers" indicates that his account is an I-mode one (see Bratman, 1999, p. 103): The singers are assumed to jointly intend to sing a duet without helping the other one if he, contrary to expectations, does something wrong. This example indicates that I-mode joint intentions need not be cooperative. In contrast, a we-mode joint intention is necessarily cooperative (see chapter 7), as the inference schema (W2) of the previous section also shows. However, no actual inference is needed, because we-intenders typically have internalized for-groupness and the substantive content of (W2) so that it has become a kind of skill.

42. Bratman's (1999) account, discussed in chapter 3, is a case in point.

43. One can, however, cooperate in the I-mode and to achieve a shared goal and act for a group, and one can also value the other group members' company—see chapter 7 for I-mode cooperation.

44. See Velleman (1997) and Stoutland (2002). Bratman's relevant article is reprinted as chap. 6 in his 1999 collection.

45. See Bratman (1999), pp. 148–49.

46. See the discussion earlier in this chapter and in Tuomela (2005b). Stoutland (2002) proposes the Responsibility condition as conceptually valid.

CHAPTER 5

1. I have earlier discussed and analyzed joint action in several works; see Tuomela (1984, 1995, 2000c). Below some of my earlier ideas will be presented, but in a somewhat improved and enriched form.

2. However, in general I take collective action to cover more than joint action (see section 5). For instance, mass actions and mob behavior can be regarded as cases of collective action but not joint action. Similarly, action with respect to a shared goal described without reference to any specified agents need not be joint action.

3. Put slightly differently, joint action in the we-mode can be said to be action based on a shared we-mode reason (more precisely, joint intention in this case), while an I-mode joint action is based on a shared I-mode reason (recall chapter 1).

4. Versions of this account are to be found, e.g., in Tuomela (1984, 1995, 2002b).

5. See Tuomela (1995), chap. 2.

6. Tuomela (1995), chap. 2.

7. In Tuomela (2000c), chap. 2, I analyze intended collective goals as follows.

(ICG) G is an *intended collective goal* of some persons $A_1, \ldots, A_m$ forming a collective g in a situation S if and only if G is a state or (collective) action such that
(a) each member of g has G as his goal in S, entailing that he intends to contribute (at least if "needed"), together with the others—as specified by the mutually believed presupposition of the shared goal G—to the realization of G;
(b) part of a member's reason for (a), namely, for his having G as his goal, is that there is a mutual belief among them to the effect that (a);
(c) it is true on "quasi-conceptual" grounds that G is satisfied for a member A_i of g if and only if it is satisfied for every member of g; and this is mutually believed in g (Collectivity Condition with mutual belief).

To arrive at an intended joint goal (hence a joint intention) from an intended collective goal, some further conditions making the group g more like a face-to-face group are required. I have required the "communication of acceptance" condition, the "jointness of goal-directed action" condition, and the "knowledge of other participants' acceptance" condition as defeasible default conditions for intended joint goals. As said, I will spare the reader these complications in this book and regard intended collective goals and joint goals as equivalent here.

8. See Searle (1983).

9. See Richerson and Boyd (2001, 2005) and Tomasello et al. (2005) for evidence and arguments.

10. See Tomasello and Rakoczy (2003) and Tomasello et al. (2005).

11. Cf. the collective pattern-governed behaviors discussed in Tuomela (2002b), chaps. 3–4, and recall the discussion of circularity in chapter 4.

12. There are joint actions also in humans that involve preconceptual elements. For instance, playing a duet is joint activity in which there is fine-grained nonconceptual interaction. I would claim, however, that these actions still are based on conceptual mental states, although they involve many routine elements as well as anticipatory expectations and reactions, and although in some cases there is much spontaneous joint action (for instance, jam sessions in jazz). We-willings seem to have an important role in these kinds of actions, which may lack prior we-intentions. (See Knoblich and Jordan, 2003, for anticipatory control in joint action.)

13. In my "purposive causal" account of joint action in Tuomela (1984), an intentional joint action token, x, of a certain, possibly compound type, say, X, was taken to be composed

of the agents' intentional part action tokens x_i having the form $<t_i \ldots, b_i, \ldots, r_i>$, where t_i represents the agent's we-intention (to perform the achievement type action X connected to a result event of type R), b_i, represents the bodily behavior required by X, and r_i the result event of the agent's part action X_i. The joint action token is taken to have the structure expressed by the ordered sequence $<t \ldots, b, \ldots, r>$, where t refers to the ontological (mereological) sum of the agents' we-intentions (actually, more, generally to their relevant underlying motivational states) t_i, b refers to the sum of the bodily behaviors b_i that the action type X required on that occasion; and r is assumed to have been generated by the sum of the result events or states r_i. More precisely,

> (PCS) The agents $A_1, \ldots, A_m$ *performed an action x jointly intentionally* if and only if
> (1) the results r_i, $I = 1, \ldots, m$, of the agents' part action tokens x_i together purposively generated r;
> (2) there was a joint action plan of $A_1, \ldots, A_m$, which involved an end that the agents effectively we-intended (we-willed) to realize then by their bodily behaviors (of the kinds they took their behaviors b_i to be) such that they believed their respective behaviors would at least tend to bring it about or be conducive to it;
> (3) the agents' effective we-intendings (we-willings) plus the beliefs referred to in clause (2) together purposively generated their behaviors in the x_i's, and inter-mediately, the results x_i.

In the case of fully intentional joint actions, of which it is assumed that all the agents actively participate and intentionally perform their parts as parts of X, the following is also required:

> (4) each agent A_i performed his part-action x_i intentionally as her part.

By an effective we-intending is meant a we-willing, with the content of a present-directed intention now to do, by one's bodily behavior, whatever is needed to satisfy the joint end referred to in (2). We-willings are agency-exercising, present-directed we-intentions having the full content "We will do X jointly now."

Purposive causation (generation) is a "purpose-preserving" relation holding between the willing event t (with the relevant belief) and the overt behavior (in this case b simpliciter). This character of willing is an expression or consequence of the fact that willing is an act-relational notion—the agent wills by his bodily behavior to do something. In the context of (PCS), the agent willed by the behavior b to do that something. The willing caused the behavior (movements) in the action (obviously, the willing did not cause the action x_i).

14. See Sandu and Tuomela (1996) and Belnap et al. (2001). Let me also note that in Tuomela (1984) I have argued that a joint action token $x = <t, \ldots, b, \ldots, r>$ can be understood to some extent without dependence on a clear and specific notion of an action type. Why one can have—to an extent—an independent handle on (joint) action tokens is because one can have de re beliefs concerning partly imagined result events. Thus an artist may figure in her mind how a certain sculpture is going to be like. This agent need not have a clear notion of type in her mind when she proceeds with her activity. This idea can be generalized to a social context where the agents are facing a common task—to take a trivial example, the task of shaking hands or hugging each other. This point shows that action types are not that important.

15. See section 5.

16. It was specified in the account (PCS) of note 13 that, related to a joint action token $<t, \ldots, b, \ldots, r>$ of a joint action type X, the agents' effective we-intendings (we-willings) plus the beliefs referred to in clause (2) of (PCS) together purposively

generated their behaviors in the x_i's, and intermediately, the results r_i. Purposive generation entails acting in accordance with and in part because of a jointly accepted plan of action to perform X. The participants jointly controlled their activities so that r came about as planned. They thus jointly brought about something that was not there beforehand but that required their activity in the right plan-based sense.

17. See the account by Seumas Miller (2001), to be discussed in the next section, as an example of this kind of analysis. I have earlier given an account of a kind of I-mode joint action as "coaction" (CO), as follows (see Tuomela and Bonnevier-Tuomela, 1997).

(CO) Agents A_1 and A_2 *coact compatibly in a situation S relative to their I-mode goals* G_1 and G_2 (or, briefly, act jointly in the I-mode) if and only if

(1) their respective primary goals (namely, action-goals) in S, that is, types of states or actions, G_1 and G_2, which relate to the same field of action dependence in S, are compatible, in the sense of being satisfiable without making it impossible for the other agent to satisfy her goal;

(2a) A_1 intends to achieve G_1 without his means-actions conflicting with A_2's attempts to satisfy his goal and believes that he can achieve it, at least with some probability, in that context, although his relevant G_2-related actions are dependent on A_2's relevant G_2-related actions, and he acts successfully so as to achieve G_1; and

(2b) analogously for A_2,

(3a) A_1 believes that (1) and (2), and

(3b) analogously for A_2.

(A more rudimentary version of coaction need not even satisfy clause (3).)

18. This account is rather similar to Bratman's (1999) account (recall section 3 of chapter 4). If we add the meshing subplans requirement, we almost have his account, except that in his account there is an idle mutual knowledge requirement, while above there is a reason-giving mutual belief requirement.

19. Another possible account is given in terms of the notion of "coaction" defined in note 17.

20. See the account given in Tuomela and Bonnevier-Tuomela (1997) and Tuomela (2002b), and recall chapter 3 here. Note that it does not matter much, if at all, in this context whether plain we-attitudes or reason-based ones are meant. In the former case, a social attitude is a reason for a person's action; in the latter case, his social attitude is already reason-based. Then the reason for the attitude will, at least normally, also be the agent's partial reason for his action. (The so-called toxin puzzle may be taken to be problematic here, but actually it is not, for my account does not depend on the assumption of the sameness of the social reason for the attitude and the reason for the ensuing action.)

21. In particular, the subclass that in Tuomela and Bonnevier-Tuomela (1997) is called coaction with compatible goals might serve to characterize I-mode joint action.

22. This extension is made in Tuomela (2002a), chap. 4.

23. Schmitt (2003).

24. I draw on Tuomela (2003c).

25. Miller (2001), p. 57.

26. See, e.g., Tuomela (1995, 2002b).

27. See Miller (2001).

28. See my points in Tuomela (2003b).

29. Miller (2001), p. 57.

30. Miller (2001), p. 56.

31. See Tuomela, (2002a, 2002b, 2005).

32. For my recent discussion of this, see Tuomela (1995, 2002b, 2003a).

33. See Tuomela (1995), chap. 4, where this is taken to be even a kind of a conceptual truth of groups (also cf. chapter 1 of this book).

34. See Tuomela (2002b, 2003a).

35. Gilbert (1989).

36. Schmitt (2003), p. 151.

37. See Tuomela (2005b), and recall my discussion of the jstit approach and the general viewpoint that the content of a joint intention can be a state supposed to be *jstit*-ed.

38. See chapter 4 and Tuomela (2005b) for further discussion and defense of the joint settle condition as the only acceptable settle condition in this joint intention context.

39. Gilbert (2000), p. 19.

40. Gilbert (2002a), p. 68; also see (1990), p. 9.

41. Schmitt (2003), p. 155.

CHAPTER 6

1. Premisibility is the idea of taking p to be correct or to be assumable in the context in question. But a group member does not really have to (experientially) *believe* it is true. (Nevertheless, premisibility in g can be viewed as a notion in the belief-family, construed in a wide sense of typically having mind-to-world direction of fit.) To accept a proposition as true or correctly assertable entails that one has the right to use the sentence as a premise and sometimes one ought to use it. Suppose the sentence p = "The earth is flat" has been collectively accepted by group g. Using it as a premise means accepting it as a premise in one's practical inference or using it as the basis for one's action. While one cannot rationally accept p and –p, one can to some extent rationally accept p *qua a member* of g without accepting p *as a private person*. (It can be proposed that what, strictly speaking, is accepted is a Sellarsian dot-quoted sentence, .p., taken to represent a proposition; recall chapter 2.) The notion of a group's treating something as correctly assertable is central. In the case of *descriptive* sentences, however, correct assertability is simply truth, and then we are speaking of the group's taking s to be true in this context. My approach, accordingly, can and does make use of the notions of truth and satisfaction condition, and from a logical point of view even roughly in the Tarskian way. (See Tuomela, 2002b, chap. 5, for simple examples of practical inferences using the above view of premisibility as a group member.)

2. See, e.g., Searle (1983) for the notion.

3. There are different kinds of mental states with which the same direction of fit is associated. Thus, e.g., promises, intentions, directives, and wants seen as mental states have the same direction of fit. If the differences between these mental states are shown to be relevant to collective acceptance, an enriched account is called for.

What is being compared here are two facts, namely, the fact of someone's having a mental state with a certain direction of fit and the fact of the satisfying state of the world being such-and-such. In the wide sense, we are dealing with propositional mental states, but they can well be nonlinguistic, and they can even be states that goal-directed animals like lions have.

4. In logical symbols, we have "for the group":

$$CA(g, p) \leftrightarrow Com(g, stit(g, Prem_g(p, df)))/_{pr}KWH(g, p, df))$$

"Com" means group commitment, which may but need not be based on the group's intentional action. The formula $stit(g, Prem_g(p,df)$ reads "group g intentionally sees to it that p, with the df appropriate to it in this context, is premisible in group contexts." $KWH(g, p, df)$ means that g knows what the direction of fit of p is (namely, whether it in this context is wm or mw), and $/_{pr}$ means "given the presupposition that thus and so." CA can be logically treated as an operator, and we can distinguish in the standard way between de re and de dicto collective acceptance, the former having roughly the form (Ex) CA(g, p(x)) and the latter CA(g, (Ex)p(x)).

In the case of intentionally acquired and held commitment, the group has to see to it that it is committed as in (i). We then have "for the group":

(i*) CA(g, p) $\leftrightarrow$ stit(g, Com(g, stit(g, Prem$_g$(p, df)))/$_{pr}$KWH(g, p, df)))

The outer stit is primarily meant to be one involving intending as a group (and thus joint intentionality). The inner stit will here involve that the group intentionally stit-s as a group.

    5. To use the terminology of Tuomela (2002b), we can also say, letting ATT be the set of attitudes relevant to acceptance, that ATT = {I, B}, where I = intention and B = belief, both in the we-mode. We arrive at the following idealized "we-attitude thesis" for g.

(WA) CA(g, p) $\leftrightarrow$ (for all i in g)(WI$_i$(p)) or (for all i in g)(WB$_i$(p))

We must here "nonstandardly" assume that WI marks the fact that s expresses a we-intention in the we-mode and WB marks that p expresses a we-belief in the we-mode. Given this, (WA) says that collectively accepting that p is noncontingently equivalent to the following fact: We, the members of group g, share a relevant we-attitude—indeed an acceptance-involving attitude—about s in the we-mode (more specifically an attitude in the intention family WI or an acceptance belief WB) and—as attitudes involve action dispositions—are disposed to collectively act on the basis of this shared we-attitude. This analysis is basically equivalent to the one propounded and defended in the text.

    6. In logical symbolism, we have Com (g, stit (g, Prem$_g$(p, df)))). We have individual commitment, Com, in the I-mode case, whereas in the we-mode case, which is actually what (i) deals with, we must have collective commitment, Cocom, and group reason (for-groupness). Cocom can be taken to entail full-blown for-groupness; see Tuomela (2002b), chap. 5.

    7. More precisely, if mutual knowledge is symbolized by MKWH (g, p, df), we have the following "for the group."

(ii*) CA(g, p) $\leftrightarrow$ SWA(A$_1$,...,A$_m$, p, df) & Cocom(A$_1$,...,A$_m$,

stit(g, Prem$_g$(p, df)))/$_{pr}$MKWH(A$_1$,...,A$_m$, p, df),

where SWA means shared we-attitude satisfying the Collectivity Condition and is thus a genuine joint attitude.

    8. In logical terms, we have "for the group":

(ii*) CA(g, p) $\leftrightarrow$

Cocom(A$_1$,...,A$_m$, stit(A$_1$,...,A$_m$, Prem$_g$(p, df)))/$_{pr}$MKWH(A$_1$,...,A$_m$, p, df)

    9. We-mode collective acceptance can be "simulated" by means of I-mode collective acceptance, which, however, requires the postulation of several features (like counterparts of the Collectivity Condition and collective commitment) the we-mode versions of which are conceptually inbuilt into the we-mode.

    10. See Tuomela (1995), chaps. 4–7, for authority systems in the case of group action, intention, goal, belief, etc.

    11. Cf. Seumas Miller's (2001) functionally similar notion of a joint mechanism and Cristopher McMahon's (2005) related idea of a mechanism for choosing a cooperative scheme.

12. See Raz (1986). McMahon (2001, 2005) uses this account, and what I say below is also indebted to his article.

13. See Bratman (1987), chap. 2.

14. McMahon (2001) argues that his individualistic principle of collective rationality (PCR) gives the kind of justification in question. In a way, my present idea of justification of authority in terms of group reasons (we-mode reasons) is a kind of group version of (PCR), for we-mode reasons (thinking and acting as a group) will lead to solutions of collective action dilemmas (see chapter 7 below and Tuomela, forthcoming b, for my account of this).

15. I have earlier presented roughly the same account; see Tuomela (1989a, 1989b) and Tuomela (1995), chap. 5. Weaker kinds of group action were commented on in section 5 of chapter 5 here.

16. This is what I have argued especially in Tuomela (1991) and Tuomela (1995), chap. 3; in section 5 below there is a more detailed discussion of this matter.

17. The term "positional account" is used in Tuomela (1992, 1995). Positions are taken to be defined by "task-right systems" in the sense of Tuomela (1995), chap. 1. See also Tuomela (1992, 1995, 2000a) for the positional account.

18. Such group views are called "acceptance beliefs" in Tuomela (1992, 2000a).

19. See chapter 8 and especially Searle (2003).

20. See Tuomela (1992, 1995).

21. The requirement of continued acceptance is subject to the constraints stated in section 5 of chapter 1.

22. Group knowledge in the full sense can be taken to amount to justified true group belief. My partial analysis of justification can be sketched as follows (as elaborated in Tuomela, 2004).

(GB) Group g is *justified as a group in believing that* p in the normative group-binding sense in the social and normative circumstances C if and only if in C there are (authorized) operative members $A_1, \ldots, A_m$ of g in respective positions $P_1, \ldots, P_m$ such that

(1) the agents $A_1, \ldots, A_m$, when they were performing their social tasks in their positions $P_1, \ldots, P_m$ and due to their exercising the relevant authority system ("joint intention formation" system) of g,

(a) (intentionally) collectively accepted p as true or correctly assertable in g (as a group) and because of this exercise of the authority system they ought to continue to accept and believe it positionally, thus in the we-mode (being collectively committed to p, which they have collectively accepted for g); and

(b) p relates appropriately to the realm of concern of the group and is epistemically justified for g in C;

(2) there is mutual knowledge among the operative members $A_1, \ldots, A_m$ to the effect that (1);

(3) because of (1a), the (full-fledged and adequately informed) nonoperative members of g tend to tacitly accept—or at least ought to accept—p in the we-mode;

(4) there is mutual knowledge in g to the effect that (3).

Here the justification of a proposition in a group is analyzed in terms of the following starting point.

(EJ) A proposition p is (rationally) *epistemically justified* for group g (in a situation C) if and only if (in C) g accepts p in virtue of p fitting and being supported by (a) the relevant data available to the members of g, and (b) the relevant laws and general principles accepted by g that pertain to data of these kinds.

Here beliefs are divided into those that can be broadly described as not depending totally on "us" (factual belief, e.g., belief about the external physical world) and those entirely dependent on us (e.g., institutional belief).

23. In Tuomela (2000c) I argue about the relationship of (experiential) belief and acceptance in the single-agent case that (1) "if agent A wholeheartedly accepts as true that p and if this acceptance is not an intentionally performed action, then he believes that p at least to some nonnegligible degree" (p. 129) is true. I also argue that the thesis (2^*) "If an agent A has the flat-out belief that p in language-involving sense, then he accepts that p" (p. 131) *seems* to be true. Now I would like to take acceptance here to involve also the possibility of mere disposition to accept, and given this, I would take the thesis to be strictly true. Acceptance in (2^*) can be intentional or nonintentional. Now I suggest that A can be a collective agent, a group. Given (2^*), with this interpretation, it (given (GB)) comes to entail my claim in this paragraph, namely, that the belief must involve the acceptance of "We believe that p," at least in a dispositional sense for the group members. The voluntary acceptance of this judgment makes the group belief an acceptance (an acceptance belief) rather than a genuine belief.

24. Gilbert (2002b) analyzes collective beliefs as follows: The members of a population, P, collectively believe that p if and only if they are jointly committed to believe that p as a body. She asks (p. 45): "How are people to act so as to constitute, as far as possible, a body that believes that p?" Her answer is that "they are to act as would anyone of several *mouthpieces* of the body in question, thus uttering its beliefs, as opposed to the beliefs of any of its members, including the utterer." This seems to allow that collective beliefs amount to something like shared we-mode beliefs (thus shared beliefs qua group members). But it seems, contrary to the claim by Gilbert (p. 65), that collective beliefs in this "mouthpieces" sense must be taken to entail acceptances, because the members cannot, on conceptual grounds, properly utter such beliefs as "We believe that p" without accepting this belief-expressing sentence, or its cognate, as true for the group, and this amounts to the group's acceptance of the belief content.

25. This I have argued in view of the account of social institutions in Tuomela (2002b), chap. 6. See also the account (SI) in chapter 8 here.

26. One can of course belong to and identify with several groups and have different acceptance beliefs relative to those different groups, although this may create problems of inconsistency.

27. See Tuomela (2002b), chap. 5.

28. See, e.g., the article by Gilbert (2002b) and the references in it.

29. This requires some qualifications; see Hakli (2006).

30. I am inclined to accept a functional role account, although not a "topic-neutral" account, of mental states—also in the case of groups and their attitudes and states. Thus it is primarily the relationships among wants, beliefs, intentions, other mental states and perceptions (inputs), and actions (outputs) of the "system" that matter. This kind of account amounts to a kind of broad psychological theory. As I have argued elsewhere, it is important not to reduce away the mental state notions in terms of a topic-neutral Ramsey sentence. (David Lewis, 1972, tries to do this in terms of explicit definitions; my counter-argument is in Tuomela, 1977, chap. 4.) On the contrary, multiply denoting mental state predicates are to be accepted, in part because they may do some work in ruling out some observational states of the world that the Ramsey sentence of the theory is not capable of ruling out, i.e., the full theory may have semantic models that are not expansions of models

of the Ramsey sentence. (This discussion in the text and in this note gives my response to Deborah Tollefsen's charge, 2004, of circularity concerning my approach.)

31. The operatives are assumed to continue to accept $ATT(p)$ until (new) reasons for ceasing to accept it emerge (recall section 5 of chapter 1).

32. Using our earlier logical symbolism and letting $/_{pr}$ stand for presuppositional reason, we have this:

(ii^*) $ATT(x, p, agms)$ if and only if $ATT(x, p)$ &

$Cocom(x, ATT(g, p), E/_{pr}ATT(g, p))$.

33. The account above simplifyingly assumes that every operative member has committed herself, as a group member, to the group's decisions and views. This is actually not a conceptual requirement for acting as an operative group member, provided that enough of them currently accept the group attitude. What is strictly required is that every operative member be obligated to binding herself to the group's having $ATT(p)$.

34. Recall the discussion in section 4 of chapter 1 and in section 2 above. Broome's (2000) detailed discussion is relevant here.

35. I take the conceptual framework of agents and persons to presuppose that persons have bodies and bodily sensations, as well perceptions and feelings, and can refer to themselves by the first-person pronoun "I." Groups are not this kind of entity.

Carol Rovane (1998) argues that groups are persons. She ends up proposing the following necessary and sufficient condition for the identity of a group person (pp. 164, 180).

There is a set of intentional episodes such that

(1) these episodes stand in suitable rational relations so as to afford the possibility of carrying out coordinated activities;

(2) the set includes a commitment to particular unifying projects that require coordinated activities of the very sorts that are made possible by (1);

(3) the commitment to carrying out these unifying projects brings in train a commitment to achieving overall rational unity within the set.

I take these conditions jointly to be true of we-mode groups, namely, groups that can act as groups. Whether or not they are sufficient and necessary for a we-mode group depends on how we-notions can be taken to be involved in the conditions. I cannot speculate about that here. Instead, I wish to point out that group persons in Rovane's above sense do not have to be ontological agents "in their own right." It does not follow from (1)–(3) that there are in the social world group agents in a sense going beyond (or being "over and above") joint agency. Thus, if (1)–(3) were all that group persons require, this is compatible with my account.

Philip Pettit (2003) claims that groups are indeed persons, but his ontological view remains somewhat unclear. He says that groups may be entities supervening on their members' states and what have you. This still entails, given that supervenience is nonreductionistic, that groups have an existence sui generis. Pettit's view seems ontologically stronger than my view of we-more groups, but because I find his view unclear, I will not here comment on it.

36. In the case of a we-mode group, this will involve the members' mentally constructing them as forming a group (recall chapter 1).

37. My definitions of we-mode and I-mode groups basically serve to give specific content to the G-predicate. The subjective aspects related to group membership (in those definitions) can also be included in its content.

38. See Tuomela (1995), chap. 1, for task-right systems.

39. A singular group entity, g, can be connected to several ethoses and several group aspects G, G', and so on, and thus is "intensionally aspectual." Gilbert (1989), chap. 4, gives a related example (also recall chapter 5 here).

40. I have earlier formulated a nonentity view in chapter 4 of Tuomela (1995); see also the 1984 book for essentially the same view. We can now formulate the view in terms of the above account. The basic change that has to be made, obviously, is to remove the assumption of a real entity. Below I will try to preserve the common-sense phrase "g is a group" instead of directly using the ontologically more parsimonious locution "$A_1, \ldots, A_m$ form a group g," which was my phrasing in Tuomela (1995). My view in that book grounds a group ontologically, although not conceptually, on its members' actions and interactions in terms of irreducible supervenience (see chapters 4–6 and 9 of the 1995 book).

41. Let me still mention another line of argument against the entity conception of groups. Schein (1993) argues against the existence of plural objects, claiming that postulating their existence leads to Russell's paradox. His linguistic-logical discussion is interesting, but I am not totally convinced of his approach because of the assumptions that he makes. So I still allow for the existence of plural objects, although my approach does not strictly need them. Recall, too, that I have accounted for "we" as a predicate, not as a plural object. (I thank Kirk Ludwig for the reference to Schein's work.)

42. In Tuomela (forthcoming c) I discuss the views by Keith Graham (2002), chap. 3, on social groups and his so-called phenomenon of the clique. My discussion in that article thus expands my discussion here.

43. See Mathiesen (2003).

CHAPTER 7

1. It has been argued, for instance, that human beings are less social than monkeys but more social than chimpanzees (see Turner, 2000, chap. 1).

2. For instance, chimpanzees seem to have the ability to cooperate but not the motivational disposition, except concerning some situations requiring cooperation for instrumental reasons. (See Tomasello et al., 2005.)

3. For the innateness assumption, see, e.g., Richerson and Boyd (2001) and Tomasello et al. (2005), and see chapter 9 below. Richerson and Boyd's thesis is this (p. 190): "Humans evolved to be innately prepared to commit to the institutions and projects of their tribes, but culture dictates how to recognize who belongs to the tribes, what schedules of aid, praise, and punishment is due to tribal fellows, and how the tribe is to deal with other tribes—allies, enemies, and clients."

4. See Gintis et al. (2005), p. 8, for the notion.

5. See Sripada (2005) and Gintis et al. (2005) for results that dramatically show that mere reciprocity is not sufficient to generate sustained cooperation.

6. Somewhat more precisely, in we-mode groups, acting as a group member with collective commitment entails strong reciprocity. What is more, strong reciprocity gets a partial justification and explanation from the group's authority over its members regarding their we-mode activities: The group members qua group members ought to act as group members and promote the ethos. This kind of group reason is missing from the Gintis et al. (2005) I-mode approach (see also Schmid, 2005, for a similar point in terms of identification with the group). Such a group reason leads to a strengthened disposition to at least intragroup cooperation even in large groups. (But see Kollock, 1998, and Goette et al., 2006, for experimental investigations that indeed show the effects of a group qua a group, as one might say.)

7. Richerson and Boyd (2005) favor a view of cooperation as largely based on *cultural evolution* and, in addition, involving "*moralistic*" *punishment*, which indeed amounts to strong reciprocity in the sense of Gintis et al. (2005).

8. What I call *full* cooperation is intuitively the dictionary sense. For instance, Collins Cobuild Dictionary defines "cooperate" thus: "1. If people cooperate, they work or act together for a purpose. 2. If you cooperate, you help willingly when they ask you for your help."

9. See Tuomela (2000c) for a comprehensive discussion of cooperation. This chapter, while self-contained, presents an improved version of some aspects of the theory developed in that book. The improvements concern especially I-mode cooperation and cooperation in a group context.

10. See Tuomela (2000c).

11. In the well-known ultimatum game, people tend to see the situation as a group situation involving moral or group-social considerations, such as fairness (see e.g. Gintis et al., 2005, for empirical results speaking against selfishness and game-theoretic prediction).

12. See Bratman's (1999) and McMahon's (2001) I-mode accounts of cooperation.

13. Bratman's sophisticated account of cooperation concerns a somewhat stronger idea of (I-mode) cooperation than what my account, given in terms of (CIM) below, involves (see Bratman, 1999, chap. 5). He requires that the features of mutual responsiveness, commitment to the joint activity, and (private) commitment to mutual support hold true of cooperation. As my example of the cooperating businesspersons shows, actual mutual behavioral responsiveness should not be required, but I find the other requirements acceptable for I-mode cooperation. However, these features should be understood in the weak sense that (CIM) involves. I discuss Bratman's theory in detail in the appendix to chapter 3 of Tuomela (2000c).

14. See R. Tuomela, and M. Tuomela (2005).

15. See Tuomela (2000c), chaps. 3 and 4, for a discussion of the willingness aspect of cooperation. It contrasts with reluctance and with coercion. Taking on extra costs includes the cost of sanctioning defectors (including those who do not sanction first-order defectors).

16. See Zlotkin and Rosenschein (1994) for this kind of cases.

17. That the commonality of goals, interests, and preferences is central for cooperation has been argued for in Tuomela (2000c), chap. 9, where a technical index of correlation, corr, is used to measure the correlation or correspondence in question. This measure is a normed Pearson coefficient ranging from -1 to $+1$ and defined by $corr = 2\mathrm{cov}(A,B)/(s_A^2 + s_B^2)$, namely, the covariance of utilities normalized by the variances of these utilities. The statement $corr > 0$ represents, roughly, cooperation, and $corr < 0$ represents conflict. In Tuomela (2000c) the following *Commonality Thesis* is defended: Other things being equal, the more commonality of interest (as measured by the index *corr* and preferences) there is in a situation, the more likely cooperation is to be initiated and carried out successfully and— speaking of reward-based cooperative situations—to give the expected rewards, understanding this to mean rewards from acting together (relative to not acting so).

That cooperation is successful in the sense of the Commonality Thesis has to do with improvements related to (a) the selection of a collective goal and the means of reaching it, (b) the stability of the commitment to the collective goal-directed action, (c) the possibilities of helping, and (d) flexibility concerning the change of a collective goal when it is called for. In relation to (CIM) we can speak of its clauses (1) and (2) constituting a cooperative goal (in the thin sense discussed in the text), and this goal qualifies as the kind of goal spoken about above. (See also appendix 4.)

18. See chapter 2.

19. See Tuomela (1995), chap. 1, and Tuomela and Miller (1988) for this kind of analysis and justification for clause (3).

20. The dominance principle is a collective principle concerning the players as a unit. While not a priori true, I regard it as a plausible a posteriori rationality principle. Harsanyi and Selten (1988), p. 356, propose this principle as an acceptable rationality principle in their comprehensive theory.

21. See Tuomela (2000c), chaps. 11–12, for discussion. My notion of collective action dilemma is somewhat broader than is common in this field. For comparison, let me quote what Liebrand et al. (1992) say about "social dilemmas" (p. 4): "Formally, social dilemmas are defined by three properties: (1) a noncooperative choice (D) is always more profitable to the actor than a cooperative choice (C), regardless of the choices made by the others; (2) compared to a cooperative choice, a noncooperative choice is always harmful to the others: and (3) the aggregate amount of harm done to others by a noncooperative choice is greater that the profit to the actor himself." This account fits, e.g., the central types of dilemma explicated by the PD and Chicken, but, primarily because of clause (1), it does not fit, e.g., the Assurance Game. Collective action dilemmas of the above kind are often divided into *commons* (or "take-some") situations and *public good* (or "give-some") situations.

22. However, a centipede game (an extended PD) offers a partial exception to this, for "long term" rationality in conjunction with progroup I-mode action can lead to a cooperative solution. Players can get to the last choice node with long-term rationality (in a sense involving assurance of the other's cooperation), but the last choice requires taking progroup action and acting on I-mode (or possibly we-mode) utility, against one's initial I-mode utilities. See Tuomela (2000c), chap. 11, for the centipede game, and see chapter 8, section 4, here for comments on iterated collective dilemma situations.

23. Of course, game theory concerns only rational action. However, normal humans are rational—boundedly rational if not rational in the game-theoretic sense. In any case, noncooperative game theory has been used in empirical research, and the general result is that its predictions do not fit real behavior well. Thus, in a recent survey, Elinor Ostrom (1997), p. 5, summarizes the relevant results of empirical collective action dilemma research as follows: "1. High levels of initial cooperation are found in most types of social dilemmas, but the levels are consistently less than optimal. 2. Behavior is not consistent with backward induction in finitely repeated social dilemmas. 3. Nash equilibrium strategies are not good predictors at the individual level. 4. Individuals do not learn Nash equilibrium strategies in repeated social dilemmas." Noncooperative game theory basically deals with I-mode cooperation, whereas cooperative game theory can to some extent be connected to my theory of the we-mode. (See Tuomela, 2000c, chap. 12.)

24. See Gintis et al. (2005), especially for interesting experimental results related to strong reciprocity.

25. DC and CD are not rational group choices here, as they give less to the group than all members performing C. However, in some cases with division of tasks in the group DC and CD are also possible combinations of we-mode actions as a group member.

26. The term "valuation" is used in a nonnormative sense here. Utilities and preferences may, however, be based on values, which, in contrast to the former, are normative in nature. Below, however, I will concentrate only on preferences and utilities, independently of their possibly reflecting the participants' values. This is in line with my general view that cooperation is not inherently normative. (See McMahon, 2001, for a discussion of the normativity of preferences.)

27. See, e.g., McClintock (1972), p. 447, and the references to experimental literature given there.

28. See my earlier treatments in Tuomela (1984), chaps. 2 and 12, and (2000c), chap. 10.

29. Falk and Fischbacher (2005), in their technical account of strong reciprocity, in effect add two multiplicative parameters in front of u_{ij2}, a parameter representing strength of agent 1's reciprocal preferences and another one for "kindness" of partner 2's action. Thus, our (iii) comes to represent the special case of strong reciprocity with maximal reciprocity strength and full cooperativeness ("kindness") of the partner's action.

30. See Hakli and Tuomela (2003) for other examples of the effects of utility transformation.

31. See Harsanyi (1976).

32. Note that the joint gain transformation can be implemented in various other ways than the sum transformation used above. For instance, the multiplicative joint gain transformation would produce similar results in many respects. In contrast to the sum transformation, it will also take into account the distribution of utility by preferring utility distributions that are as close to equal as possible. Hence the product transformation may sometimes give a solution to a collective action dilemma when the sum transformation fails. The reader is referred to Hakli and Tuomela (2003) for details and for further discussion of utility transformations.

33. Note here that cooperation is not an intrinsically moral notion. Moral considerations such as fairness and justice often are de facto involved in cooperative contexts, but there can clearly be unfair and unjust cooperation. See McMahon (2001), for recent discussion.

34. See chapter 6. Note, however, that the agents $A_1, \ldots, A_m$ in this context are not assumed to collectively accept the preference in a normative sense of acceptance. Collectively intentional joint acceptance can even be based on mutual belief and be unconscious. I am not aware of other similar accounts of group preference, but for a similar, but explicitly normative, account of group beliefs see Gilbert (1989).

35. As to group values, it is plausible to argue that group values supervene on members' we-mode values but not on their I-mode values—at least in the short run. Furthermore, group values supervene on members' stable we-mode preferences, interests, and beliefs (etc., whatever the supervenience basis involves). When (collective) rationality is based on values it is of a stronger kind (*Wertrationalität*) than when based only on the preferences (and interests) involved in them. Given the above, it would be easy to formulate a precise account of group values in analogy with (GP).

Bratman (2004) discusses shared values from a kind of progroup I-mode perspective, thus weak we-perspective. Similar considerations can be applied, mutatis mutandis, to the we-mode case.

36. See, e.g., Pettit (2001, 2002, 2003) and chapter 4, section 2 of this book.

37. See the discussion of this kind of "authority systems" in Tuomela (1995), chap. 4, and in chapter 6 above.

38. These and related patterns of inference are discussed in Tuomela (1984), chap. 11, and (2000c), chap. 5.

39. Colman (2003) has recently discussed "team reasoning." He says (p. 150): "A team-reasoning player maximizes the objective function of the set of players by identifying a profile of strategies that maximizes their joint or collective payoff, and then, if the maximizing profile is unique, playing the individual strategy that forms a component of it." Here, however, a group and group preference does not occur in a genuine way, and, what is worse, the level of thinking and acting as a group member is totally absent from his discussion. Had this central dimension been taken into account, all his criticisms against team reasoning would have vanished (see pp. 150–52).

Also Sugden and Gold (2004) have recently investigated and developed "team game theory," partly on the basis of ideas by Bacharach. Some aspects of thinking and acting as a group member (e.g., the compromise character of many group preferences) are taken into account in their progroup I-mode theory.

40. If group authority would always yield preemptive reasons—as, e.g., Joseph Raz seems to require—the combination of group utilities and private ones would be impossible (recall the discussion in section 2 of chapter 6). However, in this respect Raz's view is not

realistic. While there can be preemptive group reasons related to fundamental matters in the group (e.g., matters strictly required of group members) this need not be taken to hold for all group reasons.

41. I discuss the notion of a cooperative attitude (willingness) somewhat more in Tuomela (2000c), where also more detailed analyses of several kinds of cooperation, weaker and stronger, are discussed. The willingness of the performances can be assumed to be contingently based on the participants' preferences, more precisely their final preferences concerning outcomes from their part performances or contributions. If they correlate positively, it is more rational to exhibit a cooperative attitude, although that is not at least fully a voluntary matter.

42. This is the central thesis in my earlier theory of full-blown, namely, we-mode, cooperation. Thus, in chapter 4 of Tuomela (2000c) I present some arguments for the thesis that full cooperation must be based on a shared collective goal. According to the basic thesis of cooperation of chapter 1 of that book, (1) full-blown cooperation entails acting jointly as a group (in the sense (AT^*) of chapter 5 of this book) toward a shared collective goal, namely, we-mode cooperation, and conversely (2) we-mode cooperation (assumed to entail joint action as a group) entails full-blown cooperation. Subthesis (1) actually contains the following two claims: (a) Cooperation in the full sense involves a collective goal (end, purpose), and (b) a collective goal entails that the participants must act jointly to achieve the goal. Given the above, I present a "conceptual" argument for the necessary presence of a shared goal in full-blown cooperation, a "group-perspective" argument, and a "normative" as well as an "instrumental" argument to this effect (see Tuomela, 2000c, pp. 112–15).

43. Essentially this account is defended in R. Tuomela and M. Tuomela (2005).

44. Let me note that Conte and Castelfranchi (1995) present a goal-based account of cooperation based on dependence and a common (or "identical") goal. This account bears some resemblance to this account. An identical goal in their sense is roughly a we-mode goal in my sense. They require strong dependence between the agents and their actions. For a detailed discussion of their account see Tuomela (2000c), chap. 4.

45. Rational cooperation implicitly makes reference to noncooperation, which includes the following possible situations: (a) a situation in which X is performed by no one; (b) a situation in which only one of the participants does X; (c) a situation in which A_1 and A_2 each perform X but separately (or at any rate not jointly in the full-blown sense); (d) a situation in which one of the participants is forced by the other's threat to do something, Y, which may be worse for the threatened agent than his doing nothing or either one doing nothing or his—the threatened person's—performing X separately or alone.

46. In view of the arguments in chapter 4, Bratman's (1999) theory of cooperation is best regarded as an I-mode one. In it the notion of joint action need not yet be cooperative. Only the addition of a condition of "minimal cooperative stability" makes it so. Bratman's case of "unhelpful singers" indicates that his account is an I-mode account. We recall that here the singers are assumed to jointly intend to sing a duet without helping the other one if she, contrary to expectations, does something wrong. They act jointly, but this can be only I-mode joint action; and I-mode joint action in my account (AT#) in chapter 5, which resembles Bratman's account, need not be cooperative, either. In contrast, a we-mode joint action is necessarily (at least "minimally") cooperative, being based on joint intention as a group. Such joint intention involves the collective commitment to the joint action that serves to exclude the case of the unhelpful singers. The inference schema (W2) assumed to apply to we-intenders also shows this; recall chapter 4, section 4. When there is a (strong) cooperative attitude at work, fuller cooperation comes about.

47. That the ethos can in general be seen as a goal is due to the fact that for the group members it basically has the world-to-mind direction of fit concerning its satisfaction (recall the discussion in chapter 1).

48. The reader is referred to R. Tuomela and M. Tuomela (2005), where the relationship between cooperation and trust is examined in detail from the perspective of the account of trust developed by Maj Tuomela (e.g., in her 2003 article). The participants of rational (I-mode or we-mode) cooperation can be argued to trust each other concerning the other's participation. They need to have at least "rational predictive trust" in each other. This includes that they believe that the other will perform the expected action with goodwill toward the partner and they themselves have an "accepting attitude" about being dependent on the other's action. Both (CIM) and (CWM) can be understood to satisfy these conditions because of the participation beliefs involved and, as for the accepting attitude, because of clause (2) of (CIM), and in the case of (CWM), simply as a conceptual feature of the we-mode.

More specifically, the following three theses are argued for in Tuomela, R. and Tuomela, M. (2005): (1) at least "predictive" trust is needed for rationally initiating and maintaining intentional I-mode or we-mode cooperative action; (2) successful rational intentional cooperation promotes rational "genuine" trust that is based on the participants' mutual respect of each other; (3) given some contingent qualifications, when some participants rationally cooperate in the we-mode, where the members hence are sincerely collectively committed toward the others to performing one's part, and where they mutually believe that this is the case, their relationship is characterizable as one involving mutual respect and genuine trust concerning their part-performances.

49. In Tuomela (2000c), chap. 4, I discuss some versions of orchestrated cooperation, including the operation of a spy organization. My discussion there was influenced by the account of Conte and Castelfranchi (1995). (See also Tuomela, 1984, chap. 5.)

One problem that would deserve a fuller treatment is the status of hired persons in a collective. In general, they are required to do only what they are paid for, and this will not, at least not always, require functioning as a proper group member.

50. For a fuller discussion of this kind of situation, see Tuomela (forthcoming b).

51. Recalling chapter 3, we may assume that people in general are disposed to act on the basis of shared we-attitudes (a similarity feature generated by social capital); thus, in particular in our present context, we may assume that they take as their reason to cooperate and comply that the others also do so. This may look like the kind of circular situation already considered in chapter 3 and above: I cooperate because you cooperate, and you cooperate because I do, and so on ad infinitum. However, while that is right, we saw in chapter 3 that there are many ways out.

52. I will below consider free-riders only in the context of a simple PD without attempting to analyze the notion of free-riding. As Amartya Sen has pointed out to me, this kind of context does not allow a free-rider to publicly threaten the others, which, in contrast, is the case in the "threat games" studied by Nash in the context of bargaining (Nash, 1950). However, even in the simple public good case to be discussed below, it may be the case that a player believes that there will be sufficiently many contributors so that the good will be produced (assuming it is a step good) and that there thus is something to free-ride on.

53. See Tuomela (2000c), chap. 10.

54. This is an institutional case—see chapter 8.

55. When E amounts to the joint outcome CC, we have CC > CD v DC v DD. Thus there is no PD anymore. However, if we allow that E can be achieved also alone, E would amount to CC v CD v DC and we have a dilemma for the members, for while they are

collectively committed to avoiding DD, each will prefer in the I-mode to choose D over than C. (I thank Kaarlo Miller for emphasizing this to me.) In the general case, however, it is rare that a public good can be produced by a single member.

56. Some social psychologists have investigated situations in which an n-person PD is embedded in a social context where the ingroup formed of those n persons is competing with another group (outgroup) for the same continuous or binary public good (for recent discussion and experimental results see Bornstein, 2004). This is called an intergroup PD game. In it, the more the players contribute to the public good, the more the group gains (the "cake" the group gets is bigger), but on the other hand, free-riders will always do better than cooperators. This game has the following central strategic properties:

(1) Withholding contribution is the dominant individual strategy. In each group a player's payoff for defecting is higher than her payoff for contributing, regardless of what all other (ingroup and outgroup) players do.
(2) The dominant group strategy is for all group members to contribute. The payoff for a player is highest when all ingroup members contribute, regardless of the number of outgroup contributors.
(3) The collectively (i.e., Pareto-) optimal outcome, the one that maximizes the collective (or summative) payoff to all players in both groups, is for all of them to withhold contribution.

The first and second properties, taken together, define the intragroup payoff structure of the IPD game (for any number of outgroup contributors) as an n-person PD game or a social dilemma. The second and third properties define the intergroup payoff structure as a two-party PD game between the two groups.

I cannot in this context discuss intergroup dilemmas, but I wish to point out that here we have an invitation to both we-mode and I-mode thinking. Properties (1) and (3) encourage subjects to think and act in the I-mode, while (2) invites we-mode thinking and acting.

57. See Tuomela (forthcoming a) on acting for a reason in the case of joint action.

58. Collective commitment is bound to change the probability assignments in the expected utility formula. Thus with full collective commitment a member acting as a group member will give zero probability to another member's choice of D. In actual life, the probabilities hardly change so dramatically.

59. Here is what Boyd, Gintis, Bowles, and Richerson (2003) say about the second-order dilemma basically in the case of an I-mode group. We assume a population (group) of size n. There are contributors and defectors. Contributors incur a cost c to produce a total benefit b that is shared equally among group members. Defectors incur no costs and produce no benefits. If the fraction of contributors in the group is x, the expected payoff for contributors is $bx - c$ and the expected payoff for defectors is bx, so the payoff disadvantage of the contributors is a constant c independently of the distribution of types in the population. Next add a third type, punishers, who cooperate and then punish each defector in their group, reducing each defector's payoff by p/n at a cost k/n to the punisher. If the frequency of the punishers is y, the expected payoffs become $b(x + y) - c$ to contributors, $b(x + y) - py$ to defectors, and $b(x + y) - c - k(1 - x - y)$ to punishers. Contributors have higher fitness than defectors if punishers are sufficiently common so that the cost of being punished exceeds the cost of cooperating $(py - c)$. Punishers suffer a fitness disadvantage of $k(1 - x - y)$ compared with nonpunishing contributors. Thus, punishing is altruistic, and mere contributors are "second-order free riders." The payoff disadvantage of punishers relative to contributors approaches zero as defectors become rare because there is no need for punishment.

A crucial question here, of course, is how costly punishing is. At least in the case of expectation-based or "proper" social norms, the group members typically are well socialized and the cost of punishing may not be high and may even be based on involuntary expressions of negative ("moralistic") feelings toward the free-riders. This is just an example of a case in which second-order free riding may be easy to avoid. Recent neuro-physiological research suggests that the caudate nucleus—known to be involved in reward processing—gets activated in punishing norm violators (see Dominique et al., 2004). Thus punishing in norm violators would not be a cost but a reward after all. (Also see Boyd et al., 2003, for cultural evolution and cheap punishment.)

60. Goette et al. (2006) present interesting experimental results on cooperativeness of "groupness." They studied groups (officer trainees during a four-week period) into which the members were selected by the experimenters. Yet there was a clear group effect: Cooperation and cooperation expectations concerning fellow group members were signifi-cantly higher than concerning outgroup members.

61. There is some work in the I-mode case on this mixture problem, namely, under which conditions defectors can win over the cooperators in a population, and vice versa; see the discussions in Gintis et al. (2005).

62. For central arguments, see especially chapters 2, 4, 6, and 8. For the case of social institutions, see also Tuomela (2002a), chap. 6.

63. See Boyd and Richerson (2004).

64. See e.g. the anthology edited by Gintis et al. (2005).

65. See Blackmore (1999).

66. See McMahon (2001) and my 2005 review of his book (Tuomela, forthcoming b).

67. See Tuomela (2000c), pp. 270–73.

68. See Nida-Rümelin (1991).

69. See Tuomela (2000c).

70. I thank Raul Hakli and Martin Rechenauer for their comments on a version of this chapter.

CHAPTER 8

1. See Barnes (1983), Bloor (1997), Kusch (1997), and Searle (1995). My account has affinities with Searle's theory. For a detailed discussion and comparison see Tuomela (2002b), chapter 6.

2. See Tuomela (2002b) for a child's acceptance of a view in terms of "pattern-governed behavior."

3. See Cohen (1992) and Tuomela (2000a).

4. See Tuomela (2000a) and Hakli (2006) for discussion.

5. For simplicity's sake, I will below mostly speak of collective acceptance without mentioning its possible context-relativity. Collective acceptance in general applies only with some constraints, but I will not below explicitly consider them. If wanted, they can be taken to be in-built into the notion of collective acceptance in each situation in question.

6. What will be called *constitutive* collective acceptance results in collective commit-ments with the world-to-mind direction of fit—see below in the text.

7. While my account in a sense is in the same camp as Searle's (1995), it should be emphasized that Searle does not present a detailed account of his key notion of collective acceptance, whereas my theory has a broader scope and is based on a well-defined notion of collective acceptance. More important, my account makes institutionality and institutions we-mode group phenomena and gives reasons for doing it.

8. As said in chapters 2 and 6, what a proposition here amounts to is a Sellarsian (1968, 1969) dot-quoted sentence.

9. As seen, e.g., in chapters 2–5, in the I-mode there are ways to simulate we-mode collective construction and the Collectivity Condition, but those constructions fail to capture the we-mode concepts they simulate.

10. Pretending seems to be an evolutionary adaptation in humans. Even small children in their second year of age start to exhibit pretending in their play (consider "(Pretend that) this cup is a cap"). See Rakoczy (2004).

11. Searle (1983), chapter 6, takes this kind of performatives—in the single-agent case—to be declarations. A declaration has not only the world-to-mind direction of fit but also the mind-to-world direction of fit. Thus "We hereby take squirrel pelt to be money" also represents the collectively created fact that squirrel pelt is money.

12. It has earlier been discussed at length in Tuomela (2002b), chap. 5 (also see Searle, 1995, for resembling ideas). The account below has been considerably improved.

13. For instance, what is money in an autonomous group is entirely up to the group members to decide about. If the group then comes to accept, by decision or perhaps by just acting in the appropriate ways, that squirrel pelt is money in the group, that was something entirely up to the group. However, this concerns types or concepts or other similar things. Whether this particular object that a person takes to be a squirrel pelt is money depends in part on the world, that is, on whether this object indeed is a squirrel pelt. See the discussion of the central concept of what it is up to the group to determine and the entailed collective mind-dependence in Tuomela (2002b), chap. 5.

14. The general view I am relying on here is the account of group acceptance sketched in chapter 6, section 1. Here my formulations are simplifyingly geared to egalitarian, unstructured groups. Group acceptance as action is to be analyzed in terms of (IGA), and group acceptance as a kind of state is to be analyzed in terms of (GATT) of chapter 6.

15. The *narrow* sense of institutionality concerns what essentially pertains to a social institution in the sense to be precisely characterized by (SI) below.

16. Recall that collective acceptance in the squirrel pelt example has both the world-to-mind and the mind-to-world direction of fit.

17. The discussion in this and the next section makes use of chapter 6 of Tuomela (2002b).

18. See Tuomela (2002b), especially chap. 4, for more details.

19. Douglass North (1998, 2001) has advocated this view (2001): "Institutions are the humanly devised constraints that structure human interaction. They are made up of formal constraints (for example, rules, laws, constitutions), informal constraints (for example, norms of behavior, conventions, self-imposed codes of conduct), their enforcement characteristics. Together they define the incentive structure of societies, and specifically, economies" (p. 248).

20. See Tuomela (2002b), chap. 7.

21. See Searle (1995).

22. See Tuomela (2000c), chaps. 10–13.

23. In modern Western societies, the collective acceptance related to social institutions has typically been *codified* (consider the performative print "This note is legal tender for all debts, public and private" on a U.S. dollar note).

24. See Searle (1995), chap. 4, for this, and see analysis (SI) below.

25. See Tuomela (2002b), chap. 3.

26. I am inclined to think that normative relationships can be analyzed nominalistically in terms of a suitable kind of trope theory. That cannot, however, be attempted in this work.

27. My account of social institutions is in a different camp from Barry Smith's (and partly also Searle's recent account; see Smith and Searle, 2003). Smith's view seems to allow for endless amounts of abstract entities like debts and loans or marriages.

28. See my earlier discussion in Tuomela (2002b), chap. 6.

29. See Tuomela (1995), chaps. 1 and 8, on positions as contrasted with roles.

30. See Tuomela (1995) for social norms and task-right systems.

31. See the treatment of concept institutions in Tuomela (2002b), chap. 6.

32. Let us briefly consider Searle's (1995) deontic power account. The deontic powers collectively conferred on people are enablements and requirements. Searle's basic hypothesis is as follows (p. 111): "There is exactly one primitive logical operation by which institutional reality is created and constituted. It has this form: *We collectively accept, acknowledge, recognize, go along with, etc., that (S has power (S does A))*." Searle thus takes many different kinds of activities to be power-creating (or power-maintaining, as the case may be). For convenience, I will below mostly use only the first term, namely, "collective acceptance." Searle says rather little about the aforementioned different acceptance-related notions, and this leaves the theory somewhat vague. For one thing, the theory is supposed to account for the rise and maintenance of social institutions, but it seems that, e.g., "going along with" will not suffice for the first of these tasks and perhaps not always for the maintenance task either.

33. See Tuomela (2002b), chap. 6, for a detailed account of reflexivity, and see below for institutional status.

34. For instance, Schotter's (1981) account belongs here.

35. Thus I assume that the correct analysis of them will involve reflexivity. I will not here consider the possibility that there are or could be cases of a new deontic institutional status that would not involve reflexivity. (Case (d) is considered in detail in Tuomela, 2002b, chapter 7.)

36. See Tuomela (2002b), chap. 6. The constitutive norms may be either authority-based or mutual-belief-based.

37. For discussions that somewhat similarly emphasize the reflexivity feature, see, e.g., Barnes (1983), Searle (1995), and Bloor (1997).

38. See Searle (1995), chap. 1, for constitutive rules. I also accept constitutive mutual-belief-based social norms.

39. As to education, here is how Turner (2003) summarizes it: "Education is the systematic organization of formal student-teacher instruction, revolving around an explicit curriculum and involving ritualized student passage, that has consequences among the members of a population for social reproduction, cultural storage, social placement, conflict management, and social transformation" (p. 95). As for economy, he says: "The economy as an institution can thus be defined as the use of technologies, physical and human capital, entrepreneurial structures, and property systems for the gathering of resources, the conversion of resources into usable commodities, and the distribution of these commodities to members of a population" (p. 58). Both of these examples of institutions as social systems clearly are very complex. For an account of economic institutions mainly in game-theoretic terms, see Schotter (1981).

40. This is not a very restrictive assumption in principle, depending on what kind of entities one allows in the domains of the logical models of the theory.

41. See Carnap (1966) and my discussion of it in Tuomela (1973).

42. Such a complex theory of an institutional system is a matter for the future. However, this kind of treatment can be used to illustrate the conceptual situation with respect to institutional notions, although I will below speak only of simplified cases.

43. The critical points directed by Barry Smith against Searlean constitutive rules of the kind "X counts as Y" thus do not concern my account at all. For Smith's criticism and Searle's response, see Smith and Searle (2003).

44. See Searle (1995), chap. 4, for this form as the characteristic or typical form of a simple constitutive rule.

45. Hindriks (2005) presents a kind of account of social institutions that he terms the "XYZ conception." Here X (e.g., a certain kind of piece of paper) represents the noninstitutional basis of the institutional predicate Y (e.g., money), and Z is supposed spell out the behavioral consequences or content of Y. For Hindriks, they are concerned with powers, as is the case also with Searle (1995). However, Hindriks seems only to consider cases where the meaning of Y is antecedently given, but in such cases Z does not add anything new to the picture. The interesting cases are those in which the new institutional theory introduces totally new institutional predicates and in the very formation of the theory comes to implicitly define those predicates (recall what was said about T′ and its M-predicates above).

46. Searle emphasizes this feature: "The move from X to Y in the formula X counts as Y in C can only exist insofar as it is represented as existing" (Searle, 2003, p. 202).

47. In logical terms, the analysans amounts to: $FG(CA(g, s) \, \& \, N(CA(g, s) \leftrightarrow s))$ or, equivalently, $FG(CA(g, (O \rightarrow_N M)) \, \& \, N^*(CA(g, (O \rightarrow_N M)) \leftrightarrow (O \rightarrow_N M)))$. The necessity operator N^* is a conceptual one governing the meaning of CA and may differ from what we have in (2).

48. Searle's account of deontic social status emphasizes the symbolizing nature of a status and the language-dependence of social institutions. My account largely agrees with this aspect of his theory, but my notion of an institutional status is clearly broader than his notion of institutional status (or status function).

49. See Searle (1995), chap. 4.

50. See Searle (1995), p. 105.

51. Using the symbols O = squirrel pelt, M = money, and P = possessing, and supposing that $s = N((x)(O(x) \rightarrow M(x)))$, we have $s \rightarrow (y)((Ez) \, (P(y, z) \, \& \, \text{Participant}(y) \, \& \, O(z)) \rightarrow \text{Power}(y, (Ex)(x \text{ is buyable } \& \text{ y buys } x)))$.

52. As Searle (1995) has argued, institutions require language with syntax. For instance, promising and properly obeying norms requires syntactic language and normative vocabulary, and already for this linguistic reason falls beyond, e.g., chimpanzees' capacities (not to speak of other, cognitive and moral, capacities needed here).

53. See Searle (1995), p. 39.

54. See, e.g., Atkinson and Birch (1970) and Atkinson and Raynor (1974) for the theory of achievement motivation that is based on this trio of motivational factors.

55. This clause has been formulated to best fit the case of we-mode group. As argued earlier, we-mode groups allow for some amount of I-mode norm obedience.

56. When applied to all members or rather to all members functioning in the I-mode, we are in effect dealing with a shared reason-based we-goal to do X in C, assuming that values appropriately yield corresponding goals. I have the goal to do X in the we-goal sense if and only if I have that goal for the reason that I believe that the group members expect that everyone should do X in C and that this is mutually believed among the group members. This is a case of a shared we-attitude where a person's attitude—intention, goal, or action—is reason-based on the others' expectation that he have that attitude (recall chapter 3).

57. A subjective version of this premise says that I believe—correctly or not—that (3). This allows for pluralistic ignorance, in the sense that the members of the group might incorrectly believe that the others expect them to conform.

58. Pettit (2002), pt. 3, also interestingly discusses what I call I-mode norm obedience in terms of social approval.

59. For a more extensive discussion, see Tuomela (2002b), chap. 6.

60. See Tuomela (2002b), pp. 176–77, for a detailed argument to this effect.

61. An extreme example of acting on one's group identity is voluntarily sacrificing oneself and dying for one's nation, e.g., in war. On the other hand, a group member may "quasi-identify" herself with the group for instrumental or selfish reasons and function in all public respects as a proper group member. Notice, too, that a person may identify herself with the group in a private, I-mode sense, but this does not amount to the kind of full group identification presently under discussion.

62. In Tuomela (2002b), chap. 6, several arguments for the thesis that social institutions require at least some amount of we-mode thinking and acting are given. Let me here without further discussion produce a quasi-deductive argument for the we-mode requirement based on what the group's ethos, E, implicates:

> (1) It ought to be the case in g (and for g) that E is fulfilled (that is, satisfied by the group members' actions qua group members).
> (2) The group (and group members collectively), perhaps via their operative members, ought to see to it that the ought-to-be norm expressed by (1) is satisfied.
> (3) The group members ought to commit themselves to (possibly recurrently, as the case may be) intentionally performing actions conducive to E.
> (4) The group members indeed have collectively committed themselves to E in view of (1)–(3), and they act purporting to fulfill and promote E.
> (5) Intentionally performed actions purporting to fulfill E are actions qua a group member involving for-groupness (that together with the assumption of collective commitment in (4) will satisfy the Collectivity Condition).
> (6) In view of (4) and (5), the group members' (intentional) actions conducive to E in this case are we-mode actions.
> (7) The institutions of g must not contradict E and must in general be conducive to E.
> (8) An institution of g must involve at least some we-mode acting, which by definition must be based on we-mode beliefs or we-mode we-intentions and possibly on other we-attitudes, purporting to uphold E.

63. For instance, when squirrels become almost extinct, squirrel pelts cannot anymore be used as money. Group decision-making, in principle, seems necessary for effectively changing the unit of money. As a recent example, recall the case of Sweden changing overnight from left-hand traffic to right-hand traffic. Without we-mode decision-making chaos would have resulted. See Tuomela (2002b), chap. 6, for the change argument.

64. I have argued that the functionally best institutions must involve some we-mode intentionality. See Tuomela (2002b), chap. 6.

65. I am here assuming that if they act in the I-mode they do not act for a progroup reason and do not, e.g., transform the PD into a coordination game, as some authors—for example, McMahon (2001)—have tried to solve the problem.

66. See Binmore (1994), chaps. 2 and 3, for the folk theorem.

67. I thank Maj Tuomela for helping me with some formulations in this section.

68. See the "duality models" of Giddens (1984), Bhaskar (1989), and Tuomela (2002b), chap. 7.

69. This is essentially the formulation of Tuomela (2002b), p. 251.

CHAPTER 9

1. Here is a recent textbook formulation of these postulates (Boyd and Silk, 2003, p. 6): 1. The ability of a population to expand is infinite, but the ability of any environment

to support populations is always finite. 2. Organisms within populations vary, and this variation affects the ability of individuals to survive and reproduce. 3. The variations are transmitted from parents to offspring.

2. See Boyd and Richerson (1996).

3. In their recent two-volume anthology on imitation, Hurley and Chater (2005) characterize imitation more specifically as follows (p. 2): "Imitation may be presumed to require at least copying in a generic sense. The observer's perception of the model's behavior causes similar behavior in the observer, in some way such that the similarity between the model's behavior and that of the observer plays a role, though not necessarily at a conscious level, in generating the observer's behavior." I find this a plausible characterization as such, but it forgets about the various cognitive presuppositions pertinent to the human case—think, for example, of the imitation involved in the case expressed by "When in Rome, do as Romans do." The Hurley and Chater anthology, at any rate, gives a good survey of the present-day scientific investigation of imitation. See also Tomasello (1999) for an emphasis of the copying kind of imitation as partly opposed to the emulation kind of imitation in the case of humans.

Ethologists have mentioned song dialects of some birds and foraging behaviors (practices) in apes as examples depending on imitation-based social learning. Thus, Boesch (1996) found socially transmitted, including imitation-based, behaviors in chimpanzees that, furthermore, are solutions to tasks that can be solved in more than one way and in which individual, nonsocial learning typically leads to different results. Special kinds of leaf-clipping, leaf-grooming, and knuckle-knocking are cases in point.

4. It can alternatively be said, in view of the developments in chapter 6, that culture consists largely of shared contents or propositions that are premisible in a group and have certain specific directions of fit of semantic satisfaction. However, also nonpropositional knowledge typically is involved (think of specific cultural skills).

5. The norms involved here are typically functional for the group and learned as a child, often as "pattern-governed behaviors"—recall the comments in chapter 1 on this notion by Wilfrid Sellars and see the use made of it in Tuomela (2002b), chaps. 3 and 4.

6. Three general accounts of cultural evolution have recently been developed. Barrett et al. (2002) speak of them as the gene-culture coevolution model, the phenogenotype coevolution model, and the dual inheritance model. These differ in what is assumed of the interaction between genetic and cultural ("memetic") fitness. In this chapter, I will make some use of the dual inheritance view that Richerson and Boyd have developed during the past two decades. Their view allows most independence to cultural items.

7. The genetic and neural sources of prosociality have been long studied. E.g., lesions in the frontal lobe and the level of certain neurotransmitters like oxytocin, dopamine, and serotonin are factors relevant to prosocial (and asocial) behavior.

8. See especially Boyd and Richerson (1985) and Richerson and Boyd (2001, 2005) for their theory and arguments. This section makes use of the research of these two authors. There are points of difference between my and their approaches, for example, my use of the we-mode and emphasis on we-ness is not to be found in their work. See Tomasello (1999) and Tomasello et al. (2005) for the claim that collective (or "shared") intentionality is coevolutionary adaptation. For similar claims concerned especially with biological evolution, see Kurzban and Neuberg (2005) and Ahn et al. (2004).

9. As to social insects like ants, they do form large cooperative societies, but all of their cooperation is based on kin (genes) and coresidence and lacks the plasticity that human societies have. Their societies are not based on collective intentionality.

10. Cooperation within societies that are nation-based and that also are states or are disposed to become states seems more likely to come about than within societies that are

not nation-based or are not organized into states. Accepting Max Weber's basic ideas, we may say, in rough terms, that a nation is formed out of a group of people that are unified by their tradition, culture, and history and accept that they share a common destiny, where the members desire to form or maintain a state and where they also typically share a certain territory.

11. See Tomasello et al. (2005) for discussion. Chimpanzees' cooperation rather seems to resemble the kind of behavior that lions engage in when hunting jointly. The scarcity of proper cooperation in chimpanzees seems to relate to the generally known fact that chimpanzees are not able to synchronize their motor activities. They cannot make music together and have no "work songs," for instance.

12. See Tomasello et al. (2005) and Kurzban and Neuberg (2005). See also Richerson and Boyd (2001), Richerson and Boyd (2005), chap. 7, and Barrett et al. (2002), chap. 13, for coevolutionary aspects of adaptations.

13. Even the kinds of primitive symbolic and linguistic capacities required for living in large groups involve the use of conventional symbols and, perhaps, a kind of protolanguage based on two-word sentences and the like (even if language with proper grammar came about only much later). Whatever the right account is, collective intentionality seems to be involved—perhaps even as the most basic underlying factor.

14. See Tomasello et al. (2005). Here are two citations from p. 687 and a third one from p. 688, to document what is said in the text: "Based on all of these data, our proposal is that in addition to understanding others as intentional, rational agents, human beings also possess some kind of more specifically social capacity that gives them the motivation and cognitive skills to feel, experience, and act together with others—what we may call, focusing on its ontogenetic endpoint, shared (or "we") intentionality. As the key social-cognitive skill for cultural creation and cognition, shared intentionality is of special importance in explaining the uniquely powerful cognitive skills of Homo sapiens." These authors' phylogenetic hypothesis says: "In addition to competing with others (and coordinating with others generally, like all social animals), humans evolved skills and motivations for collaborating with one another in activities involving shared goals and joint intention/attention." As to ontogeny, they say: "If our phylogenetic hypothesis is correct, selection for good collaborators means selection for individuals who are (1) good at intention reading and (2) have a strong motivation to share psychological states with others. Our ontogenetic hypothesis is that it is precisely these two developing capacities that interact during the first year of life to create the normal human developmental pathway leading to participation in collaborative cultural practices."

15. Boehm (1999) argues that, indeed, large-game hunting was an evolutionary factor that led to cooperation in the fuller sense of sharing meat in a fair, egalitarian way (in contrast to what seems common among, e.g., chimpanzees).

16. See Richerson and Boyd (2001, 2005) for this and the references to their work in the paragraphs below.

17. Hamilton's rule says this: An (altruistic) act will be favored by selection if (and only if) $rb > c$. Here r = the average coefficient of relatedness between the actor and the recipients, b = the sum of the fitness benefits to all individuals affected by the behavior, and c = the fitness cost to the individual performing the behavior. To arrive at a kind of social version, I suggest we take $r = corr$, that is, we let the relatedness be the degree of correspondence between the actor's and a recipient's interests or (rational) preferences. Then we have: $corr > c/b$, where b represents the benefit to the group, namely, for-group-ness quantified.

We can assume that the group, defined basically by its ethos, has preferences and views about the topics of concern of the group. We can speak of quantified preferences in utility matrices that represent or at least "respect" the ethos. These matrices show what value different items, including beliefs and goals, have for the group. If a group member's personal preferences concerning those same matters are close to the group's utilities or values, then she is close to the group, and while she then "rationally" acts in a progroupish way, it may be acting selfishly (if her personal preferences are selfish), and it can be acting in the I-mode rather than in the we-mode. The reinterpreted Hamilton rule says whether and which progroup action is "rational" for the person in question to perform. Rational actions here are those actions for which $bcorr > c$. So the closer or more like the group (or, for that matter, and ideal, ethos-obeying group member) the person is, the more she should act for the group (or, respectively, for such a group member). There is also another factor, not to be seen in the Hamilton rule-analogue: In many cases, a group member can further her own private preferences by acting jointly with group members in a progroupish way—especially in cases where she cannot achieve those gains alone, without joint action, given, of course, that she indeed sees those outcomes as gains for herself.

The average degree of correspondence between all the group members' private preferences concerning group topics and the ethos of the group measures the cohesion (homogeneity) of the group. In the case of a group with voluntary membership, one can expect higher cohesion (and smaller intragroup variation) than in the case of a group with involuntary membership. The degree of correspondence, $corr$, between the ethos E of a group g and the ethos E^* of another group g^* measures the degree of correspondence and similarity between g and g^*. Similarity can enhance cooperation between the groups but can also lead to competition.

18. See Henrich and Boyd (1998, 2001), for some results showing that an equilibrium can be reached at some level.

19. The meme theory leads to a similar view (see Blackmore, 1999). Recall appendix 1 in chapter 7.

20. The advantages of the we-mode over the I-mode have been discussed in several places in this book; recall especially the points made in chapters 2, 7, and 8; also see Tuomela (2000), chapter 12. Somewhat similarly, Richerson and Boyd (2001), p. 192, say, "Our social instincts hypothesis requires that cultural group selection be strong enough to counter individualistically motivated selfish decision making in order to avoid tribal scale cooperation and as a corollary to favor a measure of unsecured commitment to the group's practices and projects." They require some amount of initial cooperativeness in the group before cultural evolution can do its work; thus their approach and my approach are largely compatible: Cooperation must be started to be able to spread, and unless sufficiently many (a "critical mass") do cooperate, others do not risk doing it in situations of collective action dilemma (notice that as coordination equilibria are self-enforcing, those cases do not involve the risk of being cheated). To argue for the existence of some amount of initial cooperation in the group, we note that the group members will often face tasks for which cooperation is practically necessary or at least useful. Thus, unless some cooperation comes about, the group may perish or lose out to competing groups (or some other bad consequence will result).

21. See, e.g., Richerson and Boyd (2005), chap. 6.

22. The issue of negative attitudes toward outgroups is a complex one, however, and depends on many factors. For recent surveys, see Turner and Reynolds (2003) and, from an evolutionary perspective, Kurzban and Neuberg (2005); also recall the comments in chapters 1, 2, and 6 here. The capacity and motivational disposition to think of our group as "we" and to contrast it with outgroups ("they") seems to be a coevolved feature.

23. Also the capacity for music making seems to be a cooperative evolutionary adaptation, or at least this is what the musicologist Steven Brown (2000) argues. Here is his central argument (p. 257–258): "The human capacity to make music is a group-level

adaptation that evolved, in large part, by group selection. What this implies is that the group, more so than the individual, is the appropriate level of analysis in thinking about the fitness consequences of music. Music's fitness advantages come about from its ability to promote group-wide cooperation, coordination, cohesion, and catharsis, and this operates to increase both the absolute and relative fitness of groups. It functions to promote group welfare and group warfare. The fitness benefits of music-making at the group level far outweigh the costs of individual participation in musical activities; music is, on balance, a low-cost system for the individual. There is little conflict between within-group and between-group fitness consequences, and little motivational conflict between self-interest and musical participation. Music has a host of design features that strongly reflect its role in group function, the most prominent being pitch blending and isometric rhythms. Finally music functions as a type of neural 'reward' system, serving to emotively reinforce cooperative behavior during group ritual activities. Music evolved as ritual's reward system." Similar points are to be found also in Benzon (2001).

24. Richerson and Boyd (2001) point out that arranging military armies so that they take tribal groups into account will increase their fighting power. As van Crefeld (1982) has shown, after controlling for the quality and amount of equipment available, for example, the German forces were about 20 percent more effective than the U.S. forces in World War II. One decisive difference was that the German soldiers were recruited so that men from the same local areas ("tribal groups") were included in the same small units. The same was true in the Finnish army, sometimes with the sad side effect that almost all the men from the same village were killed in battle.

25. One can debate about whether shared mental states in the I-mode developed first or only after the we-mode developed, to the extent that the distinction even is clear in the rudimentary cases (see the comments in chapter 2, section 3).

26. My claims about the partly biological nature of the we-mode get partial support from recent neuropsychological investigations related to "mirror" neurons and "shared we-centric representations of space" that also indicate the biological basis of sociality, especially conformity. Such we-centric processes are unconscious, automatic, and structurally impersonal and develop well before a child acquires a "theory of mind" (to use a current term of art), which starts happening roughly by the age of four. Mirror neuron research shows that on a subpersonal level neural mechanisms are operative that seem necessary for human imitation and through that to conformity and empathy. Mirror neurons fire when an agent (human or ape, or perhaps primate) acts. The more interesting thing about them is that they also fire when the agent observes another person acting or even only sees a picture of another person acting. This makes mirror neurons relevant to imitation and cooperation.

27. The genetic disposition to live in tribes and to act as a tribe (and ingroup) member is "blind" as to specific content, that is, it is the function of culture to specify who belongs to the tribe, what kinds of help, reward, and punishment can be expected from tribal fellows, and how the tribe is to deal with other tribes—outgroups, be they allies or enemies.

28. In recent literature on cooperation, evolutionary game theory has been used to give arguments for cooperation. I have elsewhere, in Tuomela (2000c), chap. 12, discussed this theory, especially Skyrms's (1994, 1996) correlational version, and presented some critical points against it.

29. See especially Richerson and Boyd (2001, 2005).

30. Tuomela (2002b), chap. 7, gives the full mathematical details of the dynamic model here adapted to evolution.

31. The treatment in Tuomela (2002b), chap. 7, makes this assumption.

32. See Tuomela (2002), chap. 7, and also the somewhat different treatment in Tuomela (1995), chap. 10, both incorporating only deterministic change functions.

33. This model serves to make precise and also to improve on the central aspects of the "structuration theory" of Anthony Giddens (1984). My model is an obvious improvement, in the sense that it takes into account the joint attitudes and actions that the participants have. This is accomplished primarily through the central notion of a shared we-attitude, taken to be partially definitory of "core" social practices (recall chapter 5).

34. See the discussion in chapter 7 here, Tuomela (2002b), chap. 6, and Searle (1995).

35. What I have called "collective pattern-governed behaviors" represent a typically nonintentional kind of routine-like activities based on such conformist transmission. See Tuomela (2002b), chap. 3.

36. ATT could also be a conjunctive attitude concerning, e.g., preferences. Thus in the two-choice matrix for two persons it could be, e.g., the attitude CC > DC > DD > CD of personal preference over joint outcomes (matrix cells), in the case of the choice alternatives C and D. The first agent, the "row player," and an altruistic second agent, the "column player," might accept and fully share this ordering, which means maximal similarity of preferences over joint outcomes (or, more generally, over the certain set of states). So interpreted and measured, the similarity of preferences is likely to generate rational joint intention to cooperate.

37. See Henrich (2001).

38. Henrich and McElreath (2003) present the following classification of the elements of social learning that are involved in cultural evolution. They divide the biases involved into those related to content (e.g., a natural preference for sweet things) and context. The context factor is divided into "model-based" biases and "frequency-dependence" biases. The former includes the factors "prestige," "success," "similarity," "others." These are features of the model person(s) imitated. As seen from the presence of the "others" category, the list needs further specification. The latter context factor consists of conformity and rarity. (The rarity factor appears to allow for opposition against the majority of the group.)

39. Consider a simple two-person two-choice coordination game with the alternatives p and –p and the case of imitating successful persons. In chapter 3, this was rendered as follows (in section 1), where the member variable y has been relativized to an idol M (or to idols M).

$$WATT_x(p) \rightarrow ATT_x(p/_r(y)(M(y) \rightarrow ATT_y^*(p)) \, \& \, MB_g((y)(M(y) \rightarrow ATT_y^*(p))))$$

where M means idol or model. There might, e.g., be only one such model in the group, e.g., the leader. At the other extreme, M might not restrict anything, and we would be back where we started, namely, the standard conformative notion of we-attitude.

We can now make the following simple observations (recall chapter 3).

(1) For all ATT and all p, A's and B's disposition to share a we-attitude (SWATT) relative to a content set {p, –p} entails that in the corresponding desirability matrix the agents' attitudes are perfectly correlated (namely, $corr$(A, B, Att({p, –p})) = 1, where corr is my measure of attitude correlation amounting to a normed version of the Pearson correlation coefficient; recall chapter 7).

(2) Taking Imit(A, B, ATT({p, –p})) to mean that A fully imitates (copies) B with respect to ATT({p, –p}), we have that
Imit(A, B, ATT({p, –p})) entails $corr$(A, B, Att({p, –p})) = 1, which, ceteris paribus, disposes A and B to cooperate with respect to {p, –p}.

(3) Imit (A, B, ATT(p)) entails WATT(A, p) but it does not by itself entail shared we-attitude SWATT(A, B, p), relative to any content p. (Imitation here

could as well concern not only p but the set {p, −p} in which case WATT would have either the content p or −p.)

(4) SWATT(A, B, ({p, −p})) −> *corr*(A, B, ATT({p, −p})) = 1.

We can also say, without presenting a strict analysis of conforming, that under my wide notion of imitation, (mutual) imitation amounts to (mutual) conformism.

40. See Henrich (2001).

41. See Henrich (2001).

42. See Henrich and Boyd (1998, 2001).

43. See Henrich (2001), formula (7) in his article.

44. See Richerson and Boyd (1999, 2001, 2005). Recall the earlier points on the role of mirror neurons in giving a kind of neural foundation of conformity and we-ness.

45. See Richerson and Boyd (2001).

46. This is largely the setting that, e.g., Boyd and Richerson (1985) use in their theory. It can be noted here (also in relation to the points below in the text) that my formal developments above focus on the process where one attitude wins over another one rather than the outcome. The latter, however, is what the famous Price's equation primarily concerns (see, for example, Okasha, 2006). His result, interpretable either in biological or cultural terms, involves interacting subpopulations and selection between them. For such selection to involve a group effect (in an individual average, thus I-mode sense) there must be positive covariance between a trait (e.g., cooperativeness, extensionally considered) and fitness (in terms of growing subpopulation size). Thus cooperativeness can be fitness-positive for the population while fitness-negative (because of the cost effect) for the individual members.

47. See Tuomela (2000c), chap. 9.

48. See Tuomela (2004) for a discussion of group knowledge relevant to the present concerns.

49. See chapter 7 and Tuomela (2002b), chaps. 5–6.

50. I thank specifically Joe Henrich and Tomi Kokkonen for comments on this chapter.

CHAPTER 10

1. This account makes use of a manuscript I wrote in 2004 with Maj Tuomela. I gratefully acknowledge her permission to use material from that manuscript. My account also makes use of some ideas in the accounts by Mäkelä and Tuomela (2002) and R. Tuomela and M. Tuomela (2003). However, there are also differences with respect to the Mäkelä-Tuomela account. One is that, in contrast to it, I will here consider also I-mode group action and not only we-mode group action. I thank Maj Tuomela and Pekka Mäkelä for critical comments on this chapter.

2. In general, groups can be responsible for actions and attitudes. I will not below discuss the attitude case in particular (but see clause (6)(b) of (NRGB) below). The importance of this aspect of group responsibility has been emphasized by Larry May (1992).

3. Recall the point about single-ethos and multiethos groups made in section 2 of chapter 1. I will below continue to speak of the ethos of a group and mean by it the nuclear ethos in the case of multiethos groups.

4. It is justified to hold an agent responsible for some action only if the agent has certain capacities (e.g., rationality, capability of intentional action) and the agent freely exercised these capacities in acting. Thus, there are both internal and external factors to be taken into account here when deciding whether the action was "up to the agent" in the

right way. These remarks hold both for single agents and groups when treated as agents (persons).

5. As far as I can see, the basic elements of this account also apply to societies, nations, states, and other groups into which one is born. As pointed out earlier in this book, for instance, the constitution of a state is precisely what I mean by a group's ethos; such a constitution normally obligates the citizens to obey the ethos.

6. The account in Mäkelä and Tuomela (2002) concentrates on internally authorized groups, which is also the case in this chapter and, in general, in this book.

7. In R. Tuomela and M. Tuomela (2003) this dissidence-allowing sense is called the responsibility sense.

8. For a detailed presentation of cases that (5) here in a somewhat generalizing way is taken to represent, see sections 5 and 6; also see Mäkelä and Tuomela (2002) and M. Tuomela (2003), as well as R. Tuomela and M. Tuomela (2003).

To comment on an intentional dissident's commitments in view of chapter 1, the following kinds of actions are possible in their case. There may be private commitment to the topic of concern of g while there is no commitment to the group's ethos (a violator might be a rebel purporting to change the group's ethos). Hence there is no commitment to ethos-congruent action or type. However, a dissident (violator) may be committed to himself to act for himself in ways related to the topic of concern of g (and perhaps to his "modified" ethos), but that commitment need not be more than commitment before himself and only to himself. There is possibly no commitment to the group or to the other group members, although a violator may be committed to the group, apart from the aspect of its ethos that he purports to violate. When the dissident is still committed to the bulk of the ethos, he is a reformist; but he is a revolutionary if he is committed to an essential change of the ethos. The two variables of obeying-violating and maintaining-changing allow for four possible cases.

9. Recall chapter 5, and see Sandu and Tuomela (1996) for a logical analysis of some of these.

10. The same holds true of Mäkelä and Tuomela (2002).

11. See Tuomela (1995), p. 242, and chapter 6, section 2, of this book.

12. My verbal formulation of course does not fit the special case $m = 1$, but the phrasing is for simplicity's sake.

13. See the closely related treatment in Mäkelä and Tuomela (2002). Let me emphasize here that a group task comes with underlying, possibly implicit presuppositions, expressing the conditions under which task performance can reasonably be required— think, for example, of the "revocability" conditions of promises and contracts. Such revocability conditions are intimately related to the conditions under which a group ultimately can be regarded as responsible for its normative commitments—see (NRGB).

14. Note that here and elsewhere a group's foreseeing or believing (generally: "attituding") something is to be understood in terms of its (operative) members functioning as group members in the standard, we-mode sense (see Tuomela, 1995, chaps. 6–7).

15. See May (1992) for discussion. I take affecting in (6)(b) to be understood as a control-involving notion entailing that the members qua members ought to have changed their S-violating attitudes but did not.

16. See David Copp (forthcoming) and also Kirk Ludwig (forthcoming) and Seumas Miller (forthcoming).

17. In a case of overdetermination, such as when a man is killed by the shots of agents A and B such that each agent's shot or shots is/are sufficient for the death, we should presumably say that each agent is fully responsible for the bad outcome. This is just private full responsibility for the same outcome.

18. In the collection edited by May and Hoffman (1991) and in the monographs by Mellema (1997) and Kutz (2000), various problems related to group responsibility, especially distributivity problems, are discussed. I use a special conceptual framework (especially the we-mode/I-mode distinction) that these authors do not employ and cannot here use the space required to comment on this discussion.

19. Here is a list of cases that show what kinds of actions are possible when private (or I-mode) responsibility gets involved in addition to we-mode responsibility. There are both actions that the member erroneously takes to be ethos-compatible and there are ethos-violating actions.

A. Actions possibly believed by the acting member to be ethos-compatible:
(1) "incorrectly" performed permissible positional actions related to action class (1) of section 2;
(2) "wrong" manner of action, especially of obligatory positional action (cf. aforementioned class (1));
(3) freely chosen action (not ultimately collectively acceptable although meant by the author to be; cf. class (4) of chapter 1, section 3);
(4) refraining from participation in monitoring and punishing dissidents.
B. Ethos-violating actions:
(5) actions attempting to change the ethos, thereby violating it;
(6) exiting the group (which need not amount to giving up membership literally).

20. See, e.g., Mellema (1997) for discussion.
21. See Jaspers (1947/2000), for a classic discussion of the Nazi case.

REFERENCES

Adenzato, M., Becchio, C., Bertone, C., and Tuomela, R., 2005. "Neural Correlates Underlying Action-Intention and Aim-Intention." Poster presented at the Cognitive Science 2005 conference, Stresa, Italy, July 21–24.

Ahn, T., Janssen, M., and Ostrom, E. 2004. "Signals, Symbols, and Human Cooperation." In R. Sussman and A. Chapman, eds., *The Origins and Nature of Sociality*. Hawthorne, New York: de Gruyter, pp. 1221–39.

Aronson, E., Wilson, T., and Akert, R. 2005. *Social Psychology*. 5th ed. Upper Saddle River, N.J.: Pearson Education.

Asch, S. 1987. *Social Psychology*. Oxford: Oxford University Press. Originally published 1952.

Atkinson, J., and Birch, D. 1970. *The Dynamics of Action*. New York: Wiley.

Atkinson, J., and Raynor, J., eds. 1974. *Motivation and Achievement*. Washington, D.C.: Winston.

Aunger, R. ed. 2000. *Darwinizing Culture: The Status of Memetics as a Science*. Oxford: Oxford University Press.

Bach, K. 1995. "Terms of Agreement." *Ethics* 105, 604–12.

Baier, A. 1997. "Doing Things with Others: The Mental Commons." In L. Alanen, S. Heinämaa, and T. Wallgren, eds., *Commonality and Particularity in Ethics*. New York: St. Martin's Press, pp. 15–44.

Baltzer, U. 2003. "Social Action in Large Groups." *Protosociology* 18–19, 127–36.

Balzer, W., and Tuomela, R. 1997a. "A Fixed Point Approach to Collective Attitudes." In G. Holmström-Hintikka and R. Tuomela, eds., *Contemporary Action Theory II*. Dordrecht: Kluwer Academic, pp. 115–42.

Balzer, W., and Tuomela, R. 1997b. "The Structure and Verification of Plan-Based Joint Intentions." *International Journal of Cooperative Information Systems* 6, 3–26.

Balzer, W., and Tuomela, R. 2003. "Collective Intentions and the Maintenance of Social Practices." *Autonomous Agents and Multi-agent Systems* 6, 7–33.

Bardsley, N., and Sausgruber, R. Forthcoming. "Social Interaction Effects in the Laboratory and Society: Conformism and Reciprocity in Public Good Provision." *Journal of Economic Psychology*.

Barnes, B. 1983. "Social Life as Bootstrapped Induction." *Sociology* 17, 524–45.

302

Barrett, L., Dunbar, R., and Lycett, J. 2002. *Human Evolutionary Psychology*. Princeton, N.J.: Princeton University Press.

Bates, F., and Harvey, C. 1975. *The Structure of Social Systems*. New York: Gardner Press.

Belnap, N., Perloff, M., and Xu, M. 2001. *Facing the Future: Agents and Choices in Our Indeterministic World*. Oxford: Oxford University Press.

Benzon, W. 2001. *Beethoven's Anvil: Music in Mind and Culture*. Oxford: Oxford University Press.

Bhaskar, R. 1989. *Reclaiming Reality: A Critical Introduction to Contemporary Philosophy*. London: Verso.

Binmore, K. 1994. *Playing Fair: Game Theory and the Social Contract*. Vol. 1. Cambridge, Mass.: MIT Press.

Blackmore, S. 1999. *The Meme Machine*. Oxford: Oxford University Press.

Bloor, D. 1997. *Wittgenstein, Rules and Institutions*. London: Routledge.

Boehm, C. 1999. *Hierarchy in the Forest: The Evolution of Egalitarian Behavior*. Cambridge, Mass.: Harvard University Press.

Boesch, C. 1996. "The Emergence of Cultures among Wild Chimpanzees." In W. G. Runciman, J. M. Smith, and R. I. M. Dunbar, eds., *Evolution of Social Behaviour Patterns in Primates and Man*. Oxford: Oxford University Press, pp. 251–68.

Bornstein, G. 2004. "Cooperation in Intergroup Social Dilemmas." In R. Suleiman, D. Budescu, I. Fischer, and D. Messick, eds., *Contemporary Psychological Research on Social Dilemmas*, Cambridge: Cambridge University Press, pp. 227–47.

Boyd, R., Gintis, H., Bowles, S., and Richerson, P. 2003. "The Evolution of Altruistic Punishment." *Proceedings of the National Academy of Sciences USA* 100, 3531–35.

Boyd, R., and Richerson, P. 1985. *Culture and the Evolutionary Process*. Chicago: University of Chicago Press.

Boyd, R., and Richerson, P. 1996. "Why Cultural Evolution Is Rare." In W.G. Runciman, J. M. Smith, and R. I. M. Dunbar, eds., *Evolution of Social Behaviour Patterns in Primates and Man*. Oxford: Oxford University Press, pp. 77–93.

Boyd, R., and Richerson, P. 2004. "Solving the Puzzle of Human Cooperation." In S. Levinson and P. Jaisson, eds., *Evolution and Culture*. Cambridge, Mass.: MIT Press, pp. 105–32.

Boyd, R., and Silk, J. 2003. *How Humans Evolved*. New York: Norton.

Bratman, M. 1987. *Intention, Plans, and Practical Reason*. Cambridge, Mass.: Harvard University Press.

Bratman, M. 1992. "Shared Cooperative Activity." *Philosophical Review* 101, 327–41.

Bratman, M. 1993. "Shared Intention." *Ethics* 104, 97–113.

Bratman, M. 1999. *Faces of Intention*. Cambridge: Cambridge University Press.

Bratman, M. 2004. "Shared Valuing and Frameworks for Practical Reasoning." In J. Wallace, P. Pettit, S. Scheffler, and M. Smith, eds., *Reason and Value*. New York: Oxford University Press, pp. 1–27.

Brewer, M. 2001. "Ingroup Identification and Intergroup Conflict." In R. Ashmore, L. Jussim, and D. Wilder, eds., *Social Identity, Intergroup Conflict, and Conflict Reduction*. New York: Oxford University Press, pp. 17–41.

Brewer, M. 2003. *Intergroup Relations*. 2nd ed. Philadelphia: Open University Press.

Broome, J. 2000. "Normative Requirements." In J. Dancy, ed., *Normativity*. Oxford: Blackwell, pp. 78–99.

Brown, R. 2000. *Group Processes*. 2nd ed. Oxford: Blackwell.

Brown, S. 2000. "Evolutionary Models of Music: From Sexual Selection to Group Selection." In F. Tonneau and N. Thompson, eds., *Evolution, Culture, and Behavior*. Perspectives in Ethology. Vol. 13. New York: Kluwer Academic, pp. 231–81.

Capozza, D., and Brown, R., eds. 2000. *Social Identity Processes*. London: Sage.

Carnap, R. 1966. *Philosophical Foundations of Physics*. Edited by M. Gardner. New York: Basic Books.

Castelfranchi, C. 1995. "Commitment: From Intentions to Groups and Organizations." In *Proceedings of ICMAS '95*. Cambridge, Mass.: MIT Press, pp. 41–48.

Cohen, J. 1992. *An Essay on Belief and Acceptance*. Oxford: Oxford University Press.

Cohen, P., Levesque, H., and Smith, I. 1997. "On Team Formation." In G.. Holmström-Hintikka and R. Tuomela, eds., *Contemporary Action Theory*. Vol II. Dordrecht: Kluwer Academic Publishers, pp. 87–114.

Colman, A., 2003. "Cooperation, Psychological Game Theory, and Limitations of Rationality in Social Interaction," *Behavioral and Brain Sciences* 26, 139–153.

Conte, R., and Castelfranchi, C. 1995. *Cognitive and Social Action*. London: UCL Press.

Copp, D. Forthcoming. "The Collective Moral Autonomy Thesis." *Journal of Social Philosophy*.

De Quervain, D., Fischbacher, U., Treyer, V., Schellhammer, M., Schnyder, U., Buck, A., and Fehr, E. 2004, "The Neural Basis of Altruistic Punishment." *Science* 305, 1254–58.

Durkheim, E. 1965. *The Elementary Forms of Religious Life*. New York: Free Press. Originally published 1912.

Durkheim, E. 1982. *The Rules of Sociological Method*. 2nd ed. Edited by Steven Lukes. New York: Free Press. Originally published 1901.

Falk, A., and Fischbacher, U. 2005. "Modeling Strong Reciprocity." in Gintis, H., Bowles, S., Boyd, R., and Fehr, E., eds., *Moral Sentiments and Material Interests: The Foundations of Cooperation in Economic Life*. Cambridge, Mass.: MIT Press, pp. 193–214.

Gallese, V. 2001. "The 'Shared Manifold' Hypothesis: From Mirror Neurons to Empathy." *Journal of Consciousness Studies* 8, 33–50.

Gensler, H. 1996. *Formal Ethics*. London: Routledge.

Giddens, A. 1984. *The Constitution of Society*. Cambridge: Polity Press.

Gilbert, M. 1987. "Modelling Collective Belief." *Synthese* 73, 185–204.

Gilbert, M. 1989. *On Social Facts*. London: Routledge.

Gilbert, M. 1990. "Walking Together: A Paradigmatic Social Phenomenon." *Midwest Studies in Philosophy* 15, 1–14.

Gilbert, M. 1993. "Agreements, Coercion, and Obligation." *Ethics* 103, 679–706.

Gilbert, M. 2000. *Sociality and Responsibility*. Lanham, Md.: Rowman and Littlefield.

Gilbert, M. 2002a. "Acting Together." In G. Meggle, ed., *Social Facts and Collective Intentionality*. Frankfurt: Deutsche Bibliothek der Wissenschaften, pp. 53–71.

Gilbert, M. 2002b. "Belief and Acceptance as Features of Groups." *Protosociology* 16, 35–69.

Gilbert, M. 2002c. "Considerations on Joint Commitment: Responses to Various Comments." In G. Meggle, ed., *Social Facts and Collective Intentionality*. Frankfurt: Deutsche Bibliothek der Wissenschaften, pp. 73–101.

Gintis, H., Bowles, S., Boyd, R., and Fehr, E., eds. 2005. *Moral Sentiments and Material Interests: The Foundations of Cooperation in Economic Life*. Cambridge, Mass.: MIT Press.

Goette, L., Huffman, D., and Meier, S. 2006. "The Impact of Group Membership on Cooperation and Norm Enforcement: Evidence Using Random Assignment to Real Social Groups." Forshungsinstitut zur Zukunft der Arbeit (IZA), Report No. 2020.

Graham, K. 2002. *Practical Reasoning in a Social World: How We Act Together*. Cambridge: Cambridge University Press.

Grice, P. 1989. *Studies in the Ways of Words*. Cambridge, Mass.: Harvard University Press.

Hakli, R. 2006. "Group Beliefs and the Distinction Between Belief and Acceptance." *Cognitive Systems Research* 7, 286–87.

Hakli, R., and Tuomela, R. 2003. "Cooperation and We-Mode Preferences in Multi-agent Systems." Presented at the First International Workshop on Social Life (SOLI 2003)

European Conference for Artificial Life, September 14–17. Available at: *www.valt. helsinki.fi/staff/tuomela/papers/soli03.pdf.*

Halpern, J., and Moses, Y. 1992. "A Guide to Completeness and Complexity for Modal Logics of Knowledge and Belief." *Artificial Intelligence* 54, 319–79.

Harsanyi, J. C. 1976. "Cardinal Welfare, Individualistic Ethics, and Interpersonal Comparisons of Utility." *Journal of Political Economy* 63, 309–21.

Harsanyi, J. C., and Selten, R. 1988. *A General Theory of Equilibrium Selection in Games.* Cambridge, Mass.: MIT Press.

Heidegger, M. 1980. *Being and Time.* Oxford: Blackwell. Originally published 1928.

Henrich, J. 2001. "Cultural Transmission and the Diffusion of Innovations: Adoption Dynamics Indicate That Biased Cultural Transmission Is the Predominate Force in Behavioral Change." *American Anthropologist* 100, 992–1013.

Henrich, J., and Boyd, R. 1998. "The Evolution of Conformist Transmission and the Emergence of Between-group Differences." *Evolution of Human Behavior* 19, 215–42.

Henrich, J., and Boyd, R. 2001. "Why People Punish Defectors: Weak Conformist Transmission Can Stabilize Costly Enforcement of Norms in Cooperative Dilemmas." *Journal of Theoretical Biology* 208, 79–89.

Henrich, J., and McElreath, R. 2003. "The Evolution of Cultural Evolution." *Evolutionary Anthropology* 12, 123–35.

Hindriks, F. 2005. Rules and Institutions: Essays in Meaning, Speech Acts and Social Ontology. Doctoral diss., Erasmus University, Rotterdam.

Hofstede, G. 1994. *Cultures and Organizations.* London: HarperCollins.

Hogg, M., and Abrams, D. 1988. *Social Identifications.* London: Routledge.

Hogg, M., and Abrams, D. 2001. *Intergroup Relations: Essential Readings.* Hove, England: Psychology Press.

Hogg, M., and Tindale, S. 2002. *Blackwell Handbook of Social Psychology: Group Processes.* Oxford: Blackwell.

Hollis, M. 1998. *Trust within Reason.* Cambridge: Cambridge University Press.

Hume, D. 1965. *A Treatise of Human Nature.* Edited by L. A. Selby-Bigge. Oxford: Clarendon Press. Originally published 1740.

Hurley, S., and Chater, N., eds. 2005. *Perspectives on Imitation I–II.* Cambridge, Mass.: MIT Press.

Insko, C., and Schopler, J. 1987. "Categorization, Competition and Collectivity." In C. Hendrick, ed., *Group Processes.* Beverly Hills, Calif.: Sage, pp. 213–51.

Insko, C., Schopler, J., and Kennedy, J. 1992. "Individual-Group Discontinuity from the Differing Perspectives of Campbell's Realistic Group Conflict Theory and Tajfel and Turner's Social Identity Theory." *Social Psychology Quarterly* 55, 272–91.

Jaspers, K. 1947/2000. *The Question of German Guilt.* New York: Fordham University Press.

Katz, D., ed. 2002. *Evolutionary Origins of Morality.* Thorverton, England: Imprint Academic.

Knoblich, G., and Jordan, J. 2003. "Action Coordination in Groups and Individuals: Learning Anticipatory Control." *Journal of Experimental Psychology* 29, 1006–16.

Kollock, P. 1998. "Transforming Social Dilemmas: Group Identity and Co-Operation." In P. Danielson, *Modeling Rationality, Morality, and Evolution.* New York: Oxford University Press, pp. 185–209.

Kurzban, R., and Neuberg, S. 2005. "Managing Ingroup and Outgroup Relationships," In D. Buss, ed., *The Handbook of Evolutionary Psychology.* New York: Wiley, pp. 653–75.

Kusch, M. 1997. "The Sociophilosophy of Folk Psychology." *Studies in History and Philosophy of Science* 28, 1–25.

Kutz, C. 2000. *Complicity: Ethics and Law for a Collective Age.* Cambridge: Cambridge University Press.

Lagerspetz, E. 1995. *The Opposite Mirrors: An Essay on the Conventionalist Theory of Institutions.* Dordrecht: Kluwer Academic.

Lewis, D. 1969. *Convention, A Philosophical Study.* Cambridge, Mass.: Harvard University Press.

Lewis, D. 1972. "Psychophysical and Theoretical Identifications, *Australasian Journal of Philosophy* 50, 249–58.

Liebrand, W., Messick, D., and Wilke, H. 1992. *Social Dilemmas,* Oxford: Pergamon Press.

Ludwig, K. 1992. "Impossible Doings." *Philosophical Studies* 65, 257–81.

Ludwig, K. Forthcoming. "The Argument from Normative Autonomy for Collective Agents." *Journal of Social Philosophy.*

Mäkelä, P., and Tuomela, R. 2002. "Group Action and Group Responsibility." *Protosociology* 16, 195–214.

Mathiesen, K. 2002. "Searle, Collective Intentions, and Individualism." In G. Meggle, ed., *Social Facts and Collective Intentionality.* Frankfurt: Deutsche Bibliothek der Wissenschaften, pp. 187–204.

Mathiesen, K. 2003. "On Collective Identity." *Protosociology* 18–19, 66–86.

May, L. 1992. *Sharing Responsibility.* Chicago: University of Chicago Press.

May, L., and Hoffman, S. 1991. *Collective Responsibility.* Savage, Md.: Rowman and Littlefield.

McClintock, C. G. 1972. "Social Motivation—A Set of Propositions." *Behavioral Science* 17, 438–54.

McMahon, C. 2001. *Collective Rationality and Collective Reasoning.* Cambridge: Cambridge University Press.

McMahon, C. 2005. "Shared Agency and Rational Cooperation." *Nous* 34, 284–308.

Meijers, A. 2003. "Can Collective Intentionality Be Individualized?" In D. Koepsell and L. Moss, eds., *John Searle's Ideas about Social Reality.* Malden, Mass.: Blackwell, pp. 167–83.

Mellema, G. 1997. *Collective Responsibility.* Amsterdam: Rodopi.

Miller, K. 2003. "Collective Reasoning and the Discursive Dilemma." *Philosophical Explorations* 6, 182–200.

Miller, K., and Tuomela, R. 2001. "What Are Collective Goals?" In M. Kiikeri and P. Ylikoski, eds., *Explanatory Connections.* Available at: http://www.valt.helsinki.fi/kfil/matti/.

Miller, S. 1992. "Joint Action." *Philosophical Papers* 21, 1–23.

Miller, S. 1995. "Intentions, Ends and Joint Action." *Philosophical Papers* 24, 51–67.

Miller, S. 2001. *Social Action: A Teleological Account.* Cambridge: Cambridge University Press.

Miller, S. Forthcoming. "Against the Collective Moral Autonomy Thesis." *Journal of Social Philosophy.*

Mithen, S. 1996. "The Early Prehistory of Human Social Behaviour: Issues of Archeological Inference and Cognitive Evolution." In W. G. Runciman, J. M. Smith, and R. I. M. Dunbar, eds., *Evolution of Social Behaviour Patterns in Primates and Man.* Oxford: Oxford University Press, pp. 145–77.

Moscovici, S. 1985. "Social Influence and Conformity." In L. Gardner and E. Aronson, eds., *The Handbook of Social Psychology II,* New York: Random House, pp. 347–412.

Mulligan, K., 2001. "Phenomenology: Philosophical Aspects." In N. J. Smelser and P. B. Baltes, eds., *International Encyclopedia of the Social and Behavioral Sciences,* Oxford: Pergamon, pp. 11363–69.

Nash, J. 1950. "The Bargaining Problem." *Econometrica* 21, 155–62.

Nida-Rümelin, J. 1991. "Practical Reason or Metapreferences: An Undogmatic Defense of Kantian Morality." *Theory and Decision* 30, 133–62.

North, D. C. 1998. "Five Propositions about Institutional Change." In J. Knight and I. Sened, eds., *Explaining Social Institutions.* Ann Arbor: University of Michigan Press, pp. 15–26.

North, D. C. 2001. "Economic Performance Through Time." In M. Brinton and V. Nee, eds., *The New Institutionalism in Sociology*. Stanford: Stanford University Press, pp. 247–57.

Okasha, S. 2006. *Evolution and the Levels of Selection*. Oxford: Oxford University Press.

Ostrom, E. 1997. "A Behavioral Approach to the Rational Choice Theory of Collective Action." *American Political Science Review* 92, 1–22.

Pettit, P. 2001. *A Theory of Freedom*. Oxford: Polity Press.

Pettit, P. 2002. *Rules, Reasons, and Norms*. Oxford: Oxford University Press.

Pettit, P. 2003. "Groups with Minds of Their Own." In F. Schmitt, ed., *Socializing Metaphysics: The Nature of Social Reality*. Lanham, Md.: Rowman and Littlefield, pp. 167–93.

Preyer, G. 2006. *Soziologische Theorie der Gegenwartsgesellschaft: Mitgliedshaftstheoretische Untersuchungen*. Wiesbaden: VS Verlag für Sozialwissenschaften.

Rakoczy, H. 2004. "Pretend Play and the Development of Collective Intentionality." Paper presented at the Collective Intentionality IV conference, Siena, Italy, October.

Rawling, P. 2002. "Decision Theory and Degree of Belief." In S. P. Turner and P. A. Roth, eds., *The Blackwell Guide to the Philosophy of the Social Sciences*. Oxford: Blackwell, pp. 110–42.

Rawls, J. 1971. *A Theory of Social Justice*. Cambridge, Mass.: Harvard University Press.

Rawls, J. 1993. *Political Liberalism*. New York: Columbia University Press.

Raz, J. 1986. *The Morality of Freedom*. Oxford: Clarendon Press.

Richerson, P., and Boyd, R. 1999. "Complex Societies: The Evolutionary Dynamics of a Crude Superorganism." *Human Nature* 10, 253–89.

Richerson, P., and Boyd, R. 2001. "The Evolution of Subjective Commitment to Groups: A Tribal Instincts Hypothesis." In R. Nesse, ed. *Evolution and the Capacity for Commitment*. New York: Russell Sage Foundation, pp. 186–220.

Richerson, P., and Boyd, R. 2005. *Not by Genes Alone: How Culture Transformed Human Evolution*. Chicago: University of Chicago Press.

Richman, B. 1987. "Rhythm and Melody in Gelada Vocal Exchanges." *Primates* 28, 199–223.

Rifkin, J. 2004. *The European Dream*. New York: Penguin.

Rizzolatti, G., Fadiga, L., Gallese, V., and Fogassi, L. 1996. "Premotor Cortex and the Recognition of Motor Actions." *Cognitive Brain Research* 3, 131–41.

Rousseau, J. 1960. *The Social Contract*, edited by E. Barker. Oxford: Oxford University Press, pp. 167–307. Originally published 1762.

Rovane, C. 1998. *The Bounds of Agency*. Princeton, N.J.: Princeton University Press.

Ruben, D.-H. 1985. *The Metaphysics of the Social World*. London: Routledge.

Sandu, G., and Tuomela, R. 1996. "Joint Action and Group Action Made Precise." *Synthese* 105, 319–45.

Sartre, J.-P. 1966. *Being and Nothingness*, translated by H. Barnes. New York: Washington Square Press. Originally published 1943.

Scanlon, T. 1998. *What We Owe to Each Other*. Cambridge, Mass.: Harvard University Press.

Scheff, R. 1967. "Toward a Sociological Model of Consensus." *American Sociological Review* 32, 32–46.

Schein, B. 1993. *Plurals and Events*. Cambridge, Mass.: MIT Press.

Schelling, T. 1960. *The Strategy of Conflict*. Cambridge, Mass.: Harvard University Press.

Schiffer, S. 1972. *Meaning*. Oxford: Oxford University Press.

Schmid, H. B. 2005. *Wir-Intentionalität*. Freiburg: Alber Verlag.

Schmitt, F. 2003. "From Individualism to Supraindividualism." In F. Schmitt, ed., *Socializing Metaphysics: The Nature of Social Reality*. Lanham, Md.: Rowman and Littlefield, pp. 129–65.

Schotter, A. 1981. *The Economic Theory of Institutions*. Cambridge: Cambridge University Press.

Schutz, A. 1967/1932. *The Phenomenology of the Social World*. Evanston, Ill.: Northwestern University Press.

Schutz, A. 1962. *The Problem of Social Reality: Collected Papers 1*. The Hague: Nijhoff.

Searle, J. 1983. *Intentionality: An Essay in the Philosophy of Mind*. Cambridge: Cambridge University Press.

Searle, J. 1990. "Collective Intentions and Actions." In P. Cohen, J. Morgan, and M. Pollack, eds., *Intentions in Communication*. Cambridge, Mass.: MIT Press, pp. 401–15.

Searle, J. 1995. *The Construction of Social Reality*. London: Penguin.

Searle, J. 2001. *Rationality in Action*. Cambridge, Mass.: MIT Press.

Searle, J. 2003. "Social Ontology and Political Power." In F. Schmitt, ed., *Socializing Metaphysics: The Nature of Social Reality*. Lanham, Md.: Rowman and Littlefield, pp. 195–210.

Sellars, W. 1963. *Science, Perception and Reality*. London: Routledge and Kegan Paul.

Sellars, W. 1968. *Science and Metaphysics*. London: Routledge and Kegan Paul.

Sellars, W. 1969. "Language as Thought and as Communication." *Philosophy and Phenomenological Research* 29, 206–527.

Sellars, W. 1981. "Mental Events." *Philosophical Studies* 39, 325–45.

Skyrms, B. 1994. "Darwin Meets 'The Logic of Decision': Correlation in Evolutionary Game Theory." *Philosophy of Science* 61, 503–28.

Skyrms, B. 1996. *Evolution of the Social Contract*. Cambridge: Cambridge University Press.

Smith, B., and Searle, J. 2003. "The Construction of Social Reality: An Exchange." In D. Koepsell and L. Moss, eds., *John Searle''s Ideas about Social Reality*. Oxford: Blackwell, pp. 285–309.

Sober, E., and Wilson, D. 1998. *Unto Others: The Evolution and Psychology of Unselfish Behavior*. Cambridge, Mass.: Harvard University Press.

Sperber, D. 2000. "An Objection to the Memetic Approach to Culture." In R. Aunger, ed., *Darwinizing Culture: The Status of Memetics as a Science*. Oxford: Oxford University Press, pp. 163–73.

Sripada, C. 2005. "Punishment and the Strategic Structure of Moral Systems." *Biology and Philosophy* 20, 767–89.

Stamenov, M., and Gallese, V., eds. 2002. *Mirror Neurons and the Evolution of Brain and Language*. Amsterdam: John Benjamins.

Stangor, C. 2004. *Social Groups in Action and Interaction*. New York: Psychology Press.

Storr, A. 1993. *Music and Mind*. London: HarperCollins.

Stoutland, F. 2002. "Review of Michael Bratman, Faces of Intention, Cambridge UP 1999." *Philosophy and Phenomenological Research* 65, 238–42.

Sugden, R. 1993. "Thinking as a Team: Towards an Explanation of Nonselfish Behavior." *Social Philosophy and Policy* 10, 69–89.

Sugden, R. 2000. "Team Preferences." *Economics and Philosophy* 16, 75–204.

Sugden, R., and Gold, N. Forthcoming, "Commitment and Team Reasoning." In F. Peter and H. B. Schmid, eds., *Rationality and Commitment*. Oxford: Oxford University Press.

Tollefsen, D. 2004. "Collective Intentionality." In *The Internet Encyclopedia of Philosophy*. Available at: http://www.iep.utm.edu/c/coll-int.htm.

Tomasello, M. 1999. *The Cultural Origins of Human Cognition*. Cambridge, Mass.: Harvard University Press.

Tomasello, M., Carpenter, M., Call, J., Behne, T., and Moll, H. 2005. "Understanding and Sharing Intentions: The Origins of Cultural Cognition." *Behavioral and Brain Sciences* 28, 675–735.

Tomasello, M., and Rakoczy, H. 2003. "What Makes Human Cognition Unique? From Individual to Shared to Collective Intentionality." *Mind and Language* 18, 121–47.

Triandis, H. 1995. *Individualism and Collectivism*. Boulder, Colo.: Westview.

REFERENCES 309

Triandis, H., and Trafimow, D. 2003. "Culture and Its Implications for Intergroup Behavior." In R. Brow and S. Gaertner, eds., *Blackwell Handbook of Social Psychology: Intergroup Processes.* Oxford: Blackwell, pp. 367–85.

Tuomela, M. 2003. "A Collective's Rational Trust in a Collective." *Protosociology* 18–19, 87–125.

Tuomela, R. 1973. *Theoretical Concepts.* New York: Springer Verlag.

Tuomela, R. 1977. *Human Action and Its Explanation.* Dordrecht: Reidel.

Tuomela, R. 1984. *A Theory of Social Action.* Dordrecht: Reidel.

Tuomela, R. 1989a. "Collective Action, Supervenience, and Constitution." *Synthese* 80, 243–66.

Tuomela, R. 1989b. "Actions by Collectives." *Philosophical Perspectives* 3, 471–96.

Tuomela, R. 1991. "We Will Do It: An Analysis of Group-Intentions." *Philosophy and Phenomenological Research* 51, 249–77.

Tuomela, R. 1992. "Group Beliefs." *Synthese* 91, 285–318.

Tuomela, R. 1995. *The Importance of Us: A Philosophical Study of Basic Social Notions.* Stanford: Stanford University Press.

Tuomela, R. 1997. "Searle on Social Institutions." *Philosophy and Phenomenological Research* 57, 435–41.

Tuomela, R. 1998. "A Defense of Mental Causation." *Philosophical Studies* 90, 1–34.

Tuomela, R. 2000a. "Belief versus Acceptance." *Philosophical Explorations* 2, 122–37.

Tuomela, R. 2000b. "Collective and Joint Intention." *Mind and Society* 1, 39–69.

Tuomela, R. 2000c. *Cooperation: A Philosophical Study.* Dordrecht: Kluwer.

Tuomela, R. 2000d. "Reasons for Action." In B. Brogaard, ed., *Rationality and Irrationality: Contributions of the Austrian Ludwig Wittgenstein Society.* Kirchberg, Austria: Austrian L. Wittgenstein Society, pp. 193–98.

Tuomela, R. 2001. "Shared Belief." In *International Elsevier Encyclopedia of the Social and Behavioral Sciences.* Oxford: Elsevier, pp. 14039–43.

Tuomela, R. 2002a. "Joint Intention and Commitment." In G. Meggle, ed., *Social Facts and Collective Intentionality.* Frankfurt: Deutsche Bibliothek der Wissenschaften, pp. 385–418.

Tuomela, R. 2002b. *The Philosophy of Social Practices: A Collective Acceptance View.* Cambridge: Cambridge University Press.

Tuomela, R. 2002c. "Searle, Collective Intentionality and Social Institutions." In G. Grewendorf and G. Meggle, eds., *Speech Acts, Mind, and Social Reality.* Dordrecht: Kluwer Academic, pp. 293–307.

Tuomela, R. 2003a. "The We-Mode and the I-Mode." In F. Schmitt, ed., *Socializing Metaphysics: The Nature of Social Reality.* Lanham, Md.: Rowman and Littlefield, pp. 93–127.

Tuomela, R. 2003b. "Collective Acceptance, Social Institutions, and Group Beliefs." In W. Buschlinger and C. Lütge, eds., *Kaltblütig, Philosophie von einem rationalen Standpunkt.* Stuttgart: Hirzel Verlag, pp. 429–46.

Tuomela, R. 2003c. "Review of Miller, S., Social Action: A Teleological Account." *Australasian Journal of Philosophy* 81, 300–301.

Tuomela, R. 2004. "Group Knowledge Analyzed." *Episteme* 1, 109–27.

Tuomela, R. 2005a. "Review of C. McMahon, Collective Rationality and Collective Reasoning." *Ethics* 116, 242–46.

Tuomela, R. 2005b. "We-Intentions Revisited." *Synthese* 125, 327–69.

Tuomela, R. Forthcoming a. "Motivating Reasons for Action." In M. Timmons, J. Greco, and A. Mele, eds., *Rationality and the Good: Themes from the Epistemology and Ethics of Robert Audi.* New York: Oxford University Press.

Tuomela, R. Forthcoming b. "Cooperation and the We-Perspective." In F. Peter and H. B. Schmid, eds., *Rationality and Commitment.* Oxford: Oxford University Press.

Tuomela, R. Forthcoming c. "On the Ontological Nature of Social Groups." In S. Pihl-ström, P. Raatikainen, and M. Sintonen, eds., *Approaching Truth: Essays in Honor of Ilkka Niiniluoto*. London: College Publishers.

Tuomela, R., and Balzer, W. 1999. "Collective Acceptance and Collective Social Notions." *Synthese* 117, 175–205.

Tuomela, R., and Balzer, W. 2002. "Collective Acceptance and Collective Attitudes." In U. Mäki, ed., *Fact and Fiction in Economics*. Cambridge: Cambridge University Press, pp. 269–85.

Tuomela, R., and Bonnevier-Tuomela, M. 1992. Social Norms, Tasks, and Roles. Reports from the Department of Philosophy, University of Helsinki, no. 1. Department of Philosophy, University of Helsinki.

Tuomela, R., and Bonnevier-Tuomela, M. 1997. "From Social Imitation to Teamwork." In G. Holmström-Hintikka and R. Tuomela, eds., *Contemporary Action Theory*. Vol. 2. *Social Action*. Dordrecht: Kluwer, pp. 1–47.

Tuomela, R., and Bonnevier-Tuomela, M., 1998. "Norms and Agreement." In E. Attwooll and P. Comanducci, eds., *Sources of Law and Legislation*, Stuttgart: Franz Steiner Verlag, pp. 87–93.

Tuomela, R., and Miller, K. 1988. "We-Intentions." *Philosophical Studies* 53, 115–37.

Tuomela, R., and Tuomela, M. 2003. "Acting as a Group Member and Collective Commitment." *Protosociology* 18–19, 7–65.

Tuomela, R., and Tuomela, M. 2005. "Cooperation and Trust in Group Context." *Mind and Society* 4, 49–84.

Turner, J. C. 1987. *Rediscovering the Social Group: A Self-Categorization Theory*. Oxford: Blackwell.

Turner, J. C., and Reynolds, K. 2003. "The Social Identity Perspective in Intergroup Relations: Theories, Themes, and Controversies." In R. Brown and S. Gaertner, eds., *Blackwell Handbook of Social Psychology: Intergroup Processes*. Oxford: Blackwell, pp. 133–52.

Turner, J. H. 2000. *On the Origins of Human Emotions*, Stanford: Stanford University Press.

Turner, J. H. 2003. *Human Institutions: A Theory of Societal Evolution*. Lanham, Md.: Rowman and Littlefield.

van Crefeld, M. 1982. *Fighting Power: German and U.S. Army Performance. 1939–1945*. Westport, Conn.: Greenwood Press.

van Vugt, M., Snyder, M., Tyler, T., and Biel, A. 2000. *Cooperation in Modern Society*. London: Routledge.

Velleman, J. 1997. "How to Share an Intention?" *Philosophy and Phenomenological Research* 62, 29–50.

Walther, H., Adenzato, M., Ciadamidaro, A., Enrici, I., Pia, L., and Bara, B. G. 2004. "Understanding Intentions in Social Interaction: The Role of the Anterior Paracingulate Cortex." *Journal of Cognitive Neuroscience* 16, 1854–63.

Weber, M. 1968/1921. *Economy and Society*. New York: Bedminster.

Webster's Third New International Dictionary. 1966. Chicago: G.&C. Merriam.

Worchel, S., Rothberger, H., Day, E., Hart, D., and Butemayer, J. 1998. "Social Identity and Individual Productivity in Groups." *British Journal of Social Psychology* 37, 389–413.

Wrangham, R. 1980. "An Ecological Model of Female-Bonded Primate Groups." *Behaviour* 75, 262–400.

Zaibert, L. 2003. "Collective Intentions and Collective Intentionality." In D. Koepsell and L. Moss, eds., *John Searle's Ideas about Social Reality*. Malden, Mass.: Blackwell, pp. 209–32.

Zlotkin, G., and Rosenschein, J. 1994. *Rules of Encounter*. Cambridge, Mass.: MIT Press.

INDEX